Spectacular Nature

Spectacular Nature

Corporate Culture and the Sea World Experience

Susan G. Davis

UNIVERSITY OF CALIFORNIA PRESS

Berkeley / Los Angeles / London

University of California Press
Berkeley and Los Angeles, California

University of California Press, Ltd.
London, England

© 1997 by
The Regents of the University of California

Library of Congress Cataloging-in-Publication Data

Author name. Davis, Susan G., 1953–
Spectacular nature: corporate culture and the Sea World experience / Susan G. Davis
p. cm.
Includes bibliographic references and index.
ISBN 0–520–20031–4 (cloth: alk. paper). ISBN 0–520–20981–8 (pbk: alk. paper)
1. Sea World. 2. Amusement parks—Social aspects—California—San Diego. 3. Amusement parks—Economic aspects—California—San Diego. 4. Corporate culture—California—San Diego. I. Title.
GV1853.C22S434 1996
790'.06'8'09794985—dc20 96–44902

Printed in the United States of America
9 8 7 6 5 4 3 2 1

The paper used in this publication meets the minimum requirements of American National Standards for Information Sciences—Permanence of Paper for Printed Library Materials, ANSI Z39.48–1984.♾

For Mary Ann
and Dan, Lucy, and Ethan

my beautiful reward

Contents

Illustrations

Maps

Figures

Acknowledgments

Like any long project this book has intersected the lives and work of many other people. A full accounting would be impossible, but I'd like to mention my debt to John Berger and the late Raymond Williams. This study of nature as mass entertainment was possible because of their creative and committed work.

A grant from the John Simon Guggenheim Memorial Foundation helped me find time for sustained research and contemplation. The University of California Humanities Research Institute at Irvine offered a chance to try out some ideas, and my colleagues in the Department of Communication at the University of California at San Diego provided a critical context and food for thought. Lucia Ruedenberg, Kay Mary Avila, Judith Gregory, Rivki Ribak, Yalonda Lofton, Maria Foley, Sarah Banet-Weiser, and Barbara Dahlke helped with library and photo research, tape transcription, and the daunting job of filing my endless Sea World materials. Krista Camenzind and Joy Hayes at UCSD and Megan Liles at the Union-Tribune Publishing Company researched primary materials; and Larry Cruse, Elliot Kanter, and Jim Jacobs of UCSD's Geisel Library provided bibliographic support. At the University of California Press, Naomi Schneider and William Murphy guided this project with skill and enthusiasm; in the final stages, sharp editing by Scott Norton and Bonita Hurd has saved readers no end of confusion.

Jackie Hill, Dan LeBlanc, and Diane Oaks of Sea World, and Carter Dunkin of Fleishman Hillard in St. Louis, Missouri, helped make possible my interviews with Sea World personnel. The management of Sea World, Busch Entertainment Corporation, and Anheuser-Busch will probably disagree sharply with the arguments I present here; disagreements don't take away from the fun I had interviewing Sea World of California's staff and managers or my respect for their energy, knowledge, and skills.

Dan Schiller has given me logistical, moral, and intellectual support from the first research trip until the last. Without his help, I'd still be searching for my road map. Margaret Crawford, William Cronon, Steven Jay Gould, Robert McChesney, Vincent Mosco, Catherine McKercher, Stuart Ewen, Janet Francendese, Rachel Klein, George Mariscal, Marjorie Millstein, Carol Padden, Roy Rosenzweig, Ann Spirn, Herbert and Anita Schiller, Zach Schiller, Ellen Seiter, Roger Showley, David Sternbach, Alan Trachtenberg, and Richard White gave valuable encouragement and criticisms. Some selfless souls, including Lisa Hirschman, Elizabeth Colwill, Jay Mechling, George Lipsitz, and several anonymous readers commented constructively on the entire work. Barbara Kirshenblatt-Gimblett helped by giving me time and space to start this project, and Joan Hansen and all the staff of UCSD's Early Childhood Education Center supported me during the last big push. Each in her own way, Stephanie McCurry and Nancy Hewitt said the right thing at a critical moment. Marcus Rediker hauled me back to the land of the living with an on-time blues transfusion.

Lucy, Ethan, Dan and Mary Ann, Herb and Anita, and all the rest of my family gave me the best reasons to finish up. My father, David, lived scrupulously and avoided the prepackaged emotions of much contemporary commercial culture. He would have liked Yeats's epitaph for Tom O'Roughley: "An aimless joy is a pure joy."

Introduction

Since 1964, Sea World of California has occupied a swath of carefully sculpted and lavishly landscaped acres at the southwestern edge of San Diego's Mission Bay Park. In amusement industry terms, Sea World is a marine park, a careful organization of shows, displays, rides, and concessions coordinated around the theme of ocean life. On any summer day, thousands of customers gather in Sea World's stadiums to watch its nature performances; thousands more wander through the larger park, a botanical garden larded with aquariums, souvenir stands, and corporate advertising.

In any year, the vast majority of Sea World's nearly 4 million customers come to see Shamu the killer whale. The park's trademark animal performs four times daily (five or six times daily in the summer) in its own six-thousand-seat stadium. Indeed, Shamu is the most important, best known, and most iconic animal in Southern California, and Sea World is one of the region's prime tourist attractions. But Sea World contains more than whales. A visitor can also encounter the synchronized dances of dolphins, sea otters rehabilitated after the great Alaskan oil spill, pettable sea stars, and stingless sting rays. Marine and freshwater aquariums house colorful fish and striking sharks. Zoological displays show rare Commerson's dolphins, breeding penguins, wallowing walruses, and nesting flamingos. Among the humans one can find stunt-diving Olympic acrobats, competitive jet-skiers, ballet troupes, Russian choristers, clowns, mimes, do-wop singers, and beauty queens. A gondola ride, a stable full of Clydesdale horses, gift shops, restaurants, vendors' carts, concession stands and more gift shops, a multistoried children's play area, amphitheaters, and an auditorium round out a continually changing landscape. Outside everyday life, Sea World offers a carnival of visions and colorful, if not exactly novel, experiences. Indeed, as the Sea World publicity slogan goes, "It's not just a park, it's another world."

Viewed from the perspective of tourism and the mass entertainment industry, Sea World of California is a specialized variant of the theme park form, the foremost occupant of the marine animals and ocean nature niche. One of a chain of ten U.S. theme parks and four Sea Worlds, it is owned by the Anheuser-Busch corporation, the world's largest brewer and a packaged-foods and agribusiness conglomerate.[1] Like all theme parks, it is a corporately produced space where entertainment and retail sales can be creatively combined and effectively organized around a core attraction, in this case the performing whales and dolphins. Just as important as admissions for each park's profits are the almost endless concession stands, boutiques, and gift shops offering refreshments and souvenirs of many sorts. As a student in one of my undergraduate classes aptly put it, "Sea World is like a mall with fish," and underwater life is the story that helps us keep shopping. But viewed from another perspective, this theme park is a hybrid public-private institution. Sea World styles itself an urban public resource, a site of animal rehabilitation, marine conservation, research, and education. Hundreds of thousands of San Diego school children and millions more nationwide are exposed to its ocean-themed educational products.

I first became interested in Sea World in 1986. After publishing a book on street performance in the nineteenth century, I was interested in public space in the contemporary city and especially curious about how the processes of privatization were remaking its older collective uses and experiential qualities. Although the streets and squares of American cities have been shaped by commercial and capitalist uses for centuries, by the 1980s the process of the commodification of space had become much more intense. On one hand, older common and residential areas of the city had been weakened and, in some cases, destroyed by the freeway and the exurban shopping mall. On the other hand, these same emptied districts were often reinvented as culture and history malls for tourists, as the image of place was commodified by developers and entrepreneurs. Meanwhile, new private "public" spaces protected from the life of the street sprang up inside monumental corporate towers.[2]

As I thought about the relationship between commercial culture and the popular uses of space and place, I kept returning to theme parks.

They seemed to me emblematic of the spatial-urban problems I was wondering about, the extremity of the transformation of vernacular and local meanings of place into a standardized product. Searching the literature on architectural history and mass entertainment spaces, I found conflicting emphases in the ways scholars had treated the parks. In the mid-1970s, critical communications scholars had analyzed the Disney media empire, including its theme parks, as part of a critique of the political economy and ideology of American entertainment. The work of Michael Real and Herbert Schiller recognized that Disneyland was a special kind of medium, a space where the older contours of collective recreation were recast into something new, an integrated landscape of meanings unified around consumption. Real and Schiller insisted that even as the theme park has come to be seen as a culturally central site, in a strong sense it must also be recognized as cultural production from the top down. In Schiller's view, since the Disney parks were tied closely to the world of the mass media conglomerate, they served to combine recreation with advertising, marketing, and mass consumption within a framework that misleadingly claimed the neutrality of entertainment. From Real's perspective, Disneyland was a morality play that rehearsed the perspective of a largely white and mainstream American audience within ideological bounds set by the corporation. In the communications critique, places like Disneyland were reinforcements for the status quo.[3]

This sharp and radical cultural critique was explicitly rejected in the theme park studies that emerged after the late 1970s. The 1980s saw a tide of anthropologists, semioticians and, later, postmodernists who conducted textual readings of theme park landscapes. Little effort was made to explore the political and economic workings of the themed spaces or connect the parks directly to their social history.[4] There was no shortage of sophisticated discussions of Disneyland, for example, but like so much of contemporary cultural criticism, these studies were often based only on a quick visit and depended only on the interpreter for their validity. For the most part, the anthropological tradition celebrated theme parks as marvels of semiotic play, a move that protected them and many other fixtures of the mass tourism landscape from political economic and social historical analysis and, to a degree, from social criticism.[5] At the same time, however, social historians followed a different trajectory, giving the forerunners of the theme park—the World's Fair, the industrial exposition, and the amusement park—serious attention and investigating the history of American patterns of leisure and recreation. Roy Rosenzweig, Kathy Peiss, and John Kasson, for example, had traced the cheap but profitable entertainments of the commercial public sphere and argued that they had been a significant force in the transformation of American culture in the early twentieth century.[6] But little work in the emerging cultural studies literature or in American studies linked the social historians' concerns about the growth of amusements for a mass urban public to theme parks as a consumer good for a contemporary mass market, or to the work they do for their corporate owners.

So I started this work on two fronts. I read widely in the literature on commercial spaces and themed spaces—shopping malls, amusement parks, and world's fairs, in particular. At the same time, I began to study themed amusement spaces on the ground by reading business journalists' reports on the industry. This economic and industrial coverage helped me understand the current and, as it turned out, quickly changing shape of what insiders call the parks industry. As the eighties lurched into the nineties, what I thought of as a seriousness barrier around theme parks was being eroded by changes in scholarship and, no less, by events. In part due to the explosion in the 1980s of an economy of accelerated consumption, in part because of the deepening structural crisis of American cities, architectural historians, geographers, and sociologists turned their attention to the relationship between social life and the intensified commercialization of space.[7] In the face of continuing urban crisis, it has again become harder to see the theme park as a joyful ritual of national identity. Rather, it is a physical expression of wishes about the urban, social world, and scholars have looked at the Disney theme parks in particular as more than exemplars of capitalist culture. They are literal heralds of a new kind of city made up of spectacular privatized spaces. In his cogent introduction to *Variations on a Theme Park,* for example, Michael Sorkin argues that the logic and techniques of the high-consumption spaces have erased the boundaries between theme park and city and, in the process, emptied urban space of memory and history. Sorkin and his colleagues explore the design ideas and social ideals expressed in Disney's parks and the ways these ideas have been exported into other realms of the built world: shopping malls, resort complexes, planned and gated communities. The process these architectural historians and critics trace has by no means exhausted itself. As I write this introduction, the Disney Development Company is moving into the production of totally planned themed communities.[8] Cloning controlled recreational space into a corporately built company town, the theme park does more than define places for leisure. It helps redefine the potential for meaningful activity in social space, and social space itself.[9]

In addition to the growing literature on the city as high-consumption tourist district, there has been a surge of interest in the world's leading theme parks, Disneyland and Walt Disney World, due in large part to the international expansions of the Disney company and in part to political and cultural controversies surrounding what is now the world's largest media conglomerate. Writings by Michael Wallace, Alexander Wilson, Susan Willis, Stephen Fjellman, and others critically explore the workings of the landscapes that help create the company's global visibility and bring in vast profits. Scrutinizing the Disney parks' visions of society, their celebrations of the power of technology and corporate creativity, and their constructions of gender, race, and history, these scholars take up again the theme announced by the critics of the 1970s. Although I did not have it to draw on as I began my own theme park project, this perceptive literature is growing quickly. It is no longer confined to readings of the parks, valuable as these are, but increasingly uses ethnographic techniques to explore the multiple and overlapping relationships between mass media–based recreation, mass tourism, and the structures of everyday life.[10]

As my background knowledge grew, I thought it would be helpful to study one park closely, watch it in operation, and compare what I was learning about theme parks as mass entertainment and mass communication in general with a particular case. I kept thinking about Sea World of California: I'd only been there once, had gotten a terrible headache, and hadn't wanted to go back. But now I was looking for a site for a case study, and Sea World seemed to me a good one. It was large, part of a chain then owned by the publishing conglomerate Harcourt Brace Jovanovich. With over 3 million visitors per year, it was popular and conveniently located in San Diego, where I usually lived and worked. My research could be continuous and sustained. And since it was not a Disney park, it had not found fame among academics. Not even business journalists had paid it much attention.

When I turned to Sea World of California in 1987, I hoped to unpack the connections between public meanings, mass entertainment, and private enterprise. My observational fieldwork began with a positive, scholarly openness to understanding the theme park form and its appeal to its customers, as well as critical questions about Sea World's cultural meanings and effects. Early on, my scholarly attitude toward the park was a mix of fascination and suspicion. My fascination rose because the landscape was rich and complicated and I was ready to look at it. Suspicion persisted, growing out of my own background and my assessment of the contemporary cultural scene. I had a contradictory sense that Sea World and places like it were at once important to study and faintly laughable, and this sense was part of a widely shared, joking disbelief about things Southern Californian. But joking signaled awareness of cultural historic change. Thirty years ago the well-educated, middle-class social world I grew up in viewed theme parks as vacuous junk culture, but this has changed. The social critics and countercultures of the 1960s viewed theme parks as mainstream or "white bread" at best, or worse, authoritarian. But by the mid-1980s, the predominance of the Walt Disney Company had helped redefine theme parks as culturally central sites all Americans (indeed all the world) should aspire to visit. At the same time, mass tourism has drawn a huge proportion of the American population into travel, and themed resorts are prime, even prestigious, destinations. My suspicious attitude was also part of an intellectual tradition. On the one hand, my training as a folklorist undermined condescension. No serious student of popular culture would write off the theme park. On the other hand, my folklore background and personal convictions also place positive value on informal and noncommercial modes of cultural production, privileging them over centrally produced, market-driven culture. While there is no pure place to stand here, no folk-cultural world free from influence by the market and mass media, this distinction between the vernacular and corporately or officially produced culture forces the analyst always to ask what cultural alternatives have been foreclosed, as well as which left open. In short, my critical view of Sea World and theme parks generally included the question, how might things be different, how would culture look and feel if it were produced differently?

I focused first on the ways Sea World constructed its spaces, on how the park represented people and cultures, and how people used the park. Since I saw it as an interesting variant of Disneyland, it didn't occur to me to wonder too much about Sea World's own peculiar qualities. I assumed that studying any large park would help me pose and answer questions about the way crowds were moved around, and about the relationships between people, performances, and spaces. In the first year of fieldwork, I wrote several papers—one on a reconstructed urban neighborhood that Sea World had just built, a kind of mockup of the Lower East Side of Manhattan, with ethnically diverse natives singing and dancing a paean to the city and community. I found the "City Streets" show (located at what is now the Bird Showplace) silly and felt distanced from the other customers, most of whom seemed to take it for an accurate recreation of an eastern, urban past. In a second paper, I explored the representation of another kind of foreignness and mystery at the park by looking at a Japanese pearl-diving show.

These tentative analyses tried to unpack the economics of entertainment in the theme park and to account for the subjects and peculiar qualities of the performance. Reading them to friends and colleagues at academic conferences was fun. I always got laughs as I described in a deadpan way the odd seriousness and lack of irony with which the theme park mixed and matched mass cultural materials. How funny it was that Sea World sandwiched its own recast version of *West Side Story* in between the dolphins and the whales. How ironic and sad that the suburban audience cheered a song-and-dance tribute to city life in a geographical context where urban is a foreign if not dirty word. How hilarious that the "authentically costumed Japanese *ama* girls" had names like Cheryl and Tracy, and how telling that the most important performer in their show was the gemologist who weighed and certified the planted pearl! While Sea World's human performances certainly revealed much about the shallowness of representation in mass culture, they were just that, shallow, and this made the question of their appeal all the more compelling. The peculiar construction of exoticness and ethnicity, whether Asian or American urban, was World's Fair lite, a recycling and recombination of midway entertainment staples. Finally, it was hard to stay interested. Anything Sea World borrowed from Disneyland was probably done better at Disneyland, and *West Side Story* looked and sounded better on film. These human performances left me thinking that Sea World was essentially a shopping mall without the talented piano player, an advertising shell in which American mass culture's odds and ends were recombined.

But I was focused on what Sea World's managers regard as filler. It took a good friend to point this out and redirect my attention. Sam Schrager supported my view of Sea World as a complex spatial machine for extracting profits from its customers, and he agreed with me that I should try to understand it as a cluster of performances dealing with central and contested social relations. But I wasn't looking at the park's key performers, he argued, and so I was missing the point. I had to start watching the killer whales because what was really important and completely unexplored about Sea World and places like it was its way of dealing with nature in general and marine mammals in particular. This helped explain why visitors did not seem to greet the park's landscape and performances with the ironic detachment a postmodernist might predict. Indeed, from what I could observe and the conversations I could join in, most customers entered the theme park with a sense of purpose and high seriousness, determined to contact something rare, special, and powerfully meaningful. Visitors to or residents of a city focused on the Pacific coast, they were going to meet Nature in the form of reconstructed reefs and coves filled with approachable sea creatures, commemorated in a rich variety of commercial souvenirs. Sam was right: I was missing the point. To say that Sea World is a powerful, profit-generating machine and leave it at that was to miss something. Even if I thought that representations of people were a more important part of American commercial culture than performing animals, Sea World's audience doesn't agree. For them, the oceans and their animals are the central story, and class and labor, race, ethnicity, and gender—Sea World's representations of humanity—seem peripheral to the nature plays being performed all around.

But I had not thought much about the problem of the representation of nature in commercial culture, and I began to ponder how to study a theme park built around animals and environments. In one way, Sea World and places like it are the most ersatz cultural artifacts possible. They are carefully constructed, expensively maintained artificial worlds that most of the time fairly successfully conceal their own extreme artificiality. According to Western common sense thought, *nature* denotes a sphere of authenticity and purity, an anticommercial world outside the marketplace.[11] In the late twentieth century, the oceans might seem the last remote place, an anticultural world teeming with nonhuman life and free from the burdens of history. This sense of the isolated authenticity, even the sacredness, of wild nature as a cultural category, was probably one reason audiences found my papers so hilarious. When I juxtaposed descriptions of singing, dancing urban natives with descriptions of synchronized back-flipping dolphins, the profane and the sacred became obscenely confused. And this confusion is one of the things that makes places like Sea World so fascinating: a theme park about wild nature is either so peculiar that it makes no sense, or contemporary culture is so thoroughly rationalized that it makes perfect sense. One friend said to me after watching Shamu the killer whale perform, "This is the worst thing I've ever seen in my life." But his minority opinion might be irrelevant, at least from the point of view of the cultural analyst. The Shamu show is a standardized experience, in which a very large, paying audience has a vivid and visual encounter with a huge, tamed-wild animal. As such, it is an amazing cultural phenomenon. Operating on the same principles as the core show, all of Sea World is an immediate, see-able, touchable consumer experience, a spectacular story about nature in general and oceans in particular. It is one of the most popular and available versions of the wild that contemporary American and international tourists can encounter.

I had started out resistant to Sea World's appeal because it is so intensely commercial, but as an analyst I had an obligation to try to understand the pleasures offered by its product. Now, as I tried to follow my friend's suggestions, I felt another tug of resistance. I'm not an "animal person," and I couldn't easily access the sources of the audience's enthusiasm for the trained animal shows. I knew nothing about whales and dolphins, so I'd have to learn to be interested in them. But the more I watched them, the more significant and compelling they seemed, not, from my point of view, inherently interesting as creatures but as occupants of an odd social space in California culture. I noticed that images of whales and dolphins suffused the commercial material culture of Southern California, from postcards and murals to charity appeals to designs cast on wedding rings. As the tidal zone is a margin between life on land and in the sea, whales and their kin, as mammals, occupy a similar liminal space between humans and the living ocean. Since the mid-1970s, whales and dolphins have been caught up in a tide of popular spiritualism and cross-species identification, prompting imaginative writing, art, music, and healing.[12] There is a kind of cult of the marine mammal abroad—but did the successful theme park create this popular commercial celebration, or did it just profit enormously from a vernacular enthusiasm? I felt drawn in and intrigued by the carefully crafted environment of the entire park even while I was alternately horrified and bored by the animal performances. But the question kept coming up—how would one study a nature theme park? What questions were worth asking and what methods should be used?

Like theme parks, nature's circulation in commercial entertainment culture has hidden, mostly unnoticed, behind a gravitas barrier. While the humanities have developed a long tradition of studying representations of nature, for the most part this scholarly tradition has, until recently, ignored nature's place in contemporary popular culture. There are several reasons for this neglect. While a great deal of inventive work has been done on the history of landscape painting and wilderness photography, and on nature in early advertising imagery, in modern commercial culture nature still has the status of a backdrop.[13] Nature's uses in the mass media are safe, and marine nature may be even safer since it is seemingly removed from the human environmental conflicts expressed on land. The ubiquity of nature programming on PBS and cable networks, to take an example from television, is due in part to its reputation for being wholesome, inoffensive, and cross-generational in its appeal, which perhaps also makes it seem boring and trite.[14] In studies of advertising, the pervasive use of the natural to sell products has come in for little critical examination, perhaps because nature seems to lie outside the important, contentious terms of race and gender.[15] The pervasiveness of the use of nature in commercial culture is exactly why we should study it. Cultural history and cultural studies have begun to provide a basic, orienting framework for viewing these representations.

One piece of the framework is Raymond Williams's insight that ideas of nature naturalize and help obscure relations of power. In Williams's general view, the idea of nature itself and the way it has been worked out in poetry and painting are part of a selective cultural tradition encoding a long history of deeply exploitive social relations.[16] Ideas of nature both express profound social longings and help conceal the unequal relations on which industrial societies are built. If they do not explicitly follow in Williams's tradition, groundbreaking works by feminists have detailed the close relationship between general cultural constructions of nature and conceptions of gender. An eclectic but growing tradition of work destabilizes the notion of nature as authentic, emphasizes its connections to relations of power, and encourages examination of the whole range of cultural practices for producing, showing, and using something called nature. In particular, Donna Haraway deals with museum exhibits and traces the ways the study and display of primates sustain cultural narratives about women and "primitive" peoples.[17] In the case of mass consumer culture, nature's reach, diversity, and popularity means that however formulaic the artifacts—nature theme parks, for example—the stories they tell are stories to be reckoned with. They are there, in part, because the producers of mass culture have a lot of knowledge about how nature appeals. And however we define it, the mass-produced, popular-culture version of nature is a major source of imagery and information shaping public understandings of environmental and scientific questions. The pervasiveness of nature as mass media content ought to attract the interest of cultural studies and communications scholars. But while communications scholars have extensively tracked the representations of violence, races, genders, and professions in the mass media, it is striking that they have not given such categories as nature, wilderness, or the environment more than the most rudimentary analysis.[18]

To take Sea World seriously, we have to view it as one stream of a flood of nature representations that greets North Americans daily. These images and stories percolate in entertainment, advertising, television, news reportage, film, consumer goods, and shopping malls, as consumer culture and the mass media make the nonhuman world visible to an unprecedented degree. On television, nature programming that bridges vast stretches of space and time is an enormously popular staple, ranging from inexpensive filler shows employing stock footage to high quality nature documentaries such as *Nature, The Nature of Things, NOVA,* and *National Geographic Explorer.* And everywhere, and more diffusely, in genres of commercial mass culture ranging from the television advertisement for Clorox bleach to the scenic postcard at the drugstore, images of the pristine pastoral and the untouched wild add to an ever multiplying stock of visual representations of nature.

Outside the visual media, the culture of tourism has also developed a wide range of ways of showing and knowing about nature, from aquariums, zoos, dioramas, and performing animals to packaged adventures and ecological tourism. At the relatively inexpensive end of the market, nature tourism includes old-fashioned camping and hiking at state and national parks; at the high end, it includes catered and guided tours for the very wealthy to such exotic sites as the Galapagos Islands.[19] Present-day tourism powerfully reproduces older imperial and colonial relationships between the first and third worlds, very often through the medium of mass consumption of exotic nature.[20] Americans also experience nature through the world of everyday material culture, especially decor and fashion. Highly successful retail chains such as the Nature Company offer mass-produced fashionable clothing and custom-made home decorations themed "nature" and "the outdoors" to a carefully studied, upscale audience.[21] Although its emphasis is strongly on seeing, Sea World also joins these experiential and retail constructions of nature. All these diverse phenomena are connected by the ways they circulate arguments about what nature is and how humans ought to think and feel about it, through the culture of consumption. On one hand, these products and media appeal to and even embody contemporary popular concern with nature and the environment. On the other hand, popular culture, mass media, and consumer goods play a profound although mostly unexamined role in shaping people's understanding of and relationship to the biological world. In her study of the Nature Company, Jennifer Price argues that shopping for nature commodities is a safe way to express environmental concern within the familiar satisfactions of consumerism, even while this activity is structured to dampen awareness of the environmentally exploitive aspects to mass consumption itself. In the representation of nature, it is this problem of the gaps between what we are shown and what we can't see, between what can be thought and what might be imagined, that frames the problem for studying Sea World.[22]

Armed with these thoughts, over the next several years I focused on Sea World's nature displays and especially its performing animals. Wondering where the theme park's traditions of animal display had come from, I read about the history of zoos and circuses, the performative structures of carnivals, and the ideology of natural history museums and national parks. I taught courses on tourism, animal performances, and nature and the environment in the mass media, using my teaching and discussions with students to try to understand what was happening in the whale shows. (The students were usually intrigued, and I learned a great deal from their comments and questions.) At the park, I tried to combine the historical and anthropological perspectives I'd gained with fieldwork, spending countless dollars on admission passes, film, and sunscreen, and endless hours watching, photographing, and recording whale, sea lion, dolphin, and bird shows. I asked my undergraduate students to tour Sea World, the zoo, or a museum and write papers about their impressions. I dragged my infant daughter, relatives, and friends through the park.

At the same time, I collected the unending flow of local San Diego press and television coverage of park events. The predictable and regular reporting on Sea World announced new animals, exhibits, and landscapes, charity events, and special performances, and it described animal research at the park. Less predictably, there were animal rights demonstrations outside the park and disputes between management and employees to follow. And life and death matters at Sea World could occasionally break into the national news, as when whales were born or killed in accidents, when trainers got seriously hurt, or ownership changed corporate hands. My bulging archive of press clips, local documents, and Sea World ephemera, along with the files of local governmental agencies, disclosed the history of the tourist attraction's interpenetration with the city and region, as well as the development of a national theme park industry. Surely this history was also part of the context shaping the theme park, its performances, and the perceptions of its audience. I became aware that Sea World had a local history of its own, one that was characterized by a close relationship to the growth of San Diego. And as I tracked Sea World in the popular and specialized business media, I saw that the park devoted prodigious effort to building a local, public identity for itself. The relationship of this identity construction to nature needed to be traced in its own right.

In 1991–92, a year's release from teaching allowed me to begin sustained fieldwork. Since I was now familiar with the park and its workings, I needed to test my understandings against the knowledge of the people who made Sea World run, and so I sought permission from its administrators to conduct interviews with management and personnel. This access took a discouragingly long time to obtain, as I was forced to work my way up from the park's public relations office in San Diego to the highest levels of Anheuser-Busch in St. Louis (and word had it, to members of the Busch family themselves). There was no reason for Sea World or its corporate owners to give me permission to do interviews. My repeated visits would take up considerable staff time and, I insisted, they could have no right of review or editorial control over my manuscript in return. (Sea World repeatedly requested this prerogative.)[23] Three things conspired, I think, to get me the access I sought. First, I provided management with a general description of my book project and assured them truthfully that I was not an animal rights activist.[24] Second, I assured them that I would respect "off the record" disclaimers and would not disclose sensitive information that might disrupt a marketing plan. This was not a hard promise to make since nearly everyone I would talk to had experience dealing with journalists if not academics, and as I pointed out, the pace of scholarly publication is so slow that it would be very unlikely that I could inadvertently unveil sensitive facts. Third, I was unthreatening but persistent. I told the managers over the phone, in writing, and in person that I sought to understand more about the park's place in the life of San Diego, and how they understood their work. Once I had gained formal access, I still faced resistance from a series of public relations directors in the form of endless unreturned phone calls and long delays in meeting my requests. My goal of finding out as much as possible conflicted with the public relations department's job, which, as in any industry, is not to give out information but to carefully control it. Here the basic fieldworker's techniques of reading up on the details and refusing to go away proved powerful. When I was able to display expert knowledge of the economic ups and downs of the industry, it was harder for theme park representatives to refuse to talk with me or brush me off as a neophyte. The formal permission from St. Louis headquarters helped a great deal: it gave me license to keep coming back with more questions. Finally, over several months I got the interviews I needed with Sea World administrators and employees in the marketing, food services, curatorial, animal training, public relations, education, and entertainment departments.

As noted above, my access was formal and sponsored, and the information derived from the interviews should be read with this in mind.[25] Nonetheless, I found that after an initial chat, most of the employees I met were happy to talk to me, even flattered, as people usually are when someone is interested in what they do all day.[26] These interviews were supplemented by in-depth discussions with several former employees who had worked at Sea World over a long period of time and could give me a strong sense of the park's evolution.[27] All these conversations allowed me to test the ideas I'd developed in reading and observation against the understandings of insiders. During this same year, I also conducted a field study of elementary school children to approach what Sea World meant to them and their families and in the classroom. I interviewed a small number of teachers, school administrators, and, with Sea World's permission, some of the instructors, parents, and volunteers who participated in Sea World's education programs.[28] And I attended Sea World's assemblies and special programs and wore out my shoes following along on school field trips and guided tours.

The result of these years of archival, observational, and interview research is a detailed account from several different angles. *Spectacular Nature* looks at Sea World from economic, local historical, spatial, and experiential perspectives, as well as from the point of view of its management and at least some of its customers. It is not possible to understand the park and its performances without this layering of context and perspectives. Two key trajectories are woven together in my exploration of Sea World's work and meanings: the problem of public space in an era of advancing corporate privatization is entwined with the problem of the representation of nature and the environment in the contemporary mass media. If at first I thought these topics were distinct, over time I understood that at Sea World they were not separable. Sea World, it turns out, represents new private institutional uses for nature. While it produces ocean-life stories for mass consumption, it is also inventing a public educational role for itself by providing curricular materials, classroom programs, teacher training, and media products to San Diego schools. When I looked at Sea World as a corporately produced public space, I saw a business offering a blend of information about marine animals and their environment in a commercial form that increasingly claimed the legitimacy of the traditional public educational domain. It seemed centrally important that this didactic product had as its main subject the appeal of wildness and the popular fascination with marine mammals. Nature was Sea World's educational product, and its entrée into schools and public life. Conversely, when I examined Sea World as a collection of arguments about the nature of the nonhuman world, it was impossible to cordon off the park's performed stories from their corporate origins. The peculiarity of Sea World is, in fact, how well and tidily these dimensions—the private, corporate, and the transcendent natural—fit together most of the time. Each facet of the park infuses the meanings of the other. Sea World is full of corporate stories about nature, and nature stories about the corporation.

The first part of *Spectacular Nature* traces Sea World as a place and an experience in a local and national tourist economy. In chapter 1, "Another World: Theme Parks and Nature," I sketch the theme park industry that is the context for Sea World and begin an exploration of the appeal of the other world that is its special nature product. Against a very general background of the social history of the representation of nature, I argue that Sea World is a unique case and a central example of the nature stories that are told through the American commercial media and mass-produced popular culture. These stories have a long past, and they carry particular class, ethnic, and gender codings and implications. Chapter 2, "The Park and the City," traces Sea World's local history and development as an institution straddling the public-private boundary. The workings of the park's landscape, its structure as time, space, and human effort, are traced in chapter 3, "Producing the Sea World Experience: Landscape and Labor." I take up Sea World's entry into the expanding market for nature and science education in chapter 4, "Enlightenment Lite: The Theme Park Classroom." Education and instruction make up Sea World's other, less material landscape, one that can be exported far beyond the physical park. Since Sea World's education products are explicitly built around the park's spectacular animals, they serve, in addition to their didactic function, as a way to market the park to its audience and thus to reproduce the park as paying attraction and going concern. The ways Sea World's spectacular entertainments are produced, and the peculiar constraints of working with live animals and a variety of species, are taken up in chapter 5, "Routine Surprises: Producing Entertainment." The central and paradigmatic animal event at Sea World, the Shamu show, I analyze in detail in chapter 6, "Dreaming of Whales: The Shamu Show." Here, I pay attention to the embedding of gender and ethnicity in the performance and, especially, to the relationship between the celebrity whale and its corporate parent and sponsor. From different directions, each of these chapters adds to the picture of Sea World's work with landscapes, plants, animals, and people, and of the ways it communicates its ideas about nature, science, and the environment. In a conclusion, I assess the general messages about nature and the environment that Sea World sponsors for its large public, and I return to the problem of the private, corporate production of public discourse around nature and the environment. Despite its emphasis on the specificity of local cases, my argument is that Sea World is resolutely a part of contemporary American and increasingly transnational corporate culture—its arguments are not just recyclings of older cultural patterns and ideologies. Rather, they sit and fit neatly in a contemporary context of the realignment of much of public life and cultural meaning in the United States today.

As the reader will have no trouble telling, *Spectacular Nature* has a political reference point. A basic premise of this work is that theme parks and tourist attractions are never mere entertainment and recreation. No matter how much Sea World's operatives insist on the innocence of entertainment, it represents and shapes the world in ways that have implications.[29] Selectively interpreting reality to and for their customers, the park's producers try to discover and respond to what they think their customers want. In the case of Sea World the reality to be interpreted is named marine nature. But implied in the notion of nature is a set of contested problems, including local and international histories, environmental problems, and people's relationship to the physical environment generally. In this light, Sea World's entertainments, as materials to help make sense of the world, have important consequences.

I began this introduction by telling a story about how I refocused my guiding questions in the process of research. It was not only my perspective that changed during the course of fieldwork. The park and its larger social context changed, too. Sea World got physically bigger, changed corporate hands, revised its landscape and architecture several times, and reassessed its market. Its managers shifted their rhetorical strategies to meet popular protest and suit their changing evaluation of their audience. The popular environmental politics of the 1980s and early 1990s increasingly forced the theme park's managers to perceive their customers as "caring about" nature, animals, and the environment, and it encouraged them to align the park's entertainments the same caring way. At the same time, as I detail in the chapters to follow, a series of deaths and serious accidents involving the orcas and their trainers in the late 1980s forced Sea World to adopt a very aggressive strategy of portraying itself as a rational, educational institution. In particular Sea World became more explicitly environmental and educational during the years I documented it, although "environmental" and "educational" have a very limited sense in the park. Changes in both dimensions responded to public relations pressures and reflected new corporate marketing strategies.

All this might seem like a story of progress: a strictly money-making institution decides to become more "educational," the better to serve its customers and a general public. For me it is not so easy to see the transformation this way. As my Sea World study progressed, conservative electoral and cultural politics and social policies gathered strength in California and the United States, turning even more sharply right in fall 1994. As I write this in 1996, Southern California now seems set to lead the way in accomplishing a radical governmental and cultural agenda that will include the privatization of public property and institutions, including much of education, as well as the restriction of immigration and citizenship rights, the dismantling of social welfare programs, and the mangling, if not overthrow, of environmental protections. Is it preposterous to locate a nature theme park in this social political context? At the very least, if a visit to Sea World expresses concern about the environment (as Sea World's advertising proposes), Sea World's affluent audience acts on this sentiment in a thoroughly private and corporate context, and one where the definitions of nature and environmental problems seem reassuringly separate from other political issues.

In the middle 1980s, when I began this project, the theme park as public space seemed like an intriguing metaphor. By 1996, it is less a metaphor than an incipient reality. I have already noted that the theme park suffuses entertainment with advertising and public relations. But there are more boundaries to blur. In the current context of discussions about dismantling public education, when Sea World argues that it produces a sound environmental-educational product, it is not hard to imagine that the theme park might soon replace the classroom. Indeed, I argue here that in some ways it has already done so. Similarly, given the growing enthusiasm for subcontracted, long-distance instruction via video and computer, Sea World's education and media departments may soon find themselves producing courses for schools and colleges, a project that is already well under way in San Diego. Given the increasing commercialization of formerly public functions and the swollen rhetoric claiming that private enterprise can always do public work better, such scenarios are entirely plausible.[30] Sea World's entrance into the schoolroom would be another step in the injection of a corporate view into the content of education, as well as an extension of control over the educational process. Such incursions could and arguably already do limit and distort democratic control over education, over what can be taught and learned.[31] Whether or not such scenes come to pass, Sea World and places like it have had an important role to play in heralding the growing role of the private corporation in producing public services for a profit, just as they have been important in promoting the private corporation as environmental activist and educational philanthropist. Sea World is successful in its public roles in part because it has occupied the entertainment space of nature so well and mobilized the universalistic meanings of nature so aggressively. Whether this corporation and others like it ought to occupy such an ample space is a different question, and I hope this book will help educators, parents, and citizens address it.

Sea World's versions of nature—carefully produced, manufactured, and coordinated from a mega-corporate point of view—are, of course, not the only ones available. But never before have images of nature had such a direct and powerful link to corporate capitalism or such wide dissemination through the mass media. The same forces involved in the biosphere's exploitation have an important stake in nature's definition and representation. Let's explore these unexplored connections.

CHAPTER ONE

Another World

Theme Parks and Nature

Sea World's experiences are manufactured by a relatively small number of people working for a very large organization; they are disseminated from a narrow point of origin for wide reception and consumption. In this sense, the theme park is industrially produced popular culture. Viewed this way, from its landscaping to its performing whales to its television commercials, Sea World is more than just another example of a universal human tendency to enjoy nature. Rather, the theme park's oceanscapes are an example of the private production of visions of nature and ideas about animals, images and ideas that spread out into the larger culture. To unpack the meanings of places like Sea World, it is useful to speak of theme-parked nature as an industrial product and to look closely at the industry that produces it.

At the same time, of course, the Sea World parks are popular culture in the sense that a large number of people, more than 11 million a year in fact, enthusiastically enjoy them. But what has created this enthusiasm? Fascination with nature and animals has deep roots in Western culture, and so, while the industrial history of the theme park needs analysis, Sea World's manufactured marine visions must be located in this cultural history. The present-day surge of commercial nature imagery is not a transparent matter of commerce bringing the previously unseen into focus, but a case of selecting natural things to see and inventing ways to see them.[1] Sea World adds to this history, producing and mobilizing a stream of intertwined ideas. Its innovation is to make remote ocean worlds visible to a mass public and bring previously little-known sea animals to fame, even as it folds these novelties into older nature stories.

Sea World's Forebears

The beginnings of this industry are usually dated from the 1955 opening of Disneyland in Anaheim, California, but its roots run deep in the history of popular and commercial culture. Theme park ancestors include the older amusement park and its peripatetic forebears, the circus and carnival, and the industrial expositions and world's fairs of the nineteenth and twentieth centuries.[2] Historians consider turn-of-the-century Coney Island prototypical, a mass commercial recreation synthesizing carnivalesque fun with the celebration of technological progress.[3] Urban resorts like Coney Island, along with smaller pleasure gardens, were inexpensive, widely popular gathering places for European immigrants, working people, and youth, providing a shared experience of the freedoms of the industrial city and offering connections to the new meanings of the culture of consumption. Their proprietors profited from the freeing up of leisure time attendant on the ten-hour day, and they catered to a large working and middle class seeking cheap amusements.[4] Social historians' evaluation of the amusement park is complex. These pleasure worlds provided a realm of liberty that undermined older gender barriers and allowed unmarried women, in particular, freedom from the constraints of factory and family. They gave a wide spectrum of Americans a place to shed harsh work discipline and self-restraint, a public place to learn to play. But at the same time, like much of the rest of commercial recreation, amusement parks and World's Fairs were racially segregated. Their displays carefully connected leisure to the basic lessons of white superiority and American imperialism. In this sense, there was nothing innocent about their pleasures.[5]

Between about 1900 and 1920, organized amusement zones modeled on Coney Island's resorts sprang up in most metropolitan areas in the United States. During the Great Depression, the amusement park business suffered, and it did not rebound until its wide working- and middle-class audience found itself amid the unparalleled post–World War II economic boom. Higher per capita income, the reemergence of leisure time in the 1950s, and the advent of the paid vacation in the 1960s gave the amusement park business new energy and direction. In the first two decades following the war, a building boom nearly doubled the number of amusement parks, from 400 counted in 1954 to 786 tallied in 1967.[6]

As American prosperity and the amusement park industry expanded, the parks themselves were profoundly reorganized. By all accounts, Disneyland, completed in 1955, was the model. At Disneyland, the amusement park shed its petty commercial connections, and the principles of the theme park were decisively laid out. In the late 1960s and early 1970s, many large national corporations followed Disney into the theme park industry, seeking the profits to be made from entertainment, mass leisure, and the expanding tourism industry.[7] Enthusiastically aided by local and state governments, this "minor stampede" resulted in a U.S. landscape dotted with elaborate, themed leisure zones as development corporations absorbed older parks, built new ones, and cloned successful single ventures into chains of similar parks.[8] By 1993, *Amusement Business,* the industry's leading trade journal, estimated that the more than seven hundred theme and amusement parks in North America had an attendance exceeding 255 million. Attendance at the fifty largest parks was about 143.3 million in that year, or more than half the combined Canadian and U.S. populations.[9] In the 1980s and 1990s, waves of corporate mergers, takeovers, and leveraged buyouts gathered under the wings of still larger corporations the chains constructed in the 1970s, so that in 1993 about 40 percent of all theme park visits were made to parks owned by conglomerates. In 1995, corporately owned chains accounted for 90 percent of attendance at the fifty largest North American parks.[10] Meanwhile, many small and locally owned amusement parks, some of them survivors of the thirties, continue to go out of business.

Disneyland's designers had sparked the two-decades-long theme park boom by inaugurating not just a new park style but a new kind of cultural product. The structure of the theme park and its cultural ingredients differ in some important ways from those of its forerunners. The early parks were certainly completely commercial ventures, making their profits from a high volume of admissions, rides, games, and concessions, all offered at low prices. But the first theme park was commercial with a new intensity: it built advertising and modern marketing into its amusements, and in fact it placed them at the core of its activities. As is well known, Disneyland's success derived from its founder's foresighted connection with the fledgling ABC television network. Together, Disney and ABC developed *The Disneyland Show* to showcase the Anaheim park: the show promoted the park while the park promoted the show and the network. Disneyland imagistically and physically converted Disney media products into tourist attractions. This new genre was a medium of mass communication, one that literally made film physical and spatial.[11]

As it has developed, the theme park is exhaustively commercial, a virtual maze of advertising, public relations, and entertainment. Whether Sea World, Disneyland, or Six Flags Over Texas, the theme park is the site of carefully controlled sales of goods (food and souvenirs) and experiences (architecture, rides, and performances) "themed" to the corporate owner's proprietary images. But theme parks are advertising culture in another way too, and here again Disneyland led the reworking of the amusement park's economy and organization. While the early amusement park was often built by metropolitan capital (for example, railway companies had trolley parks and brewers had beer gardens), Disney followed the example of the twentieth-century world's fair or industrial exposition and involved national corporations as investing partners. Consumer goods manufacturers like Carnation received exclusive sales, marketing, and advertising rights at Disneyland in return for cash investments to help start up particular displays or rides.[12] As at the world's fairs, these displays in many cases promoted a product, a technology, or a corporate vision of the future.[13] This pattern has been expanded over several decades, and the theme park has been used to concretize and demonstrate visions of the social future. Today corporate sponsors collaborate in promotions, sharing advertising costs while they fold their general social stance into the recreational landscape.[14]

The contemporary theme park is, in theory, open to all who can pay. In contrast to the amusement park, where raucous mixing was framed by racial hierarchy, it appears broadly democratic. But spatial and locational changes altered the meanings of the amusement park and defined the theme park as a new kind of experience, in some ways more restricted than before. Where early twentieth-century amusement parks had been built within short distances of urban neighborhoods or connected to them by cheap public transport, the new theme parks went up far beyond the outskirts of town. In the 1950s, land in the exurb was cheap, federal policies dictated the connection of vast interurban areas with the new interstate highway system, and housing policies set the stage for massive suburban growth.[15] By the 1980s, Anaheim, San Diego, and Orlando were no longer the sleepy outskirts but the centers of vast tourism districts.[16] From the beginning, this geographical pattern in tourism development tended to cut the urban and inner-city working class out of the theme park market. As one park marketing director put it, not mincing any words, "Once you got out of those old neighborhoods, you left a lot of trouble, a lot of tough people and rowdy teenagers behind. That was the real breakthrough." The new audience would be mainly white, suburban, and middle-class, although in this manager's opinion the important social dimension "wasn't color so much as class."[17] Navigating the interstate to the theme park required, of course, a car and a parent free to drive it, which limited the access of the amusement park's younger and poorer audience.

Similarly, pricing strategies helped shift the cultural meanings of the theme park as they revealed the developers' conception of their customers. Whereas the older amusement park charged no admission but collected a separate fee for each ride or attraction, in the 1960s the Six Flags parks initiated "pay-one-price," a high admission fee allowing unlimited access to rides and shows.[18] Although a convenience for the visitor, the single price eliminated nonpaying access, and the meaning of a visit to the park shifted from a casual, often spur-of-the-moment recreation to a planned excursion. Pay-one-price tended to define the customers as those who could save enough to pay a high fee, and it tended to define them as families—or groups under parental control.[19] The theme park offered families on vacation a carefully packaged tourist experience whose meanings were based on recombinations of familiar content, novel location, and the expanded technologies of perceptual control.

It was this corporately shaped product that became so widely popular, promoted through the 1970s and 1980s as the focus of middle-class travel plans and, increasingly, business conventions and professional-society meetings. As the parks steadily flourished, they influenced the landscape around them. While in the 1970s theme parks were stand-alone tourist attractions, by the 1990s they became the core of vast leisure and resort complexes such as those in Orlando, Florida; Orange County, California; and Las Vegas, Nevada.[20] Theme park companies are now involved in developing entire urban entertainment districts. The famous Universal Studios Tours parks in Hollywood and Florida (owned by MCA) have expanded outward into malls surrounding them. Called CityWalks, these are in fact attempts at small, themed residential and working cities.[21] Similar zones are being built in Germany and France, and in Tokyo and Osaka, Japan.[22] At the same time, urban planners and shopping mall designers draw heavily from theme park technique.

In the 1990s, the theme park industry's most striking development has been the integration of the chains built in the sixties and seventies into enormous conglomerate corporations. The "big five" owners are Disney, Anheuser-Busch, Time-Warner, Paramount-Viacom, and Universal-MCA, a subsidiary of Seagrams Co. Together these five chains comprise twenty-nine parks in North America, with combined attendance totaling more than 119 million visits in 1995. Four of these chains are nestled within mass media conglomerates, with Disney dominant; its American parks alone account for 47.2 million visits in 1995.[23] Time-Warner's attendance, an estimated 24.3 million, probably ranked second in 1995; the company estimates that 85 percent of the U.S. population lives within a day's drive (three hundred miles) of a Six Flags park.[24] The Busch Entertainment Corporation's nine parks garnered about 20 million visitors in 1995; about 13 million people visited a Paramount park and 12.7 million visited an MCA park in the same year.[25]

The Cash Machine

The theme park is a good investment for a corporate conglomerate, since it is a machine for the rapid generation of cash. Immediate profits are made in much the same way as in other mass entertainment industries, such as movies, rock concerts, and big-league sports. Admissions make up perhaps as much as 50 percent of revenues; roughly another 50 percent comes from sales of food, drinks, souvenirs, and other merchandise inside the park. But unlike the rock concert and more like the shopping mall, the theme park depends heavily on the construction of a landscape and the careful planning of human movement through space. The spatial rationale of the theme park is to cluster commercial opportunities represented by concessions, including everything from hot dog stands to designer boutiques, around attractions, which can range from rides and simulator theaters to animal, human, or robotic performances. Event scheduling, architecture, and landscaping help move customers through concessions at speeds and intervals that have been carefully studied and determined to enhance sales.

Because of the overriding importance of concession sales measured in sales per capita, or "per caps," managerial and perceptual control are central to any theme park. The old amusement park was a complex mix of often sleazy entertainments run by subcontracting performer-entrepreneurs or concessionaires. By all accounts it was this cheap and explicitly carnivalesque heritage that Walt Disney rejected as he planned Disneyland. By contrast, the theme park specializes in experiential homogeneity.[26] Replacing the petty carnival and midway entrepreneurs with the corporation's own centrally produced and managed attractions, Disney and his followers gained control over profits, the quality of concessions, and—just as important to advertisers and sponsors—image and style. This totalizing effort is captured in the industry phrase "to theme." Surface stylistic characteristics are highly coordinated in "theming," but more important, the meanings the park contains are centrally produced to be as nonconflictual as possible. Paradoxically, this overall uniformity is expressed as a rich variety of artifacts, cultures, histories, styles, texts, architectures, and performances.

The production of an environment that pays so much attention to experience is costly, requiring centralized monitoring of a range of factors. Temporary and long-term problems demand solution: theme park companies are divided into departments filled with specialists in traffic flow; design and signing; maintenance and sanitation; interaction between the park and its patrons ("guest relations"); the quality, tone, style, and content of performances; food and drinks; and souvenirs and concessions. One theme park designer writes that "in the final analysis everyone views the design of the theme as a complete unit in which all elements, major and minor, work together in a harmonious relationship. This means keeping contradictions to an absolute minimum."[27] Indeed, the concept of the "themed environment," the fully designed, highly coordinated "land" with all services, performances, and concessions designed and provided in-house, was arguably Disney's major contribution to the industry and perhaps to American culture.[28]

As is well known, park themes vary. The industry leader Disney's overarching theme is the corporation's imaginative work and media products, "The Magic Kingdom." During the 1970s the other park chains could not draw on an animated film heritage, but they did find pieces of cultural history to mine as themes. National history, once over lightly, was the original narrative of the Six Flags company; now it specializes in mind-blowing roller coaster rides themed to action movies.[29] As I will show, the Sea World chain discovered the charisma of marine mammals and the benefits of specializing in marine nature and wildlife. Media conglomerates' acquisition of most parks located in large markets has resulted in a wave of retheming as parks display and cross-promote the entertainment products of the parent companies. These products include a wide variety of animated films and live-action film and television, television cartoon and comic strip characters, books and magazines, sports teams and sports heroes, music and music television celebrities. The promise of limitless opportunities to cross-promote (in entertainment industry terms, to "support") goods and imagery and the vast potential for interlocking products and overlapping promotional activities is what has attracted MCA, Viacom, and Time-Warner to theme parks.[30]

Cross-promotional possibilities have been evident for at least three decades, but only the recent merging of huge media companies and the collation of a wide range of media products have allowed its full promise to become clear. Today, the overlap of marketing, advertising, and content has become the essence of media profitability, especially since licensed merchandise sales can now far outstrip the revenues from the original media product.[31] In the marketing language of the 1990s, each product—the television show, the animated film, the rental video, the theme park, and the Pocahontas pajamas—adds value to all the others.

In an industry dominated by mass media conglomerates, Sea World is both typical and an anomaly. Its parent company, Anheuser-Busch, stands out for its lack of major media holdings and Hollywood connections.[32] Although Sea World was a relative latecomer when it opened in 1964, its history parallels that of the parks industry as a whole. Begun as a single park developed by a group of Southern California investors, Sea World was quickly expanded into a chain which then changed corporate hands several times: The publishing, real estate, and insurance firm Harcourt Brace Jovanovich (HBJ) bought the first three Sea Worlds in 1977 in hopes of combining the marine exhibits with its own extensive educational publishing and filmstrip enterprises. This promise was never realized. When HBJ was threatened by a takeover attempt from a consortium put together by the predatory British publisher and financier Robert Maxwell, HBJ pulled all the available cash out of the theme parks division, sucking the Sea Worlds dry of funds for anything beyond day-to-day operations. The parks raised admissions prices and laid off nearly half their on-site workers, but when fiscal restructuring failed to right HBJ's ship, the Sea Worlds were put up for sale and purchased by Anheuser-Busch in 1989.[33]

Anheuser-Busch had been in the amusement parks industry in the old days, setting up brewery tours and picnic grounds around its plants in Tampa and Pasadena. The Tampa amusement park was expanded into a botanical and zoological garden in the 1970s (felicitously called Busch Gardens: Africa: The Dark Continent).[34] Later, Anheuser-Busch diversified by building Busch Gardens: The Old Country, a history park near Williamsburg, Virginia, and acquiring Sesame Place, a TV-themed children's play park in Langhorne, Pennsylvania.[35] With the purchase of the HBJ holdings, Anheuser-Busch owned the largest group of theme parks in the United States.

Anheuser-Busch's parks are very successful. While none of the biggest theme park chains report attendance figures, it is likely that Anheuser-

Busch's nine parks together have the third largest total attendance of the five United States theme park conglomerates.[36] At a conservative guess, the four Sea Worlds together entertain about 11.6 million paying visitors annually, and most of these are North Americans.[37] These visits alone evidence wide exposure to and interest in Anheuser-Busch's colorful worlds of the sea. And Busch Entertainment is expanding abroad with the Gran Tibidabo theme park in Salou, Spain.

The theme park business is ancillary but important to the brewer. As a giant beverage and food producer, Anheuser-Busch controls 43 percent of the U.S. beer market. In 1993 the company saw about $11.6 billion in sales worldwide, and in 1995 it bought a half interest in China's national Tsing-Tsao brewery and announced an aggressive plan to expand into beer making in all of Asia.[39] Although the parks appear only tangentially related to the beer product, with their *Sesame Street* character tie-ins and their nature education theme, they do help provide a useful "family image" for the Budweiser brand in particular. The Sea Worlds also help further beer's association with the great outdoors, picking up a longtime Busch family association with wildlife management.[40] By associating the brewing conglomerate with conservation, the parks help deflect concern over industrial pollution and large-scale waste production.[41]

Unlike other theme park owners, Anheuser-Busch has no significant media holdings or outlets to help integrate its parks into a cross-promotional marketing and merchandising strategy. Sea World has never had a film product or long-running television series to make up the core of its marketing, although it airs annual television entertainment specials and buys prime-time advertising.[42] Lacking a Mickey Mouse or Bugs Bunny, Anheuser-Busch and Sea World rely heavily on Shamu, the trademarked killer whale, which is also a licensed image, park logo, and corporate icon. But Anheuser-Busch's ability to exploit the whale mascot is limited, at least compared to what Disney can do with one of its characters. Although the company bought the rights to an animated, feature length film that would promote Shamu and the parks to movie and television audiences, licensing rights have been tied up in a legal Gordian knot.[43] Meanwhile, Time-Warner, owner of the Six Flags parks, has done well with two action adventure films starring a killer whale named Keiko. *Free Willy* was spun off into *Free Willy 2: The Journey Home* and an animated Saturday morning television show. Following an imbroglio over the treatment of Keiko at a theme park in Mexico, Time-Warner helped invent a "Free Keiko/Free Willy" rehabilitation campaign that not surprisingly also promotes the film products. Ironically, despite the

Warner films' anti-theme park, anticaptivity story lines, Sea World claims that all their parks have profited from an increased general interest in killer whales stirred up by the movies and the Keiko controversy.[44]

Industrial Nature Magic

The lack of a direct film or television tie-in has encouraged Sea World to carefully cultivate nature as the theme park's central story. Although the park always includes human and land animal entertainments, recreated ocean environments and marine animals—from invertebrates to birds to mammals—are the central theme of the Sea Worlds; the performing whales are the central attractions, and management calls them its "core product." Superficially, the ways that the different Sea World parks present nature seem varied; the oceans' rich variety is one theme at all the parks. Occasionally there are regional variations. Sea World in Orlando, for example, features manatees that cannot be seen at Sea World in San Diego; conversely, the killer whales are on display at all four parks. But despite the detail in the dioramas and the range of species within individual parks, Sea World's nature is standardized. As we will see (in chapters 3 and 5), nature displays for mass audiences rely on stock techniques and the corporate search for a consistent product. Indeed, in addition to being visually dazzling, Sea World's nature spectacles must be consistent and predictable precisely because they express a corporate worldview.

In the theme park–world's fair tradition, other corporations are involved with Sea World. The park subsidizes some of its displays through corporate partnerships, and park brochures refer to the Sea World "family of sponsors." In San Diego, ARCO helps present the Penguin Encounter, the Skytower Ride is brought to you by Southwest Airlines, and am/pm mini markets helps fund the Shark Encounter. But many other businesses and manufacturers, from Kodak to Pepsi-Cola, take part in joint promotional and advertising ventures inside and outside the park. Southwest Airlines also provides Sea World with a "flying billboard" in the form of *Shamu One,* a black-and-white-painted Boeing 737 lined inside with wall-to-wall paintings of Shamu. Through sponsorship arrangements all the Sea World parks reduce their advertising costs; sponsors gain exclusive merchandising rights (for example, Kodak and Pepsi-Cola are "official suppliers"), cross-promotional advantages such as the ability to offer Sea World discounts along with their products, and association of their name in connection with animals and children, the environment, and family entertainment.[45]

Sea World gives the most thorough service to its parent company. The park integrates advertising, public relations, and political argument for Anheuser-Busch. For example, besides selling Anheuser-Busch's Budweiser beers and Eagle snack foods, all the Sea Worlds' "Hospitality Centers" feature a microbrewery and free beer tasting in what amounts to direct product promotion. In San Diego, the modern beer garden houses museum exhibits of brewing history and video screens that cultivate Anheuser-Busch's identity as an environmental and conservation-minded company. Pamphlets and posters exhort customers to recycle aluminum, drink sensibly, and resist increased excise taxes. Next door, in a huge stable are Anheuser-Busch's trademark Clydesdale draft horses, the registered trademark of one corporate division converted into an attraction at a wholly owned subsidiary. Anheuser-Busch-themed merchandise, from beer steins to T-shirts and baseball caps, not only generates concession sales but circulates the corporation's image, as customers pay to wear its advertising and logos. And of course, associating Anheuser-Busch and its products with animals, nature, education, and families positions the world's largest brewer as a socially concerned firm.[46]

The company uses the theme park as an environment for its messages, and this can be useful, if it is not directly related to theme park profits. Anheuser-Busch's walk-through advertising may be especially important in a time of rising anti-alcohol sentiment in the United States. Brochures promoting responsible drinking through slogans ("Know when to say when") and urging parents to talk frankly with their children about alcohol can deflect if they can't defuse widespread concern about the health and societal effects of alcoholism and alcohol abuse among children and adolescents. Similarly, by relentlessly stressing the values of recycling in its theme parks, this huge manufacturer of bottles and cans can displace the discussion of the effects of the American system of disposable packaging and stave off attempts to legislate limits on the production of waste.[47] The theme park can be turned to many public relations uses, in fact; the more diverse the conglomerate, the more issues it may need to address. In any case, at the Sea World theme parks, advertising, marketing, and public relations are so thoroughly part of the landscape that they are collapsed into entertainment and recreation, until it is very hard to tell what is publicity and what is "just fun."

In the case of Sea World, the live nature of the oceans and coasts is the heart of the successful entertainment-promotional mix. Nature—living creatures in harmonious environmental balance—exists at Sea World as a commodity for sale in its own right, in order to sell other things and to help people feel good about larger social projects and arrangements, including the high-consumption economy typified by the theme park itself. On one hand, Sea World shares this use of nature as a surface with much of the rest of American consumer culture, and in this sense, nature is just another industrial product or symbolic commodity, available today to anyone who can afford the poster, the T-shirt, or the ticket. But of course, in another sense, nature is not just another product—not only is it the basis of all human existence but culturally it carries meanings that seem special and magical. It is a world beyond the human that is invented out of inevitably human meanings and desires, an escape from the limited, the routine, and the mundane. Here the oceanic nature on display at Sea World may have special salience. As we shall see in chapter 3, there is something special about the underwater worlds the theme park constructs for viewing. They can seem especially remote, deep, and endless, free of boundaries and limits. Such nature visions promise transcendence of the polluted and conflictual social world on land, even while we realize that they are in fact terrestrial and artificial, highly processed commodities.

As a piece of industrial magic, Sea World represents an enormous contradiction. Using living animals, captive seas, and flourishing landscapes, the theme park has organized the subtle and contradictory cultural meanings of nature into a machine for mass consumption. At the same time and despite its best efforts, Sea World makes nature—one of the ideas most taken for granted in Western culture—into a problem that leads to questions. Why should nature in general and ocean life in particular be so central to the workings of this hypercommercial space? How does nature work as a commodity in the late twentieth century? In what way is what we see at Sea World "natural" or unnatural? Who wants to see it and buy it, and why?

A first way to approach these questions is, of course, to acknowledge that "nature" is not natural but social and cultural. It's not new to argue that nature is a cultural construction. Anthropologists, historians, and scholars of literature have been at pains for decades to show that every culture uses nature metaphorically and the natural world provides not only all means of material life but a common, human currency for representing ideas about that life as society and culture. Rather than a simple reflection of popular taste or fascination, nature is often deployed as part of a definition of the world, as a way to convince ourselves and others of the rightness and inevitability of the world as known. It has been used to create authority for the social arrangements of gender, for example, in ideas of woman's "nature." It is invoked to justify family structures, sexual orderings, and racial and imperial hierarchies. But how particular constellations of ideas and images of nature become current and what social relationships they represent are questions that need to be examined with an eye for social and historical specificity.

The American mass media in general and Sea World in particular give nature a seemingly universal appeal that helps obscure its specific class and ethnic connotations. In this project, mass entertainment joins a grand tradition. For at least the last two hundred years Europeans and European-Americans have made nature a transhistorical category that paradoxically contains both fundamental human qualities ("human nature") and that part of the biological universe that is intractably separate from humankind and society.[48] During the eighteenth and nineteenth centuries, European and American artists, writers, and poets increasingly treated nature as a visual, touchable, "out there" object, literally "another world," endowed with cultural and spiritual properties. As Raymond Williams has pointed out, this tradition of rendering nature opposed it to human social organization and poised it emblematically against the industrial city.[49] At the same time, art and literature emphasizing labor and the complex interactions between humans and the biological world became more marginal to the Euro-American tradition.[50] Appreciation of a separate, aesthetic version of nature suppressed awareness of class exploitation and was used to distinguish people from each other and normalize the differences between them. For example, in the eighteenth century, as Williams argues, the gentry justified their expanding property rights and dominance over the rural poor through artistic practices. Sculpting nature into country estates, celebrating it in pastoral poetry and painting, manipulating it in the form of lovingly landscaped gardens, the wealthy literally naturalized the vast social and economic power they derived from the enclosure of agricultural lands and forests, even while they consolidated their control in the laws and courts.[51]

A related and similar process of aestheticizing nature took place in the nineteenth century, as an urban, manufacturing upper class developed for itself a wide range of practices for appreciating nature. As ethnographers Jonas Frykman and Orvar Lofgren have shown in their study of the cultural self-definition of the Swedish bourgeoisie, viewing mountains, sketching trees and flowers, photographing scenery, and hiking through wilderness helped factory owners and financiers define new identities for themselves. Exposure to nature through new touristic practices and visual cultural forms helped these men become rational and sensitive, in explicit contrast to rural farm laborers and urban workers.[52] Frykman and Lofgren argue that this new conception of nature as an empty, wild place where a man could connect with his soul and his nation offered consolations for the dislocations of industrial life. Once thoroughly mastered, the conception of the wild landscape as spiritual space became a form of cultural capital that the bourgeoisie could transmit to their heirs.[53]

Much of the European tradition of nature appreciation was adapted to the American setting. At the turn of the twentieth century, Peter Schmitt shows, amateur scientists, journalists, and novelists moved a campaign for scientific knowledge out of museums and translated it into a movement for nature appreciation.[54] Turn-of-the-century nature appreciation was located in an imagined "Arcadia," a not-too-faraway wild, and was in part a project of earnest reformers, in part a comfortable town-dweller's enthusiasm. This loose movement developed curricula for classrooms, organized summer camps and bird-watching clubs, and lobbied for parks and greenbelts. While Schmitt describes nature appreciation in the Arcadian vein as having a fantastic tinge, the urge to preserve open spaces and help urban children spend time outdoors surely had many democratic and socially progressive uses.[55] But under the surface, nature appreciation could fit with "Americanization" campaigns and efforts to model a hierarchical social order. The right sort of person, as advocated by nature educators, was an English-speaking, self-controlled, property-respecting, refined middle-class citizen. Whether this "right sort of person" was actually produced is another question. But if we look at rhetorics of nature whether benign or authoritarian, we can see that for at least two centuries they have belonged to the powerful. The propertied have used nature as a material resource, a symbolic resource, and a tool of prescriptive improvement aimed down the social scale at class and racial others.

No one would mistake Sea World for a Swedish forest or a trail in the Sierra, but this theme park tries to connect with the long tradition of adventurous exposure of the sensitive self to nature, a tradition that signifies property and privilege. When Sea World's advertising constructs the park as a worthwhile recreation and a place to learn, for example, it draws on this sense of nature knowledge as cultural capital. The connections to the nineteenth-century tradition are strong and direct, while the objects of vision reveal an important difference in emphasis: Sea World allows views into coastal and marine worlds, whereas the nineteenth-century tradition of nature appreciation gazed on garden scenes and terrestrial animals and landscapes. By giving us glimpses of the landscapes underneath the oceans, Sea World asks its customers to orient themselves to the future in unexplored realms as well as to cultural capital formed in the past. A long tradition of science fiction writing and film imagines the oceans as it has treated outer space, as a future on which to work with the tools of science and technology.

While Sea World partakes of a genteel history of nature appreciation, as commercial recreation it also draws on Euro-American traditions of displaying animals. On one hand, there is a long-standing pattern of displaying scientific control by presenting animals to the public; on the other hand, animals have been caught up for centuries in less rational shows. On the scientific side, as Victorian England consolidated its global economic power, the exotic animals of the old royal menageries were relocated in the new institution of the zoological garden founded by gentlemen in the interests of research. But despite their royal and learned origins, zoos were also popular displays. For scientists and public alike, animals were interpreted in explicitly imperialist terms; as tokens of conquered peoples and metonymic extensions of the geography of empire, they were illustrations of racial inferiority and difference.[56]

In related ways, in the period from about 1800 to 1900, natural history museums popularized the global scientific worldview and integrated nature into a Euro-centered colonial map. These institutions organized nature and displayed it as the subject of Western rationality, underlining the connection between scientific knowledge and the imperial organization of the world. The classification of animals, for example, was evidence of this combined intellectual and geopolitical control. An edge of domestic social management and cultural uplift also marked the prominent institutions promoting natural history and nature education in the cities of the eastern United States. The museum's boards of directors hoped to bring rationality to a wide spectrum of the newly arrived immigrant working classes, whom they saw as having anarchic, un-American ideas. Animal dioramas and natural history exhibits, especially, were aimed to help teach immigrant workers and their children respect for law and "natural order" at home and abroad.[57]

The founders of the London zoo initially saw their institution as opposed to the city's plebeian menageries, where crowds heckled, teased, fed, and baited the animals. They restricted membership to gentlemen and issued passes only to "respectable" nonmembers. Nonetheless, the zoological society garden became enormously popular with the people of London, and as limits on visitors were worn away it became a tourist attraction. The public found their own uses for these spaces and sometimes caused concern. Crowd behavior at the zoo was hard to distinguish from that at Wombwell's Menagerie or the London Exchange. The zoo's scientific mission was revised, in part through the recognition that since the irrational recreations of the urban working class were proving difficult to suppress or control, they could in some way be made edifying. But in theory, the zoological garden was a mechanism by which scientific knowledge and the understandings of experts could be disseminated to social inferiors with, it was hoped, improving results. In the twentieth century the zoo remains a preeminent popular learning and research space as the display of animals as exotic oddities has fallen to the circus and sideshow. But perhaps the lines of demarcation between the zoo and the old menagerie sideshow, or the zoo and the theme park, are less clear-cut than they seem. For example, the modern zoo still retains some marks of its early history. It is still a geopolitical map, a display of living curiosities framed as parts of exotic worlds and foreign cultures, albeit in much less overtly racist ways than in the nineteenth century. In the twentieth century, zoos, like theme parks, are powerful tourist attractions and resoundingly popular recreations, and they have not eschewed either the themed gift shop or the trained performance.[58]

Whether or not they are aware of it (and they often seem unaware of it) the crafters of Sea World's nature stories draw on this mixed and selective tradition of representation and thought about nature, on traditions of constructing nature in order for it to be consumed, contemplated, and experienced.[59] Sea World's nature magic partakes of the uplifting tradition in which contact with nature creates or affirms a customer's identity as a caring, sensitive, and educated person, even while its origins in the amusement park and midway give it strong ties to the less rational traditions of animal display. We might think of Sea World as a braid of genres, incorporating the rational and the irrational—blending the controlled and seemingly scientific display of the perfect natural, underwater or on land, with what are often frankly circuslike decontextualizations and exaggerations. Both circus and carnival sideshow isolate animals from their wild context to individualize rather than catalogue them. In the circus animals are often humanized (and thus exquisitely dominated) in performance; in the old-fashioned sideshow they were made gigantic and threatening.[60] A visit to Sea World offers ocean visions and tamed-wild animals as rational pleasures, but, in consumer culture's revision of Carnival, it is also constructed as a cut-loose spending spree that begins with the outrageous admission prices and finishes up with throwaway souvenirs. True, there are no gut-wrenching, mind-blowing roller coasters here, but there is a crazy quilt of cultural materials, a promiscuity of the serious and the unserious. And of course, the customers too draw on and participate in this mix of museum, zoo, and carnival in a new, watery key. As nature consumers, they are paying homage to one of the most complex ideas in Western industrial culture, even while they are also getting away from it all in a world of planned leisure and structured consumption.[61]

But Sea World puts nature through a further transformation. Here the nineteenth-century idea of the sensitive and rational self discovered in communion with nature persists, but it has been translated from a process of romantic national definition into an emphasis on the individual and the discovery of individual feelings in contact with nature. At Sea World, animals from another world are displayed in ways designed to bring forth positive emotions, and these emotions depend on contact, on the bridging of distances between the alien species, the faraway, and the self. Sea World specializes in and defines ways people can contact marine animals as well as see them, and this contact is offered as personally transforming in overlapping, multiple ways. Among the most popular attractions at all the parks are the pools holding dolphins, sea stars, rays, and skates that visitors can handle and feed. Similarly, the whales and dolphins perform to scripts that emphasize themes of loving, caring, and closeness between animals and people. The themes of "touching" nature and "making contact with another world" emphasized in Sea World's print, billboard, and television advertising certainly refer to the problem of crossing boundaries between terrestrial and marine environments, of creating closeness between people and animals, but they also circle around to imply that a visit to the theme park creates closeness among people, especially in families, between parents and children.[62] Sea World's spectacular nature is a medium that connects customers to nature and, in the ordered theme park world, to each other and to themselves. In this way, it both continues and revises the quasi-religious nineteenth-century tradition of nature as self-discovery and gives the domination of nature a gentle, civilized face.

Finally, Sea World's predominant language is that of reason, and the visitor to its worthwhile recreations travels a distance from the insensitive and irrational, best represented by the circus, to a more learned, forward-looking place.[63] The class messages of the long tradition of nature appreciation are reconfirmed at Sea World, as the general portrait of Sea World's audience reveals. The customers are largely white and upper-middle class. For example, the park describes its clientele as consisting heavily of "parents" who are "usually college educated and . . . interested in learning about ocean life."[64] Although managers of Sea World of California, like most white Americans, are reluctant to speak in terms of social class at all or to acknowledge a racial pattern among their customers, their own market research reveals that in general the Sea World audience, drawn heavily from Southern California, is older, whiter, wealthier, and better educated than the average San Diegan.[65] In 1992, the park's market research interview data showed that only 15 percent of customers reported family annual income under $30,000; 51 percent of customers claimed more than $40,000 annual income and 33 percent stated that their family earned more than $50,000. During this same period, median income in San Diego County was about $35,000; a similar median prevails for neighboring Orange County. Even allowing for the many problems inherent in self-reporting, this is obviously an affluent audience. Fully 43 percent of those interviewed claimed a college or higher degree, while 22 percent had a high school diploma or less. Market research for the same period reports that 89 percent of customers interviewed were "Anglo" and 11 percent "non-Anglo" (only these two categories were used).[66] This figure diverges noticeably from the general ethnic makeup of San Diego County, where "whites" comprise about 75 percent of the officially counted population, and it fits with my observations of the paying audience over many years.[67] The average audience member is a "baby boomer," about thirty-eight years old, and nearly 65 percent of the audience are between the ages of twenty-five and fifty.[68]

Although other theme parks in California use dress codes and profiles to discourage the presence of "gang members," to my knowledge the people who run Sea World do not do anything active to keep ethnic minorities out of the park.[69] Indeed, the education department's programs recruit minority children via public school field trips. Considering the multiethnic demographics of San Diego and the rest of Southern California, the wealth and whiteness of Sea World's paying audience seem to indicate extreme self-selection, despite Sea World managers' claims that "we're here for everyone."

The appeal of Sea World to children and families with children gives another clue that consuming Sea World's nature spectacle is in part about social class. As we shall see in chapter 4, a large part of Sea World's marketing effort is aimed at elementary school children, and this too fits with a great tradition of defining nature. The positive association between children and animals, children and nature, is a long one.[70] In white middle-class culture, children are supposed to gain special things from contact with nature, but perhaps these special things are related as much to social ideals and cultural capital as they are to problems of growing and learning.[71] In long-standing theories of education, nature and the outdoors teach the child about the inner self, and nature confers the good childhood.[72] And, at a more mundane level, contact with nature is thought to lay the groundwork for the child's future success in biology or some other important science. It is not that any of these ideas are entirely false. But in this ideal of childhood, nature, social mobility, and the sense of self all run together. The connections between nature, children, and social class identification are expressed in the century-old, middle-class emphasis on suburban yards, summer homes, summer camps, and nature study in the classroom.[73] That many of Sea World's advertisements feature children learning underscores the theme park's claim that it helps produce the right sort of person. That the theme park is designed for children to learn in the context of the family implies that the park also helps reproduce families and their social position.

In the end, it is hard to show how or whether the general economic standing and class makeup of Sea World's audience is an artifact of the park industry's search for an affluent audience, or whether nature is a commodity with special, important meanings for white people. It seems most likely that Sea World has constructed its nature spectacles with appeal to the educated, upwardly mobile, and wealthy in mind, that is, it has increasingly styled its displays and shows according to the long-standing canons of nature appreciation in order to secure an audience with disposable income. The following chapter reveals that this was not always Sea World's style. At the same time, it is very likely that price helps keep poor people and minority customers out of the park.[74] But since other theme parks in Southern California, most notably Disneyland and Six Flags–Magic Mountain, have strong followings among people of color and charge roughly the same admission prices, the cultural meaning of Sea World's product has to be considered as a force shaping its audience. It is possible that the version of nature marketed by Sea World appeals positively to white people as part of being appropriately white and middle class. Sea World draws on the tradition of thought connecting nature to self-improvement and social uplift, albeit mainly in the context of private consumption. Perhaps Sea World constructs its version of nature to appeal to consumers as much in terms of who they want to be, as in terms of who they are.

Is it possible that, conversely, Sea World's aestheticized, uplifting version of nature can seem unfriendly or irrelevant to working-class people and nonwhites? A recent study by the National Park Service at least bears out the possibility. Designed to explore why visitors to the American national parks system are so disproportionately white as compared to the larger national population, the study found that the parks were seen as unfriendly, even hostile, to nonwhites. The study took into account the costs of travel to parks and historic patterns of leisure for minorities, but found that the experience that was offered, especially the emphasis on being in the wilderness and contemplating spectacular scenery, was regarded as foreign and unappealing. Further, travel through rural areas to get to national parks and incidents of racial discrimination and hostility experienced there helped define this experience of nature as unwelcoming and even threatening for urban nonwhites.[75] It is possible that a trip to Sea World, though embedded in an urban tourism network, shares some of this meaning for minorities, for the historical reasons cited above. There is another demographic aspect to consider. Sea World has very carefully used its rhetoric of nature to pattern its attractions to appeal to "families," especially nuclear families. It has avoided adding "metal" rides and musical attractions that would bring in large groups of unsupervised teenagers—again, for white Southern Californians the presence of minority youth in groups almost automatically raises the spectral image of the "gang."[76] Despite the declarations of Sea World's marketers that "the park is for everyone," its pricing, location, mix of attractions, and the historical-cultural meanings of its nature theme have clearly marked out its audience.[77]

While the desires and identities of Sea World's customers have a long past, they are not unchanging, and the theme park reaches out to meet its customers' evolving desires. Touching Sea World's ocean magic is a way of making contact with a world of possibilities as well as affirming a social identity. All of the Sea World parks and their publicity materials, as well as the advertisements of Anheuser-Busch, appeal strongly to the environmental interests and worries of the American public. (Most recent public opinion polls show that the general public is more worried about environmental issues and in favor of stronger governmental action on environmental problems than either business or governmental leaders.) Corporations like Anheuser-Busch and multinational capital generally must deal with unprecedented environmental concern and a popular sense of local and global crisis; sponsoring spectacular nature in commercial entertainment serves corporations well.[78] Underwater visions, especially, transport the viewer to a world neither agricultural nor urban, a space teeming with colorful life that seems free of history and culture. Sea World's reconstructed marine environments seem total, unfettered, and of course beautiful.

Sea World expresses, in part, its customers' desires for nature and their worries about the future. But the job of the theme park is also to transform these longings. Customers want to see the amazing, performing killer whale and the pristine antarctic wilderness, of course, but they also hope to feel agency, that is, that however indirectly, a visit to the theme park is an act of caring. That they can do so is, in part, a result of the fact that in the late twentieth century, American business has worked hard to define consumption as a form of concern, political action, and participation. At Sea World, customers are explicitly asked to see consumption this way. As one of the killer whale show scripts puts it: "Just by being here, you're showing that you care!" In this logic, a visit to the nature theme park is a form of action on behalf of the environment.

Presenting Sea World as environmental commitment and Anheuser-Busch as an educational and philanthropic force, the theme park creates a closed circle of participatory spectatorship in which "being there" is the main form of doing. Entertainment, recreation, public relations, marketing, social mobility, and environmental concern run together to become essentially the same thing: the theme park. Certainly the circle is not closed yet, but this innovation on the traditions of showing and seeing nature is important. Untangling the Sea World versions of nature and tracking their connections to other parts of contemporary life, including American corporate culture, is the task for the rest of this book.

CHAPTER TWO

The Park and the City

Although the Busch Entertainment Corporation is headquartered in St. Louis, Sea World is very much a part of the city of San Diego. Since it opened in 1964, the theme park has played a defining role in San Diego's development into a destination, a network of mass tourist attractions. In turn, the city's rapid population growth, promotional strategies, and fiscal resources have helped Sea World expand from a local business into a national chain.

This pattern of shared growth and interdependence means that in a strong sense the city and the theme park have shaped each other. While San Diego's growth has been driven by military spending, federally supported science and technologies, and real estate speculation, its long post–World War II expansion has placed heavy emphasis on tourism. As part of the process of modernizing the city, tourism promotion helped reshape physical and perceptual geography—changing San Diego's identity from "Dago," as Navy men slurred the port and its small commercial core, to "America's Finest City," a sprawl of suburban housing, decentralized industry, and high-scale mass consumption.[1] Sea World was key to an expanding commercial resort district and became a fixture of the city's economic landscape, helping San Diego focus its image and providing an identifiable sight to attract visitors.[2]

Sea World's landscape reflects this history, as well as the effects of a series of ownership changes. More important, changes in the theme park's physical space disclose the evolution of the narratives of nature that Sea World offers to customers. These successive, rethemed nature stories trace the park's relationship with its audience of locals and tourists, different but overlapping audiences to which Sea World must thoughtfully respond. The theme park's managers report to Anheuser-Busch headquarters in St. Louis, and design and management decisions are increasingly made there, but Sea World is tightly connected to a national and international tourism market and necessarily rooted in a local and regional environment.[3] By virtue of its sheer physicality it must appeal to residents of Southern California and San Diego, who relate to the park as customers, neighbors, voters, and citizens. While the theme park may seem a quintessential postmodern spectacle, it is also a space, a place, and a performance with an audience.

San Diego, the Attraction

In 1996, San Diego County, with a population of about 2.4 million people, anticipated more than 35 million tourists. Swollen by a massive influx of delegates to the Republican National Convention, the flood of visitors was expected to dump almost $3.9 billion into the local economy. As billboards, television, and radio ads insistently reminded San Diegans, tourism is the county's third largest generator of income, after manufacturing and the military.[4] Boosters claim that tourists are vital to the vulnerable local economy which, like the rest of Southern California, has been shaken by a weak housing market, unrelenting manufacturing layoffs, and slashed state funding.[5]

San Diego's promotion of tourism to itself, although intense, is nothing new. As one executive put it, "[T]he local tourism industry didn't just grow. It has been pushed, cajoled, bullied, bled for, and wet-nursed" for more than a century, as San Diego has developed tourism by inventing resorts, attractions, and cultural images for visitors.[6] From the 1880s, when San Diego papers carried reports of numerous excursionists traveling south from San Francisco and Los Angeles to experience the city of "bay and climate," editorialists urged locals to make the city hospitable. And they exhorted for good reason. As early as 1887, the city experienced a severe shortage of hotel rooms, caused by the record number of ten thousand tourists per month arriving during the winter season. In 1888, the completion of the Hotel del Coronado on Coronado Island in San Diego Bay provided rooms for more than one thousand guests. Then the largest West Coast hotel, the Del Coronado helped turn San Diego into a major resort destination.[7]

From the beginning, the beaches provided a staple resource for tourism and real estate development. In 1914, a real estate syndicate began restructuring the peninsula between Mission Beach and Mission Bay by platting commercial, residential, and resort neighborhoods. Eventually tent cities; bath houses; piers; and Luna Park, an amusement zone with rides, a roller coaster, a plunge, and a dance hall, turned Mission Beach into San Diego's Coney Island. Bordered by Pacific Beach and La Jolla to the north and Ocean Beach to the south, the spit of land became an important commercial node for the city.[8]

When city fathers organized the 1915–16 Panama-California Exposition, San Diego took another major step toward consolidating a tourism economy. The temporary Spanish-Colonial city built on a mesa to the east of the downtown contained the animal collection that would become the city's celebrated zoo and the "Spanish Renaissance" structures that would later become the heart of San Diego's official architectural heritage. The exposition grounds, renamed Balboa Park, would become a centerpiece of both the town's civic culture and its developing tourism industry.[9]

The city's first tourism promotion group, the San Diego–California Club, formed in 1919, began by hailing the city in the Midwest and the East as a winter tourist spot, but by 1920 it was advertising the city's cool summers across the Southwest. As San Diego aimed at a wider and more mobile group of tourists, its proliferating attractions expressed class differences. On one hand, resorts for the wealthy were a staple. The building of La Valencia Hotel in La Jolla; the La Jolla Beach and Tennis Club; and the Agua Caliente Resort in Tijuana, Mexico, expanded San Diego's appeal as an elite destination. On the other hand, where wealthy tourists had traveled in luxurious sleeper trains, beginning about 1920 the expansion of automobile travel opened tourism to those of more modest means. The wider availability of car travel in the twenties was accompanied by a surge in the popularity of camping and, subsequently, by the rise of cabin camps, "motor courts," and state and national parks as tourist accommodations and destinations.[10] The increased number of visitors in the 1920s encouraged San Diego's city fathers to refresh the exposition grounds and expand the San Diego Zoo, setting the template for the tourism infrastructure.[11] By the 1930s the zoo and its animals were the center of a national public relations campaign for the city.[12]

Although tourism slowed during the Great Depression and almost came to a halt during World War II, the work of the San Diego–California

Club in promoting the city and coordinating local governmental support for tourism development assured the industry's firm place in the economy. After the war, this pattern of private associations in economic planning for the whole city was vigorously reasserted. County funds were channeled into tourism and convention organizations to promote the postwar city, as planners and developers alike saw rising incomes in the nation's future and increased mobility via automobile and air travel, as well as local growth linked to the military-industrial complex.[13] But promoters faced a challenge. San Diego's zoo and Balboa Park faced competition that was, at best, unsavory. The city's heavy dependence on the navy, and its fortuitous international border, meant that during Prohibition gambling and prostitution ranked among its major attractions. Its reputation as a wide-open town rivaled its celebrated beaches and climate.[14] After World War II, San Diego's tourist promotions would have to stress a cleaned-up and wholesome "family" profile in order to erase or at least modify the legacy of sailor-town. For example, a burst of promotions in the 1950s aimed to refresh the colorful Spanish image that had served the city so well in the past. A 1954 article in *San Diego Magazine* explained that "Eastern papers go for 'Spanish' type shots, picturing San Diego and Old Mexico as romantic historical spots still suffused with the gaiety and charm of the old Spanish dons."[15]

The city's postwar rehabilitation was also material, as San Diego's planners sought to recast the old commercial downtown of department stores, "travelers" hotels, and cheap shore-leave pleasures. City leaders working with property owners and entrepreneurs pursued a double strategy in which tourism was central. They planned a downtown convention center and visitor's concourse and used state and federal redevelopment monies in a two-decades-long project to clean out the red-light and hotel district. Second, they used redevelopment projects to shift the weight of commercial life northward. Beginning in the late 1950s, Mission Valley, a concentration of resort hotels, shopping malls, freeways, and a sports stadium, was built in the San Diego River valley floodplain. The river issued into the ocean through Mission Bay, a complex estuary and marsh, parts of which had long been used for dumping industrial wastes. Here a massive recreation development turned the "unused" city lands into a new commercial and public playground.[16] Improvement of the river's floodplain and dredging of the estuary began in 1945, when voters approved a $2 million bond. The city also received congressional funding and assistance from the Army Corps of Engineers for this massive environmental reorganization.

The plan for the new Mission Bay Park had been circulating since well before the war. Early versions projected a recreation area to rival Balboa Park and amplify real estate values in Mission Beach by building public beaches, water sports and picnic areas, camping facilities, boat slips, a ball park, and an aquarium. As articulated in the mid-1940s, the plan's focus was on local recreation more than commercial tourism, since San Diego already had a relative abundance of fancy resort hotels. But as the project took concrete shape, it was seen as a resource for the growing tourist industry. Contemporary planning maps show that by the late 1940s, commercial hotels, resorts, trailer parks, and restaurants had been added to the plan. By mid-decade, the project was defined as the city's link to a national tourist economy. In his 1954 report on Mission Bay, city planning director Glenn A. Rick declared that "Mission Bay is San Diego's answer to America's search for a place to go. It's the 'Mecca' for tourists' dollars in an age of longer, paid vacations and earlier retirement."[17] The 1958 master plan by the city Planning Department proposed leasing 25 percent of the land around the bay for hotel, motel, and other commercial developments.[18]

Around the newly dredged bay, tourist attractions spread and intensified. A new structure of highways and a cloverleaf interchange tied the dredged-up islands and beaches of Mission Bay to the old beach neighborhoods, replacing the pedestrian pathways and streetcars that had connected Luna Park to the open space of the estuary. By the early 1960s, a separate, bayside zone of high-rise hotels, vacation villas, marinas, yacht basins, and restaurants tapered off into the mixed residential-tourism-service neighborhoods of Ocean Beach and Pacific Beach.

In retrospect, planners would admit that the vast alteration of the city's relationship to its open spaces accomplished in 1950s and 1960s led to a double disaster. Cleaning up much of the older city and building freeways through older commercial and residential districts to support suburban expansion began a dispersal of people, housing, and energies away from the downtown, from which San Diego has not yet recovered. Channeling the river, filling in its floodplain with automobile-dependent hotels and malls, and destroying the estuary made an environmental disaster that so-called mitigation may improve slightly but cannot undo.[19] It is hard to overstate the magnitude of the environmental damage recorded in the transformation of Mission Bay into Mission Bay Park: by one estimate, dredging the park reduced the expanse of the estuary's natural wildlife habit from 4,600 acres to 46 acres—that is, the space available for the reproduction of species and the basic biological process of the wetlands was reduced by 99 percent. The result of the dredging and channeling was the extinction of much marine and plant life in the bay, pollution and sewage runoff problems, and water of doubtful safety.[20] At the time, mastery of the landscape and the quality of life seemed inextricably linked in the logic of growth.

With the Mission Bay plan, San Diego's local recreation and tourism now had modern heartland, away from the old downtown, separate from the scattered beach resorts, and close to the new freeway. The bay project spurred more attractions. Mud and sand from the bay went to make a new resort, Shelter Island in San Diego Harbor. In the mid-1960s, the State Parks and Recreation Department barred car traffic from a small residential district just south and inland of the bay, near the nexus of Interstates 5 and 8. Here, over the next two decades, San Diego's original site was excavated and reconstructed into Old Town State Park and Heritage District, a complex of historic government buildings, houses, churches, restaurants, and Mexican-themed boutiques. Within a fairly short time and within a small geographical area bounded by Mission Bay on the north, Shelter Island at the south, and the famous zoo in Balboa Park to the east, San Diego had constructed a highway-linked network of tourist attractions and accommodations.

The tourism forecasters were right: the postwar strategy of building vast infrastructure and extending national promotions worked well. Tourism had long been a power, ranking second only to the navy as an economic force from the 1920s until World War II. But now the scale and basis of the city's economy was changing, riding the swells of federal spending. By 1955 tourism held third place after the federally subsidized aerospace industry and the military, a position it has maintained ever since.[21] The city entered a new tourism boom: Between 1950 and 1960, money spent by tourists in San Diego County more than doubled.[22] This growth fed the hotel and construction industries: the early sixties saw a huge burst of building activity, especially at bay side and in the Mission Valley corridor. By 1964, San Diego had "more than twice as many rooms for visitors as the entire state of Hawaii," a close competitor for tourists, and rooms did not sit empty.[23] At mid-decade the average daily visitor population was about seventy-eight thousand, up more than 15 percent over 1960. Drawn to elegant new hotels like Mission Valley's Town and Country, these visitors were riding the West's expanding economy: in the fifteen years since 1950, tourists' annual spending had quadrupled, from $60 million to nearly $246.7 million.[24] Corporate and civic conventions hosted at the Mission Valley hotels and

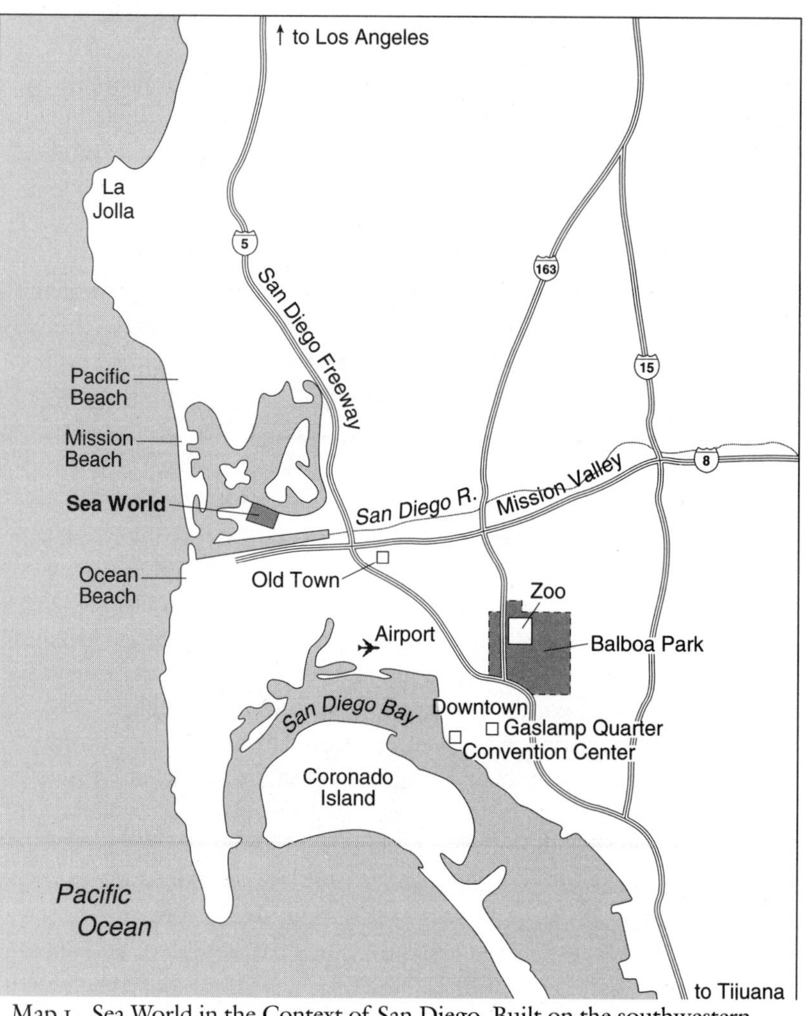

Map 1. Sea World in the Context of San Diego. Built on the southwestern edge of the newly dredged Mission Bay, Sea World took its place in San Diego's emerging tourism infrastructure. When it opened in 1964, the theme park was strategically located close to Interstates 5 and 8, near the airport and the cottages and motels of Mission and Ocean Beaches, and convenient to the new resort hotels on Mission Bay and Mission Valley. Old Town, the site of the original San Diego settlement, would soon be reopened as a state park and historic site, while downtown San Diego suffered the onslaughts of urban renewal.

Mission Bay resorts helped fuel these increases: San Diego nearly tripled the conventions it hosted between 1950 (152) and 1965 (410), and spending at conventions seems to have increased by a factor of eight during the same period.[25] Between 1966 and 1969, the county experienced the largest growth burst yet, with tourist spending rising by almost 70 percent.[26] San Diego's Convention and Visitors Bureau, also known as "ConVis," was now the nation's second largest tourist bureau in both membership and investment, and with the dawn of jumbo jet travel San Diego's entrepreneurs speculated that their city would become the most popular vacation spot on the West Coast. As the head of the Royal Inns hotel chain commented, "I think San Diego already is becoming sort of the Miami Beach of the West Coast."[27]

By the late 1960s, San Diego's growth machine had dramatically transformed the relatively compact and small city. Once focused on the navy and its superb harbor, in the 1970s and 1980s the city would expand its suburbs, its military-based, high-technology industries, and its universities.[28] Physically, the city would spread outward, adding tens of thousands of housing units and nearly fifty thousand new residents annually during the 1980s. And while recessions in the 1970s and 1990s would slow the growth in numbers of visitors, with solid support from the city government, speculators, and planners, tourism always remained central.[29]

Tourism is based on images of cultures and histories.[30] In San Diego's case, from the very beginning boosters and entrepreneurs built attractions based on mythologies of other times, places, cultures, or ways of being, and in turn, these images have shaped the city's cultural identity.[31] San Diego has drawn on and recombined four overlapping themes—the city's Spanish colonial history, its links to Europe, its closeness to Mexico, and the natural gift of the city's climate and beaches. In general, San Diego's touristic representations of history have centered on Spanish connections as opposed to the Mexican and Native American presence; its past, whether styled European or Californian, has been a veneer applied to monumental buildings, while much of the city's real and recent history has remained unexplored.[32] This has to do, of course, with the narrowly colonial and military focus on American history in general at tourist attractions, and the heavy emphasis on the mission period in California tourism in specific.[33] But it also has to do with the domination of Western tourism from about 1880 through 1920 by wealthy health-seekers. Grand hotels and luxurious resorts styled "Old World" appealed to these travelers, as San Diego's climate could be linked to the prestige of the European tour via a Mediterranean motif. The city's fledgling tourism and real estate promoters stressed the area's "Mediterranean climate" and the charm of its beaches, plunges, and cottage colonies.[34] In an 1895 promotional book, the Chamber of Commerce described San Diego as "Our Italy," an ideal destination for "capitalists, home-seekers, tourists, and invalids."[35]

In fact, climate, nature, and health form the strongest continuity in San Diego's century-long promotion of itself. Today the city offers itself to tourists as an outdoor-lover's paradise, a spacious, lushly planted, blue-skied, sunny playland, where history struggles to play a supporting role. The most important touristic sign of San Diego is still the beach, where a seemingly endless variety of outdoor sports and recreations unfold, from surfing, swimming, and sunning to sailing, kayaking, hang gliding, biking, roller-blading, and running. But San Diego's more commercial and constructed attractions also help define the city as a nature-oriented, conservation-conscious outdoor place to be. The San Diego Zoo, Wild Animal Park, and Sea World make up a powerful tourism triumvirate, presenting reconstructed natural environments and conserved animals to the tourist audience. Color photographs of birds, fish, animals, and plants are prominently displayed throughout the city and heavily used in mass media tourism marketing. As San Diego has carved an outdoor-sports and nature niche in the national tourism market, so animals and animal performers have become extraordinarily closely identified with the city.[36] In every mass media frame, from local news and weather programming to tourist brochures to airport billboards, the spectacular images of nature recur. Touristic images of nature tell a San Diego story sharply at odds with much of the reality its residents experience, a daily reality of polluted air, homeless people living in canyons, beaches closed due to sewage contamination, bitter fights over open space and planning issues, toxic hot spots in the harbor, and far-flung suburbs linked by clogged freeways. But they do re-create the touristic reality of warm weather, luxuriant blossoms, and vivid sights. The latest in a long line of images of place created to attract people from elsewhere, glorious nature and exotic animals are signs of both modernity and the future.[37]

Jewel of the New Mission Bay

If the centerpiece of San Diego's multidecade tourism expansion was Mission Bay, from the beginning Sea World was its jewel.

Public relations versions of Sea World history stress the entrepreneurial vision of its founders. But the theme park's arrival is more accurately located in the collaboration of San Diego's public and private interests in creating the growth machine. Sea World served the Mission Bay complex as its key attraction, a showplace to divert and occupy the conventioneers and vacationers in the new hotels and motels, while also appealing to the local audience and their guests. The theme park was the bay's largest concession; along with the zoo, the beaches, and Old Town, it provided convention planners, travel agents, and guidebooks with a way to speak to tourists about San Diego as a cluster of family attractions. Each of these tourist spots supported the whole: each attraction, along with the new concourse and hotels, helped ConVis advertise San Diego as a place for modern recreation.

The idea for an oceanarium, as it was called then, probably came from the San Diego Aquarium Society. As the Mission Bay plan came up for discussion in the late 1940s, the small nonprofit Aquarium Society reintroduced a decades-old plan for a modest marine life display. By 1954, the society was urging the city to build a $1 million marine exhibit including a snack bar, cocktail bar, and a motel on thirty-five acres of land. Although none of the versions of the society's proposal was accepted, they did spark enthusiasm for a commercial attraction on the bay. Five years later, the city Planning Department solicited and received several proposals for marine parks. A group of entrepreneur-developers won out, and in 1962 construction began on leased public land, at Perez Cove on the southwestern edge of the newly dredged bay.[38] There is no evidence of any public debate over the Sea World plan, although it is clear that public financial support was being directed to the private entrepreneurs of the tourism economy.[39] The oceanarium had been first suggested and drawn up as a public amenity, with an important open space component and provisions for a wildlife preserve, but it quickly followed the template of the private concessions ringing Mission Bay. Sea World opened in 1964 at a peak in the tourism swell. The park's importance to the local economy was marked by the presence of the mayor and congressmen at its opening. Presidential candidate Barry Goldwater made a backdoor landing in a speedboat to avoid a union picket line.

The field was wide open for Sea World's growth in the mid-1960s. The park's lease from the city gave Sea World advantages that few if any theme parks in the region had. It specified a certain rate of return on profits to the city, guaranteed long-term access to valuable city real estate, and left

Fig. 1. Sea World under Construction, circa 1962. The park was built on mudflats at the southwestern edge of Mission Bay. The pop Japanese Theater of the Sea (now the Commerson's Dolphins display) is in the center of the photograph; the performance lagoon is just above it. At the right, surrounded by newly planted palms, is the Hawaiian Punch Pavilion. Courtesy San Diego Historical Society, Photograph Collection.

open a door to future expansion of the theme park.[40] Sea World has used this door often, expanding its original allocation to more than 150 acres. While the original agreement between Sea World and the city called for a marine life display with some educational functions, the theme park was seen by the city as well as its developers as a revenue-generating concession with great potential, rather than an aquarium for the public.

From the very beginning, the developers envisioned their "aquatic extravaganza" as a rival to Disneyland.[41] They had an advanced understanding of the Southern California tourism market. Sea World's first president, George Millay, had been a restaurateur in Long Beach: his plan to build an underwater seafood eatery cum aquarium at the mouth of the Los Angeles River in Long Beach Harbor was foiled by engineering and water clarity problems, but it contained the germ of the theme park project.[42] Another two of the original investment group had extensive experience with marine life and theme parks: Ed Ettinger had worked as public relations director for Disneyland, and Kenneth Norris, a biologist trained at the University of California at Los Angeles, was curator of marine mammals at Marineland of the Pacific in Palos Verdes. Scripps Institute of Oceanography ichthyologist Carl Hubbs was another investor in the park, adding further scholarly legitimacy and scientific weight to the project.[43]

Adventures in Paradise

Despite the claims that Sea World would help San Diego step forward into the future, what the developers actually built on the Mission Bay site closely resembled some of San Diego's earlier tourist attractions. On one hand, the park was new and sparkling, a far cry from the tatty Belmont Park amusement zone on Mission Beach. On the other hand, Sea World initially had more in common with Balboa Park's cultural pavilions of the 1915 and 1935 international expositions than it did with the television and movie world of Disneyland or the natural history displays of a public aquarium. The early Sea World specialized in presenting homegrown exoticism, and in this it was much like older amusement parks and world's fairs. Just as the Spanish Renaissance–styled expositions had featured displays of the natives of other cultures, so Sea World's world was fashioned of fanciful Japanese and Polynesian villages, tropical greenery, women performing as underwater sea maids, and trained animals: it was distinctly faraway, antimodern, and fantastic.[44] But while the expositions had used so-called primitive peoples as counterweights in a nationalistic argument for the progress of humankind through racial evolution and imperial conquest, at Sea World culture was framed in nature to make an exotic environment seemingly outside of history, industry, or politics. As one journalist put it, "If it were possible to pick up and move a 22 acre chunk of the Pacific Ocean, complete with tropical fish and swaying palms on small islands, the builders of Sea World would do it."[45] While the expositions had used grandiose civic architecture to present a vision of political order and destiny, Sea World offered an extrapolitical garden paradise of leisure and consumption.

And in fact, the notion of paradise, a geographically remote and bounded realm of sensual and spiritual perfection, was much at hand for tourism promoters and pop culture entrepreneurs of the late fifties and early sixties. Hawaii had just become a state, and as part of this process the islands began a jarring transition from the agribusiness monocultures of sugar and fruit to the mono-economy of tourism.[46] In the process, the commercial culture of film, television, music, architecture, and fashion thrust Hawaii into popular awareness.[47] South Sea images were everywhere, and at San Diego and Sea World, Pan-Pacific theming was a careful tourism marketing strategy. During the mid-1960s the Convention and Visitors Bureau viewed Hawaii as a major tourism competitor and marketed San Diego as a closer-to-home, budget version of this American "paradise." A proliferation of Polynesian images throughout the city helped bring San Diego into the national mass tourism competition, even while they folded America's newest acquisition into the nation's consciousness.[48]

On the ground, San Diego's Hawaiian-ization took place stylistically and architecturally, as well as through national tourism marketing. As white, affluent San Diego grew northward past Mission Valley and westward to the open spaces of its harbor islands, it began to model parts of its suburbs after the tropics of Hawaii and Miami Beach. Shelter Island sprouted dense tourist accommodations, almost all of which followed a Polynesian motif, and Mission Valley developers opened the Hanalei Hotel and Islands Restaurant. The Polynesian theme had the strongest grip on Mission Bay, however, where Sea World's Pacific Island motif, designed by noted Los Angeles architects Victor Gruen and Associates, was repeated by the Catamaran, Ocean House, Vacation Village, and Islandia hotels.[49]

To its first visitors, the early Sea World aimed to present a Pan-Pacific and preindustrial world. The customers' gateway resembled an enormous, inverted war canoe. Roofs were rounded, thatched, curving, sloping, or swooping in Oriental style; pillars were carved with totemlike faces. This Western Pacific–East Asian theme was taken up again in corporately sponsored concession stands, in a Hawaiian Punch Pavilion (now the Harborside Cafe) that served nonalcoholic "Polynesian cocktails," and in an architecturally authentic Japanese village (now the site of Forbidden Reef) transplanted by Japan's Murata Pearl Company.[50] The early live performances, too, resolutely stressed the premodern. For example, at the village "real Japanese Ama girls" demonstrated their traditional pearl-diving occupation in an underwater oyster bed. At the Lagoon, friendly dolphins rescued a shipwrecked sailor, enacting an ancient folk idea about animals and their relation to humans. Tourist promotional films of Hawaii, booths selling Polynesian souvenirs and clothing, and corporate luaus held after hours filled out the picture.[51] The odd modernity of the tourist paradise depended on returning visitors to a dehistoricized, geographically remote extramodern world. Visitors were encouraged to feel like thoroughly up-to-date, sophisticated travelers and appreciators of other cultures, through the consumption of tokens of domesticated primitivism.

Culture and Nature Underwater

Next to this vision of a more natural, premodern culture for consumption, Sea World built a version of nature as another, underwater world that could be seen through novel means of vision.[52] And here, cultural fantasies old and new could be realized with the help of new or what seemed like new technologies. Again, this was very much in the Disney vein, from the Walt Disney Studios' early definition of the field of nature films for theaters and television, to its movie and underwater theme park adventure, *20,000 Leagues under the Sea.*[53] In its own World beneath the Sea aquarium exhibit, the theme park's initial performances constructed a mythical narrative about human relations to nature, couched in references to scientific investigation of the natural world. Friendly humans penetrated the mysterious world of the deep and found it colorful and hospitable, another world made completely visible by viewing and breathing technology. Behind Plexiglass barriers in the underwater theater, audiences watched while submerged "sea maids" with hi-tech vocal and breathing apparatuses performed a three-act script with trained dolphins. In another sunken "Sea Grotto," "maids" spoke through hydrophones to onlookers, offering tidbits of information about the tropical fish. The Sea World image of science was a precarious blending of the technological and the fabulous—more in the mode of Disney's interpretation of Jules Verne than the later productions of Jacques Cousteau. (Interestingly, the "life and work underwater" exhibits paralleled a 1965 navy experiment with a long-term underwater human colony in the offshore trench near La Jolla. Sea World's publicity materials speculated that in the future, millions of people would live in underwater colonies.) Sea World's vision of the underwater future was untypically female. In the early years, with the exception of the shipwrecked sailor, all the humans performing as trainers, investigators, and members of exotic cultures were female.[54] But here, in human presentations of natural "facts" and powerful visual access to another world, were the origins of Sea World's present-day claims to represent ecologies, environments, and solutions to environmental problems.

Part of the draw of the underwater paradise was the park's physical separation from the city and its contrast to urbanism. Whereas the 1915–16 exposition had converted open land into Balboa Park, making a public center for the city's first suburbs, Sea World's construction paralleled the suburbanization, dispersion, and emphasis on consumption of the 1950s and 1960s. As San Diego's development departed from central urban spaces and older industrial neighborhoods in favor of new construction in the previously undeveloped coastal mesas and rural hinterlands, Sea World and Mission Bay made up a new fantasy region poised on the Pacific, remote from the city's downtown and cut off from its cumulated past.[55] This isolation and symbolic distance were underlined in Mission Bay's physical form. Mudflats were dredged up and scraped into curvy islands; inside Sea World, paths wound around sculpted amoeboid knolls. The hot scrub and sand of the estuary's dunes were replaced by cool ponds and small streams as landscapers planted shady palms, ferns, and exotic shrubs to soften the brutal San Diego sun. The major performing area, a lagoon bordering the open bay, gave a view to the hills beyond, but most of the theme park views were turned inward.[56]

At the same time, the park's claims to present a sort of scientized investigation of a world beyond the terrestrial fit in many ways with mid-1960s culture, with San Diego as a specific context. References to knowledge were necessary to justify the provision in Sea World's public lease that some educational content, however vaguely defined, be provided to the paying public. At the same time, pop culture images of science powerfully if hazily signaled a future tied to military-industrial research, a future in which many San Diegans saw themselves as direct participants. In 1966, Lockheed Corporation, the powerful Southern California military contractor, sponsored a "Man and the Sea" exhibit, which explored ways the oceans' resources could feed terrestrial economies.[57] In this sense, silly as they sound in retrospect, Sea World's underwater exploration dramas spoke to the self-awareness of an influential part of the local and touristic audience.

Meanwhile, as all this exoticism was being constructed on the former mudflats, San Diego's downtown of commercial hotels, department stores, small service establishments, and tattoo parlors languished, undercut by competition from the resorts and the movement of commerce to Mission Valley's shopping malls. And from the 1960s onward, the southern and southeastern residential, working-class neighborhoods supporting the shipyards, docks, tanneries, plating factories, and military bases remained in their industrial and unbeautified state. Tourism development was not taking place in or near the neighborhoods from which it drew many of its support workers.[58] The city's eyes and development activities were usually focused elsewhere.

Sea World Takes Off

For all their strategic understanding of postwar San Diego tourism, Sea World's original partners knew that if they hoped for real growth for their company, their attraction needed greater national visibility. Simultaneously, San Diego's convention and tourism promoters recognized the park as a key part of the national destination they were aiming to expand. The park's opening year, 1964, saw a highly coordinated tourism promotion as a local television station briefly produced a Sea World series for syndication.[59] Television was central to the construction of the attraction and the city. For Sea World, it directly helped create exoticism and visibility. The park's developers learned well from watching Disneyland: they connected the park to the dominant national medium by making its landscape resemble that of popular network programs like *Adventures in Paradise.* And from the beginning, they filmed TV shows in the park.

Over the next years, Danny Thomas, Hugh Downs, Lloyd Bridges, Perry Como, and Bill Burrud, of *Wild Kingdom*—to name just a few personalities—would be recruited by the marketing executives to use Sea World as a backdrop for their programs or program segments. The result was to insert Sea World into an impressive range of daytime and prime-time television programming, from news and variety shows (*Today*) to music and entertainment specials (Danny Thomas's, Perry Como's) to dramatic series (*Sea Hunt*) to the well-established nature-adventure show format (Burrud's *Wild Kingdom*). (The park must also have been helped by the success of a new prime-time television drama, *Flipper,* filmed for NBC at the Miami Seaquarium.)[60] These presentations positioned the theme park on the powerful national medium, before a family audience, bringing it visibility and air time much more cheaply than paid advertisements could.

Historians of early theme parks have stressed how "televisual" the physical environment of Disneyland was, how closed, visual, controlled, domesticated, and commercial.[61] As early as the 1960s, theme parks fit well with the suburban living room version of the world presented on the small screen. At Sea World this principle was extended. The imperative of developing a nationally recognizable commercial tourist attraction meant that Sea World quite literally joined itself to television. In a sense, television didn't represent the theme park, and the theme park didn't lobby to get itself on TV. Rather, from the beginning Sea World invented itself as safe, clean, family-oriented television content, even as it produced itself as such a space and place. Television used this content, and in the process the city of San Diego itself became more visible as a tourist destination, connected to the nation through the television nexus of Hollywood's human celebrities.[62] Today this strategy continues to be important to the chain of Sea World parks; marketing directors, along with public relations officers and corporate sponsors, spend prodigious amounts of time and energy designing and producing extravagant network television "Sea World Specials" that feature performing animals (especially the whales), recruited talent (in recent years, TV serial, pop, and country music stars), beauty queens, and tourism tie-ins for the host park and host city. In 1995, for example, Sea World of California's performances tied-in with the top-rated *Baywatch* and *Full House* television series. At the same time, in addition to slick commercials produced by the marketing department with ad agencies, the vigorous public relations department works at keeping Sea World visible in the local, regional, and national news media through charity events and animal-saving stories sent out via frequent print, satellite, and computer press releases.[63]

The problem of celebrity lay at the center of Sea World's early promotional strategies. When in 1965 Sea World acquired one of the first captive killer whales, it gained a striking creature around which to build its attractions and entertainments.[64] The celebrity killer whale, quickly named Shamu, opened another avenue for touristic distinction. Sea World had been a collection of exotic fish, dolphins, and masquerading humans. Now it would be a "show park" built around animal performances. And while its reputation would be made by its celebrated captives, the park would also be shaped by tensions between the zoological display and circuslike spectacle. As I will show, although captive animals provide the basis for the park's uniqueness, their volatility as

Fig. 2. Sea World's First Shamu Is Lowered into Its Original Tank, 1965. Courtesy San Diego Historical Society, Photograph Collection.

political and cultural symbols poses formidable challenges to the park's marketers and managers.

By the late 1960s Pan-Pacific theming, the use of television, and the creation of an animal celebrity had helped Sea World achieve a national reputation, wide visibility as a tourist destination, and enormous economic success. In 1968 Sea World became a publicly held corporation, and by 1970 it had surpassed Marineland of the Pacific, its forerunner and closest competitor, in paid admissions and profits.[65] After this, according the park managers from this period, there was no looking back. Although Sea World came nowhere near the fame or profitability of Disneyland, by this time its future and San Diego's were knit together.[66]

Fig. 3. Dolphins and Sharks Arrive by Plane, 1971. Sea World drew on an international network of animal traders as well as its own scientists to build its display collections. Courtesy San Diego Historical Society, Photograph Collection.

Retheming the Park

Sea World had to keep expanding spatially to assure steadily growing profits. In the theme park industry, new attractions whether "hard" or "soft" (that is, built or human), new rides, or "rethemed" shows have to be developed on an almost yearly basis to assure return visits and to lengthen the average time spent in the park. Since theme park profits are based in large part on concession sales, and sales per capita are strongly related to length of stay in the park, expanded amusements and rising sales go hand in hand: as Sea World became physically bigger and diversified its attractions, its "concession opportunities," in the language of industry analysts, multiplied.[67] As Sea World's developers faced their success and the changing dynamics of the theme park industry, their efforts at expansion began to revise the park's landscape and imagery. And the "retheming" of the park reflected changes in San Diego as a place as much as the demand for growth and profits.

As the park negotiated more acreage from the city, designers tried to blend new ideas into the older park. Trading the need to expand and intensify attractions against the homogeneity of its original landscape, Sea World began to break up the Pan-Pacific architectural consistency of Gruen's design and gradually adopted a more scientific approach to themed nature. The mass cultural South Pacific resolved into architectural diversity and sometimes dissonance, held loosely together by the tropical plantings.

The process was piecemeal. Sea World saw bursts of construction in the mid-1960s after the introduction of Shamu, and as early as 1966 it had nearly tripled its original acreage. Another wave of construction in the middle seventies added more structures and spaces for mass viewing, including two large stadiums for animal performances. (Shamu had originally been kept in a very small circular pond.) Shows and exhibits multiplied. While designers continued to use botanical displays to soften the concrete of the animal tanks, they shifted the tone of the environment by including such supermarket-futuristic forms as the Skytower Ride sprouting an American flag and a Water Fantasy Pavilion (now the Window to the Sea Theater) shaped like an inverted Tupperware bowl. And the always-sponsored environment of the park intensified. Sea World financed its expansion with the help of more corporations that followed the lead of Murata Pearl and Hawaiian Punch and subsidized the construction of new exhibit areas or the development of new performances. The mix of local and national corporate sponsors, including Sparklett's Water (a dancing-water-and-light show), Pacific States Airways and, later, Southwest Airlines (the Skytower), local banks, dairies, Coca-Cola and, later, Pepsi-Cola, and Kodak, preferred their pavilions styled clean to meet the space age, as they were at Disneyland and the New York and Seattle World's Fairs. In return for their support, they gained exclusive sales and liberal advertising privileges inside the park.

Profits from the park and capital from the public stock offering allowed the original group of owners to spin their ideas and expertise into a chain, starting with a new park in Aurora, Ohio (near Cleveland), and, following Disney, a Sea World in Orlando, Florida, a sleepy citrus town on the verge of becoming the country's largest tourist destination. In 1977, Harcourt Brace Jovanovich acquired the Sea Worlds and planning began for a fourth Sea World, which opened in San Antonio, Texas, in 1987. Under the direct supervision of president William Jovanovich, the HBJ parks division acquired several other amusement parks, including the venerable Cypress Gardens in Winter Haven, Florida, to build the largest portfolio of theme parks in the United States at that time. When

Robert Maxwell's buyout attempt nearly bankrupted HBJ, the park chain and its animals were sold to Anheuser-Busch, the beverage giant.

The Theme Park as Local Culture and Resource

Even as Sea World grew nationally, to be snapped up by corporate conglomerates, it retained a San Diego identity. And while the park increasingly reached out to remote tourist markets, its local market grew too and, in some ways, became critically important. Like San Diego's tourist economy generally, Sea World depended on significant numbers of customers drawn from Southern California as well as the greater west and the United States as a whole, and it depended on a solid base of local customers.[68]

The marketing, televisual, and celebrity strategies that defined Sea World as a national commodity also helped promote it as a place for San Diego residents. For many San Diegans, Mission Bay represented a cleaned up version of the natural wonders of Southern California, improved with the amenities of public slips and docks, campsites, and picnic grounds. It gave them a place to play away from older, urban parks and provided outdoor space and water access for those who lived far from the coast. Set in the midst of this playground, Sea World heralded the city's modern future. For residents who could afford to go there and pay its modest prices (under $2 in the first years it was open), Sea World found use as a carefully controlled parklike space, a close-to-home tropics for children and families.[69]

From early on, Sea World built a community image for itself, with programs such as "graduation nights" for high schools, "date nights" for college students, and "kids' days." In the 1960s and 1970s, real sea lions, as well as performers costumed as seals, walruses, and dolphins, opened local shopping malls, visited the Del Mar Fair (Southern California Exposition), and kissed local beauty queens. In its turn, the city government produced rituals which communicated its view of the park's importance to the local economy and culture. For example, in 1965 the mayor proclaimed "Shamu Day" to mark the first orca's arrival. Civic leaders and the city elite—their own interests firmly tied to economic growth through tourism—saw supporting the park as their responsibility. They set fashionable events and charity benefits in the exotic landscape. In 1966, for example, a group of society women "reinterpreted" a Japanese spring festival for a charity benefit. From its beginning, Sea World enjoyed exceptionally friendly treatment from the local press, which followed the lead of the public relations department and covered Sea World personalities, from the innovative curator of mammals and the salty old sea captain who served as collections director to the "Japanese" divers and the wholesome high school girls who played the sea maids. This coverage highlighted claims for the park's beneficial economic and recreational effects on the city.[70] Newspaper columns stressed the park's importance for the local economy. Not only would Sea World's visitors add revenues through sales and hotel taxes, its rent agreement added to city coffers. All these activities and claims established the theme park as an important local place.

For Sea World, community goodwill was important to justifying the favorable terms of the lease, to passing city bonds and ordinances allowing such critical improvements as a major freeway off-ramp and access roads. Goodwill helped when Sea World asked the city council for more park acreage and permission to build on it, and it countered the bad publicity of trade union pickets outside the park's nonunion construction sites. From the late 1970s onward, Sea World's community identity would also be important in deflecting the criticisms of animal rights activists and protesters, who were frequently at Sea World's gates.

But most of all, the regional and local audience was important economically. After Sea World's first decade of growth, Southern California tourism markets had become intensely competitive. Customers from the larger cities of the West were indispensable, but by the mid-1970s rising gasoline prices and airfares, as well as the general slide in the standard of living, showed that tourism economies were not immune to national and world conditions. And theme parks had multiplied in Southern California until the regional market was near saturation. In a 1972 interview, Sea World president George Millay cited intensified competition from newer tourist magnets such as the Wild Animal Park, near Escondido; the Queen Mary, Long Beach; Lion Safari Country, Irvine; and Magic Mountain, Valencia, plus such "seasoned crowd pullers as Disneyland, [the nonprofit] San Diego Zoo and Marineland." "We have three times more competition than we had five years ago," he asserted. There were two ways around this problem: One was to pursue the most affluent portion of the market. The other was to attract and keep local, repeat business.[71]

To reach out to San Diego County audiences, Sea World developed several strategies that would stand the park in good stead into the 1990s.

Sea World's marketers began to work on expanding uses for the park. They began to add temporary, or "soft," entertainment to their roster of long-running performances.[72] The marketing division tried booking adult concerts and dances mixing musical and entertainment styles to pull in audiences across age and taste groups. These experiments led, in the 1980s, to the successful "Summer Nights" program, which keeps the park open late during summer evenings. Most important, marketers stepped up their pitch to conventions and meetings and developed the park's uses for businesses, corporations, religious, and civic groups. A pavilion was built to house meetings, banquets, and high school graduations; new arenas made room for ballets and concerts, ceremonies and services.[73] All these uses crossed the boundaries between the local and the touristic, and they brought in a higher-spending audience.

Sea World began to absorb some of the uses of the city's older core. With its new facilities, the park could position itself as a local public resource offering culture as well as diversion to San Diegans. For example, in 1977, the San Diego Symphony performed at Sea World.[74] As a gathering place and banquet spot for conventioneers, an auditorium and concert and dance hall rolled into one, the theme park drew events away from the foundering downtown. Ironically, this intensification of the theme park's role as public space began just as San Diego's planners were realizing that suburban and coastal developments were killing the city's center: in 1974, Mayor Pete Wilson inaugurated a plan for Horton Plaza, a shopping complex cum historic district that would lure department stores back downtown.[75] But in contrast to the mixed uses of the older city, these activities, from the aircraft carrier picnic to a performance of *Swan Lake,* were conceived first and foremost as ways of marketing the theme park.

The park's most innovative strategy for exploiting the local audience was to define itself as an educational institution. Developed in the early 1970s, a constellation of educational programs began to recruit growing numbers of school children into the park; in chapter 4 I will discuss in more detail how these programs define Sea World as instructive recreation. Staff scientists first prepared sheets of answers to commonly asked questions; they went on to work up teacher information packets and three-hour seminars with the ambitious intention of integrating Sea World into the public elementary school nature study curriculum.[76] At the same time, the park acquired a small publication, the *Journal of Ma-*

Fig. 4. Dolphin in a Bikini Takes It Easy: "Hot Weather Art" for the Newspapers, 1964. Sea World's early promotions frankly humanized its animals and often used human bathing beauties. Courtesy San Diego Historical Society, Photograph Collection.

rine Education, and hired a curator from the prestigious New England Aquarium to be director of education.[77]

From the mid-1970s to the mid-1980s, the education department initiated a program of free hours for school groups, sponsored a summer reading program with the countywide library network, and developed an "outreach program" of elementary school and high school seminars on marine life and ecology.[78] In its early years, the education department fell under supervision of the marketing division, and each of these initiatives was designed to fit in with Sea World's marketing goals. The library and outreach programs featured the park's licensed characters,

Shamu and Seamore the sea lion, and company president George Millay spoke revealingly of school children as "future audiences"—a kind of long-term investment.[79]

Whatever their educational benefits, the outreach programs undoubtedly familiarized many families with Sea World as an "educational entertainment" through the legitimacy of school participation and the conduit of the teacher. But despite its publicity value, the education department had to scrounge for corporate support, and no park space was dedicated primarily to the school programs. A look at what Sea World planned but did not build reveals the choices that were made and decisions that were taken in shaping the park's relationship with the city. In 1968, four years before the education offensive, Sea World announced the construction of a "World of the Sea" oceanographic museum on its grounds. To be produced jointly with the nonprofit San Diego Natural History Society and sponsored by ARCO, the exhibit would cost $3 million and feature twelve to fourteen exhibit areas, an Imax big screen theater, walk-through scale models of fish and whales, and displays on topics from ecology to desalination. The oceanographic museum was to have been a no-admission exhibit, adjoining the boundary of Sea World but with a free entrance through the parking lots.[80] The plan, therefore, envisioned a public amenity in line with the free uses of Mission Bay and much of Balboa Park.

While Sea World's plans for expansion were approved by the city council and local leaders began fund-raising drives, the museum sat on the drawing board for a long time, to be replaced in 1975 by a children's amusement center called Cap'n Kid's World (now Shamu's Happy Harbor Playground), themed around the licensed images of a local fish restaurant chain.[81] The proposed museum never materialized, but the co-venture with the petroleum refiner resurfaced in 1983 as the ARCO Penguin Encounter.

The museum project was, in a way, the ghost of the Aquarium Society's long-forgotten proposals. The case of the disappearing public museum reveals where the line was drawn in the theme park's efforts to be a public institution. Since theme park space is measured in spending per square foot, a free-entry or semipublic museum was a bad use of acreage for Sea World. Hoping for expansion of the park perimeter, its planners saw that a public exhibit could limit growth and draw off spending customers. If the project was jointly produced with the nonprofit Natural History Society, who would control exhibit content? In a theme park (as

Fig. 5. Miss World Contestants with Dolphin and Chimpanzee, 1968. Sea World's early marine mammal shows grew out of the circus and boardwalk carnival traditions. Here, Chester, a chimpanzee that performed in shows with the dolphins and whales, helps welcome beauty queens. Courtesy San Diego Historical Society, Photograph Collection.

in all commercial media) content must be more or less consonant with the views and goals of corporate owners; in retailing, content must consistently amplify sales.[82] As Sea World's profits boomed in the 1970s its directors likely foresaw that the paid attraction, with its corporate-size advertising budget, public relations machinery, and city backing, would outstrip any competition from the struggling Natural History Museum in Balboa Park.[83] Sea World was a public resource only insofar as this furthered the process of building an audience of customers.

Fig. 6. Grand Opening of the ARCO Penguin Encounter, 1983. A "people mover" carries observers past the illuminated, living diorama. Overhead are photographs of the penguins on display, with taxonomic information. Courtesy *San Diego Union-Tribune,* photo by Peter Koeleman.

Nonetheless, the period from the late 1970s through the middle 1980s was a period of physical and rhetorical transformation for the theme park. Its management tried, at first tentatively and later decisively, to move Sea World away from its animal show identity toward the image of a more nature- and science-oriented recreation. Sea World worked to build on its identity as a public educational resource by styling itself a site of private research, animal saving, and species conservation. A souvenir brochure issued in 1978 highlighted the park's autorevision: "We must learn not only how to conserve and manage the populations occupying the oceans, but to properly conserve and manage their environment as well. We believe a deepening knowledge and understanding of the oceans, based on extensive scientific study, represents the only real hope of preserving the living resources of the sea. . . . [A]nd the future of mankind may well depend on our success. . . ."[84]

The process of redefinition was not without contradictions, because finally Sea World was a structure built to return profits to its corporate owners by drawing large audiences and keeping them happily spending. Retheming the park "science," however, fit well with the tastes and

Fig. 7. School Children Make Contact at the Sea Lion Exhibit, 1986. Sea World's education programs bring poor and minority students into the park. Elementary school teachers in underfunded districts go to great lengths to give their students the Sea World experience. Courtesy *San Diego Union-Tribune,* photo by Joel Zwink.

interests of the higher-spending audience Sea World sought. A deep transformation was impossible, but a theme park can always find new themes and construct new surfaces.

The educational transformation of Sea World's public image and physical environment was in no small part a response to a series of internal and external crises that began to unfold in the mid-1970s, placing pressure on the theme park to become more museum-like and scientific for both local and touristic eyes. First, the popular environmentalism of the 1970s played a large role in forcing the new image. Sea World had helped create widespread interest in the orcas, but now it was faced with a public that had been exposed to popular scientific literature that speculated about the intelligence and communicative abilities of whales and dolphins and even their psychic or spiritual qualities. Was there a "mind in the waters," as anthropologist Joan McIntyre and psychologist John Lilly suggested, and if so what was it?[85] Gradually the park's writers stopped producing scripts like "Shamu Goes to College" and "Yankee Doodle Whale," because, they felt, the customers had begun to see these shows as humiliating to the animals.

Popular environmentalism had a more direct and antagonistic impact, calling into question the validity of Sea World's need to capture wild whales, train them, and keep them in concrete tanks. By the late 1960s, the celebrity animals were essential to the theme park and Sea World's entertainment reputation. But killer whales, unlike dolphins and sea lions, did not survive well in captivity in the early years, nor did they reproduce successfully. Since Sea World was expanding into a chain of parks, it needed a reliable way to add to its stock of trademark star performers. In its start-up days the park had formed its collection of performing marine mammals in the same way circuses, sideshows, and zoos form animal collections, buying them from animal dealers or circuses or trading with other zoological institutions. In the case of killer whales, which were unknown in captivity until the mid-1960s, they went on collecting expeditions off the coast of Washington State. But the passage of the Marine Mammal Protection Act in 1972 reflected the strength of a vocal movement to save whales, dolphins, and endangered species from whaling, overfishing, destructive fishing techniques, and human harassment. The Act seemed to show that public sensibilities about whales wild and tame were shifting unpredictably.[86] By establishing a rigid oversight process and setting limits on the capture, import, sale, exchange, and display of marine mammals, the Act threatened Sea World's access to wild orcas.[87] The park bitterly resisted the National Marine Fisheries Service's interpretation of the Act and other animal protection legislation as "anti-zoo," "irrational," and "needless over-regulation."[88] At the same time, Sea World tested the law. In 1976 theme park curators launched a whaling expedition in Puget Sound but were foiled by Washington State environmental activists and Senator Warren Magnussen;

the expedition turned into a public relations debacle when Sea World was roundly criticized in the national press by environmental activists. The incident had the disastrous effect of opening up to public scrutiny the kinds of techniques necessary for the capture of killer whales, and giving the activists the chance to air the views that captivity injured and endangered the animals, disrupted social groups, and weakened orca populations. Although Sea World' s management called on local politicians to support them in dealings with the Fisheries Service and in congressional and court hearings, the whale capture controversy dragged on for years in Washington, D.C., Seattle, and Alaska courts. It was finally resolved in the wild orcas' favor in 1985.[89]

The whaling issue forced Sea World to undertake a public relations offensive to convince their regional and national audience that they had the orcas' best interests at heart. Early Sea World public relations had celebrated a rugged "bring 'em back alive" ethos of open-ocean collecting, but clearly, since the public's attitude toward capturing killer whales had shifted, this was no longer working. The managers hoped that a more rational image of study and science would help counter the activists' assertions that keeping whales in captivity was simply commercialism pushed to its cruelest limit. Press releases celebrating collecting trips stopped, and reporters were offered briefings on research at the theme park and the fledgling education programs. For the park's customers, killer whale and dolphin performances began to include segments on the interpersonal (so to speak) relationship between animals and their trainers, as well as educational tidbits and scientific claims.

The introduction of a nonprofit adjunct was important in recasting Sea World's image, especially in San Diego. A small program begun in 1963 as the Mission Bay Research Foundation was reorganized in the wake of the whaling uproar and renamed the Hubbs–Sea World Research Institute (Hubbs–SWRI) after the well-known local marine biologists Carl and Laura Hubbs.[90] From its early years, Hubbs–SWRI has been funded by donations from Sea World, other corporate donors, and local fund-raisers.[91] It also solicits donations from Sea World's customers. Hubbs–SWRI scientists have conducted contract research for Sea World, state and federal governmental agencies, and corporations. Most of this research has an applied aspect; for example, it deals with questions pertaining to such subjects as the nesting habits of the least tern (a matter of importance to coastal developers) or whether sea lions are disrupted by sonic booms (an environmental problem for the navy). And it deals heavily in issues of captive-animal care, medication, training, and rehabilitation.[92] Located outside the park's grounds, Hubbs–SWRI is invoked and referenced in many of the texts and photographs on billboards, signs, and exhibit labels which work to show that Sea World is "much more than entertainment." Indeed, the Hubbs–SWRI programs are the supports for research as a new kind of theme park performance. Frequent mention of the institute in theme park exhibits constructs Sea World as a place of responsible scientific investigation and unfolding knowledge, and emphatically not a site of animal exploitation.[93]

From the early 1980s onward, the orca-breeding program was the most important feature of Sea World's new public face. These efforts were celebrated and powerfully reinforced after 1988, with the first successful delivery and survival of a baby orca.[94] Curators had found that much larger tanks and the presence of a second female with the birthing mother increased the chances for a newborn's survival. The whale shows shed some more of their sideshow heritage and began to emphasize captive reproduction and conservation through research on captive animals. In this way, Sea World's institutional image converged with that of the San Diego Zoo and Wild Animal Park, which in the 1980s also began to extensively publicize claims that captive reproductive was the answer to the problem of preservation of endangered species.[95]

However, the public relations pressures on the park did not let up. The late 1980s saw a spate of what seemed like uncontrollable controversy and bad publicity. When a trainer was almost killed in a widely publicized accident in 1987, a history of many previous near-disasters was disclosed.[96] Then, in 1989, there were two highly visible whale deaths. In the worst of these, a mother whale bled to death in front of a crowd of August tourists. National media attention, including the broadcast of agonizing video footage, kept animal rights protesters outside the park gates and forced Sea World's managers to insist even more vigorously that the park was engaged in research and environmental conservation.[97]

The process of retheming the park "science" was expressed in the landscape as much as in public relations. Gradually the park's general architectural style had become cleaner and more austerely modern as its designers modified the old tropical core. After Harcourt Brace Jovanovich purchased the park in 1977, the in-house architects were directed to adopt a cool and functional contemporary style and a blue-and-white color scheme. The old totem faces were painted solid white, and the thatched roofs gradually began to vanish, to be followed by the sea maids and pearl divers.

And park spaces became bigger and more open. In part this was due to attendance, which rose from about 2.62 million in 1980 to roughly 3.75 million in 1990.[98] During its twelve-year tenure, HBJ management built more civic-styled open spaces, and the newer, eastern part of the park worked less to call up a foreign culture (with the exception of the reconstructed urban neighborhood, "City Streets") than it tried to use monumental spaces, flagpoles, sculpture, and huge maps of the United States to convey the importance and authority of the parent corporation. But the most important large-scale construction, and perhaps the most important way to communicate corporate authority, has been a new kind of display. In the last decade, under both Harcourt Brace Jovanovich and Anheuser-Busch, Sea World built several total environments, or ecosystem replicas. Following the fashion in zoos, the theme park moved away from the relatively sterile, small animal cages, pools, and tanks to exhibits that tried to represent whole worlds.[99] The ARCO Penguin Encounter began as an experiment in aviculture, an attempt at fostering the reproduction of Adelie penguins in a simulated antarctic environment.[100] Eventually the behind-the-scenes hatchery evolved into a living, multispecies penguin colony diorama—produced at enormous cost and complete with water and ice. This multimedia exhibit stresses exploration and research as videotapes narrate the daunting voyage of Sea World ornithologists to the wilds of southern Chile to collect penguin eggs for the hatchery. Display panels in and outside the building stress the importance of understanding the Antarctic ecosystem, especially since Antarctica is figured as a "last frontier," full of "resources."[101] Under Anheuser-Busch, Sea World has added the Forbidden Reef, comprised of Bat Ray Shallows and Moray Eel Caverns; a new Shark Encounter; and Rocky Point Preserve. This last display is, of course, not really a preserve at all but a bit of molded rock coastline with a wave machine and sound track. The Rocky Point Preserve houses dolphins and otters in separate tanks but represents the notion of ecology, of whole and interdependent systems of life.[102] These are complex and expensive exhibits, and the opening of each one shows up as a spike on the longitudinal attendance charts.

In aid of its science and research theme, Sea World has increasingly added texts to its landscape. Visitors can draw on aural or written cues to interpret exhibits and guide them through the park, although these texts are much sparser than those at science museums or aquariums. From the late 1970s, brochures, exhibit labels, explanatory signs, and small handbooks referenced the animals. From the mid-1980s, education

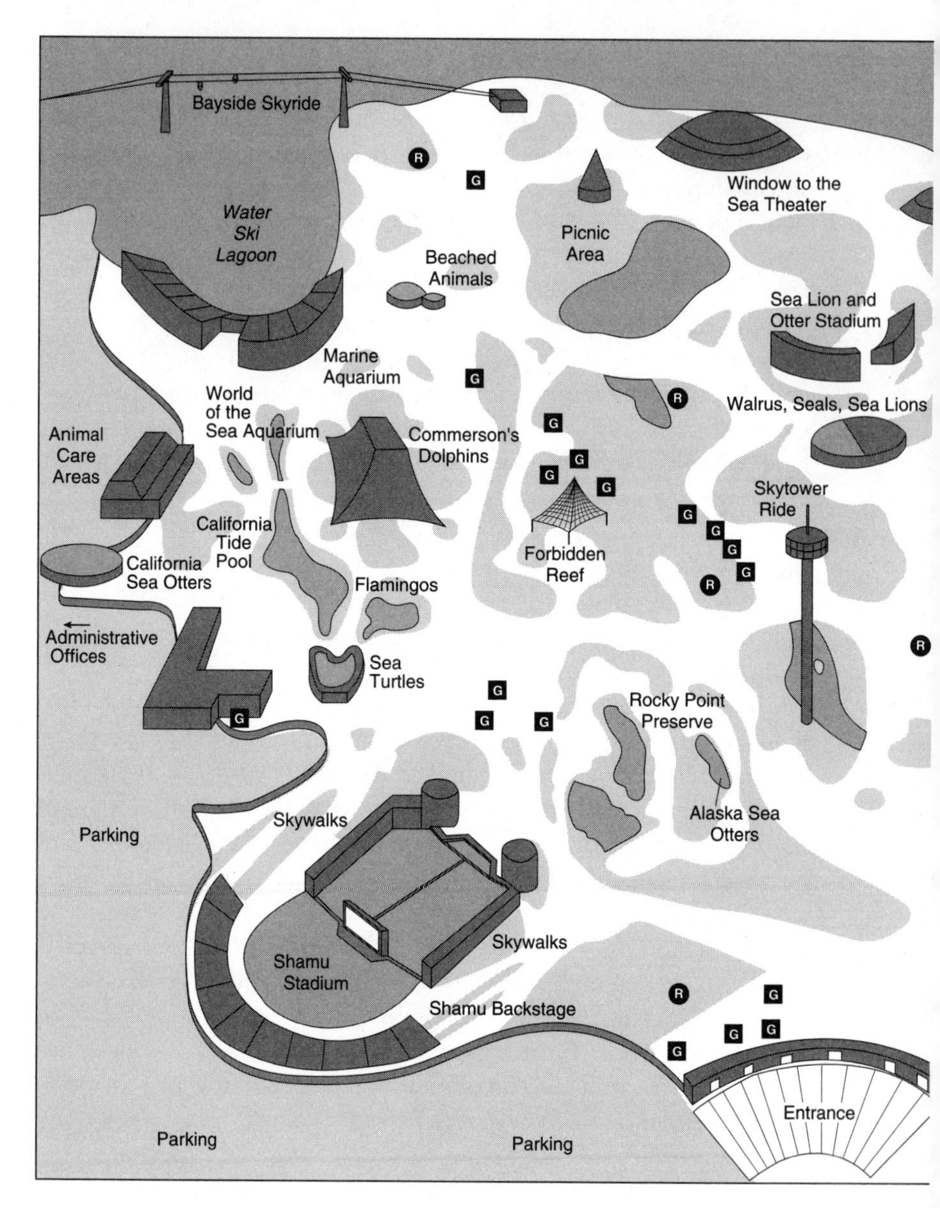

Map 2. Sea World, 1996. Sea World claims to give its customers entry to "another world," to offer an encompassing vision of marine nature. In fact, the park provides a tour of regions and sights predefined as exotic by the mass media and tourism industries. At the same time, the park landscape presents some incongruous displays—such as the Clydesdale Hamlet—closely tied to its function as advertising for Anheuser-Busch. Shamu's Happy Harbor and nearby Games Arcade aim to extend the length of customers' stays in the park. Walkways funnel customers from animal performances in stadiums through a nearly endless array of carefully placed gift shops, concessions, restaurants, and snack bars.

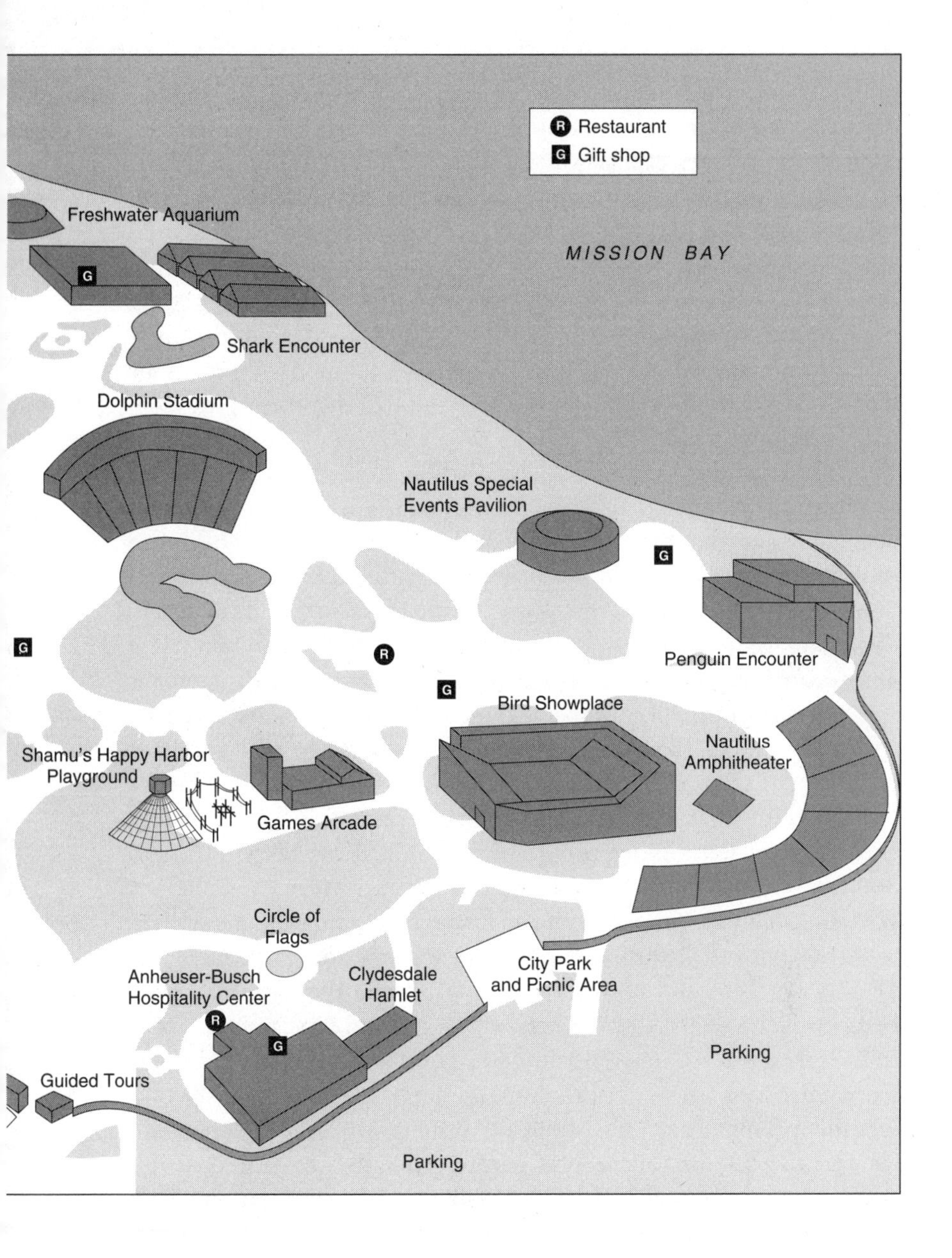
Restaurant
Gift shop
MISSION BAY
Freshwater Aquarium
Shark Encounter
Dolphin Stadium
Nautilus Special
Events Pavilion
Penguin Encounter
Bird Showplace
Nautilus
Amphitheater
Shamu's Happy Harbor
Playground
Games Arcade
Circle of
Flags
Anheuser-Busch
Hospitality Center
Clydesdale
Hamlet
City Park
and Picnic Area
Parking
Guided Tours
Parking

department workers served as "interpreters" and personal tour guides; the park also adopted explanatory video and audio installations. The concepts of the seas as a resource for human management "based on scientific study" and of the need for wildlife conservation were grafted onto already existing surfaces like the California Tide Pool exhibit, where children at play became student researchers, and the old dolphin petting pool, where placards about tuna industry research reassured customers that the canneries cared about the chances for dolphin survival. As at the world's fairs or Walt Disney World, these texts tell the story of the company's good works.

The last decade of changes at Sea World not only reflected the public pressures brought by activists, they revealed a shift in the park's understanding of the sensibilities of its larger audience. As Sea World shed its fantastical paradise identity for a representation of rationality and modernity, its managers seem to have realized that they could appeal to their San Diego and Southern California customers in a new way. Here architecture provides a clue: The hard-edged architecture of the 1980s was, of course, much like that being built in San Diego's industrial parks, strip malls, and condo complexes. It not only seems "new," it speaks of the power of science and technology to solve environmental problems. In a sense, it helps coordinate the park with the professional, technical, and scientific sensibilities of the highly trained migrants drawn to Southern California by the explosive growth in the 1970s and 1980s of government and military science and research programs.[103] These white migrants, with their businesses and technology parks, have filled San Diego's northern and northeastern suburbs, and they help make the bedrock of Sea World's local audience. Upscale and educated, they have to a degree absorbed the relatively new notion of ecology and the holistic popular consciousness of the 1970s, if not the animal rights ideologies that prompt uneasiness about performing whales. They are familiar with the cultural valuation of nature, while they remain identified occupationally, economically, and socially with the corporations shaping the city's high-technology defense systems and biotechnology sector. Thus, the gradual and piecemeal process of architecturally, textually, and performatively retheming the park "science" and "education" has not only helped fend off criticism from environmentalists and animal rights activists, it parallels the social identifications of San Diego's white, affluent residents.[104]

Over thirty years, Sea World has become part of and helped build the city's culture and identity. The local appeal of the park is reflected in its ability to draw more than half of its nearly 4 million annual visitors from within a hundred-mile radius.[105] Its presence is felt as it positions itself as a good citizen and provides spaces for a number of well-understood services and functions, along with thousands of full-time and seasonal, part-time low wage jobs.[106]

Sea World's location in the touristic landscape is as important as ever before, if not more so. A short drive away, merchants and developers are struggling to give the city center that nearly collapsed in the 1960s new life. New downtown hotels and spectacular banking towers have recast at least part of the central city's profile, but except for a few lively blocks of expensive restaurants, the downtown still struggles.[107] A massive convention center along the harbor front and a postmodern-styled, urban-themed shopping center mark opposite ends of a narrow channel of streets, through which, it is hoped, crowds of conventioneers can be pushed back and forth. This Gaslamp Quarter is decorated with historical remnants and reinventions of mercantile San Diego at the turn of the century; indistinguishable from other turn-of-the-century tourist areas, along with Old Town it makes up the history pole of San Diego's tourism map. Although the downtown is in many ways becoming a theme park, the story it wants to tell is not yet clear. San Diego's nature attractions are much more coherent and cogent landscapes.

The theme park remains an important piece of the local culture at hand. Although its admission price has risen to nearly $30 for an adult, Sea World finds use as a kind of private-public park, a controlled outdoor space that its annual pass–holders can visit casually.[108] By contrast, due to the city's growth the capacities of all San Diego's public beaches and Mission Bay Park are strained by heavy use, even as funds for maintenance and staffing are cut.[109] The context of declining care of beaches and parks makes the manicured landscape of the private, pay-to-enter facility stand out sharply. And Sea World's environmental exhibits allow no understanding of the ecological history of Mission Bay or the crises of San Diego's waters, dangerously polluted by runoff, sewage pipe leaks, and old deposits of industrial toxics. In fact, Sea World's spectacle of nature provides more anesthesia than challenge for the serious spatial and environmental problems of daily life.

Sea World's growth has been a complex process of accommodation. The marine theme park has been buoyed by San Diego's economic and population growth, buffeted by Southern California's recessions, pushed by changing customer sensibilities, and pressured by popular environmentalism. As a part of expanding corporations, it has been driven to build a national tourist attraction *and* intensify cultivation of the local audience. The interaction between these forces has been complex and at times uneven, but over time it has been answered by decisions culminating in a series of overlapping surfaces. Sea World simulates public space and a research and educational institution within the private pay-to-enter park. At the same time, it offers its commercial public a veneer of environmental concern. In a sense Sea World's history is a series of simulations: first, of the long-proposed but never built public aquarium, later, of the public oceanographic museum. It thus incorporates the notions of these older institutions and activities into itself without relinquishing any of its intensely commodified space.[110] But the theme park goes further: in addition to creating the image of a public institution, it has also invented a range of visible activities to coordinate with it—from evening concerts and educational programs to a working penguin hatchery and whale-breeding farm. Through these activities, Sea World's customers participate in its spectacle and, by extension, in its brand of social action on and for nature. In this sense, Sea World deals in more than simulations; it creates ways for people to live its spectacle. It is the profoundly material expression of a corporate point of view, a reinterpretation of nature and environmental concern, in the husk of a public space.

CHAPTER THREE

Producing the Sea World Experience

Landscape and Labor

Sea World aims to deliver a total experience to its customers. Unfolding in three-dimensional space, the park is a carefully coordinated flow of sights, sounds, and textures of something like nature.[1] Significant effort goes into park design, planning, and maintenance, and indeed the physical Sea World is literally inseparable from the continuous labor and close management required to reproduce it daily. In this chapter, I want to describe and analyze the complex ways this landscape is constructed out of human work, time, space, dirt, plants, and animals.[2] But in a sense, theme parks do not begin with blueprints. Experience-crafting starts and is maintained with the least material ingredient of all: numbers. Sea World's spectacle of nature is an experience machine that runs on a flood of market research and statistics, and so this description of the park's physical workings begins with the collection and use of information.

Sea World management's overall goal is to lengthen the customers' stay and expand their spending in the park.[3] At minimum, it is hoped, they will stay for six hours. To accomplish this objective, Sea World's customers should feel simultaneously entertained and relaxed and unhurried. Thoughtful planning of the landscape and coordination of visual style try to create a relaxed but diverted state of mind. Manipulation of time through scheduling of the flow of customers and the park's service labor are the bedrock of the parkscape; so is staff training in anticipating desires and preventing conflicts. Performances should unfold at profitable intervals, service should be efficient and friendly, safety must be maintained and accidents avoided, the animals monitored and appropriately interpreted, all within a tight budget. If the landscape is not always coherent and its performances don't run as smoothly as the managers hope, it is not for want of trying in the form of researching, forecasting, and automating. Everything about the park's structure is planned, based on a pool of numbers provided by the customers themselves. These are combined with long experience into an almost scientific formula that is applied to shape the park's physical terrain and, perhaps with more uneven success, to determine what the audience sees and feels.

By the Numbers

Management has two sources of numbers to help it shape the park and its atmosphere. Market research, collected inside and outside the park, provides a detailed demographic, economic, and "psychographic" (or lifestyle) picture of the park's customers. At the same time, a continuous count of the sheer volume of customers coming through the front gates, as well as some specific information about them, flows from the keypads of computerized turnstiles. These gate numbers are used to rationalize the day-to-day and hour-to-hour running of the park, while they also feed into the larger bank of market research and are mined later to further refine the park and its entertainments.

Sea World spends a great deal of money and energy on market research. In the early 1990s, the California park and its consultants, Leo J. Schapiro and Associates, were conducting nearly five hundred in-park interviews a month, as well as distributing mail-in questionnaires.[4] Market research is the solicitation of reactions and preferences from customers, as well as the cultivation of information about their identities and consumption patterns, and I will discuss some of its uses below. How much Sea World spends, and all the kinds of market research contracted for, are impossible to specify, since its managers are very close-mouthed about these issues. But it is clear that Sea World looks to market research for many things, including a reliable base of facts about the customers to forecast and advertise by and a kind of light to help guide the designers and entertainers as they draw and write the theme park.

The daily count is collected as customers enter. The number of people clicking the turnstiles over the course of the day is tracked and translated into the hourly increments of a "pace count." These raw numbers are simultaneously transmitted to the operations and the central administration offices, where they are used in different ways. At the operations offices the pace count is compared with projected attendance for that day and used to schedule the labor of the ticket takers, janitors, maintenance people, parking lot attendants, and ride operators. In the central administration offices, the pace count is watched closely, especially by the sales and marketing staff, since it is the most precise source of information about whether the park is ahead of or behind the attendance needed to meet Anheuser-Busch's revenue projections. Jackie Hill, a former vice president for communications, explained that the pace count travels outward and upward in the Sea World administrative hierarchy, to the large food and merchandise departments because it effects staffing there, too, and "to the boss, because he's got to explain them [the numbers] to St. Louis."

I was surprised to hear that the count was looked at hourly, but Hill noted that the park works on a very fine grid of projections: "There's a dry erase board outside the operations office that has the projections for the day, and they are hourly, too. For example, if we are projecting a ten thousand day, on the detailed projection sheets you'll see a ten thousand day, and then a pace count. Ten o'clock, eleven o'clock, twelve o'clock. What should you have at two o'clock in the afternoon if you are going to have a ten thousand day on a five o'clock close? . . . You can look and see whether you are ahead or behind."[5] Numbers are faxed daily to St. Louis as well. "There is just a sense in this business," Hill said, "that you have to know what the count is. Everybody in any administrative or management position ought to know how we are doing."[6] Indeed, Sea World's marketing director Bill Thomas told me he wears a beeper that allows him to know the pace count at any time, he said, to "keep a nice little pressure" on his sales staff.[7]

Since theme park revenues are directly tied to the numbers of customers coming in the gate, park management needs not only to be able to track attendance but to predict how many people they must convince to come to Sea World.

Hill gave an example of how the planning process works:

"You know basically how much money you get out of admissions on a per capita basis, and how much money you get out of food and merchandise on a per capita basis. Figuring that into what your financial projection for the year is supposed to be, you back out an attendance projection. . . . Let's say you are projected to make a profit of $10 million. Well, in order to do that, you need to have an attendance in 365 days of 3.6 million people. Now, you sit down with those 3.6 million people and say, okay, well, we can reasonably expect to get *x* number in January and *x* number in February and *x* number in March. And you spread that attendance over the period of twelve months . . . to try to end up with 3.6 million people and $10 million profits."[8]

Revenues are based not only on the gate prices; sales of food and merchandise are directly related to attendance and length of stay. The more people in the park, the more money will be spent on food and souvenirs. This relationship is expressed in the concept of "per caps," per capita sales, which are thought of as fixed. According to Hill, the general theory is that "if you have good attendance, you will have good per caps. You've got more people, you've got more money. If your per cap is five dollars a head [*sic*] in the merchandise shops, when you add an extra thousand people, they are going to buy five thousand dollars worth of stuff in the shops."[9]

Thus the theme park landscape is defined first and foremost as a place where people spend money. Getting spending people to the theme park sounds simple, but reaching attendance projections and financial projections is not a smooth process. Anheuser-Busch's budget planners can't always anticipate wars, recessions, bad weather, or bad publicity generated by accidents or activists, and attendance projections have to take into account the uneven peaks and valleys of the year so that seasonal promotions can be carefully timed. Projecting how many people will come and when is a nerve-wracking science—since the variables that affect attendance continually change.[10] Theme parks invest in new attractions, which are expensive to build, and flexible temporary promotions, which are much cheaper. At the same time, financial planners place great pressure on marketing and sales personnel to find ways to meet the profit projections in the face of unevenness and new expenses.

Hill described a common situation:

[I]n the budgeting process, department heads may well have budgeted all their expenses . . . and [then] St. Louis will say, "Oh, my God! Our expenses are such that in order to make our profit projection"—this is usually based on a percentage, 15 percent or 20 percent—"we are either going to have to cut expenses or increase revenues." How do you increase revenues? If you can't cut expenses, you increase attendance. They say, "Okay, well, we *have* to have 3.7 million in attendance." . . . So now your financial people are sitting there with an extra hundred thousand people they have to put somewhere over the twelve months. They say, "Okay, we'll put ten thousand people in April, ten thousand people in May . . ." So then you better go out and get those ten thousand people!

In order to satisfy St. Louis, attendance must be strong, even over the short term. When attendance counts slip more than a little, quick action is needed. If attendance is off significantly, "you try to figure out why." Hill noted that "a lot of very interesting marketing meetings have to do with people sitting around theorizing" about reasons for immediate declines in attendance. The historical depth of Sea World's data makes very detailed comparisons and insights possible, but finally, "you have to think of something to jump-start attendance."[11]

Promotional special events or special discount offers, quick marketing ploys "essentially borrowed from the retail business" are mustered to lift sagging attendance. And pressure comes down hard on group sales staff as well, Hill noted. "It really becomes a Maalox moment when you're [wondering] where am I going to squeeze another ten bodies, another twenty bodies, another hundred out of my hotel program, or seniors program, or military program or whatever program you are talking about."[12]

Despite its long-range plans, Sea World needs to be able to react very quickly to problems, and this is another reason why numbers are looked at hourly. In the operations office, the same data are used differently. Here too a day is usually analyzed according to the data bank and past experience, and an attendance projection is set that tells operations the number of staff needed to run the park efficiently. The vice president for operations, Steve Geiss, described the process: "Obviously, if your financial projection is very ambitious and you are projecting twenty thousand days, but you only had twelve thousand [customers] yesterday, you are not going to staff for twenty thousand people. You are going to staff for what you realistically expect to be in the park. Sometimes it'll be the other way. Sometimes you will be beating your financial projections, [with] your staffing projections higher than the financial projections."[13]

The pace count also feeds market research. As people come in through the turnstiles, gross numbers of guests are sorted into relatively fine categories. Computer keypads allow ticket-takers to categorize guests in terms of the way they have paid and how much they have paid. Only a very small proportion, about 10 percent, of guests pay the "full pop" of $29.95, so the electronic tabulation tells a great deal.[14] The vice president for marketing needs to know "how many came in and paid full admission. How many came in on a McDonald's coupon. How many came in on a Von's coupon. How many seniors were admitted. How many 12-Month Pass members and how many 12-Month Pass member guests, because they get a discount. All those are coded [on the key pad and printout] so we know precisely how many people come in on every one of those promotions. And how many comps [complimentary ticket holders] came in. How many kids under three who don't pay at all."[15]

From time to time, the marketers ask a percentage of customers for their zip codes. The zip code gives marketing very specific demographic information about customers, and the coupon tabulations give a good idea of what other products they buy, where they buy them, and thus, which promotions are working. In these very precise ways, Sea World's numbers help management draw a detailed picture of what kind of people are drawn to the park, how much they spend, and, combined with interview information, some idea of what they like and don't like to see.

Theme Park Pastoral

Sea World's number pool is also a foundation for engineering and landscaping decisions. The operations department is a storehouse of knowledge, much of it expressed in statistics reaching back years, about the spatial capacities of the park and the predilections of its customers. Engineers and architects draw on this knowledge directly in the continuous process of rebuilding the park's physical structure.

Managers from many Sea World divisions are concerned with the sensations created by the spaces of the theme park. The marketers tell the administration that it is primarily the park's "natural beauty," its rich and varied plantings, and its greenness that appeal to the researched audience. Sea World has a reputation for its plant collections and gardens, and its gardenlike feeling is created by using both a skilled horticultural staff and standard theme park techniques. Like all theme parks, Sea World tries to create a place both foreign and profoundly familiar. Customers enter a pedestrian zone free from the sights and sounds of cars and separated from the rest of the world by the water barrier of Mission Bay on its north side and by berms, high walls, and plantings on the others. Inside the garden, human hearing, sight, and movement are shaped and sent in different directions.

Sea World's designers and engineers focus on the problem of intensifying spending. To keep people buying food and souvenirs, they know that they must be made comfortable, kept interested, and moved at the right pace through a landscape they find appealingly different, one that neither alarms nor bores. The park's manicured and lush landscape is part of the creation of orderly, diversified, and seemingly choice-filled individual movement; the plantings themselves a key part of the construction of sensations and vision.

Ferris Wankier, the chief engineer, summarized it this way: "We know that we must make a visitor comfortable, and they have to leave with a sense of fulfillment. It involves more than just the shows and the animals. It's the experience of going through the park and having a beautifully landscaped park, a feeling of space."[16]

This sense of comfort in a nature space relies on landscaping that looks effortful (that is, polished by labor and held under control) and effortless (green, shady, abundant, and freely growing) at the same time. It is also diverse, with small pocket gardens and color spots in out-of-the-way corners allowing the sense that there is always another piece of nature to look at. To create this sense, a vast amount of construction, maintenance, and relandscaping takes place, mostly after hours or in the off-season. On any given day in the early spring, gardeners can be seen transplanting, trimming, watering, and fertilizing areas being redesigned or freshened. Frequent, labor-intensive revision of the gardens, along with repainting of buildings and revising of walkways fits with senior management's general philosophy that the overall appearance of the park should communicate what Wankier called "quality" and "class."[17] Unlike what's left of San Diego's original arid and decidedly unclassy chaparral environment, or Mission Bay's former, swampy character, the park is rich, neat, and bright, the result of careful maintenance of permanent trees and shrubs and the addition of annuals for intense, continually changing color. The older plantings of the 1960s park core provide important backdrops and vision screens never seen in the chaparral and a sense of continuity not easily found in newly planted suburbs.

Sea World is involved in building the problematic illusion that it is not a populous place. In moving people through the landscape, the engineers must consider capacity—how many people the park can hold at one time and how to arrange them in space. According to Sea World management, American tourists don't ordinarily like to feel crowded; indeed, theme park research shows that people who feel packed in stop spending. There should be as little crowding of the individual or the family group as possible, and all services should be available and efficient. Although people may temporarily experience themselves as large, even mass, audiences, it is important that they never experience themselves as an undirected, hot, frustrated crowd. While there may be tens of thousands of people on more than 150 acres of park at any given time on a busy day, most paying visitors are there to be alone with their family groups. At least that is how Sea World's advertising, with its emphasis on child-parent units, explains the park. In isolation from any larger collectivity, families should experience nature and each other; they will learn and, as Sea World's marketers put it, "make memories." An audience of families is organized, in the theme park, around viewing, experiencing, consuming. A crowd might become unruly, protest bad service or long lines, or even riot. Spatial arrangements and the structuring of activities need to support and reproduce the individual and familial definition of what the visitor's day will mean.

Spaciousness is constructed through the dimensions of the facilities. Walkways must be wide enough to accommodate large numbers of people; buildings must be able to hold clusters of people walking rather quickly through them but sometimes pausing; stadiums must be spacious enough to arrange thousands in such a way that each can see. Although the illusion of ample room can't always succeed, especially at the height of the summer, multiple pathways of escape from congested places can help give people space to be families; so can small seating areas, niches, benches, and restaurant and picnic tables designed to accommodate only four or five people.

To figure out the capacities of large open spaces, buildings, and viewing areas, Sea World's engineers rely on numbers collected by the operations department. Spatial needs are projected for a "design day," an average-to-heavy summer day, based on the annual, daily, and hourly counts. Ferris Wankier discussed the park design process, revealing that Sea World's planners think especially about movement through the park: "When [the park] started, they hoped they could get ten thousand people a day, that would be their max. . . . Say, eleven o'clock till two o'clock is your heavy influx of people. So we had to figure out what you need just to move [that many people] through the park. At that time we wanted to make walkways that were about sixteen feet wide to accommodate movement in the park."[18]

Today attendance is growing and the park is in a constant process of spatial revision. Design day keeps expanding, approaching twenty-five thousand people a day in the early 1990s, a figure that dictates twenty-four-foot-wide walkways. And the park itself has to keep growing so that, as Wankier said, people "feel like they're not all crowded in."[19]

Also considered, based on a design day formula, are access to facilities and services. Wankier noted: "You don't want people to have to wait in long, long lines to get food. You don't want to create anything that's a negative. And yet, you can't afford to build enough food facilities so that if you happen to have a forty thousand–person day, you can always accommodate them instantly."[20]

The design day formula is an attempt to balance the problem of overcrowding against the problem of overbuilding. As the park's success has grown, so has the size of the average maximum capacity, and so structures have been repeatedly expanded. But the reliance on numbers can also misdirect design. For example, although the Shamu Stadium was designed to hold sixty-two hundred people, based on a seating space allocation of eighteen inches per person, Geiss of the operations department knows that the stadium in fact seats at most fifty five hundred, since Sea World customers, like most Americans, with their cameras, packages, and back packs, require ample seating. "We know people take up twenty-four inches," he said, drawing on his own experience of the park.[21]

The Pulse

Of course, any architectural project must consider the temporal and spatial problems of capacity. But Sea World has a special challenge. Because it is a complex structure of performative attractions, it has what its managers think of as a pulse. Jackie Hill, the former public relations officer, observed that "the thing about Sea World parks that is so different from a ride park is that the movement of people through the parks is pulsed by the shows. You gather six thousand people together in the Shamu Stadium at one time, and then you spew them all out at one time. At ride parks you have a constant flow through the attractions."[22]

This pulsing, I will show, is carefully planned by the operations department. But it creates problems that engineers and architects need to consider. Hill explained that at first she didn't understand the effects of the pulse: "I kept getting 'long lines' letters [of complaint] from the guests. I finally talked to the food people and got a better understanding of what was going on. . . . What's going to happen when Shamu Stadium lets out is that the fast-food restaurant next to it is going to be absolutely jammed. Same thing with the rest rooms. No rest room in the world is going to handle six thousand people. You can't afford to build every snack bar and every rest room large enough to handle that peak which occurs, at the height of the summer season, six or seven times a day. We can't afford to build a restaurant that big."[23]

Engineers and the operations department have to work together and from different directions to solve this problem of intermittent, bunched crowding. Numerous small food facilities and rest rooms are offered; vendors' carts are rolled out at peak times to take the edge off customers' hunger and amplify food sales. And landscaping strategically creates multiple routes and exits away from any attraction.

In the process, the park has been cumulatively constructed as a web of walkways. Sea World's engineers have used these walks to give travel through the park a winding, weaving quality. Sight lines are usually short, ending in trees, or knolls that curve away out of sight. People will often see other families walking but, except when they are unavoidably waiting in line, it is hoped that they feel themselves members of small clusters of families, wending their way through the mildly hilly, green landscape.

When the illusion of uncrowdedness succeeds, even temporarily, it is in part because movement is shaped by the carefully arranged pulse of the shows. Structuring time is one of the least visible tasks of running the park but one of the most important. The scheduling of the park's animal shows is carried out by the operations department and is central to the smooth running of services. Since Sea World must not squander the energy of its employees and animals, nor its material resources, and since it wants to minimize the frustrations of its visitors, it must take charge of the pulsing pattern. The performative schedule that creates the pulse must also soften its effects on the spatial and temporal organization of entertainment, service, and the audience.[24]

The park literally runs around the show schedule. Each carload of customers is handed a map with a customized, "recommended" schedule computer printed on it as they pass through the parking lot gate. The map gives them an architecture of their day, so that they'll be able to see nearly everything. To produce the show schedule, operations works closely with the entertainment, food, merchandising, and animal training departments, using the expertise, and understanding the constraints, of each department. Trainers, for example, set limits on the number of times each species can do its performance in the course of a day and on how close together shows can be. Animals cannot be allowed to become overtired or to repeat their tasks too many times, or they will "shut down" and refuse to perform. The entertainment department needs to consider the human staffing of shows and technical supports. Food service staff must ebb and flow with the tides of hunger and thirst; gift shop personnel need to shift with the intake and outflow of the stadiums.

The show schedulers rely on the same hourly "pace count" that so concerns the marketing department. If the park is very full, an adequate number of shows must be scheduled, so that the audience will have reasonable chances of seeing at least the most popular ones, the Shamu and dolphin shows, during their stay. If attendance is scant, a smaller number of shows must be organized into the most efficient blocks of time. Sea World calls its system progressive scheduling: a series of schedules are written according to the day's projected attendance. If the pace count of attendance is higher than projected, the director of operations will call in a change—he or she will "go up," or accelerate the show schedule a step, to the next densest plan. Progressive scheduling is a quick formula for determining how many more shows, and then how many more support staff, are needed. Geiss said, "[I]t's just building schedule upon schedule, and we'll have a certain number of shows for a certain amount of people. More people means more shows."[25]

The Logic of the Attraction

A second point of progressive scheduling is to produce "good length of stay." Shows should not to be too close together. Too much compactness in the show schedule and customers may feel rushed through the park; length of stay may suffer if they experience the park too efficiently. Show schedulers try to create a good ratio of active times to quiet times, taking into account that the park is a physical space with activities going full tilt in one area and lulls in others. In this way, scheduling helps create Sea World's atmosphere, a pattern of rhythmic activity broken by patches of quiet. Geiss noted that it is his department's job to make this rhythm enhance concession sales: "We had done experimenting with show schedules to try and maximize [food and merchandise sales], even if it's just creating time for people to go eat lunch or creating dead times where . . . people don't feel rushed to go from show to show, and they feel they have a few minutes to go in a gift shop to do a little shopping."[26]

This same rationale is structured into the park's architecture. Although the park appears vast, show arenas are set no more than a ten-minute stroll apart from each other. Animal displays and small viewing spaces fill the distances in between. All of the winding walkways lead to clustered gift shops, each in turn themed to performing animals: Gifts From Shamu near Shamu Stadium, for example, and the Penguin Shop steps away from the Penguin Encounter.

Geiss's show scheduling works with the placement of facilities and attractions to create an alternation of spectacular excitement with leisurely looking in a nature frame. As he put it, "You want people to be able to see everything that they want to see, see all the shows and see all the exhibits, and [you consider that] they have to spend a certain amount of time doing that. You definitely don't want people to feel rushed, because that's too much like the real world. . . . We want to kind of create an atmosphere of slowing things down."[27]

Nevertheless, despite the "slowing down," the logic of the attraction dictates that certain things need to be accomplished. There is a tension between really slowing down and the theme park's need to keep sales vigorous. Shows have to be paced so that the consumption of spectacles can also be efficient for visitors who don't have all day. Steve Geiss acknowledged that this is a very regulated kind of relaxation: "Then again, when you're open from nine to five, you only have a certain amount of time and you're trying to fit in a couple of shows here. So somebody could come in at nine o'clock and see all the shows and then have the rest of the day to look at exhibits, to do what they want to do. But you try to schedule so that if somebody doesn't come in until twelve o'clock, then they still have a chance to see all the animal shows. Or maybe they don't get here until two o'clock, they are late over at the airport or something, and they still have time to see all the shows."[28]

The important shows must be far enough apart that customers are encouraged to stay longer than a few hours, and repeated regularly enough that they can feel they have had a full day, no matter when they arrive. The problem of length of stay underlies the manipulation of theme park time. In fact, despite Sea World's careful cultivation of the atmosphere of "park" and "public space," where presumably any activities could unfold in a variety of unstructured ways, its show-scheduling practices reveal that it conceives of its customers as obliged to move determinedly from performance to concession and to fill in blank spaces with more consumption.

Delivering Services, Cultivating Desires

The carefully timed Sea World experience depends also on contacts between customers and other humans. The ease, relaxation, and comfort of customers depends heavily on the skills of people who daily remake the park through physical care and maintenance. The theme park landscape is a labor intensive one; it is built by clean, friendly, helpful employees who are organized by their managers with remarkable precision to produce unproblematic cleanliness and order. And as we will see, the perception of order is not just a result of repetitive physical work, although it is that. Creating good feelings about Sea World also involves maintaining a social and emotional order that depends on the appearance, behavior, and attitudes of workers.[29]

The operations, food services, and merchandise departments comprise more than half Sea World's three thousand summer-season employees and provide most of the service labor in the park.[30] Like much of the rest of the park, the eight hundred–person operations department runs on part-time, flexible labor. Part time, seasonal labor allows Sea World to keep wages, benefits, and insurance costs low and allows the precise, progressive scheduling of its employees.[31] According to the director of operations, between 65 percent and 70 percent of the operations employees are part-time. Managers estimated the average age of employees in food service and operations at about twenty years. For many, this is their first job. Wages in food services reflect this: starting pay is comparable to McDonald's, roughly $5.25 an hour.

The youth of the service employees creates problems for Sea World's managers. The inexperience of their young, low-waged employees means that they often have to be taught how to be service employees, and although a job at Sea World is considered exciting and highly desirable, this is not easy. Low wages and flexible hours mean young workers can be unreliable. Temporary workers must be trained to show up on time, to work regular hours, and to create the right emotional atmosphere for the customers.[32]

Sea World sets dress and grooming codes. Interviewers in the personnel department are asked by management to be "prejudiced" toward a "clean-cut look." As at Disneyland, posted regulations define park standards for haircuts, makeup, jewelry, and fingernail length and care, and service employees, like all employees, are encouraged to think of themselves as performers. It is not uncommon to see small makeup mirrors nailed up next to office doors, so employees of all levels can check their appearance before going "onstage" into the park. At one of the main boundaries between the administrative complex and the park, a dogleg barrier of fence and oleander bushes divides the realms Sea World asks workers to recognize as backstage and onstage. Here a full-length mirror is positioned under a sign that reads, "You Reflect the Sea World Image!" In order to adhere to this image and bolster the park's wholesome atmosphere, employees may not smoke, eat, or socialize while in uniform in the park.

And the young, flexible employees must have the right attitude. A prime goal of service work is to create an atmosphere that parallels the park's physical terrain: one of bodily and social pleasure, health, ease, and lack of confusion or conflict. Sea World therefore must train its inexpensive, temporary work force in the demands of delivering what sociologist Arlie Hochschild has called "emotional labor," work that creates emotional states or moods in those offering *and* being offered service.[33] Sea World employees must be friendly, cheerful, helpful, and always smiling to a vast throng of stroller-pushing pedestrians. Steve Geiss explicitly contrasted these displayed feelings with what Sea World's customers experience outside the park: "I think the main business that we're in is trying to put smiles on people's faces when they walk in the gate, and I think one side to that is creating an atmosphere that is not like the outside world. Our employees are right out with the public all the time; they're friendly and they're helpful, and they go out of their way to be helpful."[34]

A posture of friendliness on the part of service workers, it is hoped, reduces the sense of mass-ness and increases the feeling of distance from the outside world.[35] But this posture of total friendliness to complete strangers is unfamiliar to most urban Americans. It's only within the suspended reality of the theme park that it makes sense.

I asked if it was hard to get across to employees the idea of being friendly. Yes, said Geiss. "It's pretty difficult. . . . I think there is a natural shyness [in] dealing with strangers. All the things that you grew up learning when you were a kid, 'Don't talk to strangers,' you have to overcome all that. And when you are a teenager and you feel shy and awkward anyway, [it is hard to be put] in a position where [you are required] to get out there and be friendly."[36]

To deliver emotional labor involves, on the part of management, not just urging teenage food servers to be friendly, but "communicating what we want"—a standardized training process in being consistently friendly.[37]

Part of what a guest ought to experience at Sea World is a sense of vigorous outgoingness, rather than just a willingness to be helpful. Sea World calls this "aggressive guest relations" and trains its service personnel to actively seek opportunities to intervene helpfully. Geiss described the sorts of "aggressive" actions he expects service employees to take: "We have to try and get our employees to realize that the guests might look a little puzzled and that's *an opportunity* for them to get in there and say, 'Can I help you with something,' or, 'Do you need help finding something?' Or when you see one member of the family taking a picture and the other four are sitting over there, to jump in and say, 'Hey, why don't I take your picture? Get in and get with the family, so that we know that all of you came here.' It's not waiting for someone to ask you something, not waiting for something to happen before you step in and help the people."

Aggressive guest relations and emotional work are standardized through constant checking. Supervisory staff continually survey the park.

> They go into shows to check the appearance of the employees, see that their uniforms are neat and presentable and they're wearing the right things that we want them to wear, [have neat] haircuts, grooming. But they also check to see that they're outwardly greeting people, and they're not just standing there. Even just smiling isn't enough of what we want. We want them to say things to people, and, as people are exiting stadiums, say, "Thanks for coming," " Have a nice day," " Anything I can do to help?" "Can I help you find something?" Or looking for people looking at their maps and looking confused and stepping in and helping them: "This way to the next show." *Just something, anything.* We have five thousand people and ten employees in each of the stadiums, so you're not going to be able to greet every single one, but greeting ten or twenty of them is something to try for.[38]

In a way, the "aggressive guest relations" Geiss described creates a sort of contagious model for how visitors are to enjoy their day. For instance, in the example of taking the photograph, the service worker is asked to help people make sure they document themselves as a family whole.

Monitoring attitude includes self-monitoring. In 1992, in all employee areas and on bulletin boards in public backstage areas, large posters read "Showtime!" a reminder that Sea World urges each worker to consider himself or herself as a performer and exemplar of important ideas, attitudes, and feelings. According to the vice president for food service, the "Showtime!" program "says you're a player on stage."[39] Showtime!

is a reward program as well. In fact, it is claimed that employees are encouraged to reward other employees, although most of the recognizing is likely done by managers.[40]

The emotional dimensions rewarded by the Showtime! program are printed on the back of a small card, to be handed to each employee caught in the act of doing the right thing:

The Buck Stops With Me;
Let Me Help;
I Am Always on Stage;
I Go the Extra Mile;
I Am a Park Team Player;
I Put Myself in Your Shoes;
I Am a Sea World Spirit;
Sure, I Have Time for You![41]

With this contest, Sea World management hopes to help employees internalize the reflex to display rather than just harbor the positive emotions of helpfulness, responsibility, peppy cheerfulness, and empathy. Display of these emotions is a condition of employment.

The laborers working on emotions are simultaneously engaged in the continual production of the physical Sea World. In addition to smiling, pointing directions, and snapping photos, Sea World employees are busy taking tickets, cooking, cleaning, removing trash, serving food, looking for lost children, and working cash registers. Their job is to make the clean, healthy, smoothly running environment in which the shows go on.

"We have," said Geiss, "a reputation of being an extremely clean park. People say it's one of the cleanest places they've ever been to, so we really strive to keep that up." But keeping it up is not a small job, since on a peak day tens of thousands of people are circulating through the park eating and drinking all kinds of foods from disposable containers. Sea World is a veritable trash factory, and if not deftly handled this fact could clash with the park's carefully managed environmental face. "The trash that happens naturally throughout the whole day is overwhelming. . . . Especially in the summertime when we're open late, my department has people here twenty-four hours a day cleaning."[42] Every night, all the walkways and sitting surfaces are scrubbed and steam cleaned. During the day, park visitors are ostentatiously solicited to help by using recycling bins.

The smooth intensity of Sea World's service labor is dictated by the show schedule. It determines how many people will show up to work, at what tasks, where, and when. Here progressive scheduling and casual employment help: janitorial, parking, security, and vending staff need to be expanded quickly when attendance is swelling, so that each service or sales area of the park delivers optimal experience and revenues. Conversely, when the audience numbers fall, part-time hourly staff can easily be sent home because, said Geiss, "you want to try and do everything with the least amount of people that it would take. So that since we are a for-profit company, we can actually make a little profit here."[43] This is the great advantage of hourly, flexibly scheduled nonunion labor. Workers can simply be told when to show up and when to go home.

The rationalized use of time and flexible part-time labor is found across the park, but it is especially important in the large, revenue-producing departments, food and merchandise. Here the goal is fast service, and the food services department, for example, has made "quite a little science" of finding out how many of their thirteen hundred peak season employees it will need on any given day.[44]

Eating is an important part of the Sea World experience: food and beverage sales account for about 25 percent of revenues.[45] Eating is constructed as both functional and celebratory. Much of the food offered is similar to the items found at a state fair or carnival: sugary, starchy, and deep-fat fried. Sea World tries to capitalize on this sense of special, festive eating and argues that people at theme parks expect and want to eat junk foods. At the same time, it offers places to sit down in small groups and fill up, even if the meal has been obtained in a cafeteria line. The park has only one "sit down," full-service restaurant, although some of its food stations present artful food displays reminiscent of those produced in restaurants.

Whether visitors are sitting or strolling, the experience of eating should follow the same rules for ease, uncrowdedness, speed, and efficiency as the rest of the park. Feedback from the computerized cash register systems, along with attendance projections, allows managers to schedule food workers' tasks and time precisely and so control labor costs.[46] And the computerized cash register allows food and merchandise managers to know exactly where in the park sales are hearty or weak, and at exactly what time of the day. Following the McDonald's model, much of the cooking is deep-fat frying, and food servers are shifted from station to station and task to task in twenty-minute blocks, as needed. Their work is limited to heating and serving pre-prepared items or cleaning equipment. The goal is to have customers spend ten minutes waiting, from the time they join a line to the time they pay for the food. But as the vice president for food services pointed out, "[O]n a forty thousand–person day, we have only seven restaurants, and people all want to eat at show break. We always compare it to forty buses coming to a McDonald's at the same time."[47]

Food service responds to the problem of lines, hunger, and crowding by fielding food vendors throughout the park. Vendors are mobile and can be located near shifting points of congestion. Just as important, vending creates a sense of festive urbanness in the theme park. With their mobile, informal, street style, carts add an air of festivity and publicness that the fast-food restaurants, so firmly tied to the everyday life of the suburb, cannot evoke. But there's nothing spontaneous about this publicness. Operations' pace counts and maps of the movement of crowds allow food services to determine where to put the novelty vendors at any time of day. The map is divided into regions and every item in the profitable "mix" of ice cream, sodas, popcorn, and *churros* is represented in each one.[48]

Movable food stands not only take the pressure off the stationary restaurants by satisfying some hungers and thirsts, they increase per capita spending by cultivating hungers the audience may not have known it had. Presenting a continually shifting stream of novel items to the walking audience was suggested by the market research. Exit interviews told Sea World that its customers differentiate between "novelties," "snacks," and "meals." According to David White, vice president for food services, "[W]hile a snack food might substitute for a meal, a novelty-type food like an ice cream bar will not. You simply make that [ice cream bar] available"; it may be purchased in addition to a meal or snack because it is "special." However, Sea World tries to make it difficult for customers to buy meal substitutes. "You'll notice we never sell hot dogs anymore at Sea World," White said. "We try to drive [customers] to a meal or a platter, a higher-priced item." The point of the food in the landscape is not to satisfy needs, but to produce and differentiate desires.[49] Overall, people should feel hungry, but they should not feel hungry long. If they are surprised by new longings, they should find satisfaction at the same time.

Looking at Animals

At the center of the experiential machine are the park's famous creatures. A great deal of the work of making the physical park involves giving the audience ways to see animals. Inside the landscape frame, animals are displayed in a range of ways consonant with ease and expanded consumption, by using ways of seeing that are well established and familiar from the zoo, the circus, the museum, film, and television.

Seeing and touching are central activities, and all the work of shaping the landscape, organizing time and movement, and sculpting the feelings of the audience helps create the ways by which customers make contact with nature. Sometimes Sea World summarizes, giving its customers a grandiose overview; at other times, it puts them in the shoes of adventurous explorers. At still others, the park reduces the distances of time and geography to bring its customers "up close and personal" (a Sea World-ism borrowed from television sportscasters) to small fish or giant whales. Among its most popular attractions are the displays that allow humans the intimate contact of touching and feeding the dolphins and fish. In each case, the park's designers and managers have used architecture, plantings, visual techniques, customer-staff interactions, and music to give the encounter between animal and human a distinctive emotional quality.

To a great extent, like many other structures of tourist experience and many other mass media products, Sea World is about looking the right way. As Judith Adler has argued, the norms of early tourism stressed the empirical and comprehensive qualities of vision. In a sense, the marine theme park carries on a centuries-long tradition of constructing visual experiences and developing sights. Sea World is a kind of machine that structures vision in highly specific and thoughtfully determined ways.[50]

The Sea World customer is immediately signaled that vision will be thorough and universal when he or she is greeted with the schematic, color cartoon map of the park's whole world. This encyclopedic wholeness echoes the park's claim to create "another world." The detailed (and hard-to-read) plan of the entire park is imprinted with the most recent show schedule, so that the visit can be exhaustive. The map shows the finer divisions of the park's encompassing theme: fresh waters, ocean waters, the Northwest Coast, California tide pools, Antarctica, Polynesia, the Bermuda Triangle are all represented. We also find a Clydesdale horse farm and a brewery, presented with Sea World's usual, unembarrassed incongruity. Should visitors want an even more overarching perspective, the centrally placed Southwest Airlines' Skytower allows a panoramic survey of the theme park, Mission Bay Park, the coast, and the city.

Below the tower, space and architecture help Sea World do what tourist attractions have been doing for at least a century: they show the customer what to see and how to see it. Architectural techniques for cultivating nature visions range from the seemingly random to the highly structured and formal. At the seemingly random end, the winding paths create a sense of intimacy, of nature as close-by surroundings. Inevitably, walkways carry the customer to a viewing site or overlook, a place where one can look past a wall, a bush, or a pool into a naturalistic pocket of space.[51] For example, near a food stand, one can lean over a stone wall to look across water to a finger of earth inhabited by small turtles. Or visitors can gather along a stone rail to look down through bushes and sago palms, into a flamingo nesting area. At many turns, one can come upon small animals or birds seemingly nestled in their own habitats. These incidental nature visions give a sense of natural riches—everywhere one looks there is something colorful and precious. Breaking up the landscape into small areal units surrounded by heavy foliage screens means that in outdoor spaces Sea World's visitors can feel they are "stopping by" animals and plants individually and casually, rather than gathering at a railing to stare along with everyone else.

Customers traveling down the walkways are usually following their printed map schedules, on their way to one of Sea World's six stadiums. Stadiums are the most important and efficient structures for seeing animals; they offer an economy of scale in viewing. A large number of people—from three thousand to more than six thousand at one time—can focus their collective attention on the animal performers for about twenty minutes. Nearly everyone gets an unobstructed if sun-beaten view of the dolphin, whale, or sea lion working with its trainers.

The mass viewing in the stadium is, in a way, spare: performance is a radical decontextualization of the animal. By contrast, the museum-style zoological displays, living dioramas, and aquariums are specialized and elaborate recontextualizations. As opposed to the stadiums, the living dioramas try to bring the viewer up close, to be intimate. But this intimacy must be carefully engineered. Indoor displays like the Penguin Encounter, Moray Eel Caverns, Shark Encounter, and the more traditional aquariums draw large numbers of people through relatively small buildings to give them a close-up look. So each structure must manipulate movement to help keep people seeing. Customers proceed at metered paces; doors and entry ways are guarded by interpreters and, at the Shark Encounter, doors are timed to a video program to keep people from bunching up in the underwater tunnel.

The result of these three viewing styles—the incidental, the mass, and controlled closeness—is an experience of alternating between being in a large group of waiting or looking people and more solitary strolling. Most people at Sea World keep moving. The spacious walkways, numerous small, open plazas and generous bench-style seating provide relief from the experience of being bunched at windows in noisy buildings with low ceilings, and the incidental nature of planting and casual views balances and relieves the organized gaze of the stadium. Greenery is compensation for the concrete and steel of the Shamu Stadium.

Making the Invisible Visible

One of Sea World's chief attractions is its museum-style synopsis of a whole wide world, in this case the other world of oceans. Here one can supposedly see some things that exist outside normal human seeing, things that would otherwise be inaccessible. This scientized and touristic claim is joined to the zoo and circus tradition of spectacularizing animals. Sea World is a masterfully constructed series of encounters with animals that until recently have had little cultural visibility to Americans, a collection of ways of walking right up to beings that are well-known from the mass media, but not part of personal experience. For example, for most twentieth-century Americans, the Antarctic or the world beneath the sea is an *other* world that they have glimpsed in print and on television, but finally it is totally foreign, just as Africa and Asia were for most nineteenth-century Europeans. And for most of the nineteenth century, penguins, seals, and sea otters were food, fuel, or trade goods, the objects of industrial slaughter. To consider penguins for a moment, in the twentieth century, most species have not survived well in captivity, or not until Sea World spent vast amounts of money simulating the cycles of light and darkness of the antarctic environment and brought a wide variety of penguins together in one place. Film, zoos, and places like Sea World have helped to popularize penguins as mascots of whimsy for late-twentieth-century first world consumers. Similarly, killer whales and sharks could not be kept healthy in captivity until filtration systems and very large-capacity tanks could be built. Only in the last thirty years have killer whales become important performers for mass audiences, filling the grandiose novelty role elephants played in the nineteenth century. In these senses, Sea World works in the very old tradition of the menagerie and circus to bring parts of an invisible wild into public view and elevate them to iconic status. As Sea World's map implies, the park rounds up a diversity of ocean animal things that, it is claimed, we have never before seen all in the same place.[52]

Making the invisible visible involves the well-thought-out structuring of vision, a repositioning of the viewer vis-à-vis nature. One of the most obvious ways of creating a new way of seeing is to place the customer close to something that in ordinary life they could rarely move physically close to. The Sea World landscape collapses great distances. As the customer walks from the parking lot, past the sweet-roll stand, and into a Polynesian atoll, he or she covers an enormous ecological and historical space in no time flat. This process of folding up distance, of getting up close to what might otherwise never be seen, is central to Sea World, as it is to all theme parks, zoos, and museums.

Indeed, the handheld map of the "world," the tower's overview, the division of the park into regions, and the stress on encounter and adventure are similar to the experience offered by other mass media, most famously *National Geographic* magazine, and strongly suggest the long history of European meetings with the non-European world.[53] But this selective tour of the globe helps define nature as found in remote places, since unlike *National Geographic,* Sea World never takes us to a European site and rarely, anymore, to a spot inhabited by humans.[54] Like the world's fair and *National Geographic*, but without ever calling up a precise history, the theme park offers its customers an implicit identification with the colonial "discoverers." And without shouting, "Put yourself in Balboa's boots!" Sea World offers customers the role of the European mappers of the non-European world. The Penguin Encounter, for example, builds heavily on the idea of a visit to the Antarctic, using cold air temperatures, sound tracks, and a passage through a series of dark lobbies to create a feeling of distance traveled from the ordinary environment.

But while adventurers might sally forth to help survey and conquer the globe, Sea World's nature views and landscape structures suggest a different kind of conquest, one accomplished aesthetically through visual intimacy. A key idea embedded in American tourist attractions from the early nineteenth century on, according to historian John Sears, is that of direct, unmediated, intimate contact as an ideal way of "really knowing," and being personally transformed by, nature. Early-nineteenth-century tourists "did" Niagara Falls, the century's most famous attraction, by progressing along a detailed tour. Not until the visitor worked through a complex structure of mediated and guided encounters and had been over, under, sideways, behind, and below did he know the falls. Visual knowing and intimate experience gave access to nature's sublime, divine power.[55]

Throughout Sea World the illusion is often one of thoroughly entering another world. For example, the old Shark Encounter, like many similar structures, placed the visitor at eye level with the swimming fish. But the new Shark Encounter takes this strategy a step further: The audience wends its way through a tropical landscape, past artificial pools holding small sharks and set against painted diorama backgrounds of South Sea atolls, into a tunnel leading to a video screening room. After a short video and lecture, visitors exit at a carefully set pace through an acrylic tunnel that enables them to look out and up—at all angles—into a tank of sharks. The acrylic tube at the Shark Encounter takes the viewer into the shark's environment, although its depiction in advertising makes it seem a vaster and more frightening environment than it really is. The tube creates a successful impression that the visitors are deeply inside the shark's colorful and illuminated environment, even while it moves them rather quickly out of the realm that would be otherwise completely obscure to the human eye.[56]

Similarly at Sea World, the paths to animals are structured in ways that build progressive closeness. Approaches are created in a range of ways. Often the customer walks toward an exhibit that is some distance lower than the main walkways. (The approach from above and the downward gaze are preferred in zoo design texts.) Special glass panels let animals and people end up at eye level. The most popular attractions at Sea World seem to contain this process of coming closer from above from several possible directions. For example, at Shamu Stadium one can look down from high stadium seats and walkways at the killer whales swimming in their tanks, and then walk around beside the Plexiglass sides of the tanks and stand next to them at eye level. On a less elaborate scale, the walrus exhibit tank makes up for its small size. One can look down at the swimming walruses, but additionally, a circulating passage near the bottom of the tank lets one come nose to tusk, through heavily scratched Plexiglass.[57]

Of course, perfect seeing and visual intimacy are a trick. Were we really to get up close in the marine environment, most of it and most of its animals would be nearly unseeable. Not only would it be hard to get up close, most of the time we would not be able to see much, water not having the transparent quality of air. Aquariums are little experiments in making the invisible visible. They give new ways to see nature, since they not only bring marine life to eye level (and more or less hold it there), but aquarium technology clarifies the environment by settling, scrubbing, filtering, stabilizing, and chemically purifying it. Manuals on aquarium building are handbooks in perceptual play, covering how to keep water transparent, how to use light, the absence of light, and perspective to create the illusion of more space.

Some aquariums create detailed and naturalistic niches for their fish. In its several aquariums, Sea World displays both "mini-worlds"—little jewel tanks holding single species and marked by simple identifying labels—and whole environments, the large tanks holding a range of species, often including some interrelated in the ocean habitat. We can look into small cabinets at precious nautiluses or poisonous lion fish or feel ourselves on the ocean bottom looking up at schools of anchovies. This is not so skillfully or brilliantly accomplished as it is at the Monterey Bay Aquarium, where the theme is the interdependent environment and one can stand at the bottom of a kelp bed and look up and out. Nevertheless, the idea of taking a fish's position is available at Sea World too, as is the idea of the ocean as a kind of totality that is foreign but visible—a working system with its own inhabitants. Sea World's aquariums offer representative slices of the unlimited, and in these intimacy and awe go together. Other tanks, especially the killer whale stadium, create the illusion of deep space. Here, no underwater scenery distracts us, and when viewed at eye level the orcas seem to float in space. Nothing impedes visual contact.

The visual rhetoric of boundless space is increasingly popular at zoos and aquariums. For example, in 1991 the Monterey Bay Aquarium announced plans for a new "Outer Bay Waters" exhibit which explicitly tries to show "the blue void, the ocean without edges you can see," where "open ocean fish, like tuna, blue and thresher sharks and 10 ft long ocean sun fish" will swim "in a world without boundaries."[58] The illusion of endless depth connects to the notion of another world—this time, it is an entirely foreign but peaceful one, without human culture. The Shark Encounter, Rocky Point Preserve, Forbidden Reef, Penguin Encounter, and killer whale pools all try to achieve the illusion of spatial depth and nature's separation from culture. From television and nature photography, we know that spaces like this exist; in the case of such underwater sights, they are otherwise completely obscure to the human eye.

Whether customers are seated in the stadium or moving through the diorama, Sea World assumes they need to feel that they have seen the real, thoroughly and in detail. But making rare nature accessible and the invisible visible is hard and expensive. Considerable technical skill, artistry, and corporate expense go into building and maintaining visibility and verisimilitude. Specialized teams of designers and curators collaborate on determining the animals' requirements for space, air, and water temperature to—in the view of chief engineer Ferris Wankier—"create something as close to nature as possible" from the standpoint of both the animals' basic biological needs and customers' perceptual needs. The aquariums are costly, dependent on aeration, circulation, and filtration systems, and on chemical purification and treatment of large quantities of artificial saltwater.[59]

When what seems to be a whole environment, including the process of reproduction, is on display, detailing becomes even more elaborate. In the case of the Penguin Encounter, attempts to mimic changes of season with light and temperature manipulate the reproductive cycle, while elaborate rock work, blown-in snow, and painted backgrounds convince the viewer that Antarctica itself has been simulated.

Wankier described the process: "'Penguin' evolved as a long-term project for our avian department. They were going to the Antarctic and studying penguins, and bringing back eggs and putting those in incubators, and hatching them. [They were trying] to develop an in-house breeding colony. Then, after six or eight years, we wanted to put the animals on display."[60]

Wankier and his staff consulted on everything from lighting and temperature to "how much space per penguin." According to engineers and animal care managers, the penguins' biological needs are well understood and controllable. What is more difficult to negotiate are the visual demands of the customers. Just making vision possible can be a challenge. Designers aspired to let the audience see penguins of several species diving and feeding underwater as well as jostling on an iceberg. But this was tricky: "[At 'Penguin'] you want water-level viewing, so you need, actually, tempered plate glass that creates the view through. On one side it's twenty-six degrees, and on the people side it's seventy degrees. With that kind of temperature difference, you'd have no view at all, so we create a big stream of warm air that prevents any fogging. It amounts to a huge defogger."[61]

Clarity of vision in the aquariums also relies on control of water, lighting, and organisms. Aquarium walls have to be scrubbed down almost daily. But these are actually the least of the engineer's problems. Wherever Sea World aims to present something otherwise unseeable, the problems of movement and capacity collide with the need for visibility. Wankier pointed out that "all of that [water stuff] is easy," but "the biggest problem you have is the display of the animals. Because the fish are in 'jewel tanks,' the very small, rectangular tanks. The philosophy [is] that you want these kids to be able to get their noses right up there and see them. Guess what? When that little boy gets up there for ten minutes, what happens to the thirty thousand people that want to see that?"

Stronger Plexiglass and new filtration technologies have made huge aquarium windows possible, easing the capacity problem. As a result, aquariums around the world now create vast underwater scenes. At the puffin display in the Penguin Encounter, Wankier had railings installed to help keep "that little boy" from pressing his nose against the glass, "so everybody gets that spectacle." The same need to spread seeing through the crowd can be met with machinery. An adjustable-speed people mover carries customers past the penguins. The speed can be calibrated according to attendance, he said, and "if the attendance is less than thirty thousand, you can give them a longer experience."[62]

Wankier designed spaces for those who don't wish to be moved: "If somebody wants to stay and just visit and look, then you create a static viewing area where they can go and look at film. That has to be behind and above the moving walkway. That kind of procedure is used on all of the things we do [at the park]."[63]

At the Penguin Encounter, there are multiple ways to look and things to see: There are penguins of many kinds, puffins, simulated rock and iceberg. Video, display panels, and texts on the walls tell the stories of Sea World's Antarctic research and adventures. There are indoor penguins, and outdoor penguins, and penguin sculptures near the ladies' room. The rationale of the attraction means that vision at Sea World abhors a vacuum. There can be no gap in the flow of things to see.

Whether or not the sublime or divine power of nature is contacted by visual exhaustiveness, by getting up close and seeing so clearly, is hard to say. The process is contradictory. As John Sears has argued, the same tourist attractions that guided nineteenth-century mass audiences to nature's thrilling sights structured and commercialized their contact with the divine and diluted its authenticity.[64] At Sea World, too, visions of the magical, unpopulated depths are thoroughly routinized. It is hard to get lost for too long in the carefully drawn wonder, and between people movers and show schedules it is almost impossible for the audience to forget the constant pressure to keep moving. The exhibits' visual rhetorics say "stay and look," while the logic of the attraction says "Keep moving! There's something amazing just ahead!" But Sea World's exhibits do try to create emotions: they call up awe, reverence, wonder, and often fear. Especially at the shark and moray eel exhibits, music, darkness, and carefully structured entry paths are designed to build a playful sense of danger. As a slogan for the Shark Encounter has it, "It's as close as you can get without holding your breath!" But perhaps reverence is induced most strongly by the displays themselves as technical feats. A great deal of the nineteenth-century world's fair tradition, with its awe of technology, lingers in Sea World's environmental reconstructions. Their intensely focused sights, their ability to take one's breath away, speak not only to the beauty of nature but the technical expert's ability to reconstruct that beauty and make it more perfect.

Interactive, Participatory, Touchable

In some ways, though, Sea World's versions of nature are wholly of the twentieth century. Although seeing nature in the nineteenth century's appreciative sense is central to the park experience, customers' times here also center on the experience of touch. The tactile emphasis at Sea World derives in part from research into factors that effect theme park length of stay. Sea World's managers have latched on to the notions of "participation" and "interaction," theorizing that people stay longer if entertainment is less passive, less dependent on just watching and more physically involving. Over and over again, Sea World's managers told me, "We are interactive," "We're participatory," "We're touchable." The vice president for entertainment explicitly compared the park to Disneyland in this way, asking, "Have you ever tried to touch anything at *Disneyland*? Have you ever tried to sit on *their* grass?"[65]

In one sense, participation is exactly about sitting on the grass verge or the bench; it is the way customers make theme park spaces temporarily their own, as opposed to being channeled relentlessly through them. And while Sea World makes a few such areas available, it does so conscious of the need to create structured antistructure, to supply the feeling that something is spontaneous. For example, at the verge of Mission Bay, near the Window to the Sea video theater, a few plastic lounge chairs are carefully scattered on the grass, as if to say, "You can sit here and just do nothing!" But generally, interactivity at the park takes more structured forms. Shamu's Happy Harbor is a water playground area set aside just for children and teenagers; it has areas where parents can sit and watch while small kids cavort on swings and tropical-colored gym equipment. Here children are provided with an environment they can physically engage, where they can play roughly, and even get wet—but the forms and kinds of engagement have been carefully planned for them. This is preshaped interaction.

In another sense, interaction is a way of going beyond seeing the displayed animals to touching and "making contact" with them. Sea World's advertising exhorts customers to "touch the magic," to reach out to "another world." Billboards and television commercials in the early 1990s regularly featured a picture of a three-year-old boy lifting a sea star out of a pool and turning it over to look at its underside. Designers give careful thought to how to create this touchy-feely interaction.

The most important structure shaping human-animal interaction is the division of the park's architecture into "display" and "show" areas. Sorted into display animals and show animals, most of the performers remain offstage, invisible to the audience most of the time. The exceptions are the killer whales who live in and are displayed in their performance stadium. Architecture is used to create a powerful awareness for the audience that unsupervised contact with the whales is off-limits. The charismatic animals need protection from unauthorized touch, and customers must keep their distance from the dangerous animals. For most of Sea World's history, barrier rails, open spaces, and high walls effectively kept humans from crossing to the whales' space, while raised walkways made viewing from above possible. By 1996, however, these constraints on interaction appeared to have been worn away, and Sea World inaugurated Shamu Backstage, an interactive, highly structured "touch the killer whale" exhibit that allowed controlled patting by a few selected customers.

Displayed animals are much more available for interaction. The California Tide Pool has a low barrier, so guests can lean over and handle different-colored sea stars. At the Bat Ray Shallows, de-spiked rays are accustomed to human touch and they cruise an irregular pool while children, parents, and school groups lean in to feel, feed, splash, and be splashed. At the shallows, tide pool, and Rocky Point Preserve, continuously cycling eco-music, a blur of instrumentation and animal noises (such as gull cries), alternates with live and prerecorded narration to offer the customer bits of natural historical information about just what he or she is touching. At each of these exhibits, what is offered is the sensation of a different, living texture. Handling of the most replaceable species is allowed full rein. For example, the California Tide Pool (no more a tide pool ecosystem than an aquarium is a life web) holds only a few maulable species. No really fragile creatures are found here, since it is designed for used by small children. Physical interactions with the larger animals must be more carefully structured. One simple technique of control is the posting of guides and interpreters near any place a crowd is expected. Geiss pointed out that "any place where there's public interaction with whales, there are also narrators or tour guides who also are specifically there to narrate, talk about the animals, and keep an eye open for that type of thing, too. It's one of the things we train our employees to do, to be very observant about everything that's going on, . . . to look for anything that might be a little unusual."[66]

Participatory exhibits use feeding to extend "touch" and "interaction." One of the central thrills at the dolphin and bat ray petting pools, especially for children, is buying small frozen fish or squid to feed the animals.[67] Feeding gives the customer a chance to lean over, pat, and look closely at the animal; indeed, the animals are so thoroughly used to being fed that it is only the purchased fish that allows the customer to get close enough to pet the animal. Children hand smelts to dolphins and anticipate a splash in return. In a way, the splash is a form of contact across species boundaries, a kind of exchange, and children are delighted by it; they seem to feel that it returns the effort of reaching out. Feeding is also an extension of training and taming. Familiar to Sea World visitors from the almost universal American practice of keeping pets, feeding dolphins or rays recalls the pet's dependence on the owner and calls up the affection that is bestowed on the dependent. The petting pool helps place the dolphin in the cultural space of the domestic animal, and so this sort of participation may subtly help soften customer discomforts about dolphins in captivity.

While participation is cast as an individual and customized activity, in fact feeling and touching are just like entering and staring: they take place in crowds and need to be organized. On busy days in the late 1980s and early 1990s, the crowds at the old dolphin petting pool were often three-people deep, with lots of noise, flying water, and excitement, but little touching or viewing for those behind the first row. At the same time, despite architectural barriers and staff supervision, unauthorized activities do take place. Sea World's employees can recount dozens of anecdotes about unplanned and unauthorized human-animal contacts, especially at the dolphin pool where enthusiasts come to dip crystals in the water and spectators have been known to strip off their clothes and plunge in, enthusiastic for the animals' touch. More prosaically, pool narrators must discourage teenagers from offering wristwatches or cigarette lighters to the dolphins.[68]

Since participation slows people down, it threatens to create so much involvement that a share of the spectacle cannot be guaranteed to the whole audience. Again, participation is a capacity problem. As the chief engineer put it, "[I]f you have anything that only one person can do at a time, if that person takes ten minutes to enjoy what he's doing, you can only accommodate a hundred people a day. When you have thirty thousand people, that's a problem."[69] In spring 1992, Sea World designers were planning a much expanded dolphin pool. A new shape with an uneven perimeter and Plexiglass panels would replace the old kidney-shaped pool that some staff called a "concrete bath tub" and provide a range of close-up opportunities.

Sea World develops interaction between humans around the animals. Guides and interpreters are stationed at exhibits to provide information and answer questions, another way of helping to make displays "less static" and easing the frustration of customers unable to get close. At some stations, narrators go beyond answering questions and call out questions to the audience, trying to engage the crowd. Guides and interpreters are a human layer of interaction and they help add text and narratives to the displays and bolster Sea World's definition as a place where customers learn something.

Authenticity and Autonomy

In the view of Sea World's designers, the customers' own, all-too-cultural and unscientific predilections shape the ways animals can be shown. From Sea World's point of view, its audience has an unfortunate tendency to project its own feelings onto animals. Managers see this "humanization" as a tendency to be resisted. Sea World's officers feel sure that as long as animal health is carefully monitored, and as long as animals are reproducing, they are in the best of all settings. (As the managers frequently commented to me: "Hey, that's a big, cold, vicious, polluted ocean out there!") So to communicate the benevolence of captivity and display, the visibility of the animals must be an appropriate visibility. While they must be secure and constrained, animals can't seem too captive or too manipulated. In fact, animals must seem to have something like the same environmental richness of landscaping and detail surrounding them that Sea World supplies to its human visitors.

The planning for the new dolphin pool provides a good example of the general problem. The park's planners and curators believe that the audience has a specific aesthetic and perceptual need for a kind of photographic naturalism in the landscape. For example, Jim Antrim, the curator of mammals, noted that the Vancouver Aquarium keeps killer whales in a "beautiful new exhibit" with artificial rock work, surrounded by "nice trees." While the Vancouver whale pool is a quarter or a fifth the size of Sea World's, "people feel better" about seeing animals in that exhibit than they do in Sea World's even though, according to Antrim, Sea World's larger pool has proved very successful in terms of the animals' breeding and birthing. "But that's the way the perceptions are," Antrim said.[70]

At the new Rocky Point Preserve, carefully simulated rock has replaced industrial ceramic tile, and a wave machine helps suggest tides, seasons, and a living ocean. The flocks of sea gulls drawn to the preserve in hopes of cadging frozen mackerel leave their white droppings everywhere—a truly realistic touch. While Rocky Point allows the brief illusion that there has been little intervention in the dolphins' relationship to their environment, there has of course been elaborate perceptual intervention to create that illusion. And the dolphin exhibit is culturally mediated in another way—it is arguably not derived from nature but is modeled directly on another dolphin display, the one at the Point Defiance Zoo and Aquarium in Tacoma.[71] The Point Defiance display and Rocky Point Preserve in turn are designed to show tourists a representative slice of the Northwest Coast they expect to see from touristic representations.[72] They are, in fact, a kind of three-dimensional postcard of an idea of nature, copied, perhaps, from other visual sources to make a representative place.

Sea World's producers and designers acknowledge that there are direct connections between other genres of nature tourism and the theme park's displays. They say that they aim to offer their customers well-defined tourist sights that they otherwise might not be able to travel to see—for example, the rugged Washington coast. The rocks surrounding the dolphin exhibit have nothing to do with the life of the dolphins—but everything to do with the idea of the rugged, austere terrestrial nature that humans expect to border on dolphin land. Animal displays are cultural as opposed to natural, not only in the sense that they are manufactured, but also in that they refer to predefined sights, to already well known ways of contemplating nature as romantically beautiful, stern, wild, and empty.[73] In this way, the preserve's craggy, uneven perimeter not only accommodates more dolphin patters, but it helps the audience see the dolphins contextualized in a familiar faraway landscape and, by extension, as more humanely treated.

Another important perception must be considered: the perception of autonomy. While humans must be able to have an unobstructed view of the animals in a recognizable setting, the animals must seem to be able to get away from the watching, petting, and probing humans. Although Antrim thought the old pool functioned adequately, he knew that both audience and staff perceived the animals "as having no sanctuary. It looks like they can't get away." In fact, the dolphins could escape to a spot in the middle of the old pool, but the seeming lack of an escape hatch called up the awareness that, in fact, the dolphins couldn't get away. So, the new pool displays a retreat, an away area where the public can not get too close.[74]

Similarly, in the case of the Penguin Encounter, the engineers had to work with an irony of perception built into their concern with verisimilitude. Wankier pointed out that "if you ever see pictures of the Antarctic, there are millions of penguins in a small space." However, in simulating a penguin rookery, the designers thought they had to keep the penguins from appearing overcrowded to their public. People are made uncomfortable by the sight of swarming animals. Crowding might indicate mistreatment in captivity, and just as bad, the engineer speculated, it might remind the viewers themselves of feeling bunched up. In this very popular exhibit, the designers did not want people who were packed on a conveyor belt to view what looked like jam-packed penguins. So the density of the rookery was modified. Audiences looking at animals are apparently always filtering what they see back through their own experience: quite literally, looking at animals is a process of reflecting on our own experiences. Are the penguins treated well? Are we being treated well? By viewing animals, how are we participating in their treatment? Realistically simulated settings help dampen awareness for both audience and presenters that the animal is in a cage; alternatively, techniques of environmental design make the enclosure seem more gentle.[75]

Most often, Sea World's planners worry that the visitor's perceptions are shaped by the animal rights and environmental activists' declarations about the conditions of captivity. Rocky Point Preserve, the newest environment exhibit, tries to deflect the captivity controversy. Crowding and issues of space are a focus of protesters, since captivity is by definition the removal of an animal from one environment and its insertion into another, smaller one. In the case of wild whales and dolphins, it is hard to ignore that this new niche is vastly more limited than the original. Spokespersons from Greenpeace, for example, have frequently and publicly compared keeping a killer whale in a tank to keeping "an eagle in a parakeet cage."[76]

Other marine animal activists claim that the orcas have been ripped from the social context of their pod and cannot be psychically or physically healthy until they rejoin it. Some claim the chlorine level in the petting pool is too high; others have argued that the orcas' sonar waves are bouncing off the pool walls and maddening them. Whatever the validity of such claims, it is clear that Sea World is on the front lines of a rhetorical war over what "natural" means and whether keeping animals in captivity has social value.[77] Its response is to design animal facilities with an acute awareness of what customers see and how they want to feel about animals, feelings that management insists has little to do with scientific knowledge. The reduction of the larger, biological environment to some few essentials adequate to sustain life should be pushed to the edge of awareness.

Sea World makes all its effort in reproducing an environment on the level of the concrete physical display, but a great deal more could be done to evoke for the audience the mysteriousness of the marine environment and the uncertainty of human knowledge about its life processes. Such imaginative work, using words, sounds, and drawings, a different kind of theatricality, might run into the problem of powerfully conveying to the audience the complexity of the environment. It might suggest the richness of what is missing from the photo-touristic slice of the Pacific Northwest, for example. It is interesting to note, however, that very occasionally the drive for visible naturalism is suspended. Visitors taking the behind-the-scenes tours in the areas where sick and surplus animals are kept view them in absolutely stark, functional pens. Dean MacCannell would say that these tourists had achieved another plane of "authenticity" and that, indeed, they have paid extra to do so! I went on guided tours and did hear complaints about the aesthetics of the rehabilitation areas. It is not surprising that Sea World's managers feel strongly that the most public of the animal exhibits must be decorative, artful, and authentically "environmental."

Like every tourist attraction, Sea World has an extensive backstage, and like most tourist attractions but unlike most theme parks, it allows selective parts of its backstage or production area to be seen. It is here that customers can occasionally glimpse the construction of spectacular nature in progress. For example, announcements of feeding time at the Penguin Encounter are printed on the show schedule; and for a brief time every day the illusion of the transplanted piece of Antarctica is broken by support staff in yellow foul-weather gear spraying crushed ice over the ice floes. Nevertheless, for the most part, the nature Sea World's animals appear in is very limited, a tight frame. Animals are not often seen mating or killing, although this has occasionally happened in shows; rather, mammals and birds are usually seen simply eating, grooming, or swimming. The complexly manipulated process of the reproduction and maintenance of their lives is more or less invisible, except when it is carefully brought forward and re-presented in selected contexts such as video tapes, guided tours, and scheduled "meet the experts" interactions.

Most of the functions that create the appropriate types of contact and seeing must be hidden. Again, this is because Sea World's management feels that although some revelation is unavoidable, visitors don't wish to know all the details of captivity. Things that must remain invisible for the comfort of the paying visitors include seriously sick and dying animals, although animals undergoing rehabilitation are carefully displayed if they don't appear wounded and can be appropriately interpreted. For example, sea lion or seal pups recovering from starvation or parasites would not be displayed, except on the "behind-the-scenes tour," where a guide can properly frame the sight. However, otters being treated after the *Exxon Valdez* oil spill form a display unto themselves: with a flourish, the exhibit label announces, "These Otters Are Survivors!" What goes on behind the scenes at Sea World can, on occasion, be inserted into a positive story that is specifically about the park.

Limited Illusions

If Sea World's exhibit areas use space, movement, and vision to consolidate the perception of entering or contacting another, wilder world, still this illusion is always limited. It is limited of course by the customer's recognition that, after all, he or she is in a theme park. But this recognition is not just due to limits of realism: Sea World actively refuses to separate the customer from the everyday, even while it insists it is providing that distance. The best example of this is the omnipresence of music. There is no greensward, display space, gift shop, or rest room in Sea World that does not have its own sound track music piped in by a set of hidden speakers. Throughout the park, musical sound is inescapable. According to the chief engineer, sound, and mainly music, is always part of the design of any building or outdoor area. Wankier noted that "all along all the walkways, you're never away from sound. . . . They say it creates ambience. It's the same as the curved walkways and landscaping. They help to create relaxation in the park."[78]

Sound falls into several rough categories—general background music that is designed to accompany a transition from one area to another or one activity to another; narrations and song lyrics that graft an explicit verbal text over music and onto an exhibit; and themed music that attempts to overlay or complement the "mood" or idea of a building or exhibit. (As we will see in chapter 5, musical sound tracks are also carefully composed and edited to help shape meaning in and drive the motion of the performing animal shows.) Most of this music might be called "lite jazz" or "New Age jazz," although some areas feature oldies-style sound tracks and what radio programmers term "adult-oriented rock." Especially around the whole-environment displays, the music is overlaid with nature sounds, like bird cries, and has a New Age, cyclical quality. It is impossible to tell when one composition ends and another begins. Not only do the jazz and New Age genres fit Sea World's upscale, older demographics but their structure helps support the landscape's sense of continuous movement without a final destination. Customized, computerized sound tracks give each area of the park a musical theme, and themes can be varied according to time of day and mood, peppy for the morning, laid-back for the afternoon, romantic at night. Sea World abhors an aural vacuum, too.

In exhibits, music cues visitors to feel a certain way about what they are seeing. Sound underlines a cultural perspective drawn largely from the mass entertainment media and reinserts it into an environment that has been visually constructed to appear at least temporarily culture-free. The goal is to supply prerecorded feelings along dimensions such as cuteness or threat. In the old Shark Encounter, for example, the background music was threatening and ominous, "strictly a takeoff from *Jaws*," according to Wankier.[79] At the Penguin Encounter, a sound track designed for the outdoor exhibit of Magellanic penguins suggests puckish waddling. In both cases, music not only supports the exhibit, it underlines conventional cultural associations to the animals. If the music in the shark exhibit really supported the idea of a naturalistic setting, for example, it would not necessarily underline the definition of sharks as ominous and threatening. In the penguin exhibit, it would not underscore the joke of the bird in a tuxedo. Sea World relies almost exclusively on popular musical interpretations of such nature themes as awe, delight, fear, or mystery.[80]

Much like the video terminals in Sea World's exhibits and stadiums, sound tracks provide a common, external focus for waiting audiences, allowing attention to be turned away from the experience of being in a crowd or the boredom of waiting. And, although they are most often without lyrics, sound tracks also provide common texts for interpretation. Some bits of music are not so much about the world of the sea or specific animals as they are a meta-interpretation offering a way to understand the meaning of the Sea World experience itself. "When I Take the Time," featured in the World of the Sea Aquarium, is about feeling the joy of leisure and looking and family closeness, a summary of Sea World's core experiential propositions. This sound track not only calls up appropriate feelings, it actually tells its audience that it is appropriate to have warm feelings, even while they are consuming the taxonomic display of the species-by-species tank aquarium.[81] Similarly, at Bat Ray Shallows, prerecorded bird calls and surf noises blend with a cyclical synthesizer composition. The singers urge listeners to "come on and get together," to "help Mother Earth" because a "new day is coming." Here, the sound track not so subtly casts the ray pool as a site of enviro-activism.

Back to the Numbers

Structuring perception and interpreting animals are long-term, evolving tasks. But Sea World's managers are concerned on a daily basis with whether vision, sound, and motion work to create financial success. To try to understand whether the experience machine will deliver profits, the park's planners and managers return to their bank of numbers. An enormous amount of market research goes into trying to discover which shows, themes, and special events programs are working and which are not, which areas of the park need to be refurbished and which can, for now, just be maintained. Within fairly narrow parameters, Sea World's market research explores the customers' reactions to the Sea World landscape, so that dissatisfactions can be preempted and successes fine-tuned. In face-to-face interviews and questionnaires, market researchers compile information that they use to rate Sea World and its attractions on a scale from 1 to 9.[82]

Thomas noted that he uses show ratings to quickly diagnose whether all is well or something is dramatically wrong: "We had a baby killer whale born here last July [1991], and we changed the show. The show became an educational presentation because they wanted the mother and baby to stay in the show pool. And for much of the summer, the whale show ratings went down. People from Iowa wanted to see this great killer whale Shamu and see this terrific show they've heard about and seen on national television. But there was nothing else we could do."[83] Thomas looks at ratings daily, and he regards them as an accurate barometer. "When we take an animal out of the show and put another animal in it, or if there is an animal problem or something, even for a couple of days, the ratings are [snaps his fingers] just like that. Instantaneous. That's what I love about the numbers. . . . It's like taking a temperature. If you're 101, you'd like to think you are 98.6, but 101 is 101. You can't kid yourself."[84]

However, allowing show ratings to dictate a major change in the park has sometimes led to headaches. One park president tinkered with a show he thought was weak, ignoring the possibility that despite its rating of 7.3, it served an important purpose. The old Sparklett's Water Fantasy show offered not much more than a cool dark place to sit for twenty minutes. Numerical measures were incapable of revealing Water Fantasy's appeal, but apparently its dancing waters, colored lights, and narration-free music soothed many hot and overstimulated customers. When Sea World rethemed the Sparklett's pavilion to tell about its animal-saving and research activities in a video called "Window to the Sea," it removed a relaxing space and "hit the science a bit too hard." Bill Thomas ruefully noted that "we spent a million dollars to bring a 7.3 show down to a 5.9."[85]

All of marketing's research is supposed to be as hard and inescapable as "98.6." None of it could be termed qualitative, that is, aimed at exploring the guest's reactions to shows and exhibits in terms of ideas, emotions, or understanding. Sea World does almost no watching or observing at their exhibits, Jackie Hill explained: "Sometimes you'll come to a management meeting and say, 'You know, I was out at the Forbidden Reef exhibit today and, gee, people really seemed to be enjoying themselves.' But nine times out of ten you don't really have time. You just have to focus your time on what needs to be done. If they are having a good time, you are doing the job, so don't worry about it. If they are not having a good time, there is something that needs to be addressed."[86]

The measures of "having a good time" are the attendance figures and numerical show ratings. If people are physically in the park, they are presumed to be having a good time. If they are not present in sufficient numbers, then something needs to be fixed. Neither does Sea World focus on how long people stay at exhibits or whether or not they read the educational graphics. Hill summed it up neatly: "You see, the reason Sea World has not focused on that is that, well, most of our research is going somehow to relate to profit: to the bottom line. Zoos and museums have different motivations and they collect different information."[87]

The education department of a zoo or a natural history museum might try to explore what visitors actually take away from exhibits, or what questions or problems they raise, but these are not the dimensions along which Sea World measures success. Market research is a closed loop, a tool for refining something that, in terms of the rationale of the attraction, is already known to be working. It closes gaps and irons out bumps in the spectacular landscape, and it identifies violations of the audience's expectations which have been shaped in large part by Sea World's own marketing. But market research is not an open-ended exploration of what the customers take away or would like to take away from the theme park.

The Sea World Experience

The rationale of the attraction means that a great deal is going on at once in the theme park. Within the overall theme of marine life, attractions and performances are disparate, sometimes clashing. Indeed, a day at Sea World can seem like an exhausting mishmash, a carnival of fish and dolphins and Clydesdale horses and gymnasts and surfers dressed like pirates. But within all this variety, most of the audience's basic perceptions, especially their perceptions of nature and animals, are being considered and carefully managed. Style, display techniques, landscaping, texts, service, and sound are mobilized to deliver the ease, comfort, and safety that frame Sea World's wide-ranging, exotic vision. One end result is a sensation of controlled novelty, of familiar diversity set in an intensively commercial frame. Although the customers have paid well for the kinetic, aural, and visual plenty laid at their feet, they should not spend too much time noticing where it comes from. Rather, Sea World's managers hope their audience receives the park's nature spectacles in an atmosphere of distracted enjoyment.

I have described the attempt to create experiences and sensations; I have not, for the most part, accounted for the sensations of the customers, except, of course, my own. The theme park ultimately has no final control over the understandings its customers bring into the park, and—so cultural theory tells us—it has little control over what they as an audience actually take away. While a range of versions of Sea World may be seen, felt, and consumed by its millions of visitors, nevertheless it is the case that Sea World tries to set firm boundaries, to limit and direct the possibilities a visit to the theme park can hold. In a strong sense, what can take place at Sea World is predetermined before the day starts and the exhibits open, by the park's location, by its pricing, and by the self-selection of its audience, which results in a general, though by no means total, homogeneity of class and educational background. Inside the park, the audience finds a kind of controlled freedom—freedom, for example, from the homeless and panhandlers in Balboa Park, or from the awareness that the world is not always clean or smoothly running.

Much at Sea World is reassuringly expectable: its ethnically and racially mixed workforce offers the friendly and deferential service familiar from hamburger chains, shopping malls, and the nearby fancy hotels. All the omnipresent mall souvenirs are available: calendars, cards, blown glass, pearl jewelry, baseball hats, T-shirts, and plush marine animals. Food and beverages come up to cafeteria and McDonald's standards, despite Sea World's claim to help us enter another world. The park is cleaned to middle-class expectations for public spaces: evidence of other people's (or even animals') dirt or living processes is removed from view (although a critical eye can spot the corporate waste).

The animals plot a continuum of familiar novelties: there are rare and unexpected animals in the familiar zoo setting, and familiar animals in visually naturalistic settings. The animals are visible with few obstructions; some even are enthusiastically touchable and feedable, practically domestic, just as television and nature photography have presented them to us for years. Always the landscape is rich, bright, detailed, and seemingly self-perpetuating. Within this closed world, the audience is free to move about, penetrating, albeit briefly, some mysteries of the natural world, only to move on, pressed by crowd management, show scheduling, and the price of admission to see everything.

On inspection, what is compelling though not at all strange about Sea World is its offer of freedom and leisure combined with the careful control of perception and the evocation of feeling. There is never anything wild, chaotic, or out of control about this theme park—except as we shall see, at moments when performing animals cause problems—despite the park's claim to show us dangerous, unrestrained, and startling nature. Indeed, all "nature" at the park, from the perennial borders to the sharks in their coral reef dioramas, is thoroughly tamed. Even the whole-environment displays show or tell very little about the complex patterns of animal life and society in the wild. To do so might emphasize how far from the wild the animals are at Sea World. To see some version of real "wildness," the audience would have to see something potentially complex and confusing, something perhaps not transparently visible or harmonious or colorful at all.

Producing this environment is a complicated series of interconnected tasks, and Sea World's management will admit that it doesn't always work so well. They get letters complaining about lines, high prices, bad food, predatory sea gulls, scheduling, impolite employees, the hot sunshine, animals that will not perform, and, again, high prices and long lines. Nevertheless, the park as a machine for moving people, showing them things, and selling them things has worked reasonably well for decades, well enough to return excellent rates of profit in most years. Although Sea World continues to refine and expand its exhibits, most of the changes in the park are at this point just that—refinements of a system that works rather well for an audience familiar with the nature theme park as a well-known commodity. Failing some severe crisis—unionization of the employees, an earthquake damaging the physical plant, or a sharp change in consumer attitudes toward animal performances—the turnstile game will tick along, supported by the electronic number-gathering technology, accumulated managerial wisdom, and low-wage labor that make it possible.

CHAPTER FOUR

Enlightenment Lite

The Theme Park Classroom

The landscape of consumption is one of Sea World's faces, regional and local tourists the largest part of its audience. But a parallel park exists simultaneously with the tourist attraction, and in fact Sea World leans heavily on it: its image as a site of education. Sea World's publicists make much of the educational role the theme park plays for its customers and the city of San Diego. They argue that Sea World's shows and displays are important sources of information about marine life and environments, and that Sea World's very existence furthers nature conservation and pro-environmental attitudes among the public at large.

Sea World claims it makes enlightenment available in a variety of ways. It can be sought in the park's landscape by the more ambitious visitors, or it can be acquired through an additional purchase, such as a book, a tape, or a behind-the-scenes tour. Enlightenment can be absorbed almost unconsciously, by simply being in the park. The managers routinely say, "Everyone who comes here gets an education, whether they know it or not," suggesting that learning may even be best when it sneaks up on the unwary customer. Rhetorically, the managers try to will for the park an identity of spectacle and enlightenment, as against the animal rights activists outside the gate who assert that the commercial performances of animals are by definition irrational.[1]

From 1990 through 1995, I spent time exploring Sea World's claims to be a kind of educator.[2] Cataloguing its activities and observing its programs inside and outside the park, I found that while thinking about Sea World as a tourist attraction can make its education programs seem peripheral, in fact they are not. School field trips take place in the winter off-season, guided tours and special classes unfold behind the scenes, and the park's narrators fill in the gaps around the antics of the feedable, touchable dolphins, but education's ancillary role is far from marginal, and the claim to deliver learning has gone beyond institutional legitimation.[3] For decades, Sea World has been vigorously engaged in using a wide range of educational programs, activities, and products to promote the theme park and extend it outward into the classroom and the community, where it becomes a part of everyday life. Both the image of education and education as practiced at Sea World are central to justifying its activities and creating public understanding of the theme park and, just as important, to cultivating its audience.

And yet, in a strong sense, there is no independent life for these products beyond Sea World. The theme park education that works its way into the life of the school and the family is so carefully crafted to meet Sea World's marketing and publicity needs that the union between spectacle and education is a lopsided one. The unevenness of this relationship can be traced in education's ambitions, uses, and content. Four descriptive excerpts from my field notes will help chart Sea World education's breadth and textures and signal some of the questions that can be raised about it.

July 19, 1990: I'm standing in the shade of four mesh nets. Hung on poles between large eucalyptus trees, they give summer customers relief from the sun and cool the California Tide Pool. Despite the fact that it is located on a route from the Shamu Stadium to the high dive show, the attractiveness of the pool's grottolike quality means people actually linger there for a while. On a hot summer day, this is one of the few refreshing places in the park. It is also a designated Kodak "Photo Spot."

The California Tide Pool isn't really a tide pool—it's more like a saltwater fountain. Several raised, oval basins of water are walled in by large chunks of reddish lava rock embedded in concrete. The tide pool is not a living ecosystem—there's no splash zone with slippery kelp attached, and the clusters of mussel shells have been artfully glued on. There is no tide, no wind and smell of the sea, no seasons. In the bottom of the shallow basin lie sea stars, bat stars, and a few sea urchins. The pool is designed so that children can reach over its edge to touch and feel the accessible inhabitants. The tide pool is one of Sea World's educational sites, the kind of exhibit the park stresses children and families can learn from.

Although the tide pool's designers intended to create a cool place where children can linger and learn and parents can rest their tired feet, it is not a relaxing spot. There are a lot of summer tourists with cameras, and they arrange their relatives in front of the Kodak marker. Over and over again, parents take pictures of their children picking up starfish and turning them over, exactly reproducing Sea World's own billboards.[4] A continual prerecorded sound track alternates between themed music and announcements. On a regular schedule, this sound track is turned off and an interpreter plugs his handheld mike into the lava and narrates the exhibit using a memorized script. Interpreter Jeff kneels to help kids see starfish and reminds them several times not remove other animals. Even at the tide pool, Sea World demands that you pay attention.

The tide pool is emblematic of the structure of education at Sea World. It is designed to impart a sense that "education is happening here," but on inspection this message seems largely superficial. For school groups visiting the park, the tide pool is a marked off as a designated "educational exhibit," a place on their "should see" itinerary; and while teachers can use it to show their students something about sea stars, the range of activities there is limited. Much of what Sea World uses the tide pool to communicate is vaguely taxonomic information, preset and prerecorded and built around the entertainment structures of the park. For regular theme park customers, the tide pool is a brief stop-off on the way to shows and souvenir stands, a place to pick up a few facts and, oddly, a place where tourists can actually insert themselves into Sea World's image by reproducing a well-known advertisement with their own cameras.

• • •

May 6, 1992: It's 9 a.m. and I'm waiting outside the Education Group Gate. I've arranged to tag along with third graders from the Louis Agassiz School, to observe how they and their teachers use Sea World.[5] As usual, there's an organized chaos of teachers and guides dealing with payment vouchers, purchase orders, box lunches, bus drivers, and hundreds of children. As if to relieve the wait, a bus goes by with its sign reading "Wrong Bus." Parents and teachers burst out laughing. Isn't there always a wrong bus?

It's gray and overcast, but the kids seem incredibly excited. I chat with the park's instructors as they give teachers and aides maps with the educational areas circled: these are the aquariums and the petting and touching exhibits. Today, five school groups will attend two scheduled "ed shows," one in the Shamu Stadium, one at the Sea Lion and Otter Stadium. The rest of the time they are free to go their own way or regroup, but there are strict rules: they must not enter the playground area, and everyone must be out by 1 p.m. or pay a "stay and play" fee. Ms. MacColl, Agassiz's leader, tells me that she "really moves out." Firmly, she tells her students, "We are here to learn and not to play," "You are *not* allowed to go to Cap'n Kid's World, and if they catch us we are *in trouble!*" and "No glass bottles!"

Suddenly, everyone is running through the gate. Ms. MacColl takes off at a spirited pace, crying "Come on, come on!" I try to keep up with her, but she's too fast. I'm not used to running with my bags of equipment, so I memorize the color of her sun visor bobbing in the crush, in case I lose Agassiz. Ms. MacColl sprints to the Bat Ray Shallows; the other half of the class splits off and where they go, I miss seeing. As the kids approach the shallows they get excited—there's a lot of room to lean over, touch rays, and get wet. They throng the pool, creating an earsplitting noise.

I lean against a text board listing ray species to take notes. From a walkway above the pool, a narrator is saluting Agassiz with a peppy cheerleader cry: "How are you *doing* out there?! Good *morning* everybody! Can you say *good morning?!* Do you want to pet *bat rays* yet?!"

From the kids, at top volume: "Yay!"

All day I see this cheerleader call-and-response pattern, a standard technique at Sea World for creating something that looks like interaction. "Are they *slimy!?* Yes! They *are!* Can you say *mucous! membrane! coating!?*"

Ms. MacColl reads the bat ray panels to the kids. She takes the kids to the narrator to ask questions and moves them from spot to spot around the amoeboid pool. She talks with them, waving her arms, about the ways the rays swim.

The next time I look up from my notebook, something unexpected is happening. Ms. MacColl is next to the narrator, complaining to her. The narrator has her hand over the microphone, the prerecorded sound track is playing and now Ms. MacColl is angry, arguing. The announcer, it turns out, has covered the mike to answer questions for two adult tourists. Ms. MacColl is insistent: "If you are answering interesting questions, do it into the mike so we can all learn something." The narrator answers that she can't, because the prerecorded sound track is playing and she cannot speak over it. Ms. MacColl says that she has only a few minutes with her group at the bat ray pool before the Shamu show. She doesn't want to waste them listening to a "sappy song." "If you are here to teach us something, teach us." "Well, actually," the narrator replies blandly, "the lyrics are very educational if you listen to them."

Later, over sandwiches, Ms. MacColl tells me about her students. Most are from very poor neighborhoods and few are reading at grade level. She really makes a big effort, she says, to get field trips for the kids. Most classrooms take only one or two trips a year, but she solicits money from parents, doubles up with other teachers, and gets discounts. The parents contribute about fifteen dollars a year, and it's a big effort for them. With all this scrimping and soliciting, she takes her kids to the Natural History Museum, Sea World, Scripps Aquarium, and other places. And sometimes Ms. MacColl pays for them herself. The time is short for this once-a-year trip: she has to literally make the children run from exhibit to exhibit, to pack in as much as she can. Given the effort she makes to take her students to the theme park, it is no wonder she was angry at being told to listen to a prerecorded sound track at a supposedly interactive exhibit. From the look on Ms. MacColl's face, I don't think Sea World has heard the last of the microphone dispute.[6]

Later the same morning: Ms. MacColl's students run on to the dolphin pool to enjoy more touching, splashing, and shrieking. The scene there is wet and wild; dolphins can throw quite a lot of water. Kids spend a little money on frozen smelt to dangle in front of them, and the narrator continues the call and response, question and answer. Now the narrator says the Shamu show is starting in just a few minutes, and most of Agassiz's kids go off at a dead run to the stadium chanting, "*Sha'*-mu! *Sha'*-mu!" There they grab seats near the concrete beach where Shamu will slide out of the water. The sun has burned through the May morning clouds and now it is searingly hot. Teachers snap pictures of their classes, and one Sea World instructor stands down in front, informally asking and answering questions: "The pool is thirty-six feet deep." "The baby killer whale is over by the gate." "Nope, they only get one set of teeth in a lifetime."

Here comes the narrator, introducing the "ed show": "Good morning!!! Does anyone know . . . ?"

He presents a partly prerecorded, partly recited narration about killer whales, and then he introduces Kelly, a sandy-haired, sunburnt trainer in a red wet suit, who takes over the show.

This show is about behavior. But talking about behavior seems to be a fancy way of telling the kids what killer whales do. Kelly tells us that the killer whale behaviors, "jumping, eating, and swimming," make orcas "the top predators in their environment." She then engages the several hundred children through give-and-take questions set up so kids will easily get them right. "Do all animals do the same behavior???" "*Nooooo!!!!!!*"

Then, dispensing with questions, she gestures to the whale in the pool behind her. "It still amazes us to see the whale jump up and out of the water," she says, and the whale delivers an enormous leap and slides out to pose for photos on the concrete beach. After a brief discussion of how orcas swim and maneuver, Kelly says, "How many people would like to see Steve get into the water?" Steve, another trainer, gets into the water and rides Shamu, jumps off its nose, feeds it, and surfs on its back: this is the same coordinated routine we can see at a regular Shamu show. This display leads into a discussion of how killer whales are trained. We learn that they are praised and rewarded for good behavior and given no reward (but never punished) for bad behavior. The discussion of reinforcement and training is not developed for this audience of third graders. It seems that whales do what people want them to do because they want to obey.

The show is brief, but before it ends there is a Sea World–style mention of an environmental issue. "Do killer whales like to swim in clean water?" asks Kelly. "Of *course* they do!" A discussion of "what we can do" to help killer whales focuses on throwing away trash properly, not messing up the beach, and recycling. Then, finally, "Hey! How many of you want to see some more spectacular behaviors!?" Shamu does some more jumping, splashing, and a final slide-out. I feel incredibly weary to hear these eager students offered such a superficial environmental message.

• • •

April 30, 1992: On another day, the Seward School group and I head to the sea lion and otter educational show. The kids are excited at the prospect of getting wet, so instructor Lydia takes them through a pledge, hands over hearts: "I promise: If I should get wet . . . I will stay seated, no matter what." Despite her jovial attempt to inject some school atmosphere into the park, for the moment discipline is in tatters. And there is a lot of delightful clowning around in the show itself, with walruses spitting water at the kids, a disobedient sea lion, and a break-dancing river otter.

Despite its raucousness, the show's theme is behavior and training. It begins with practical training tips—how you can train dogs, cats, even your parents. There is a discussion of the conditioned reinforcer. A boy named Bart is selected from the audience and magically turned into a sea lion. Then the trainer shows how Bart can be trained: he learns that when he hears "Okay" he can get a reward. We see him "reinforced," learning a "bridge," and following a target across the stage. The audience throws Bart an imaginary fish. Then he is "taught" to follow a target on a pole, until he spins around like a corkscrew.[7]

Bart retires and a sea lion comes out. The trainers show us how McClain is "shaped" to "target" his face onto a map in a trick called the "map cry." McClain rubs his eyes and his nose with his flippers as he bends over the map, and in the real show, we're told, he will finish by blowing his nose on it. At the end of his training segment, McClain delights the kids by seeming to defy his trainer's command. He jumps up on the glass barrier separating stadium from stage and bays outrageously at the children.

A river otter is being trained to do the "Pepsi carry": First he learns to touch the cola can, then to carry it in his paws, to walk with it a little further each time, and eventually to take it all the way across the stage in imitation of the Michael Jackson music video "Bad." Then, to help us understand the supposedly natural origins of the show tricks, Flo the walrus spits and sprays water all over the kids. Her trainer explains that in the wild this spritzing flushes shellfish out of their shells, so Flo can eat them. Now Flo rolls on her side, exposing a vast belly, and (with help from the show's audio operator) throws the kids a huge, smacking kiss.

After the behavior and training show, Seward School tramps off toward the sea lion exhibit. I'm thinking, "Why teach them about 'training' techniques?" One reason is perhaps that it's directly related to what the park is famous for doing: training animals. And this is a subject of fascination for children. From my conversations with them, this sea lion and otter show is the one elementary school children like best: they are tickled by the idea of training their parents, they love to imagine having a break-dancing otter or a rude walrus for a pet. And training is perhaps familiar from the structures of discipline that children face and the ways they are treated in classrooms. Twelve-year-old Adela comments to me that she liked the part where the sea lion, when he is not doing what he is supposed to be doing, is given a chance to try again. He is given a time-out and another chance. This makes sense to her; it is both familiar and fair.

Later, as we leave, I walk alongside a parent who has accompanied the field trip. He shakes his head at me and looks disgusted. Although he doesn't know I've been there to look specifically at the content of the field trip, he must surmise this, because he forcefully expresses an opinion. "Really," he says, "you'd think they could teach us something we didn't already know. I mean, they say 'communicate with animals, this is how we communicate.' 'Communication is important.' We all know that already. That's basic." He waves his hand disgustedly and walks away.

Each of my education group visits at Sea World had a feeling of rushing to see something amazing that turned out to be very familiar, a feeling of frustration, and of promises undelivered. Teachers were trying to fit an encounter with every Sea World sight into a short period of time. They were pressured to rapidly move around a large number of vociferous and rambunctious children, all the while staying within the boundaries Sea World sets for "ed groups." Teachers were constantly cautioning children not to break the rules, while the children were exhilarated to be off school grounds and on a field trip to such a celebrated place.

Students brought a range of attitudes to Sea World, from calmly respectful to cynically boisterous. At the same time, the field trips' structures marked the ed groups with a different, less desirable status than that of the ordinary tourists; students and teachers felt this and knew it, despite the welcoming attitude of the education staff. School group membership meant conditional admittance to the park, where the mark of entitlement is the paid ticket. Ed groups saw nearly the same exhibits and shows, but since they were subsidized their time in the park was limited. Since ed groups were not likely to be big spenders at the concession stands, Sea World needed to limit the demands they placed on the park's staff and spaces. This conditional admission was underlined by the clear enunciation of places ed groups were to go and not go, of places not to get "caught," and these tensions were reinforced by teachers like Ms. MacColl, who felt that for all its limits a trip to Sea World might be their students' only chance to learn something about the oceans' vivid life. The feeling of being on rations in the land of plenty could turn the students' rambunctiousness into rebelliousness, as when they occasionally deserted their groups without permission, almost certainly for the gift shops. Or, as when an eleven-year-old African-American boy shouted, when I asked for his reaction to the park, "It's all a rip off!" and went on to explain very accurately to me and his friends the relationship between the park's cheap souvenirs, inflated prices, and expansive landscape.

. . .

October 7, 1994: It's very early on a Friday morning when I pull into the employees' parking lot. I've been invited to watch the broadcast of a live interactive television show about "Animal Disguises." This *Shamu TV* broadcast will be edited, mixed, and sent up live from the grounds of the theme park, beamed via satellite to school systems around the country. A student research assistant arrives, and we make our way still yawning to the cramped trailers that house the education department. From there we're escorted into the World of the Sea Aquarium. Making our way to a back door, we have a rare Sea World experience, a true surprise. We pass a huge Asian owl tethered to a concrete pad sunken in the lawn. The owl is arrestingly beautiful and its presence, its liveness, stuns us into silence, even though it is surrounded by cameras, crew, and lights.

For a broadcast that will reach 13 million people, the operation unfolding in the aquarium is surprisingly quiet and calm. I edge back in the darkness, staying out of the way, determined not to trip over a crucial cord. Kent, the program's host, has finished with makeup and is trying to relax in front of a tank of bright tropical fish. Nina from public relations is giving time cues. I thought there would be a lot of equipment, but there's very little. A single editor is hunched over the laptop computer that will patch together material from remote cameras in this park with prerecorded materials from the other Sea Worlds. Prior to going live, the show features teasers, multiple choice and true-false questions. As we will see, similar questions warm up the audience for the Shamu show. Answers must be short, and they present facts such as speed, weight, and size, reasons for behavior, or body shapes. As Kent goes into his live welcome, we stare at his picture on the large monitor, even though he's standing only a few feet away. The editing-in of remote clips means that Kent's spiel doesn't make much sense by itself; the video screen holds the integrated whole.

Oddly, the *Shamu TV* show has some of the qualities of an aquarium: brights against darks, luminous colors, constant motion. But while aquariums try to be artificial contexts for their animals, "Animal Disguises" shows its subjects decontextualized, in tight frame, removed from their environments. "Disguises" discusses the animal's relationship to its environment in terms of the animal's ability to "dress for success" and compete in a harsh world. Except for warnings about the danger of litter and pollution, the narrative does not indicate that humans have any relationship to this competitive environment. Nature is a beautiful zone outside human activity, its laws unfolding inexorably, yet aspects of modern human life ("dress for success") provide predictable metaphors for describing it. This is Sea World's staple narrative, here vividly reproduced for schoolrooms around the country.

Sea World as Schoolroom

Education here is literally about reaching millions of people with the Sea World image and message, with programs that allow the theme park to contact specific audiences located in precise and predictable environments. That these environments not only are formally educational—the school, the day care center, the college classroom, the instructional television channel and its programming guide—but also give access to families with children is a fact not lost on the marketing department. Such settings can be powerfully influential in helping parents perceive Sea World and its products as sound and fun. And these settings are underexploited, since classrooms have been traditionally free of direct commercial advertising.[8]

Sea World has worked on its school-oriented programs for decades. With their goal of reaching out to a wide public, the programs have been developed in a context of great sensitivity to public opinion and perception. Following the accidents of 1987 and 1989, Sea World's public relations department redoubled its efforts to show that the park was involved in animal rescue, research, and conservation, and in every conceivable local good work, environmental or social, as a way of reconstructing the park's image and answering the criticisms of animal rights activists. Education programs were seen as an important part of this rhetorical defense.[9] City council oversight (however minimal) of the park's lease, and continuing pressure from activists for legal regulation of the capture and treatment of whales, have encouraged Sea World to push forward in defining itself as a responsible "citizen." One key way to do this has been to formalize and materialize the park's educational identity.

But after 1989 the park could draw on Anheuser-Busch's resources to expand education. There was pressure, and there was opportunity. With this new source of funds, Sea World began to elaborate the educational surfaces inside the park and to expand efforts dedicated to specifically instructional programs and materials behind the scenes. Not only have exhibits been rebuilt to look more modern, but their texts and graphics have been upgraded. Old instructional programs and media have multiplied, while new video, computer, satellite, and information technologies and systems are rapidly being added into Sea World's educational mix. This image-building process has led the theme park to develop close connections with schools, teachers, school districts, and other institutions public and private. This pattern of connection is accelerating and still incomplete.

A large-scale role in public education for a private, for-profit theme park company seems odd. But Sea World is not alone in its advance into public education. To take just one example, Disney's Walt Disney World and EPCOT Center theme park have been offering science, social studies, and remedial studies courses for credit to high school students for the better part of the last decade.[10] "Celebration," Disney Development's planned city for forty thousand people now being built on the outskirts of Orlando, will feature Disney-produced curricula in its Disney-run school system. Somewhat more prosaic but just as important, the Disney Company is deeply involved in developing educational software, courseware, and television programming aimed at the public elementary school classroom.[11] (Now that Disney has merged with Capital Cities/ABC to form the largest media company in the world, its educational and instructional future is so vast as to be unguessable.) Entertainment companies generally are making a concerted push into the classroom and other instructional sites, as older technical limits on media dissolve, prices fall and regulatory boundaries are shattered. Whittle Communication's Edison Project is an experiment in producing corporately run schools; the K-III Corporation's Channel One broadcasts advertiser-sponsored current events programming directly into high school classrooms. Whittle, K-III, the Walt Disney Company, and Anheuser-Busch are pushing the boundaries not only of education, but of corporate involvement in education.[12]

For Sea World, the process of expansion into education has its limits. The theme park remains first and foremost an attraction, no matter how heavily it rewrites its narratives in terms of learning and science. The park's managers and executives have no doubt that their first obligation is to supply the parent corporation with what they call "a fair rate of return" on investment. Therefore, educational programs and texts have been developed only to the degree that they do not interfere with the more profitable entertainment functions. Because the theme park is fundamentally mass entertainment, the education Sea World produces is closely tied to its spectacular entertainments and always harnessed to the goal of expanding profits. So it is nearly impossible to separate education from advertising and marketing, and indeed the education department's activities are almost always subordinated to those of other divisions. Looking at Sea World's myriad education materials and performances is like looking in a fun house mirror: the fundamental structure is visible but the outline shifts wildly. The spectacular core product—Sea World's particular version of nature—persists, rearranged.

To Sea World's upper management the assertion of a close relation between marketing and education would come as no surprise. In discussions with me, they freely admitted this conflation and did not find it problematic or contradictory. Attitudes ranged from a pragmatic "That's business!" to a more developed position that Sea World's activities are at once sound strategies for profit-making and altruistic. From this point of view, private corporations and industry have an important civic role to play in revitalizing and restructuring American education. As one former vice president put it, "No one else is going to do it!" Indeed this view is widely shared in business circles, whose leaders think themselves both entitled and in a strong position to direct "reform" of American education. Since everything and any part of American culture is commercially sponsored these days, why should the classroom be any different?[13] In the education department I found another pragmatic but less positive take on the problem. The education specialists—all, in my view, energetic, experienced, and committed teachers—sometimes see themselves as redeeming an overly commercial institution by offering the public something worthwhile in addition to entertainment. Education staff see themselves as serving the public by offering it a good that cannot be obtained elsewhere: they give access to nature to people who have little access, and they foster the appreciation of animals and wildlife. But in general, there seems to be agreement at Sea World that using educational programs to promote the entertainment product is common sense and good business strategy. At Sea World education is a multifaceted strategy *and* a commodity: it can help cultivate opinion and reproduce the audience, and there is also a chance that educational products and services may in the near future be major products in their own right.[14] Questions are rarely asked about the effects of the theme park's entry into the provision of education on the shape of public science education and the contemporary public sphere generally. Indeed, when I asked such questions of Sea World's managers and public school teachers, I usually met incomprehension. Such questions do need to be asked, however, and at the end of this chapter I will return to them.

Getting to know Sea World

Much of the success of Sea World's education programs rests on their variety. San Diego parents, children, and teachers hear about the theme park in more than one way, through television and print advertising and of course word of mouth, but also through the multiple channels of a whole range of community institutions and resources for children. As part of being an "educational resource" for the entire city, Sea World "visits" these institutions, takes part in their activities, and simultaneously encourages them to bring children to visit the park.

Imagine a hypothetical child in San Diego County. It is a helpful exercise to list all the ways she might come into contact with Sea World in addition to being taken there by her family. Of course, there is no hypothetical child in San Diego County or anywhere else. Children are part of widely differing neighborhoods and social networks: income, resource, and educational disparities between neighborhoods in the county are stark. Contact with Sea World's brand of education is sharply shaped by class and ethnicity in San Diego County, so our child should not be thought of as representing an "average" or homogenized population.[15]

Many parents and small children first encounter Sea World's education through one of the county's many private day care centers or preschools. Although the majority of these are small-scale, in-home day care providers, the growing number of large centers run by churches, social service organizations, and private corporations share a need for wholesome activities for their charges. Sea World reaches out to these children in several ways. In the outreach field trip, the Sea World van comes to the day care center and an education staff member gives a brief, simple presentation and leads the children in songs, activities, and games. In 1993, preschools could choose from the following subjects: whales; penguins; sharks; or seals, sea lions, and otters. The outreach advertisement describes the latter: "Super seals, sea lions, and wonderful walruses! Preschoolers get to know and love these fine flippered friends in this high-energy, action-packed program. Role-playing, songs and dress-ups help children learn." The outreach visit is preceded by handouts, coloring sheets, and other preparatory materials sent to the teachers; the children are told, "Sea World is coming this week." Usually parents will be assessed a few dollars toward the $175 fee which covers Sea World's costs for two forty-five-minute programs per visit. Large day care centers that stress a kind of preparation for school life and learning may be especially open to the outreach visit, since they are always in search of enriching materials and events. A long history of progressive educational thought and tradition emphasizes the appropriateness of teaching through animals and introducing life sciences and nature study to small children. (This is discussed in more detail in chapter 1.) The Sea World education department, with its coloring sheets, inflatable whales, and emphasis on knowing nature and loving the animals fits into this tradition, with its "please touch" tables piled with bones, pine cones, and rocks, the Dixie cups sprouting radish seeds, and the pet rabbits.

Sea World made only forty-five preschool outreach visits in 1993. Likely, cost pushes these visits out of the reach of most of the home day care businesses. But in-park visits and classes for young children, although they cost more per child than outreach visits, are popular with day care providers and preschools. The appeal of the park itself overrides the logistical and insurance problems of taking large numbers of small children on a trip. The education department's statistics for 1993 reveal that nearly seven thousand children took part in "Ocean Discovery for Early Learners," an "interactive program . . . developed for preschool groups of [ten or more] children ages two through six." Children and teachers "visit three learning centers [the tide pool, dolphin pool, and ray pool] in the park staffed by Education Instructors, where they view animals, role-play, sing songs and participate in other hands-on learning experiences."[16] A third way Sea World contacts preschool children is through special programs aimed at ages three to five and five to seven. "[D]esigned for interaction with [*sic*] one parent and one child," Preschool Parent Participation courses feature special lectures, tours, activities, and snacks. For example, at "Good Morning, Shamu" mother and child enter early before other customers, are served orange juice and muffins, and then watch the dolphins eat their own breakfast of frozen mackerel. This is followed by a brief, customized Shamu show and an activity: in one session, kids and moms made killer whale "hats" with crayon, glue, and paper plates. These "courses" are a kind of enrichment aimed at well-off parents who wish to spend a part of a weekday, perhaps a day off from work, with their small child, enjoying a semi-private outing at the theme park.[17]

Sea World's target market is not the preschoolers. The park's management speaks of children between eight and eleven being their most important young customers. Nevertheless, preschool programs do a great deal for Sea World. They familiarize young children with the park's name and, more important, with its celebrity animals and registered trademarks. (At my daughter's preschool, two-year-olds routinely identified a black-and-white plastic orca as a "Shamu.") Access to the young child helps attach the theme park to the family, here through the essential preschool and the deeply important caregivers.

Sea World's education department reaches school-age children most efficiently. Indeed, in work with a small sample of school-age children, I could not find a school-age child who hadn't been to Sea World and seen Shamu.[18] School-age children go to Sea World with their summer camps, YMCA programs, after-care centers, and Girl Scout and Boy Scout troops. They attend their parents' employers' picnics there and, of course, they are taken there with their teachers and classmates.

The third-through-sixth graders (eight through eleven years old) are important because their recreation remains supervised within the circle of the family. For this age group, vacation and leisure choices are still made by the parents. Sea World is accessible only by car and freeway, so children cannot go to Sea World without adults, but the eight-to-eleven-year-olds are autonomous enough to help contribute to the park's length of stay and to influence food and souvenir purchases. Older children tend to be drawn off to other kinds of theme parks, such as the Family Fun Centers franchised arcades. Once teens can drive they may splurge on trips to the metal ride parks like Magic Mountain. On a more regular basis, teenagers tend to choose cheaper commercial recreations, such as shopping malls and movies. Or they head for public parks or the beach, which appeal because they are free and nearly unsupervised. For Sea World, the later-elementary-school-child audience is an efficient conduit for reaching the whole family in the years when they are most likely to come to the park.

Until recently, the field trip has been the most common way a school child would encounter the theme park. With the stated goal of "introducing" students "to the marine environment and the animals that live there," the instructional field trip is a staple of the education department's offerings, a core product commanding a great deal of staff time and energy.[19] In 1993, instructional field trip attendance was 115,265, up nearly 25,000 (or roughly 27 percent) from 90,352 in the previous year.[20] In gross numbers, however, instructional field trip attendance was still lower than among elementary and secondary students addressed by outreach programs. This is because the traveling programs reach entire schools via special assemblies, whereas field trips are organized by classrooms.[21]

The field trip is the more momentous, thorough, and expensive introduction to the park. Most school visits to Sea World take place in the late spring (March, April, May, and June), and this reflects practical constraints and the way teachers use the park. It takes time to plan and raise money for field trips, so they most often happen in the second half of the school year. And teachers often use a field trip as a reward for students to work up to, or as a time for students to get out of the classroom and blow off steam at the end of the year.

As in all of California, field trips are a luxury for the financially strapped schools of San Diego County. Field trips are discretionary, and teachers may choose from many competing sites, some of them free. San Diego Unified and other districts pay for only one field trip per classroom per year, so city school children have at most two field trips if their teachers find a way for two classes to double up and share a bus. The great expense, according to teachers, is the bus rental. For this and Sea World's admission fee of $3.90 per child, teachers must scrimp and save and either make appeals to parents or mount Parent-Teacher Association (PTA) fund-raisers. In districts with rich PTAs, this is no problem, but much more commonly it requires great effort. Several teachers told me that they paid for some of their students out of their own pocket—they felt it was important that no student be left out of the trip. Taking all this into consideration, Sea World's field trip attendance figures are astonishing. More than 115,000 kindergarten- through college-age students participated in 1993, or more than one-fifth the enrollment in public schools countywide.[22] Of course, many private schools send children to Sea World, too, but even if only half of Sea World's instructional field trip attendance was drawn from public schools, still the equivalent of roughly one in nine San Diego County public school students went to Sea World in 1993. Attendance figures and the sacrifices made to produce field trips testify to how important a visit to Sea World was to many teachers and many schools. It was so important that it called for saving and planning and it overrode many other, less expensive possibilities.[23]

The instructional field trips reveal a distinct ethnic patterning. Visiting along with school groups, it's impossible to be unaware of race. Quite unlike the rest of the theme park audience on any given day, the school groups are heavily black and brown, African American, Asian American, and Mexican American. This is remarked on by the Sea World education staff. Education Director Joy Wolf argued that although "we are here for everybody," "the people who use our [field trip and outreach] programs," are "in fact the people we are trying to target, . . . primarily the minority schools."

She went on to say, "We don't get a whole lot of rich schools coming for education programs here. . . . We do get a certain amount; the private schools seem to use a lot of enrichment programs; you get a lot of private Christian schools that come on trips that are usually parent funded. . . . But wealthy public schools are not our predominant users. A few of them will come for our gifted programs and some special things like that, but sometimes the attitude is, since they are not going to get something different than what the rest of the people get [it's not worth their while]. . . . Sometimes I think we turn them off a little bit because . . . we don't do special tours for first graders."[24]

Wolf was piqued by the elitism that can go along with the staggering differences in school district resources.[25] Whether teachers at wealthy, white public schools view Sea World field trips as not special enough for their special children is unclear, but one suburban science teacher told me that her district had a policy, since rescinded, of not spending excursion money on trips to places that children were likely to visit with their families.

Indeed, waiting outside the "ed gate," the special entrance through which student groups are routed, I noted that Sea World's customers are distinguished by race and class in an indirect but definite way. The largely white, tourist audience enters through one set of turnstiles and pays more to get in; the mainly nonwhite, subsidized education audience enters through a special gate set off to the side that, when I was conducting fieldwork, seemed almost like a back door. As elsewhere in the United States, in San Diego County the categories "poor" and "working-class" don't translate directly into "minority": there are poor white people aplenty. But, as markedly as anywhere, class, race, and ethnicity are expressed spatially, not least in school districts. The city and county's poorest school districts tend to be heavily populated with minority students, and when these children come to Sea World they are likely to come through the education gate. In the city's affluent northern and coastal districts, it can be assumed that parents can pay to take their children to the zoo, Museum of Natural History, and expensive theme parks. At schools in the southern and inland parts of the city and county, no such assumption can be made. Indeed, in the San Diego city schools, it is usually only so-called magnet schools with corporate participation that have a science lab or nature room, for example. Due to California's stringent budgets, provision of this "enrichment," like art, music, libraries, and school nurses, has been assigned either to the local PTA or the private sector. Many teachers see Sea World as a special site of nature and science and struggle heroically to bring all their children to it, as they fight to give them other essentials of learning.

Education programs, especially instructional field trips and outreach programs, have a large part to play in widening Sea World's nature audience across race and class boundaries, beyond the core, white audience described in chapter 1. The discounted school fee helps bring minority children to Sea World, and this minority attendance at a park that sees its core audience as so white, wealthy, and educated speaks of Sea World's success. The theme park has succeeded in constructing itself as culturally important and even essential for parents and teachers whose young charges are defined with horrible moral weight as underprivileged, in need of compensatory contact with nature, animals, and science. Yet this widening of the park's customers takes place in a framework of fundamental inequality. If the hypothetical child we have been following is poor or a member of a so-called minority group, he or she is very unlikely to attend Sea World as a local tourist, and so is predefined as having a nature deficit. While children from wealthy families attend the theme park as a part of more-or-less ordinary family recreation, when Sea World offers poor and minority children its version of nature, it is clearly labeled as compensation—as a gift to make up for what they don't have.[26]

Class difference is reflected in the way Sea World structures and markets its education programs. For example, recently Sea World has begun offering "Camp Sea World," a series of weeklong half-day programs for school children. The camp reflects the fact that all arrangements for child care outside of school hours must be made and paid for privately by parents, whether wealthy or poor. There is an enormous market for such camps in San Diego, especially when they are themed nature or science, and a large number of private providers fill this niche.[27] The education department cheerfully notes this desperate need for summer child care in its year-end report: "Camp Sea World courses were filled to 93% capacity. This seemed remarkable considering the number of parents who reported job layoffs, forced relocations, and other economic downturns. Parents seemed determined to give their children a week of sun and educational fun at Sea World in spite of their diminishing checkbook balances."[28] But since Camp Sea World is promoted through the 12-Month Pass mailing lists, giveaway newspapers or "shoppers," and parent magazines, it likely appeals most to the affluent families who use the theme park as a private public space.[29] The annual report discusses Camp Sea World in terms very similar to those used to advocate traditional summer camps in the country—as a way to place city children in contact with nature and animals, as an opportunity for healthy development. Although Camp Sea World has the same overt content as the instructional field trips, it has a different meaning and occupies a different social space, serving Sea World by creating another reason for the prime market to visit the park. Camp Sea World adds to the revenue stream while it reinforces the educational image.

Beyond the elementary school–age group, Sea World education programs range across grades and instructional needs, offering programs through the high school curriculum, although in-park sessions for the youngest students are the most numerous. Up to the ninth grade level, teachers may choose instructional programs themed "Behavior and Training" or "Ecology and Conservation"; from high school through college, a "Husbandry and Training" format is offered.[30] The education department also accommodates visits by GATE ("gifted and talented education") classes and produces "In-Depth" instruction for groups with a special interest or subject focus. "In-Depth" and "Gifted and Talented" offerings together accounted for more than 7,100 student visits in 1993. "In-Depth" is a further example of the ways Sea World produces education across class boundaries: only well-funded schools with special classes could plan a series of "In-Depth" sessions elaborating on a special interest, with the group leader determining "the number of visits, visit length and topics."[31] The customized elements of "In-Depth" contrast sharply with the rushed, standardized quality of the field trip experienced by, for example, Ms. MacColl's class.

Perhaps the central way Sea World connects with the hypothetical child is through the teacher. Every fall, a free Teacher Open House at the theme park promotes all levels of the education programs to public and private school teachers. In 1993, nearly eight hundred teachers attended. At the Open House, teachers meet education department personnel and preview exhibits, displays, animal performances, and programs. They can look over Sea World's curriculum materials and purchase everything from posters to videotapes.[32] Events like this and special mailings help keep the idea of a field trip to Sea World in front of the teachers. And in collaboration with local university extensions, Sea World offers the credentialing course units public school teachers need to stay certified.[33] Taking advantage of these classes helps teachers keep their classroom materials and activities varied and up-to-date.[34] The main part of Sea World's teacher market has been elementary school teachers, who are under pressure from administrators to inject more science into the classroom and across the curriculum. Elementary teachers tend to have less science training than the more specialized high school teachers, and teachers in poor districts may have less opportunity to update their skills. According to Joy Wolf, Sea World understood this need and went about filling it. "We went after that niche. We knew that they were weak in science education, and so we made it fun and accessible for them."

> The elementary teacher is the one that usually has not taken very much science, and they are weaker in their science concepts, and they're uncomfortable with teaching science because they think of it as being scary, with people in lab coats. We take the marine science aspect, . . . and we've broken it down to several different courses. One's "Take a Bite Out of Teaching Science," which is the sharks course: they learn about sharks and fishes and . . . they can come away with some background knowledge and then specific lessons that they can integrate into their classroom. We do one that's "Hatch a Batch of Classroom Fun," which is on penguins and sea turtles, both egg layers, to give them some variety. We do one that's "Science and the Sea," and we have another one that has a focus where they learn about whales.[35]

The California Science Framework has called on teachers to leave behind textbook lessons, to implement "hands-on" and "interactive" strategies, and to work on teaching science across the curriculum. Sea World's brochures for teachers mention the framework and ask teachers if they need help adapting to its new demands.[36]

Through service to teachers, in schools public and private, day care centers, youth service organizations, summer camps, special school programs such as GATE, and its own private offerings in the educational marketplace, Sea World creates myriad ways to reach out to children and, through them, to its San Diego market.[37] Pushing beyond the elementary classroom, Sea World produces special courses for the adult general public on topics of interest, such as whale seminars and whale-watching trips. In-park courses for college students (often organized through outing clubs, fraternities and sororities, and residence halls) and for retired adults (organized through senior citizens centers, churches, and clubs) contribute another portion of Sea World's educational business. Most of these educational forms help construct Sea World as a part of San Diego's families and communities. Indeed, the education department's programs have been very successful in defining the theme park as a part of San Diego and creating a high degree of trust and positive feeling in city and county teachers.[38]

Sea World's channels of contact with the hypothetical child are simultaneous and overlapping. The same girl who colors a Shamu paper at preschool may well see the velour Shamu walk-around at her day care center's fund-raising carnival. She may visit Sea World's Earth Day display at the local shopping mall. If she watches the television news at supper time, she will inevitably hear about the rescue and rehabilitation of an otter, dolphin, sea lion, or pelican. Later she may see an advertisement for the park's network special. She may help her mother shop for Shamu-themed multiple vitamins, or go with her father to borrow a Sea World videotape from the local public library. In San Diego, she will certainly be surrounded by children who are familiar with the same images and products. The theme park images she encounters at her preschool will fit tidily into an already familiar battery of characters and ideas; her much anticipated visit to Sea World on a field trip—even if it is her first—will be a visit to a novel but already well known place. It is a place she will be encountering again and again in the course of her childhood and schooling. It is hard to overemphasize the marketing potential of Sea World's educational work.

Sea World is Coming to Your Classroom!

While the theme park's conventional educational activities are taking place in the physical park and city, Sea World is expanding its educational reach electronically. Broadcast by satellite and cable, *Shamu TV* premiered in 1992 and instantly outperformed all the education department's other efforts. *Shamu TV*'s trial broadcasts reached several million students in classrooms around the United States that spring; by fall 1994, the monthly program had an in-school audience of at least 13 million registered viewers and uncounted millions more who would see videotaped rebroadcasts of its programs.

Like the education department itself and many of its activities, *Shamu TV* was proposed by the marketing department. Marketing and public relations use state-of-the-art video and satellite equipment and a staff of skilled technicians for their own purposes.[39] Video and satellite capability supports television specials, news spots, video press releases, and "B-roll" or cutaway video footage, making images and expert commentary instantaneously available to networks via satellite uplink. In the early 1990s, the education department was helping marketing publicize the park in such distant but important vacation markets as Idaho, Montana, Colorado, and Wyoming, as well as nearby Arizona. Sea World education staff traveled to major cities and spent several days or a week presenting outreach education programs at schools. It was a short step for the marketing department from investing in satellite equipment to realizing that, with the "wiring" of city and suburban school systems all over the country, "outreach" could soon be delivered electronically over long or short distances, with efficiency and consistency. Instead of reaching two to four thousand children during a week spent in one city, Sea World could simultaneously reach tens of thousands of children in each of many cities, and millions nationally and internationally. *Shamu TV* quickly drew the attention and involvement of Anheuser-Busch, which saw the broadcasts and the expansion of education as a good fit with the corporation's environmental public relations efforts. Via pre-taped segments and satellite links, the project could also enlist curators and animals from the other Anheuser-Busch parks, especially Sea World of Florida and Busch Gardens in Tampa. *Shamu TV* was efficient: in its wide geographic reach, in its ability to pull together the specialized resources of different parts of the entertainment corporation, and in its colorful publicity for the entire chain and its parts.

As the description earlier in this chapter suggests, *Shamu TV* is vibrant and visual, and it shows the park at its colorful best. The forty-minute program is a mix of "live feed," prerecorded materials filmed in San Diego and at other parks, computer graphics, jazzy music, child actors, and experts. Half the yearly broadcasts are sent up from the San Diego park, half originate in Orlando. Downlinked by PBS and scores of local instructional cable channels, *Shamu TV* is, according to a Sea World education department report, seen "in all fifty states plus Canada, New Zealand, Puerto Rico and many other major sites." Sea World Education claims that 20 percent of the nation's PBS stations receive and transmit the program, and that the Classroom Channel and Learning Channel, two quickly growing commercial cable services delivering educational programming to schools and homes nationwide, carry it to more than 6 million viewers. In October 1993, TCI (TeleCommunication, Inc., the world's largest cable company) added *Shamu TV* to the schedules of thirty-four of its stations and promoted Sea World's print materials over its X-Press electronic mail system for teachers and station programmers. During the same fall, when the New York City schools were still closed due to an asbestos removal crisis, Sea World filled the instructional breach, providing the city schools with master tapes of *Shamu TV;* these were broadcast over ITV and viewed by the students at home. In the space of a year and a half, Sea World had entered the overlapping fields of instructional television, distance learning, and cable broadcasting to become a serious provider of educational materials.[40] The convergence of satellites, cable, and school systems affords Sea World unprecedented geographic and demographic reach.

Shamu TV is not broadcast over networks in prime time but rather occupies the vast and uncharted world of cable television stations carrying instructional programming into schools and homes. Sea World therefore has no access to ratings services or market share information. The education department must estimate *Shamu TV*'s audience based on the responses of schools to their solicitations and mailings on one hand, and by estimates of potential viewership on the other. But there are ways around this problem, and the education department's attempts at tracking *Shamu TV*'s audience are interesting for what they reveal about the links between the theme park's education programs and new communication technologies. Before the first test broadcast, the Sea World education and public relations departments did a mailing to schools across several states to gauge interest in *Shamu TV*. Free instructional materials, teacher's guides, and instructions on how to tune in were sent to every teacher who registered their class by returning a postcard. This simple technique allowed one measure of viewership; requests for the teachers' handbooks were another. A few years later, Sea World had added an 800 number telephone line for live call-ins, making the show "interactive"; the call-ins help track where the show is being seen.[41] Sea World also advertises *Shamu TV* and tracks the responses and questions of viewers via a home page on the World Wide Web. Computers linked to the Internet not only help Sea World reach its audience in new ways, but allow it to gauge and measure that audience.

Anheuser-Busch hopes that the large audience for *Shamu TV* will be multiplied by rebroadcasts and off-air tapings, and it does not restrict or charge for these.[42] Since the company must search out every opportunity for profit, the free rebroadcasts have to be seen as a promotional strategy, not an openhanded gift to the public.[43] Indeed, from the corporate perspective, the immediate object of *Shamu TV* is not to sell programming or even to encourage the growing sales of educational materials and copies of tapes, although it is possible that Sea World could decide later to charge fees for broadcasts and rebroadcasts. For the present, *Shamu TV* is most important as a way to conjure the Sea World name as often and widely as possible. *Shamu TV* repeatedly mentions the theme park and defines it as educational.

Although *Shamu TV* is clearly promotional, Sea World's managers resist admitting this, at least to an outsider. So, they argue *Shamu TV* is not promotional because it is produced by trained educators, as if these two facts were mutually exclusive. For example, Director of Education Joy Wolf argued strongly that *Shamu TV* is not marketing and should not be.[44] She discussed the "Small Wonders" broadcast: "We're doing it so that it's educational. . . . We control the content, along with the curatorial staff, so it's going to be a pure education piece. It's entertaining because it is always fun. How can you not be fun, with the animals? But there will be nothing in it that is marketing, other than that it is coming from Sea World. We control the curriculum, so that teachers have a legitimate packet in there. It doesn't say, you know, come and play at Sea World. . . . I mean, Sea World's logo is on it, and that is the subtle marketing. But still it's purely educational, and it's giving back to the community."[45]

Indeed, Sea World's managers are aware that promotional strategies can backfire. Although the Sea World logo is on the video tape, Anheuser-Busch's is not, precisely because the parent corporation is very sensitive to the marketing and public relations potential of the broadcasts. Said one executive, "They are careful never to put the A-B name on" the TV program because "they do not want to be seen as marketing beer to children" via the schools.[46]

Although the "Small Wonders" science content was controlled by the education department, the whole program is developed jointly with public relations and marketing. Indeed, the first *Shamu TV* broadcast was aimed at an important target market. Sea World's management is very clear in their understanding that marketing, product positioning, advertising, and the production of educational materials are closely connected activities, with the same root goal—to bring the theme park before its audience and keep it there. In fact, *Shamu TV* contains segments that border on being commercials for the Anheuser-Busch parks; and management, while denying that the shows are a sales pitch, hopes that when families make decisions about where to go for vacation, they will think of Sea World. "Of course we hope that," said one vice president.[47]

By 1994, Sea World was advertising *Shamu TV* widely via mailing lists, open houses, e-mail networks, the World Wide Web, publications for distance learning specialists, and elementary school teachers generally. As the education department's report put it, "Our three most effective ways of promoting *Shamu TV* have been [magazine] covers, photos, and listings in various television, distance learning and educational publications. . . . *Shamu TV* has also been featured in national and local program guides through photos, logo use and articles. . . ." Company backing allows brochures to be "mailed to various mailing lists and given out at conferences," and it pays for full-page ads in magazines for educators and live uplinks to conferences of science educators and teleconferencing specialists. Sea World education staffers personally represent *Shamu TV* at the many educational conferences they attend yearly. In spring 1995, all the effort had paid off. *Shamu TV* won a Regional Emmy award for educational programming, and Sea World collected an educational award from the American Zoo Association for its 1–800-SHAMU telephone line and Internet connection.

Tuning in Shamu

Tuning in to *Shamu TV* may have many advantages for teachers. Offering a different program each month, *Shamu TV* provides a lot of flexibility: Teachers can either integrate the programs into nature study or, relying on Sea World's curricular materials, build nature and science units around it. They may choose one program that fits their semester, tape off the air to fit it into their schedule as needed, or show all the broadcasts for a marine-themed year of science. Perhaps most important is the fact that, for now, *Shamu TV* is free, as are the classroom materials Sea World sends with registration. These packets are jammed with bibliographies, colorful posters, worksheets that can be photocopied, and ideas for activities. At a time when California teachers often pay for students' paper and pencils out of their own pockets and textbooks are difficult to come by, free and affordable mean essentially the same thing. *Shamu TV* is an exciting product at the right price.[48]

The broadcasts are fast moving and lively. Musically and visually, *Shamu TV* is styled like the Nickelodeon Channel or an MTV magazine, with fragments of hip-hop in the sound track, ethnically diverse high school–age reporters who introduce segments, and colorful computer graphics. Its style is light-years away from the old-fashioned nature education slide tape or even expensively produced but staid television programs like *Nature.* And the 800 number allows Sea World to tout *Shamu TV* as interactive. Although millions of children in hundreds of thousands of classrooms are at any given moment watching a program that is largely prerecorded, the live line does connect them to the theme park throughout the broadcast, and much is made of this. Hosts repeat the important message that children have an opportunity to call in questions and see and hear answers from experts who are always ready with the accurate information. It does *seem* more interactive than most videotape, even if Sea World staffers do occasionally call in their own questions.[49]

From Anheuser-Busch's point of view, all the education programs, but especially *Shamu TV,* are a bargain. As the marketers put it, "Television shows the park" in ways print and billboards cannot. The programs are relatively inexpensive, since the technology for producing them is already owned by the park and in use for public relations communications. Up until recently the expertise to produce *Shamu TV* has simply been pulled from across organizational lines, with producers from public relations, for example, and writers from the entertainment department helping out.[50] As *Shamu TV* proved itself, Anheuser-Busch let the education department hire more technical production people, and thus reduced push and pull between departments over the allocation of staff. Finally, most of the performers are already owned or employed by Anheuser-Busch. In this sense, *Shamu TV* makes effective use of already-paid-for talent and resources. The wiring of the school districts by cable companies and ITV represents another bargain, because the vast infrastructure necessary to deliver *Shamu TV* is being installed and paid for by other corporations.[51]

Shamu TV is obviously already very successful in reaching large numbers of teachers and school children, and at the same time is creating interest in and positive feeling toward the theme park among a key part of its audience. Traveling to children and parents via the school and teacher, and carrying their imprimatur, *Shamu TV* wears the cloak of authority. It is too early to tell what *Shamu TV* will become. Could Sea World translate it into Saturday morning programming with an educational twist, supported by advertisers and networks? Children's nature and science television is currently in demand with programmers and advertisers, which reflects the revitalized concern that commercial media for children be educational and stand out as valuable and worthwhile. In this vein, SONY produced *Beakman's World* for CBS and the Walt Disney Company has recently fielded *Bill Nye, the Science Guy.* Sea World's corporate directors might plan a series similar to *Those Amazing Animals,* for example, which was filmed at Marine World Africa USA and ran on the Discovery Channel. Indeed, in spring 1996, the ABC network featured *Second Noah,* a series about a zookeeper and his family, set in the Busch Gardens theme park at Tampa.

While there might be room for *Shamu TV* to move into commercial broadcasting, for now Sea World and Anheuser-Busch seem better set up to exploit the wide-open and underdeveloped educational market. Fiber-optic cables are being wired into the schools in San Diego as elsewhere, supported by massive private gifts from companies such as Pacific Telesis and Apple. In fall 1995, the San Diego city schools received a $5 million challenge grant from the United States Department of Education for Project Triton, a multiyear project that hopes to strengthen science education by using the Internet and "virtual reality" as teaching tools. Using the seed money from the Department of Education, along with large gifts of hardware, software, and technical support from corporate partners, the project's planners aim to bring interactive video, worldwide database and computer connections, and virtual reality capability to all the district's schools. Project Triton is themed "marine science," and Sea World will be a major provider of content and curricular materials. The theme park's long history of involvement with education in San Diego, and the more recent success of *Shamu TV,* have positioned Sea World to take advantage of the explosion of interest in getting new technology into the schools. This high-tech surge is being offered as a solution to public education's slumping finances but it also bids to dramatically transform the schools by providing media and entertainment corporations electronic entry to the schoolroom.[52]

Education and Spectacle

It is too early to evaluate Project Triton, but what can be said about *Shamu TV*'s content and Sea World's education programs generally? I have criticized Sea World's education programs as being first and foremost marketing and public relations tools. In reaction to the debut of Channel One, it has been widely argued that the classroom is one place marketers and advertisers should stay out of. After all, producing future consumers is not the same thing as producing curious and knowledgeable citizens.[53] I agree wholeheartedly with these positions. But many San Diego teachers and parents do not. During interviews and public lectures, some teachers have commented, "If it is hard to tell Sea World's education from Sea World's marketing, advertising, and public relations—so what? In the current educational crisis, shouldn't we see Sea World as providing something valuable—a kind of nature education that hard-pressed and impoverished school districts otherwise can't dream of? Aren't corporately donated educational materials better than no educational materials at all?"[54] In other words, does Sea World education's use as a marketing tool automatically invalidate it as science or nature education?

Let us suppose that by itself the marketing motive ought not to disqualify Sea World from providing something useful to students. Since the theme park argues that it represents the state of the art in marine and conservation education, let us look a bit more closely at the marketing-education blend, at the ingredients that go into the materials Sea World sends to the classroom.[55] What is the state of this art that Sea World is so actively defining? What are teachers getting when they sign up for *Shamu TV*?

The history of *Shamu TV*'s first broadcast, "Small Wonders," gives a sense of the content that emerges from the interpenetration of marketing, theme park, and education. "Small Wonders" was originally the theme of an exhibit thought up by the marketing department and installed as a multistationed exhibit in 1991. A self-guided tour led children to all the areas where propagation projects, including baby otters, hatchling flamingos and penguins, and Baby Shamu, the baby killer whale, were on display. At each display, children were supposed to rubber stamp a block on a special brochure indicating that they had read the "Small Wonders" exhibit label. A completed collection of stamps could be handed in for a set of trading cards featuring the park's offspring.

Marketing expanded this popular exhibit about babies into a broadcast aimed at young children. Although the initial "Small Wonders" broadcast tape was bumpy and uneven, it was also typical of the subsequent *Shamu TV* programs. It drew on an established display, emphasized a special animal associated with Sea World (in this case, the delicate babies that Sea World "mothers"), and linked school children's learning to Sea World's research rationale. The TV version of "Small Wonders" contains segments on "Sea World family albums," which showcase the various babies, footage on the care of baby penguins and the birth of baby killer whales, and a spot on a prematurely born giraffe. There is a visit with beluga whales at the Texas Sea World park and a discussion of environmental threats to marine animals. Shots of animals being lovingly cared for by trainers alternate with footage of cuddly antics. As in each of the *Shamu TV* broadcasts, there are shots of the Sea World parks, a small lecture on taking care of the environment (put trash in its proper place and don't throw household chemicals down the sink or storm drain), and spots of children meeting whales or dolphins. In "Small Wonders," as in all the shows, school classrooms are shown and minority children are present to ask questions.[56]

At the most basic level, *Shamu TV* hews closely to the physical park and offers teachers its core attractions: its perfected ways of seeing nature, and its charismatic performing animals. The parks themselves are the raw ingredients that can be worked into curricular publications and

TV segments. Writers and producers build around the extant displays, the landscaping, and the company's expertise with animals. After "Small Wonders," *Shamu TV*'s producers offered "Dolphin Research," "Killer Whale Research," "Manatees: Preserving the Legacy," "All About Endangered Animals," and other titles built around Anheuser-Busch's collections and shows.

Other educational materials keep the celebrity animals central. For example, most of Sea World's "Teacher's Guides" have a section called "Sea World Stars," a series of pages the teacher can cut out, photocopy, and give the class to work with. Each features one of Sea World's performer species, with its common English and Latin names. In the *Animal Behavior and Training* booklet, the behavior of the "star" is also briefly described: for example, "Top predator in the ocean, killer whales often hunt cooperatively in pods. Killer whales may slide out on sand bars or ice floes to pursue prey." Although the whales' hunting and slide-out behavior have been observed in the wild, as we shall see in chapter 6 they are also celebrated in the Shamu show, and students are encouraged to match features of the whale they have seen in the park to the description in the booklet. The theme park show illustrates the worksheet and the worksheet refers back to the theme park. The centrality of animal celebrities to the education product means that children's interest in and need to know about killer whales or dolphins or baby animals is prefabricated and follows from Sea World's construction of the animals as "stars"—exactly like the humans who populate the rest of TV. They are beautiful, powerful, lucky, and worth seeing.

With this model of using celebrities to transmit facts, *Shamu TV* and Sea World education in general construct the learners as recipients of authentic and expert information. *Shamu TV* tends to define what children need to know about whales, for example, as a set of facts closely focused on the famous individual species: what does it eat, how fast does it swim, how big does it get, how are we taking care of it? Education is defined as what kids need to know, rather than as a process of observation and questioning. The outreach field trips, for example, with their fun inflatable whales and touchable bones finally deliver lively lectures on subjects like "what is a mammal?" but they don't offer much mystery or unfolding challenge.

Beneath this definition of children as recipients and education as fact delivery is a general philosophy of presentation. In all their productions, Sea World education staff follow what might be called a wildlife interpretation strategy. The general approach is, "These are the animals: how wonderful they are." This introduction is followed by a "Did you know . . . ?" approach offering facts about discrete animals. Here, in fact, it is possible to evoke wonder at the animals themselves, in the long tradition of wildlife education for children, with its rationale that children need exposure to nature and animals. Sea World has inserted itself into this tradition, making animals available for caring, and teaching people to care about them. As a quote often found on the theme park's grounds and in its print material has it: "'In the end, we will conserve only what we love. We will love only what we understand. We will understand only what we are taught. . . .' Baba Dioum."[57]

Caring feelings are especially important among children, the basis for helping them grow into conscientious adults with conservationist tendencies. Says Wolf, "We want people to preserve the environment for themselves and animals; that's an important message. It's the value of all life, man as well as animal." But in the Sea World version, this argument slides directly into a statement about managing the environment. The goal of increased caring is benign management. Wolf explains the perspective: "If we're going to all live on this planet, if we're the ones making decisions about the planet, then we have to think about the plant and animal life that surrounds us and to know as much as we can about it. If you don't understand the environment, the relationships, if you don't understand how all of this works, and know the requirements of systems in the ocean and on land, then you can't make a good decision about it. . . . Jim Antrim, our general curator, always talks about man being the top animal, about us as being judicious caretakers."[58]

The audience's good feelings about animals, then, support judicious stewardship and ratify the dominant managerial role of humanity. But Sea World's explicit educational philosophy doesn't extend much beyond fact delivery and cultivation of feeling, since very little time or energy are spent actually explaining complex ecosystemic relations (or even what an ecosystem is), or exploring relations between humans and the nonhuman living world outside the theme park.

Human relations to the biological world are reduced to individual relations. *Shamu TV* often features a brief segment about what happens when trash gets in the wrong places: individual animals suffer horribly and die as, for example, when sea lions poke their heads through plastic six-pack rings and strangle. The concept "What we need to do to protect animals" involves individuals putting trash and waste in the right places, a tidy-up slogan that can offend no one except messy children. This is the generic "Don't Pollute" injunction familiar throughout schools, but it tells children nothing about the real problems of pollution, the reasons for the massive waste stream American industry generates, or the relationships between the production of plastics, solid wastes, and toxics, for example. "Don't Pollute" identifies individuals as the sources of environmental pollution and argues that the answers to pollution involve better individual manners. Combined with materials that would raise questions about environmental crises and challenge children to raise their own questions about the social causes of pollution, "Don't Pollute" messages might be harmless. But by themselves, they do damage by giving a flat and distorted picture of the world as divided into ill- and well-intentioned individual people.[59] Real environmental problems go deeper than feelings and stewardship: they involve conflicts of interest over the gross exploitation of the earth and its resources. Staying within a very limited conservation discourse, Sea World helps obscure these real problems.

Sea World places a lot of emphasis in its education programs on one very particular process of learning, operant conditioning. This model of learning as training to respond fits oddly but appropriately with the model of education as fact storage. On one hand, this is another way Sea World can build on its theme park core. According to Joy Wolf, there is tremendous student interest in how the spectacular animals are made to do what they do, in the techniques by which they are shaped into performers, and so the education department emphasizes animal behavior and animal training in a core education program for high school and college-age students. In this sense, the department's programs are a kind of backstage for the trained animal shows. According to Wolf,

> They wanted to know what kind of husbandry things we do. [The students] come in and they sit in the stadium when the trainers come out and go through the different husbandry procedures [with the whales, such as taking blood samples and giving physical examinations]. They [tell] why this is important to do, and what we learn, and what we do with this information. . . . The training aspect is connected to it, because no matter what we teach on husbandry, the evaluation will come back and say, "But how do you train the animals?" They say, "It was wonderful but we still don't understand. We wanted to know how you train the animals." This is because we're Sea World and we train animals, we're famous for our wonderful behaviors with the animals. So we've connected those two very popular things for the high school and college students. . . . They explain that if the animal wasn't trained, you couldn't do these examinations.[60]

There's a close relationship between how students are treated and taught in schools, what they are learning, and how Sea World shows them animals learning. Wolf pointed out that high school and college students are usually being taught behaviorist theories of psychology and learning in their home classrooms, so teachers may use a Sea World show or visit to illustrate Skinnerian theory.[61] Indeed, the subject of animal training and Sea World's behaviorist methods comes up again and again, in *Shamu TV* ("Animal Behavior and Training"), in "ed shows" for younger children at the park, as we have seen, and in curricular materials such as the teacher's guides. That a place of learning places so much emphasis on training suggests that at Sea World training and learning are identical —and perhaps for the human students as well as the animals. Oddly, or sadly, elementary schools are currently full of behaviorist methods applied to teaching and discipline: rewards and prizes for good results, the "time-outs" for bad behavior that young Adela found familiar. Perhaps, Sea World is saying to its student visitors, you and the animals are not treated so differently: you have the same motivations, receive similar rewards, exist in similar structures of reinforcement.

The "interactive" part of *Shamu TV,* when students call in questions to the 800 number, suggests slippage in the view of the child as a moldable recipient of information. On one hand the interactive segments, like the touchable animals at the tide pool, help create the tenuous impression that the theme park turns children into discoverers by asking them to formulate questions. On the other hand, the format of questions fielded by knowledgeable experts, like the video interviews with experts on breeding and baby care, serve to reproduce the theme park as a dispenser of sound information. And whether because calls are screened, as they are, or simply because *Shamu TV*'s format encourages it, many questions are quantitative. Questions called in to the "Small Wonders" broadcast included, for example, "How long does it take for a killer whale baby to be born?" "How long is a baby killer whale's tooth?" and "How long does a baby penguin take to reach full size and weight?" As we shall see in chapter 6, this sort of question-and-answer format is part of the park's key performance, the Shamu show. But some viewers' questions were more exploratory, such as: "Do whales swim right away?" "How much help do the scientists provide during the birth of baby animals?" and "How did you get interested in studying baby mammals?" And at times it seemed as if the richness of controversy surrounding whales in particular and natural history in general kept seeping in through the phone lines. One child asked, "What are the ancestors of whales?" during the "Killer Whale Research" broadcast, potentially raising a sore subject in school districts where the teaching of evolution is under attack. "Do killer whales ever die in captivity?" also raised a touchy issue, and was answered disingenuously by an on-camera spokesman: "They die in captivity, yes, just like they die in the wild. Their life expectancy is twenty-five to thirty-five years, we think." In fact the question of life span is an area of great conflict between Sea World and its critics, including other scientific researchers.[62] But in general, just as *Shamu TV* and Sea World do not present any materials that focus on evolution, neither do they raise scientific controversy or reveal that any of the information they offer might be contested.

Indeed, research in *Shamu TV,* as in the rest of the park, always underlines Sea World's arguments for its own necessity. For example, the script of "Killer Whale Research" argues that "distant observation" of wildlife is "not enough." "Marine parks and oceanariums like Sea World" give researchers opportunities to "get up close" and to understand how wild animals reproduce and "what makes breeding successful." Extending this argument, if theme parks are prevented from keeping and studying killer whales the world of scientific knowledge will be the poorer. "Small Wonders," "Killer Whale Research," and the other broadcasts make it clear that the world needs these theme park places in order that knowledge might progress.

And research always remains safe. The difficult and the unknown are suppressed in the picture Sea World gives of "researchers" as people who are anxious to "find out more." There are occasional mentions of the unanswerable questions, but no discussion of the fascinating gaps in human knowledge about the life histories of whales and dolphins, the vast variety of and uncertainty about their social patterns, and even about their species identities. In fact, a sense of the incompleteness of scientists' knowledge about whales and dolphins is available from any thoughtful naturalist's writings or handbook.[63] As in the theme park, there are no breaks in the authority of scientific research and no disputes about the directions of research. And research never turns up true horrors: at best, it can only suggest possible problems. For example, in the beluga whale segment of "Small Wonders," Sea World of Texas's education director states that scientists think that chemical pollution in the St. Lawrence Seaway might be hurting the whales. In fact, as is widely known, there is no doubt that these whales suffer from industrially produced toxins. Their bodies are so thoroughly poisoned by heavy metals that when dead whales are recovered they must be disposed of as hazardous waste.[64]

In general, environmental conflicts, the complexity of science, and the vexed politics of research cannot be built into *Shamu TV:* they only seep in because they cannot entirely be filtered out. Which questions children should be asking about the natural world, and which issues they should be exploring—these are free from such vexations because they have already been decided. Education's content is shaped by the park's charismatic marine mammals, its definition of them as celebrities, and the problems of training and keeping them in captivity.

Using familiar animal celebrities to carry "clean up" messages, displaying its successes in captive reproduction, and teaching behaviorism against a colorful backdrop, Sea World builds its educational programs and materials out of the theme park material at hand. To a great degree, Sea World's education focuses on breeding animals in captivity and training them for performance, the things that Sea World does best. The overriding result of the education and marketing synthesis is the dissemination of the park's central images, the killer whale and dolphin, and their recontextualization in the classroom as nature facts to love and learn. In effect, Sea World's education department reproduces the theme park inside the school.

If we step outside the logic that Sea World is valuable and trustworthy because, as an elementary educator put it, "it has made itself part of the San Diego community," it is useful to examine Sea World's education in terms of what it might offer and what is missing. Not only do the materials treat the student as a vessel for science facts, but, as we have seen, with few exceptions complexity, local connections, and controversy are missing. Sea World's environmental messages are little different from the flat morality play of the rest of corporate environmentalism in their emphasis on individual responsibility for cleaning up litter.[65] Of course, a careful outlining of the issues involved with marine pollution would mean discussing agricultural and industrial runoff, toxic waste dumping, the trash explosion, oil spills, and undersea nuclear testing, to name a few controversial issues. As the entertainment arm of a huge corporation with extensive agribusiness operations, Sea World can appear environmental but it can't point fingers or even name issues. It can, however, suggest to its audience that corporate America has the best interests of animals and the environment at heart.

Perhaps these are unfair criticisms. Sea World doesn't claim to define the science curriculum of San Diego city and county schools, nor to provide all of that curriculum. Its job, as defined by its lease with the city, is to provide a resource, not an entire education. And teachers and students certainly can and do pick and choose between Sea World and other resources, such as the small museum, the nonprofit zoo, the state park, and the free nature walk. But they choose Sea World often, in large part because over the decades the theme park has used its landscapes and trained animals to cultivate its image as that of an important place to visit, a public place of learning and rationality. In the next two chapters, I return to the production of the nature spectacle, especially the celebrity whales and their performances, the core of the attraction.

CHAPTER FIVE

Routine Surprises

Producing Entertainment

Sea World's discourse of education frames and supports what its customers really come to see: the dolphins, sea lions, and killer whales performing with their trainers. The marine mammals are the core of the attraction, and the heart of the spectacle is Shamu and the Shamu show. On one hand, this emphasis on live nature in performance differentiates Sea World from other theme parks, especially Disneyland, where the animals are audio-animatronic robots or fuzzy-costume versions of animated creatures. On the other hand, Sea World's animal spectacles also distinguish it from most zoos. Although Sea World terms itself an "oceanarium," it is better described as a cross between a circus, an aquarium, and a botanical garden.[1]

There is never just one show. One busy spring season, for example, Sea World had at least seven, each up and running in its own large or small arena. Four animal performances were divided by a rough grouping of species: dolphins, killer whales, sea lions and otters, and birds. And Sea World was working on the incongruous "Clydesdale hitch," a parade of the massive draft horses. One all-video electronic show (the foundering Window to the Sea), one all-human jet-ski and water-ski show, and a simulator-theater movie, *Mission: Bermuda Triangle,* rounded out the picture.[2] Every summer, the schedule cranks up as performances become more frequent and special versions of the whale and dolphin shows are scripted for "Summer Nights." Human actors appeared in all these shows, of course, as animal trainers or characters, and they delivered filler as strolling, occasional singers, dancers, and comedians. Whether permanent, seasonal, or occasional, athletic demonstrations, concerts, ballets, instrumentalists, singers, and mimes are important to the Sea World mix, to the feeling that there's always something happening. But nature is the central story: in the early 1990s, managers said, they realized they had too many "people acts" and a decision was made to shift the balance by working up even more animal shows.

Over eight years, I watched live acts at Sea World. I watched them because they were the central product the park offered and because they mystified me. Like all performances, Sea World shows unfold on several different planes simultaneously. Structurally, the animal shows alternate between the awe evoked by the animals' beauty and their ability to make fools of their trainers. Some dolphin and sea lion performances are silly, made up of parodies of well-known cultural stories and ridiculous pranks. Indeed, in their cultural references all the shows are intertextual, held together by extensive cross-reference to mass commercial culture. Verbally, both animal shows and people shows are meager: the scripts the trainers and actors recite are limited to exclamations and a few simple facts and figures. The sound tracks overwhelm. I suffered through dozens of water-ski, jet-ski, and high-dive numbers, searching for something, anything, beneath their insipid, nostalgic story lines. "Beach Blanket Ski Party," for example, drew its audience in with a lively prerecorded sound track, but the premise of gang rivalry on jet-skis deadened the power and grace of the sixties rock and roll. Almost in spite of this thinness, though, the animal performances, especially the whale shows, amaze: the huge bodies are both unfamiliar to most customers and genuinely beautiful. But awe seems to swell up despite the sound tracks, scripts, and stages framing the whales.

Perhaps Sea World's shows seem slight because they struggle to do too many things at once. They are charged with diverting the audience for a brief twenty minutes, teaching them a little something worthwhile, and sustaining their mood of upbeat relaxation as they discharge from the stadiums into the gift shops. It would be easy to write off Sea World's entertainments as schlock, but their very superficiality made me wonder. The ever changing roster of shows is absolutely central to the park's success, and the Anheuser-Busch company puts money behind their production. If in some way the shows are what the parent corporation actively tries to present, perhaps probing the ingredients of theme park entertainment could tell more about how Sea World works.

In particular, I wondered about the animal shows. From reading about circuses and carnivals, I had an inkling of how complicated work with animal performers is. Animal trainers and circus performers work close to the heart of popular conceptions of animals, and they deal daily with the reality of nonhuman intellect. If Sea World's mass cultural version of nature was heavily based on living animals in performance—if it involved shaping scripts for otters and getting dolphins to jump—what was that process like? I spent time discussing these questions with entertainment managers, producers, writers, and trainers, and more time watching their shows to understand what they told me. Popular preconceptions, and the public conflicts Sea World faces over its presentation of animals, shape the shows deeply, I found, but all Sea World's performances are molded by other forces as well. The image needs of the large corporation, the managers' conceptions of their customers, and the physical limits and cultural aspects of the animals must all be taken into account in the production of spectacular nature.

Making Product

The work of the entertainment department is central to Sea World's overall atmosphere. Its shows pack the stadiums, its sound tracks help theme the landscape, and its occasional performers fill in space and time gaps. Entertainment handles the recruitment, contracting, training, direction, scheduling, and evaluation of human performers, the writing of scripts, the design of sets and show "looks," props and costumes, lighting, sound, and such special effects as fireworks and lasers. Most shows are produced by the park's full-time staff, but sometimes the entertainment department recruits temporary contract workers, usually the athletes and circus acrobats who stage special performances during the peak summer months.[3] Ice skaters, tumblers, high-wire acts, or water-skiers, for example, are located through agents or at trade shows, hired on for a season, and written into a special or ongoing script. In short, the entertainment department's job is to help fill the landscape with constantly changing, vivid performances.

Most of Sea World's permanent human actors and musicians are drawn from the San Diego area high schools and colleges, and as with the rest of Sea World's work force, they are young and all work without benefit of union or guild contracts. These human entertainers are asked to do more than one kind of job and learn more than one role: they are flexibly "bicycled" through different park productions.[4] By contrast, Sea World owns most of its core performers, the marine mammals.

And where the theme park tries to save money on humans, through the curatorial department and its animal-training division Sea World invests a huge amount of capital, staffing, time, and energy in the animals. Collaboration between the entertainment department and the training division produces the animal shows. The producers, writers, directors, technicians, and performers who help invent and carry out the shows draw advice and overlapping input from the marketing and education staffs. The curators and trainers are responsible for the health, feeding, maintenance, safety, reproduction, and behavior of the animals. Just as important, since shows at Sea World focus on the interaction between animals and human caretakers, the trainers are the most important performing humans. Finally, the efforts of all these departments lead back to the marketing offices where they are reviewed against the daily ratings and Anheuser-Busch's long-term goals.[5]

The animal shows are not only the core product of the park, they are the most difficult product to bring forth due to the limits and constraints of working with animals from a range of species. The collaborative relationship between entertainment producers and the trainers is essential, but at times strained. Producers and trainers are embedded in very different occupations and work routines, and so they often see problems differently. And because animal shows continue to be the object of social contention, they continue to be the focus of extra worry. Sea World's trainers and entertainment staff struggle with how to offer performances to an audience with changing and unpredictable views on the subjects of training and captivity. The shows they invent need to support Anheuser-Busch's image and present an untroubled view of the relationship between humans, animals, and the environment.

The Corporate Context

Overall, the corporation defines the production of entertainment, and this has been the case for over thirty years. Of course, many of the species that serve Sea World as backup animal actors, the sea lions and birds, for example, have been trained to perform for thousands of years. For at least a century, humans have been keeping dolphins alive in captivity, but they have been training them for only about the last forty years. The history of trained orcas is much shorter and dates from just after the first Shamu's arrival at Sea World in 1965. Corporate ownership of Sea World and its animals has made the killer whale shows in their present form possible; only a big corporation could afford the cost.[6]

The history of performing marine mammals helps shed light on the ingredients that go into the whale shows. In the United States, the first large oceanarium was developed as part of the film industry; Marine Studios opened in 1938, to film movies under water; it later became Marineland of Florida.[7] The oceanarium-studio was integrated into the powerful Florida tourism industry; in 1949 it began featuring short dolphin performances. In the early 1950s, Marineland spun off Marineland of the Pacific, in Palos Verdes, California, and in the early 1960s, Karen and Tap Pryor raised the money to build Sea Life Park, a dolphin research facility cum tourist attraction in Hawaii.[8] Karen Pryor was one of the first people to work in a concentrated and applied way to discover what dolphins in captivity could be trained to do. Her writings and lectures taught a generation of marine mammal trainers and researchers around the United States.[9]

Mike Scarpuzzi, Sea World of California's head trainer, learned his craft from his uncle and grandfather who had started a small dolphin show in Florida in the 1950s.[10] This family business was one of many animal attractions that existed on the periphery of the tourist economy and embodied a kind of folk knowledge of training; at times the Scarpuzzis barely scraped by. By the early 1970s, however, the industry was growing quickly and it became clear that the petty entertainments were a thing of the past. With the rapid expansion of mass tourism in South Florida (of which Sea World in Orlando was a part), the increasing governmental limits on the capture and treatment of marine mammals, and the need for larger pools and theaters, it was clear that only businesses with a lot of capital would be contenders in the game.[11] Scarpuzzi hired on with Sea World and began, along with other trainers, to apply his skills to work with killer whales.

When it came to discovering how to keep killer whales alive in captivity, the large oceanariums like Sea World and Marineland were destined to succeed over sideshows, small museums, and parks. The tourist attractions were supported by companies that could afford the construction of huge tanks and elaborate water circulation systems necessary to keep the whales alive, the expensive veterinary care, the thousands of pounds of food a day, and the lawyers to negotiate legislative and regulatory mazes.[12] And as the Sea World parks grew, they could support specialized training staffs that devoted all their time to working with the performers. The scene was quite different when Mike Scarpuzzi worked for his uncle back in the seventies. As he recalls, " . . . I took care of the water. I went and got the fish. I gave the medicine, I called the vets. I did the stretches. I trained the [dolphins]. I cleaned the pool. I painted the pool. My family constructed and built the oceanarium. My uncle, my grandfather, my dad, and I. Totally from the bottom. There's just no way you can do that now."[13]

Sea World's size, profitability, and corporate backing allowed it to produce a new commodity—the performing orca—and to dedicate staff to the behavioral shaping and physical reproduction of those performers. The progressive expansion of Sea World from a local company to a national chain, to a publisher's subsidiary, to part of the Busch Entertainment Corporation has meant ups and downs for its entertainment managers, but in general it has also provided a growing bank of financial and technical resources to draw on, and as a result, productions can be more expensive and elaborate.[14]

The entertainment department's production process is hierarchically organized with constant reference to the demands of St. Louis, and Sea World entertainment, whether animal or human, is a standardized, national product. Indeed, Sea World's shows are in this sense contradictory: because they are live and must be recreated in each performance, they have uneven and emergent qualities. Indeed, live performance is, in a way, a rarity in a prerecorded, televisual culture. The theme park's accomplishment has been to keep its performances live and "interactive" while controlling their meanings as much as possible.[15]

Anheuser-Busch's involvement means, of course, that the content of theme park entertainment is subject to intense scrutiny up to the highest levels of the company. From the moment a decision is made to experiment with an idea for a new show or to "retheme" or revise a show, top Anheuser-Busch management monitors its development. "Concept" must be sold not only to management in California but to the highest levels of corporate entertainment management in St. Louis. Like development in television and film, ideas are pitched up the management hierarchy, sometimes as high as the chief executive officer of the corporation; as with the theme park's exhibits, show ideas are shared by management across the parks. Scripts, techniques, technologies, ideas, sound tracks, writers, trainers, and performers (human and animal) are often moved from one park to another. The scale of the corporation dictates sharing and it makes organizational sense: expertise with animals or the technical requirements of a water-ski production can, if necessary, be drawn from Florida or Ohio. It would also be a reduplication of efforts and a waste of resources for producers to create with complete independence, Don Ludwig, vice president for entertainment, argued, ". . . because when you are developing show concepts for one park, and you have the same shows in other parks, there is no reason for us to individually have to invent shows. Corporate wants to know does it have a more global application for the other theme parks? Let's look, so we can help each other."[16]

Drawing on expertise inside the whole organization whenever possible also helps keep shows within budget. This standardization of shows reveals that, in fact, theme park producers' jobs are more technical, collaborative, and adaptive than they are innovative or creative in the individualistic sense.

Trainers and animal performers are subject to the same demands for standardization and interchangeability. Although each park has its own highly expert curators, veterinarians, and trainers, Busch Entertainment Corporation centralizes the supervision of animal training techniques through a corporate vice president for animal care. Mike Scarpuzzi explained that the purpose of this centralization "is really to make sure that the techniques that I am employing here with the trainers and the animals are similar to what they're doing in Texas, . . . in Florida, in Ohio." Since Sea World has developed sophisticated transport techniques to move its killer whales from park to park as needed, for breeding or to fill performance needs, standardized techniques help with the "context shift." "When we move animals around, there is a much easier adjustment and acclimation period for the animal."[17]

To insure uniformity in the animal behavior, "the [training] signals are all the same. The behaviors that we do are all approved. We talk to each other, we have conference calls every week to make sure we're all going in the same direction, and the whole department meets once a year for three days [to discuss] what's going on. [The vice president for animal care] is there to make sure that all four parks are running together, using the same techniques, and that the animals are safe. He reports on up . . . to the corporate headquarters in St. Louis, so that John Roberts and August Busch know that the training departments are taken care of."[18] This oversight is especially important since lax supervision of trainers and training procedures probably contributed to the accident that nearly killed a trainer in 1987.

Hierarchical flexibility means that all kinds of entertainment products are structured so that they can move through the corporation. Sea

World of California's sound tracks, for example, are usually commissioned from Southern California composers, but they routinely carry buyout clauses so that there are no limits or restrictions on what can be done with the original music. In theory it can be edited, remixed, played in varying contexts in different parks; in the future, the gift shops may even sell the sound tracks on cassette. The rationale of corporate mobility and flexibility means that no matter how hard its public relations department works to bolster Sea World's "part-of-the-community" identity, in fact, the tourist customers are a mobile lot, and its entertainments cannot be too local in reference. Shows are written with the mobile and detached tourist audience in mind, even though they are performed live in a particular place and time. Except where location *is* the "theme" (for example, in the "Beach Band," a roving group of musicians who play "California" oldies), Sea World's shows cannot accommodate vernacular references. This may explain some of the entertainment's thinness. Just as Sea World's exhibits and landscape are radically separated from San Diego's environment, so its performances accommodate local culture in only limited ways.[19]

Corporate Image and Family Entertainment

Since all the Sea World parks are a form of public relations for Anheuser-Busch, entertainment producers know that the core product, especially, must be "geared to the logo." Producers concede a legitimate corporate right to monitor content and "make sure we are doing what we should be doing."[20] Another use of the corporate coordination of entertainment, therefore, is control over image, message, and tone. On the negative side, the Busch Entertainment Corporation is concerned that theme park shows take great care not to present anything that might put the Sea World chain or the Anheuser-Busch Corporation and its products in a bad light. Entertainment concepts should be appropriate for both Sea World's projected market and for the park's overall image. Dissonance, controversy, and "negatives" must be avoided.

When the question is put more positively, when theme park producers are asked what they are trying to do, articulate people become curiously inarticulate. When I asked producers what kind of entertainment they were trying to produce or what specific ingredients they tried to put in their shows, they tended to answer with theme park industry catch phrases: "We think our product has universal appeal," "We want to reach the kid in you," and "We're in the business of putting smiles on peoples' faces." Similarly, when I asked producers how they thought about their audience and what their audience wanted to see, they tended to not know what I meant by the question. Some replied, "I've never really thought about that before." Sea World's entertainment is a well-known quantity for the producers; they rarely have time to question or examine it, but just work inside it.

The entertainment genre that allows theme park entertainment producers to take so much for granted is sketched in a phrase that came up over and over again: "What we do is family entertainment." With this phrase they acknowledged that theme park entertainment is marketed as wholesome, healthy, happy, and oriented toward children and families. Not incidentally, the theme park as a whole and its entertainments are supposed to reflect these same values back onto Anheuser-Busch. This is what "geared to the logo" means. I spent a great deal of time in discussion with producers trying to get them to supply a working definition of family entertainment, but, again, if there was an explicit recipe or generic outline for producing it, the producers couldn't recite it. All hesitated, expressed puzzlement, and then replied that it took developed intuition to recognize it. In generating the content and tone of entertainment, the writers work within vague but potent boundaries of appropriateness. Although their shows are checked over by corporate heads, the writers and directors are guided as much by a "feel" for doing things the "Sea World way" as they are by St. Louis. One producer called it "just a wholesomeness . . . a fine line."

Content of Family Entertainment

In line with much of the rest of American mass culture, Sea World's family entertainment is cut to fit broader, politically current notions of what children should be exposed to.[21] From this point of view, nature, animals, beauty queens, and athletes contrast positively with *Beavis and Butthead, The Simpsons,* or *Roseanne.*[22] The overall content of productions should be upbeat and provide a "positive message." It should avoid controversies that are unappealing and unentertaining from the point of view of the conservative sections of the white middle class. References to minorities and social conflict (except where these can be appropriately repackaged, as was the case with hip-hop and break dancing in the "City Streets" show) or anything that might make people feel "bad" should be avoided. Oil spills, pollution, and complicated life-webs are out, too. But as we shall see, when it comes to Sea World's whale performances and environmental politics, avoidance of controversy can be a tall order.

Producers borrow a phrase from Disney, "putting smiles on people's faces," to describe their main job. Smiling faces are conjured in all the park's divisions and departments to mean creating an entire atmosphere that is simplified, beautiful, unlike the real world, and stress and problem free; indeed, the notion of "smiles" reveals that entertainment's job, like that of the landscape designers and service laborers, is to produce an emotional state. Sea World producers talk about the "feelings" created by action, scenery, pacing, script, or music in their shows. Feelings to avoid are boredom, uneasiness, anxiety, disgust, and pity.

Sea World's vice presidents say that the park's entertainments have "universal appeal," implying that they contain something at once so acceptable and so amazing that no language, nationality, race, or gender would stand in its way. This universal appeal, like nature, speaks to the soul without words. It dissolves local, national, political, and ethnic specificities and references via a sort of universal language. And not incidentally, Sea World's shows trade in references to science, often argued to be a universal and objective value.

The universal person in Sea World ideology is the child. Entertainment producers claim that their scripts, whether for people or dolphins, address "kids of all ages" (another phrase Sea World executives borrow from Disney). The notion of "kids of all ages" is two-sided. First, it contains the idea that everyone was once a child and thus has something in common with every other child and former child. In this line of thought, differences of opinion, occupation, taste, income, and interest, even nationality, are acquired on leaving childhood. As children, people are all equal, and equal in their ability to relate to and understand certain universally appealing ideas, such as nature, the love of animals, and the power of science. Second, the notion of "kids of all ages" holds within it an idea of reversion. People can shed their acquired identities in the universal solvent of nature to return to childhood and its universal equality.

Both ideas, nature and reversion, have in them a kernel of the utopian. In the face of entertainment we travel back to our childhood selves, to be made temporarily happy. In nature's presence, we reconnect with transcendent value. When Sea World says it reaches "the kid in you," it means it hopes to reconnect its customers with the unalienated person inside, open to delight and pleasure, free from worldly concerns and able to indulge in uncomplicated and conflict-free pleasures. That Sea World managers use Disney language to discuss this magical process is no accident, since the Disney company pioneered this mass-culture definition of childhood and continues to market it in the form of vacations at its resorts and theme parks and in its media products.[23] Similarly, Sea World argues that its shows and the park as a whole offer a path to such an untroubled state.

But calling up the universal "kid" in the theme park customer is a carefully controlled process—and the framework of family entertainment is part of what keeps it in check. Family entertainment signals not just entertainment that can be enjoyed across generational boundaries, but the careful limiting of the ideas, images, and meanings that children may experience and the assertion of parental (and traditionally paternal) control.[24] As we have seen, the postwar theme park was not really invented for children and youth, but as family entertainment—that is, entertainment for youth under the supervision of parents, requiring as it did automobile travel and a major financial outlay at the gate. Sea World follows this template, with theme park authority: it is a place for children within the control of the structures of school (during tours, classes, and educational programs) and family (during planned, supervised recreational time). It is not a free space open to youth's own uses. Indeed, the park's managers point out that by not featuring "metal rides" or youth music, it actively tries to avoid autonomous adolescents. In any case, teenagers are seen by the marketing director as "an overrated market."[25] By the same token, the entertainment department thinks of its productions not in terms of what children want to see; rather, it guesses at what parents and grandparents want kids to see and not see.[26] The corporation takes pains to see that Sea World entertainment is not dissonant with the "family learning" image of the park, and shows of every kind must fit a "family entertainment" model that rejects references to sex (or death), unapproved lifestyles, and drugs.[27]

Producers emphasize that Sea World entertainment is so well-defined that writers just know what tones and emphases will or won't fit. For former vice president for entertainment Bob La Porta, positive things that can go into family entertainment include

> [t]he good-natured humor in seal and otter, and the one-up-manship of the dolphins. It's the difference in entertainment between *Married with Children*

and *Bob Newhart* or *Bill Cosby*. You don't necessarily say, "We will put these things in." You just follow a certain judgment of a sense of good taste. . . . It's just that what the rules are is self-evident, from the minute you walk into it. . . . Everything has a level. . . . So, you understand that. It's like a company ethic. It's a company personality.[28]

"Family entertainment" means avoiding sexual references. La Porta recalled that in his Sea World years, "any sexual joke or line or double entendre was out, you know. If it came up by accident, and a trainer got a big laugh on it, we would pull it. Is that censorship? No. . . . It has do to with how you set yourself up. We have a right to present what we present, our product."[29]

In particular, sexualized displays of the female body are out. Producer Janet Gotch noted that this was a change from earlier standards of propriety: "I performed [as a sea maid] in a show that was very wholesome for that period of time. That was the early seventies. But you know, the water was cold, and our legs were showing, and we had long hair. . . . It was an acceptable thing then."[30]

Today there are no sea maids at all, and female performers in the water are covered by full wet suits. Gotch went on to say vis-à-vis women in performance, "We don't want a show that is just Hollywood or Las Vegas": "We are branching out into ice-skating shows, or gymnastic shows, wholesome family entertainment. We want that. I think a good example is an ice-skating show. We look at an ice-skating show as wholesome and athletic, and we're not going to put in a Las Vegas–type show."[31]

I asked Gotch what the difference is between a Las Vegas floor show and ice dancing, since each emphasizes skillful, scantily clad female bodies. She replied that "we have families here. Ice skating is very popular in Las Vegas, but [pausing to puzzle about it] we're not an Ice Capades show either. We really try to go for athleticism. And [pausing and lapsing into self-parody], we just try to make 'em a real all-American kind of a cornball show [laughter]."[32]

Here, Gotch's temporary confusion reveals that the distinction is one of tone and cultural meaning rather than explicit content. Sea World's entertainment makes as much use of female bodies today as it did two decades ago, but her comments reveal that this use has changed. When people are on display, women as well as men should reveal athletic strength, skill, and accomplishment. "Family entertainment" means less that writers should avoid explicitly sexualized bodies in front of children than that they should insert approved role models. "Wholesome" is affirmatively crafted to fit with the prescriptive morality of the 1980s and 1990s, now aimed so heavily at children through sports, fitness, and drug-abuse prevention programs. Family entertainment sponsored by the world's largest brewer consists of the right kinds of bodies, male and female: Sea World states proudly that some of its whale trainers are Olympic-class athletes, and in 1996 it was the "official theme park" of the Olympic Games.[33]

Useful Entertainment

Despite its conjuring of smiles, universal kids, and fantastically toned physiques, Sea World's entertainment is troubled by pressure to be rational, enlightening, and useful. Most immediately, the trainer accidents and whale deaths of the late 1980s forced Sea World to be very sensitive to charges that it is simply an irrational spectacle that endangers animals and people in order to make a profit. Less immediately but just as important, the Marine Mammal Protection Act of 1972 specifies that permits may be granted to display marine mammals as long as these displays have "educational purposes," and Sea World's lease with the city of San Diego calls for a public educational function for the park (see chapter 2). The producers seem of two minds about this problem that they can't ignore. On one hand, the entertainment managers view as "deadly" anything that will make Sea World more like a trip to a museum or a classroom; they view their audience as largely uninterested in anything but a distracted good time. Several producers told me that they thought theme park customers generally "check their brains at the door" and do not want to do any heavy thinking.[34] On the other hand, they acknowledge that their customers probably share the general environmental interests and concerns of the American public, and they feel under pressure to integrate materials developed by the education department into shows for the general audience. The marketers' view on this problem is similarly divided. They are well aware that the demographic and psychographic research shows their Southern California customers as educated and information-oriented, but marketers also pronounce scientific information about the animals "boring" and call public aquariums and museums "dry as dust."[35] This divided view surfaces in debates over the extent to which shows should discuss and explain research and attempt to be explicitly educational, and whether scientific information can be smuggled into animal shows in a way the audience won't notice.

For example, Don Ludwig, vice president for entertainment, argued that while he found the results of research on killer whales fascinating, "I'm not sure that Joe and Betty Six-Pack out there care all that much about that. The fact is that we're doing something about it and we can show it in a light fashion . . . [but if we] try to wow people on our research, I think we may lose them. . . . You just don't want to cloud up your brain while you are here. Let's just have it naturally absorbed in there, and if you can remember, you know, 30 percent of the educational stuff that was presented, then we've accomplished what we need to."[36]

Despite their uneasiness, entertainment staff does have the job of helping the park present itself as a source of useful knowledge, an adjunct to Anheuser-Busch's conservation-conscious, outdoors-loving image. But given the central role shows hold in the rationale of the attraction, this is a contradictory task: If education is something the audience finds "deadly," how *can* entertainment be made educational? If conservation and ecological themes are exciting, what sort of shows should they be writing? Ludwig expressed the bind he was in and defined the solution this way: "We can put a lot of education material out there for them to grab up, for them to pull in at whatever quantity they want. But give them the choice. Don't force it down their throat." Having already abandoned some "themed" killer whale shows as a way of defusing popular concern over the captivity issue, the entertainment staff is uneasy at seeing their scripts pushed even further to promote Sea World as a research institution. Because the park is a complex for-profit environment, exhibits, display formats, printed texts, and videos worked up by the education department can carry more of the weight of rationality, and the performed spectacles "people really come to see" can be kept lighter. Otherwise, said Ludwig, "I think we could turn ourselves into a nonprofit institution pretty quickly!"[37] In a sense, it is ideologically easier to rework the physical landscape than to seriously restructure the animal shows.[38]

The constraints on entertainment tighten when management confronts the problem of anticaptivity and animal rights activism. Animal rights activism may directly affect "the ability to do business," that is, it may politically affect the ability to keep whales at all, so shows must avoid fanning the flames of animal rights sentiments. Shows need to make the strongest case for the benefits of captivity, but they must not appear self-serving.[39] Busch Entertainment Corporation screens not only concepts but specific scripts. As Janet Gotch put it, "The animals are the main focus of the show. The animals are to be treated with respect. I don't mean treated, they *are* respected. But we need to think about what the guests see when they see the show. We would never put the animals in a position where (now, this sounds like I'm anthropomorphizing) where they were humiliated. We keep the animals' pride, in that they are doing natural behaviors."[40]

Again, this statement reflects Sea World management's awareness of criticisms that the park represents institutionalized cruelty to animals in the name of profits, while it begs the question what a "natural" conditioned behavior would be. While not all Sea World's audience hold such views, the park and Anheuser-Busch have to be sensitive to the possibility that people could see performance *itself*, no matter what the content, as humiliating to the animals. The sensitivity of the audience on the questions of captivity and domination, what is "natural" and what is not, won't go away. Indeed, the questions what is natural and what is humane are continually recycled by protests, which in turn force Sea World's scriptwriters to work on reproducing arguments about naturalness and humane treatment in the shows.

For the same reasons, corporate animal care and training staff pick away at scripts in defense of the ability to do business. Ludwig described the process:

> From the animal [rights movement] point of view there is an approval process for scripts and for lines. Sometimes a line we think is great, somebody says, "Well, I'm a little concerned somebody could interpret it wrong." Okay, fine. It's not like censorship, its more like making sure that the message, particularly from the animal rights [movement] point of view, [can't be taken and used] in a totally different fashion than we intend. So we will change a line, delete a line, or we'll add more lines in some cases. So the approval process really goes through the corporate [ranks], it's not just entertainment people, but it goes through animal care and animal training as well. Corporate staff will be there, looking at what we are asking an animal to do, to make sure we're not creating any conflicting or contradictory messages to our general public or, more particularly, to the small percentage of people who prefer to think that we shouldn't be in business in the first place.[41]

Despite careful screening of show materials (and journalists and academic researchers) occasionally there is slippage and inconsistency. For example, in addition to vetting scripts, one public relations worker made it her job to regularly check the gift shops for merchandise that might reflect negatively on captivity. She found and sent back T-shirts with a striped pattern that seemed to show orcas behind bars. Staff regularly check the whale and dolphin books on sale in the gift shops to make sure no published anticaptivity opinions sneak into the park. And Sea World's training manual specifies how animals will be spoken about by tour guides and interpreters. Training is always called "learning," and behaviors, for example, may never be called "tricks."[42] Internal disagreements have raged at Sea World about whether shows and exhibits present animals and the park in the best light. But overall, this is probably a problem that Sea World can't solve. Scripts and souvenirs can be controlled but accidents can't be always be prevented. And finally, perhaps because of the popularity of whales and dolphins in the larger culture, the public's understanding of the animals and what it means to display them can never be completely harmonized with Sea World's view that animal performances foster wildlife appreciation.

Inventing Entertainment

Within the boundaries of family entertainment, limited by the corporate image and the constraints of law and popular attitudes toward animals, producers are charged with creating familiar novelties, the routine surprises fundamental to tourist attractions. At Sea World, as in the case of much industrial cultural production, creativity is a collective process, and it makes little sense to speak about it in individualistic terms. Nor are the theme park entertainers charged with coming up with unheard of ideas. Rather, they stay within well-defined boundaries and draw on a familiar cultural stock.

The main practical pressure shaping the shows is the marketing department's need to plan seasonal advertising and marketing campaigns. As suggested above, the marketing department worries about whether the park has "something to talk about." If there has been no major new show for more than a year, the vice president for marketing will be certain to press the producers. He may even offer ideas, based on how he is currently evaluating the park's audience and direction. As Ludwig explained, "Our marketing department can come to us and say, 'Guys, we need to do a new Shamu show.' We may not even be thinking about that, but they are looking at what's sellable and saying, 'We are really kind of shy over these next six months or so. Can we talk about a new show?'"[43]

Under these circumstances novelty is both prized and very relative; invention is a process of accumulating "what we know works," adding new twists, and borrowing from outside the park.[44] Although true novelties have occasionally occurred in the theme park industry—the performing killer whale was one—they are not frequent.

Ideas for new shows and exhibits are generated in several different ways. Sea World runs a cross-departmental brainstorming group called "Kaleidoscope" to spin out "blue sky" ideas that may or may not ever move into production. The idea is to spark a general creativity in the park. Individual vice presidents or directors may press pet ideas forward. But since Sea World exists in a world of other museums, aquariums, zoos, and theme parks, ideas are often borrowed from outside the corporation, as well as from within the chain. The idea for the Rocky Point Preserve was copied, as noted in chapter 3, from the Point Defiance Zoo and Aquarium in Tacoma. In the case of the "urban-themed" bird show, Gotch recalled that "corporate had been wanting another animal show, a bird show, for a long time, so we shopped around."[45] Although Sea World owns a large collection of birds, they hired a contractor—the same one who delivered a popular wild bird show to the nearby Wild Animal Park—and themed his work to fit the "City Streets" set.

The entertainment producers are not embarrassed about borrowing ideas or genres from other parks or other industries; they are concerned only about whether they have been proven popular. This is because their audience is defined first and foremost as a market. It is more important that this market, whose demographic characteristics and consumer tastes are well understood, feel inclined to come once and then come back again, than that whole new markets be discovered and learned about.[46] Sea World's marketers watch closely what has opened or is promised at other theme parks and competing tourist attractions. They travel to other major theme parks around the United States and the world to see what is new, what is working, and what is failing, and they scout contract performers and new technologies in the trade press and at amusement industry trade fairs. For these reasons, although each Southland theme park has its own niche, they are also fad-ridden: one year, suddenly, each has a new roller-blade act; the next year, a video-simulator ride. In an Olympic year, parks feature athletes in salutes to the Olympics; following the United States–Iraq War, there were patriotic yellow-ribbon celebrations.

The most efficient way for theme park producers to keep in touch with their market is through the rest of commercial popular culture. The producers work in and freely borrow from mass entertainment's metagenres—sports, television, movies, popular music, and comic books. This vast cultural reservoir is vital, shaping theme park entertainment's form and giving it specific content. The producers also pay attention to vernacular popular culture, especially the self-produced culture of youth, but always with an careful eye to the demographics. In the late 1980s, for example, when Southern California street culture and hip-hop became visible and fashionable in the pop music media, Ludwig recruited street performers from Venice Beach and Tijuana: "You know, the kids who are working in front of their hats on the boardwalk. . . . What we try to do is take an act that may be a standard act and try to wrap him in a nice package, so that it didn't appear to be a street act. You costume it, you put music behind it, you make it fit in the context of a certain theme. You wrap it in a package that is a little different than what you see on the street. You choreograph and orchestrate, and you make it make sense."[47]

Wrapping a theme park narrative around the core of vernacular performance, the producers made urban life and ethnicity recognizable to a largely suburban, white audience.[48] But the interests of the same audience dictate that rap and new rock musics, when they appear, are tamed and consigned to the peripheral spaces of the park.

Finding the Audience

The main current to stay in touch with is television. When Bob La Porta was hired as the first full-time director of entertainment in 1972, he immediately saw his job as helping to integrate the domestic medium into the park. With a degree in theater, La Porta had extensive experience in daytime and variety television. His explicit intention was to locate the park "where the audience was." The local and tourist public La Porta aimed to reach was heavily involved with television: "My early, early show [at Sea World] was a pirate show. But rather than the pirate show they already had here, I took a notion from Saturday morning cartoons. My sons were watching Saturday morning cartoons, and I took the pirate ship and made it futuristic, with futuristic pirates. This was before *Star Wars;* it would have been '73."[49]

He availed himself of other parts of mass culture aimed at children and families:

A water-ski show we did in Ohio we thought was particularly unique, in 1976 and 1977. It was a salute to the superheroes. It was taken from my boys who watched superheroes on TV on Saturday morning. My charge was to do a show that appealed to children, 'cause the ski show was dying in the demographics with children. The surveys very often helped us make certain decisions. In '77, . . . "Salute to the Superheroes" involved licensing, a deal with Dell [Comics]. Again! Mario Puzo was writing *Superman,* and Wonder Woman was coming out on television. It was one of our most successful water-ski shows. Wonderful new special effects. We began to choreograph fights, with "Pow," "Biff," and "Bamm!"[50]

And La Porta energetically mined the world of film, history, and mass culture nostalgia. "We themed another water-ski show 'The Roaring Twenties Water Frolics,' because that year Robert Redford came out with *The Great Gatsby.* The newspapers were filled with the fantasy of the twenties, a real addiction to the twenties, so we themed it the Roaring Twenties. We had Babe Ruth going around the bases, the slalom ski, and the kite flier became Lindy, and the costumes and music were themed. And this was the first themed music. [We had it composed] around Gershwin's 'Rhapsody in Blue.'"[51]

La Porta's understanding that television and film spoke efficiently to the audience set a pattern of borrowing and appropriation that Sea World's human performances still follow. In addition to using whole stories and themes from the other mass media, much of Sea World's entertainment relies on pastiche, on taking pieces of other media products and with a quick touch integrating them into well-worked-out performance genres. In this way, the audience feels perfectly at home—at home with jokes and allusions to *Star Trek* in a killer whale show, and located among the culturally knowledgeable when an Alfred Hitchcock movie is grafted onto the trained bird show. They are at the center of American culture when network sportscasting terms ("Up Close and Personal!") are used by whale and dolphin show narrators, and among their own generation as "classic" rock from two decades past is reperformed both on stage and in the inescapable background sound track to the park.

In the 1990s, the uses of television at Sea World have intensified. Rather than borrowing from a broad television genre like "action heroes," as La Porta had done, through the William Morris Agency Sea World has literally incorporated current, prime time programming and the images of specific celebrities into its entertainment products. For example, in 1992 and 1993 the Shamu show featured James Earl Jones as its video narrator; in 1994 and 1995, a rewritten Shamu show was narrated by actress Jane Seymour, star of another network hit, *Dr. Quinn, Medicine Woman.*[52] In 1995, a new water-ski and jet-ski show was tied-in to *Baywatch,* a smash prime-time hit and the most widely seen American television export in the world.[53]

The effect of this fusion is less a knockoff of mass popular culture than an integration of different commercial media (television, film, popular music, comic books, and licensed characters) into the entire Sea World environment, although this process is less intense and thorough than in a Time-Warner theme park. What looks like low-budget copying—mimicked rock bands, skits based on Hollywood classics, references to and language borrowed from popular television shows—*is* low-budget copying. But recombining genres is also a sure way to stay in line with the most desirable end of the broad audience for mass culture; almost all mainstream entertainment aimed at a white middle-class audience is fodder for the theme park. But Sea World is not a *bricoleur* sorting and combining pieces of culture to make unexpected, new meanings. Country music, Hollywood film, oldies rock sung a cappella, Olympic ice dancing, *Dr. Quinn,* and David Hasselhoff are part of a quite predictable segment of mass culture, a signal to the middle-aged, white middle class and their children that they are, in a sense, at home. These mass media staples may be unremarkable, middle-of-the-road, and overcirculated, but Sea World is loathe to offend, challenge, or ignore the tastes they represent.[54]

Working with Animals

Finally, though, the human performances only fill in around the core product, the animal shows. Animal performers present special production problems, and the killer whale, dolphin, sea lion, and otter performances are molded by the demands and limits of working with animals and by the opportunities different species present.

As noted above, the production of animal shows cannot be handled only by the entertainers: it is the animal trainers who supply the availability of the animals by literally making them, first, into malleable, trainable animals and then into performers by teaching them the specific behaviors that can be worked into shows.[55] Trainers are also important as performers, of course, since the central subject of all Sea World's marine mammal shows is the interaction between humans and animals. Sea

World managers assert that people come to the park less to see animals on display than to watch animals and trainers connect.[56]

Animal training techniques at Sea World are not very different from those developed in marine parks in the 1960s. They grow out of the ancient techniques of circuses and the folk knowledge of circus trainers, on one hand, and Skinnerian behaviorism and its straightforward operant conditioning on the other. The dolphin, sea lion, or killer whale is trained to recognize a stimulus and to respond, first to a primary and then a secondary reinforcement. This secondary reinforcement is the "bridge" that trainers use to draw forth and then shape particular, desired movements and activities.[57] At Sea World, the animals are positively reinforced according to a variable ratio schedule with reinforcement variety, the most reliable mode of operant conditioning; negative reinforcement consists of the least reinforcing stimulus, a brief total cessation of interaction or "time-out." Sea World does not use physical punishment or food deprivation, according to its head trainer.[58]

Sea World aims to standardize trained animal behavior. The trainers work with animals to achieve not only action on command but a "topography of behavior," a very precise, consistent, and measurable use of the body. (Training is also about teaching the animal to stop doing anything at all and wait.) Precision is especially important in a choreographed show. Head trainer Scarpuzzi decides what behavior he needs and then works toward a perfect topography by reinforcing only the most desired version. This depends on tightly consistent demands and rewards across trainers. As Scarpuzzi described the process,

> If you want a tail walk, so that the animal will come out of the water and move back, and you want the dorsal fin to clear the water, that's the criterion you need: come up and go back across the pool and keep your dorsal fin out of the water the entire time. It's that precise. Now if the animal comes up, goes back a little, goes down, comes up, goes back, it's no good. And if one trainer says that *is* good, then the animal . . . can start to get confused. He is allowed to do it sometimes and not other times. But if he understands the criterion is to come up, go all the way across with his dorsal fin clearing the water, out of the water, and that's what he's going to be asked to do all the time, then he knows that. Now you can start on getting him motivated to do it quicker, more times throughout a day, start to get him into that. That's when your reinforcement comes in.[59]

Training at this level of precision involves detailed record keeping. Scarpuzzi related that records of even the shortest interactions track the animals' play, training and exercise sessions, behavior and moods:

> [When you see a trainer writing on a clipboard,] she is actually recording the interaction that just happened. Was it a learning session, a show, a relationship time? Was it a play time, or was it a "vitamins"? She writes up who did it. She writes up how much food was involved, from zero to fifty or one hundred pounds, and then she rates the interaction on a scale of one to five. One would be: "The animal didn't want to interact with me at all." Two: "He interacted but with very low energy, attitude, and cooperation." Three: "That was average: it did everything that I asked and cooperated well." Four: "It was about [a high] average. It had really good energy, high motivation, did everything really well but wasn't all perfect." And five is reserved for "Man, that animal didn't do anything wrong, had high motivation, and was just excellent out there."[60]

Every interaction is made part of the database, building control and continuity over time and across Scarpuzzi's training staff, "even if I just go out there and start rubbing him down, and then I go in and write that down," he said.[61]

Fed into a computerized data bank along with health data and veterinary records, the reports on each whale's behavior are printed out and circulated so that every one in training and curatorial knows what's going on with the animal. Some killer whales' data banks reach back decades. "You could lay out Corky's past twenty-five years," said the head trainer.

> So we can go back over the last year's records and do a behavioral study on how the animals performed in certain situations with certain people under certain guidelines and techniques. . . . You see, it's [intrastaff] communication but it's also data for future research whenever we need it. . . .
>
> You can also [ask whether] you're having too many play sessions, [or] not enough play sessions, more often than not. You know how many sessions, how many shows, how many relationships, how many "plays," and if you see the animal starting to get down a little bit or serious, you can say, "Y'know, I just don't see the fun in the animal that I used to. Let's go look at how many play sessions we've been doing." . . . You find out, whew, you've only got 2 percent play times in the last month. So, let's increase the play time and decrease the amount of learning sessions . . . and see if that brings up the attitude a little bit. . . . So you use it to look back and see what, check back regularly to see what's going on with the whale, what's going on with the relationship with the whale. It also can be used for a context shift study. In other words, if we move an animal from one oceanarium in Sea World Texas to here, you have baseline behavior that is already established. You take it over here and you can study how long does it take to get it back up to there. [This lets us see] how much moving from one place to another affects behavior.[62]

Data gathering follows each animal through its life in a kind of total informational control.[63]

However, working with live animals can never be completely rationalized. Sea World has to work around its marine mammal performers as much as it works on them. The dolphins, sea lions, and whales help dictate the temporal structure of the park, for example. Ironically, while humans can be coerced into performing highly repetitive actions or replaced if they refuse, the whales are expensive and difficult to replace. Their health, energy, and boredom levels determine the length of shows and how many times they can be asked to do the same tricks. Shows need to be short enough to be repeated many times during one day, but animal boredom limits the number of repetitions. The physical availability of the animals also influences the number of repetitions, since for each species different numbers of performers can be drafted onto the stage. Killer whales, for example, are rare and expensive, need a lot of space, and are costly to maintain. In any Sea World park, there are usually only three to five orcas at any time. By contrast, sea lions are easily purchased and conveniently kept. They reproduce rapidly and without special care. In San Diego there are numerous "Clydes" and "Seamores" who can be switched around and put through their paces, so sea lion shows can be staged frequently. It is true that different whales can play Shamu, but their small numbers limit flexibility.

Animal shows have a kind of economy of scale. In the logic of the attraction a predicted number of customers needs to be able to see at least two or three animal acts for satisfactory length of stay and quality of experience. The more numerous animals, therefore, perform more frequently in smaller stadiums, bolstering the sense that something is always happening at Sea World. The rarer animals play less frequently in the large-capacity stadiums. And all the animals set an outside boundary on the time and number of performances in a day.

Animal Essences

The cultural identities of the animals also shape the shows, their styles, and genres. To take one case, Sea World producer Don Ludwig made a basic working distinction between "themed" and "here and now" shows. He pointed out that "here and now" shows focus on presenting the immediate physical reality of the animal to the audience. The animal is "here" before the audience "right now," and the power, beauty, and strength of its body seem to be unmediated by cultural narratives, even though the animal is thoroughly trained. By contrast, in "themed" shows a loose narrative based on a familiar story or historical period frames the animal behaviors and human stunts. One example would be the sea lion and otter show, "Pirates of the Pinniped," a "pirate adventure-comedy" that turns on the antics of trained sea lions, walruses, and otters.[64] The gloss of a time period (1950s), a style (oldies rock), a narrative idea (pirates), or another genre (a movie, a Gilbert and Sullivan operetta), or some combination of all three is woven around the core of elicited animal behavior. "Themed" also means an explicitly story-telling script is written for the performance; animals' behaviors are trained to the script.

Themed shows bear the closest ties to the popular media of TV, film, and advertising, and they have a long history—for example, in the circus, where inserting animal behaviors into fairy tale narratives is an old tradition.[65] Karen Pryor's first dolphin shows at Sea Life Park told bits of Hawaiian cultural history. Today's themed shows have a great deal in common with animated cartoon movies and television. "Here and now" shows have their own antecedents in circus and sideshow animal acts that stress the physical spectacle of the animal; they also have their counterparts in the educational performances of zoos, animal park guided tours, and the newspaper science pages.

Simple behavioral routines were the dominant performance form at Sea World in the late 1960s and early 1970s. Bob La Porta recalled that "when it first started, the shows were nothing but animal behaviors with organ music or organ consoles in the music booths. And the trainers just got up there, the animals went through their routines. They solicited applause and that was it."[66] But as Sea World expanded in the early 1970s from a marine animal collection into a theme park full of shows, it sought larger audiences, and producers realized they needed scripts. La Porta remembered the introduction of "themed killer whale performances" featuring story lines, dialogue, singers, and dancers.

> Just prior to my arrival, [George] Millay had gotten some Hollywood people to write some shows, and they had incorporated some props and costumes and some story lines too. They took out the organs and put in some tapes and spot masters, needle-drop music behind it, and scripts. . . .
>
> What used to drive me crazy was, they didn't start on time necessarily, and I came from television. It was so casual, it had no beginning, no middle, no end. It just kind of was cute and it was warm and Shamu did his thing. So I added stories, costumes, and a more explicit structure.[67]

Fig. 8. Shamu Performs to a Capacity Crowd in His New Stadium, 1972. In this photograph, the performing whale is wearing enormous sunglasses, as two other killer whales wait in the wings. Courtesy San Diego Historical Society, Photograph Collection.

Today, in a reversal, factual "here and now" shows are presented as the more educational, up-to-date, and civilized way to display animals in public. While a "here and now" show focuses on the animal's body and behaviors, highlighted by the trainers' commentary, the performance may also contain statements about Sea World's goals, how the staff feels about marine mammals, and especially, how the audience ought to feel.[68] By discussing research and training, however tersely, "here and now" performances also show some backstage. They purport to let the audience in on how Sea World really works, and since they can disclose the theme park's "real motives," factual shows are a useful vehicle for presenting arguments against the anticaptivity and animal rights lobbyists. Beyond this, the older themed shows, with whales wearing sunglasses, pledging fraternities, or running for mayor, were at odds with Sea World's claim to be a scientific institution. By the 1980s even some among the staff began to see props and costumes on killer whales as demeaning of the animals.

But the view that theming is old-fashioned and demeaning and that factual is better also reveals that Sea World ranks its performers in a hi-

Fig. 9. Shamu Jumps to Touch the Ball, 1971. Getting the whale's whole, huge body up and out of the water has been a staple of the Shamu show. Courtesy San Diego Historical Society, Photograph Collection.

erarchy of political sensitivity. Some species give more concern about humiliation and humanization than others. For example, entertainment and animal-training-and-care staff frequently express concern over anthropomorphism, by which they mean the tendency to attribute human emotions and motives to animals. They recognize that producing humanlike behaviors from the animals (for example, a farewell wave) encourages the audience to think of the animals as like people. The most famous and visible species—killer whales and dolphins—are promoted in part on the basis of their qualities of being similar to humans, for example in their intelligence. In performance, however, these animals must not be seen to be humanized, they must not be made to wear costumes or do what look like "tricks" because that might appear to humiliate them.[69] Killer whale and dolphin shows are frankly spectacular in their emphasis on the animals' bodies and strength, their trainers' skill, and the theme park's relation to science, but they work hard to eschew the impression that the animals have been manipulated. Meanwhile, outside the whale and dolphin stadium, otters balance Pepsi cans on their noses and break-dance, sea lions daily "cry" over confusing maps, and walruses blow big wet kisses to the audience. This mix of ways of presenting animals reflects the park entertainment producers' assessment of the audience—that it is perfectly comfortable seeing circuslike performances by some animals, even while it shares in the larger popular culture that dictates that certain special species, that is, the cetaceans, are so precious and close to human that they must be treated differently. It is a paradox: the popular view of cetaceans insists that whales and dolphins are sociable mammals with large brains and more like "us"; therefore, they should not made to appear to act like humans.[70] However, all trained behaviors at Sea World are based on captive operant conditioning, not volition: some behaviors are made to look less cultural and conditioned than others.

Producers have to take into consideration the sometimes precise, sometimes vague cultural perceptions of what the animal is or ought to be. Sea World's curatorial and training department sees itself as in possession of more accurate and scientific information about killer whales than are the customers, and all management sees the customers (perhaps accurately) as holding a variety of romantic, folkloric, or even superstitious notions about the whales and dolphins. (Such opinions are reinforced by the visitors who dip their crystals and occasionally even jump naked into the dolphin pool).[71] Apparently, customers project essential identities onto the animal. While the curators may reject this folk knowledge, however, the entertainment staff must use it and write it into the shows. If these imagined essences are obstacles to rationality, still they cannot be violated with impunity. As Bob La Porta explained,

> I was always taking into account the mystique of the particular animals. Obviously the dolphin was considered to be intelligent and romantic. The sea lion was filled with frolic and mischievousness. And this leads you into a certain pattern of how you develop the shows. . . .[72]
>
> The complex seal and otter show, with doors opening and animals coming and going,—"Spooky Kooky Castle"—was a masterpiece of timing and sight gags . . . but [it was] always putting the sea lion ahead of the trainers,

always knowing far more than the trainer knew. With dolphins, too, you had to pull out their best attributes and work with what people wanted to think about them, even though they are not as smart as the killer whale. [People] wanted to think that [dolphins are very smart] and they probably still want to think that. . . . [73]

Beyond mystiques, entertainment producers are keenly aware of the potential of the animal as a physical body. That is, they think about how each species' distinct morphology translates into human perceptions and cultural meaning. They consider the limits this perception sets on what a show can say or do about the animals. Again, Bob La Porta was especially thoughtful about this, and I quote him at length:

You have the dolphins [and that] is one challenge, the whale is another, and sea lions are another. [They require] three distinct, distinct approaches to each show. The shows are very different in their concept, in their design altogether. . . . [E]ven though people think dolphins are so intelligent, they cannot be expressive. They cannot express what a sea lion can express. We have this notion that they are so intelligent but they actually are one shape and one form, you know. They are not [changeable or malleable], they can't express anything. They can vocalize but their faces can't change, their body language can't change to the degree that a sea lion can. Sea lions really can project any kind of an emotion or any kind of anthropomorphism [*sic*].

Dolphins are like watching a sailboat. You know, you like to watch the sailboat, it's just so beautiful against the clouds, with its sail full and the water lapping up on it. But it can be boring. It doesn't emote. So [with dolphins] you pair them. You have them jump beautifully to music together, with speed, and contrive a lot of things with them in terms of one-up-manship on the trainer.

They're gray, sleek, and they go from here to there, and they move fast. The dolphin is like the corps de ballet, ballerinas. The dolphins are a force, just a force. It's very hard to get any identification of an individual. You can say, "Well, here's Aphrodite, our highest jumper in the world." Then, the minute that three of them get together, you can't tell which one is Aphrodite and which one is another. They all look the same.[74]

The static external appearance of the dolphin's body meant that it could be used to emphasize form and order, but not to express human feelings, or make jokes: "We had a show called 'Dolphins in Harmony.' . . . [I]t was a notion of 'all's right with the world,' you know. When dolphins and [humans] work together, there is a harmony: the dolphins saving the stranded boy. It was absolutely wonderful and the music gave it the mood that we're all friends and we are together. We used a lot of pairing behaviors and—again, a lot of, what's the word?

Fig. 10. “Google’s Saltwater Revival,” the Sea Lion and Elephant Seal Show, 1972. Sea lions’ flexible bodies allow them to present personalities and perform parody and comedy. Today’s sea lion and otter shows still borrow explicitly from circus and vaudeville traditions. Courtesy San Diego Historical Society, Photograph Collection.

Maybe a lot of relationship. Conclusions we’re making about relationships could be presented there.”[75]

Sea lions, in contrast, have the enormous advantage of being able to perform out of the water, whereas the torpedo-like dolphins and whales can’t maneuver on land. Since sea lions are fat, floppy, and wiggly and more individually differentiated, they provide opportunities not only for comedy, but for the development of personalities and characters. “Sea lions do look different, and they have definite personalities, and so we were able to make a difference between [two characters, named] Clyde and Seamore. The difference was very clear. I mean, Seamore would stand perfect and straight and Clyde would slouch. The whole demeanor was brilliantly orchestrated and trained. As a matter of fact, when someone would come up with a new behavior, we would say, well that’s a Seamore behavior, or that’s a Clyde behavior.”[76]

“Slouching” isn’t natural to Clyde, said La Porta, and in fact, there is no Clyde, only many animals playing the character. But “personality” and motivation can be pulled out of the sea lion bodies and motions, or projected onto them. As he described it, "The best is when you put Clyde against Seamore. You know, Seamore's absolutely perfect, he does everything right. Clyde, he's told to put the ball over the bar. Well, he doesn't jump over the bar like Seamore does, he just pushes it over and gets under it. He tries to get out of everything—you even smiled at that, Susan! What is the animal here? The animal, he's *us,* really. You know, us. Without worry, without thinking. It's just us. It's very anthropomorphic and we do that a lot with sea lions."[77]

Inventing the Killer Whale

Because the killer whales were new to the ranks of animal celebrities, the image of the orca and the stories Sea World could tell about them were open to invention, at least in the park's early years. Physically the orcas are closer to dolphins in performance possibilities. Orcas are nearly always in the water and have a torpedo shape. But they are rounder than dolphins; their chubby look and black-and-white patching has led people to call them "sea pandas." Because their thick rostrum is more foreshortened than that of the bottle-nosed dolphin and their white facial patches seem to enlarge their eyes, they have the semblance of a facial expression. Animation artists and graphic designers make use of this coloration pattern and short nose to humanize and neotenize orcas in drawings and logos. In short, live orcas can be made cute in ways that dolphins can't; in a sense, they can be animated.[78] The physical qualities of the killer whales also helped the theme park override what it claims was the older folk image of a dangerous predator, and they gave producers ideas about what the whale show should and could express.

Bob La Porta spent a great deal of time thinking about the character Shamu. He helped define the orca's personality and passed the template along to his successors: "The killer whale was majesty. I remember I had Ethel Merman there one time to look at it, and she said she didn't know whether she wanted to fear Shamu or to hug Shamu. Well, this was very important, this told me a lot about a lot of things. It was like Ferdinand the Bull, who would run through a wall and stop to smell the flowers. I had to be very careful to portray Shamu in this fashion, never violating one [quality] or the other."[79]

La Porta developed the mystique of the killer whale as a dual force,

Fig. 11. A "Yankee Doodle Whale" Performance, 1975. Early killer whale shows were a simple series of tricks, but by the mid-1970s the Shamu show was given a narrative and theme. By the early 1980s, sets, props, and costumes like these were eliminated because they called too much attention to the orca's captivity. Courtesy San Diego Historical Society, Photograph Collection.

Fig. 12. The Killer Whale Is Majesty, 1988. Shamu thrusts his trainer in the air. Courtesy *San Diego Union-Tribune,* photo by Dave Siccardi.

balanced or alternating between fearsome power and delicate gentleness. As he put it, "It was always that respect from a distance, so the music had to be filled with French horns and wonderful and majestic at times, and as simple as a music box these other times."[80]

The recurring controversies over killer whales in captivity, beginning in the 1970s, forced Sea World's producers into heightened sensitivity about how to present the orca in performance. As La Porta recalled, they were forced to realize that "at the core of the killer whale is the question: what is the image? What is the image we want to portray? What is the image that is proper to portray? And what is expected by the audience?"[81]

In fact, the image of the killer whale could not and cannot be separated from popular environmentalism nor from the controversies swirling around Sea World's whales. La Porta remembered, with some resentment, "We were moving to a new arena and we talked about a new set. In writing scripts, we always talk about a set, so we always come down to, what's the environment? Well, [suddenly in the early 1980s] we're not going to have a set any more. Sets are *wrong*. And, you know, I realized that. I agreed to that, but we [in entertainment] have certain needs [for the performance]."[82]

While the disputes about Sea World's right to capture whales off the Washington coast circulated in the national media, sets highlighted the "culturized" qualities of the Shamu show. The appearance of the wild animal being tamed was reduced by replacing humanmade objects with a more natural element, in this case, water. A pole and ball used to guide the whale in its jumps were eliminated, and the whales were trained to follow moving jets of water. Costumes and props (such as batons, hoops, or ropes) could too forcefully remind the audience that the animals were under human control. As La Porta put it, "Sometimes it just doesn't look good anymore for the animal to do something. When I got there in 1972, Shamu wore sunglasses. Later, that was verboten."[83]

From killer and curiosity to pandalike comedian to force of alternating ferocity and delicacy, the killer whale's image was recrafted over time. In the 1990s, the orcas image is shifting again. While the shows of the late 1980s had included idylls of communication between trainer and whale, currently Sea World's trainers and entertainment producers are working at "putting the killer back in the killer whale," at showing that the whale in the wild is a relentless predator. They train behaviors like the "mouth-open swim," which shows the orca's huge conical teeth, and a mock attack on a trainer. These changes are an explicit response to trainer John Sillick's near fatal accident, the bloody death of Kandu, and the public uproar surrounding both incidents. Trainers and producers argue that showing the killer whale as a killer is in the interests of realism. This is important for an audience that, they say, has been trained to think of whales in sentimental, humanized terms. When the audience sentimentally views the killer whales as gentle, they are more than horrified when humans or whales get hurt. When pressed, however, Sea World management admits that the problem they have with the killer whale's image is a bind largely of their own making.[84]

Writing for Whales

The behavioral possibilities of the trained animals present special problems for entertainment producers, because the animals' capacities affect the timing, structure, and pacing of shows.[85] Trainers play a key role: they develop the raw material—the animal that can reliably perform and its behaviors—and they generate a behavior list, the basis for the script.[86] La Porta described the script-writing process: "You say, okay, let's have a behavior list. Get us everything the animals can do. In no order, just what can they do. What can the whales do, what can the lads do, what can the dolphins do?"[87]

> The trainers would list the behaviors, and . . . I would say, "Can you do it in this order?" They would say, "*Wellll* yes, *welll,* no, because remember, he [the whale] always likes to be over there. . . ."
>
> "Oh, okay. . . ." Compromise, compromise, compromise. Once we've got the order, we enhance it with music.[88]

The trainers help the creative team work around the animals' limits, preferences, and foibles (what psychologists call "superstitious behavior"). The writers take the trainers' knowledge about the animals and work it into the show, a combination of the overarching theme, the in-place "known things that work," and new behaviors or combinations of behaviors that the animals are being trained to perform. As La Porta recounted,

> [My writers] would put it into an order, and literally write a script. Then they would come in and they would sell it, they would pitch it, they would basically perform it. They were fabulous performers, because we would all be on the floor laughing hysterically. And then I would have to smooth over

objections [corporate] people might have, knowing already what they were predisposed to worry about. . . .

Then, we would start the process. Training new behaviors or getting the animals to do it a little differently than they did it before. While they are doing the old show, they are rehearsing the new show. The producer goes out, talks to people, gets music composed, and arranged, conducted, mixed; sets built; costumes made. Then we go into rehearsals.[89]

There are special tensions in this process. Trainers "know behaviorally what can and can't happen, and they are performers in the shows [with] a lot of stage experience."[90] They continually push to have their own highly developed knowledge of the animals represented in the script, but this worries the producers: On one hand, trainer knowledge can be a source of the desirable educational angle for the show. On the other hand, the trainers' understandings of the animals and their behaviors are thought to be too esoteric for the audience. The trainers speak the language of behaviorism and operant conditioning—but is it interesting? More important, the producers think the behaviors need to be grand, clear, and narratable, interpretable by a naive audience not interested in subtle points.

La Porta recalled that "some trainer might say, 'Hey, this is a great behavior!' And I'd say, 'Well, it really isn't because *we* don't know that he never did that before.' There might be some subtle inside story that makes this, in the trainer's mind, remarkable, but to us, too much explanation is required to get this across. It will slow the show down."[91]

The fascinating, laborious process of training dolphins and whales cannot be conveyed without time and subtlety, but visible, "themeable" behaviors are the ones producers seek out. For example, La Porta says he often drew on paired swimming behavior: "I did a dolphin Olympics and teamed two dolphins against two other dolphins in competition. And it was good 'cause you knew what was happening. You could see what was happening. If one dolphin went farther than another dolphin, he won."[92]

From the point of view of entertainers, the trainers' esoteric knowledge and their passionate interest in their animals does not seem like good theater, given the twenty-minute time constraint and the huge size of the stadium crowd. Like the education department's biological and natural historical knowledge, trainers' expertise seems too serious, too deep. But from the trainers' point of view, given the popular awareness of environmental crisis and the captivity and animal rights controversies, it seems pressingly important to tell the audience how much they know. The trainers often want to convey how marvelous and unusual their animal charges are, how much they know about them, and how deeply they care. The result is sometimes conflict between the entertainment producers and the trainers over how the whales and dolphins will be presented, a conflict that is amplified when Sea World has to defend itself against charges that it is irrational. La Porta told me that in his experience trainers just "drone on and on"; "they have no sense of showmanship."[93] But trainers, he conceded, have "a stronger hand now." Although conflicts over the content of shows take place between trainers and producers, finally these too are midlevel clashes inside the corporation. Because trainers are essential workers in the process of producing entertainment, and because their knowledge is expensive and time consuming to gain, they wield some power. But finally trainers are employees, and however closely they work with their animals, they do not own them; nor do they independently create shows or make decisions about the content, tone, and style of entertainment. Over the course of the late 1980s and early 1990s, as Sea World sought to emphasize its scientific image, shows drew more on the trainers' conceptions of and relationships to the animals, but this was not the trainers' decision to make.[94]

Reliability and Uncertainty

The entertainers argue that all shows need to be constructed according to patterned expectations for introduction, buildup, interlude, and then climax. "It's just showmanship," as Bob La Porta put it. "You're not going to start with the whale ballet. You're not going to start with some of the rocket rides [in which the trainer is rocketed into the air while seated on the whale's nose]. Those are payoff behaviors."[95] But despite convention, working with animals means that the script has to be extraordinarily flexible. In fact, it must be written as a movable, shiftable set of tasks lest the animal performer become bored and stop working. This is one reason that the whale and dolphin shows use a less heavy, "scripted" narrative hand. Although repetition and regularity are demands of the theme park, over the years it has proven impossible to produce great regularity from the small number of killer whales. With trained animals, the structure and pacing of the show are problematic: structures that are too predictable create the problem of teaching the animals to anticipate cues too well. Trained animals work better with some unpredictability. Don Ludwig explained, "We find that—I don't want to say their intelligence but—their motivation is much better when they don't know what is coming next. It is better stimulation for them not to know what's coming up next all the time."[96]

For example, La Porta pointed out, show writers and trainers have to avoid a too-definitive ending:

> You have to make allowances for the animal, because they can recognize the show ending. They will just stop and refuse to perform. So you move things around, you work in modules. . . . You have to make allowances for the animals' attention, because a lot of times, they would know when a certain behavior came up: [speaking as if for the whale] "Aha! This is near the end of a show! But I don't want the show to end right now. I think I'll go over here and stay a while!" So, there are internal things that have to be done to make it interesting for the animal. You switch things around. We were able in one show, I think it was "Shamu Take a Bow," to just move whole chunks around, because it wasn't so much a story.[97]

Don Ludwig, the current vice president for entertainment, stressed flexibility and variability: "Animals are not machines and we do not want them to go from A to Z every single time or they will get bored, just like you would. If you got up and did the same thing every day, day after day, after a while you'd start saying, oh god, not another day."[98]

Ironically, the nature theme park offers its spectacles as an antidote to exactly such human routinization and boredom. For the producers, animal boredom is no more a moral issue than human boredom is for the personnel office. Human labor in the theme park is scheduled to keep wages low and efficiency high; the final reference point for animal labor is the show ratings. If "the show comes to a screeching halt," or if there are too many lulls in the action, the audience will be disappointed. So, Ludwig said, " [W]e try to kind of build segments into shows, and we allow the trainers to decide from a group of behaviors what they are going to do. You've got enough little things that [you can vary], a Head Shake No, or a Tongue Out, [so] that the animal realizes he's got to be paying attention because he never knows when these things are going to happen. We build enough flexibility in, where the trainer can do that at any point they want, or, if they need to skip a section, we build that in as well."[99]

This need for flexibility creates tension between the desire to produce a smooth spectacle and recognition of the limits of the animals. As a result, according to Ludwig,

If you went out and saw our two killer whale shows today you would see two different shows. You would see the same show, it would have the same music, it would have the same dialogue, but the behaviors would not be in the same order that you saw in the last show. [Also, t]hey'd have different killer whales [playing] different parts in the show. So, a lot of variability and flexibility is built into our shows for the animals' sake. That maintains the quality of the show, because even though you may sacrifice a bit of quality because of the occasional inconsistency, it's better than having a great show for a week and then having the animals say, "Aw, that's it, that's it, I'm tired, I'm not going to work." And they shut down for three days.[100]

For the star performers of the core product to go on strike would be disastrous. Where these performers cannot be rotated or replaced, as with the whales, variability is the key to overcoming unpredictability and keeping the show ratings high. In fact, variability and variety are structured in for predictability's sake, not for the animal's sake.

The flexible scripts maintain the illusion of flowing, effortless control, according to Ludwig: "From time to time, a trainer may have to make a call in the middle of a show, because an animal situation necessitated it. We have to believe him, he saw something in the whale's eyes that told him he was going to lose [control of the] whale, so he decided to skip over the next segment. The trainer has that control in the show. And our job is to not let on to the audience that that ever happened."[101]

In some cases, it is just not possible to hide the loss of control. Indeed, when the illusion breaks down, it has to be dealt with. On these occasions, trainers are called on to insert more "educational" facts, figures, and natural history into the show, as a way to fill in time or gloss over uncooperative behavior. The performers in the bird show do this when they resort to lectures on traits of birds to fill in when the show halts. At the killer whale stadium the problem is experienced for similar and different reasons. Sea World keeps only four or five whales in San Diego, and their performance space is also their living space. This interpenetration of stage and backstage means that matings or births or other unanticipated events can play havoc with the show structure. Janet Gotch described how producers dealt with a birth: "I worked at the killer whale show for three or four years as a producer, and we ended up having a baby being born. And right before the birth, the mother decides to shut down. She decides she doesn't want to work anymore, and that is fine. After the birth happens we kind of ignore the show as it is written, and we just go with the fact that we have a beautiful little baby there, nursing with its mother underwater. So we change the show around to emphasize that you are able to watch this."[102]

Although Gotch thought the event was marvelous, Bill Thomas, the vice president for marketing, insisted that show ratings "bomb" when entertainment stops for unavoidable biological events, no matter how skillfully narrated. In this case, there was little choice but to incorporate education into entertainment.

Mistakes Are Made

One of the best solutions to the continual uncertainty of working with animal performers has been to work it into the shows. In this way, control is built out of the lack of control. In fact, the uncontrollability of the controlled animals is an important and stable motif of Sea World entertainment, and the circus theme of nonconformity is written into scripts, so that the audience sees the animals in performance appear to defy their trainers.[103]

I told Bob La Porta that I thought the unpredictability of the killer whale show was a part of its appeal, since it allowed the audience the pleasure of wondering who was really in charge. But he replied that I was overinterpreting. Unpredictability is a "dilemma," but it is not an accident. The whales really are unpredictable, and at first glance their mistakes and defiance look spontaneous. Will the whale follow the command, or will it rebel? In fact, the real unpredictability of the whales mingles with a manufactured uncertainty about what will happen next, and there is an uneasy boundary between spontaneous and crafted uncertainty. La Porta noted,

> There *is* uncertainty in the show, because, you see, we used to write it in. This is the dilemma. If they come from L.A., they come down for the Shamu show, and there's nothing, it's a disappointment. It's terrible, a negative for them. It's not a good experience. And you say all you can: "This is what's going on here, ladies and gentlemen, there's a dominance behavior going on, and the baby is here, and da da da dee da." And that's fine. But the audience is saying, "But I want to *see* something. I want to see Shamu *do* something."
>
> Then, if everything goes perfectly, if we've done our job, the animal hits its mark, the trainers hit their mark, the music, they have seen a terrific show, they applaud—you are right, the best part *always* was when something went wrong. But not for twenty minutes. When something goes wrong, the au-

dience loves it, as long as we can get back on track again. So, we used to put it in.[104]

In La Porta's experience "mistakes" are often made out of real mistakes: "Things that . . . happened in a real situation, we kept. In other words, [it] would happen with a sea lion, where we said, 'You must go *this* way!' [pointing] and he went *that* [other] way, and came out at the wrong time. The audience fell down. We trained it and kept it in."[105]

Here, as often happens at Sea World, the mistake was written in because it helped the human performers look foolish. An inadvertent behavior was trained because it seemed to subvert training and mastery. As Don Ludwig put it, "It's okay if something goes wrong, as long as you keep it light. The audience should laugh at you [the trainer], not at the animal."[106]

Head trainer Mike Scarpuzzi asserts that "you never want unpredictability. It's not safe." But from the producer's point of view unpredictability creates useful emotions. For La Porta, whom I found unusual because he had thought deeply about what the audience wished to see, it was crucial to undermine the appearance of total human domination of the animal. Perhaps the inversion of control is enjoyed not so much for its own sake, he thought, but because it softens the implication of a total human control over the animals, a control that may seem harsh: "In the whale show [it was useful] to make it appear like it was going wrong. Because the audience doesn't want the animal controlled. No one does. Not like puppets, not like marionettes. They want to believe that the animal has a choice, and they truly do! They can walk offstage at any time! And let's all remember that, because it's going to receive the same amount of food at the end of the day, anyway [as if it had performed correctly]. There's no food deprivation at Sea World."[107]

Working uncertainty into the performances was an important way to provide the vision of the animals exercising freedom and choice, within a structure of human control. As La Porta concluded, somewhat oddly: "Let's remember they can leave whenever they want." Of course, he meant that whales and dolphins can refuse to perform. But he unintentionally acknowledged what is in the back of the viewers' minds—that the whales *cannot* swim away wherever they want. This is the other reason why too much detail about training cannot be included in shows: these details would violate the fiction that performance is self-motivated. Indeed, a show itself—the very performance of the killer whales—poses problems for Sea World because it is such clear evidence of human mastery.[108] At best, this recognition can only be softened or suppressed, it can never be eliminated.

Sensing the contradiction, La Porta wanted to experiment with less theatrical modes of displaying the orcas; he proposed "Triad," an exhibit that would allow the audience to casually watch the killer whale swimming and feeding in its tank. Support for the audience's perceptions would be provided by strolling narrators, music, and prerecorded voice-over. Triad was ruled out by HBJ president William Jovanovich as not responsive enough to the audience's desire to see whales "do something" and especially to see trainers in the water with the whales. Along similar lines, La Porta experimented with a sea lion show that had no visible trainers. All commands were given offstage, so that the animals seemed to act entirely on their own, like "a Rube Goldberg machine" or an animated cartoon.[109] More recently, Mike Scarpuzzi spoke of experiments with a sound system that would allow invisible and precise underwater cuing, removing the trainers from the performance so that the whales would seem to leap and splash spontaneously.[110] If Sea World could remove evidence of training and control, it could produce the illusion of complete free will.

Producing entertainment is a complex process of aligning contradictory notions of what the audience wants to see, with the rationale of the attraction. Sea World believes and polls bear out that the audience wants to see trainers interacting and performing with animals; however, the audience does not want to perceive animals as dominated. Therefore, all the animals, but perhaps especially the whales, must be conditioned so that their behavior appears untrained. The fact that captivity makes Sea World's performances possible remains a central, recurring problem for those performances. Maintaining the public image of Sea World's benevolence is a delicate dance. As Ludwig put it, "[T]he animal should never be put in the position of doing anything wrong," so the audience should never be reminded too forcefully of the animal's lack of freedom. He noted again, "This is all about perception."[111]

All the cases and considerations above show the complexity of the work that goes into framing the audience's perceptions, minimizing contradictions, and keeping controversies in the background. This show work takes place on many levels at once, conventionally in texts, sets, and trained behaviors. In recent years, Sea World has added complex computerized sound and video systems to bolster its control of audience perception in performances.

Music is as central to shaping the audience's understanding of performances as it is to the landscape. The entertainment producers use music to help ascribe meaning to motion, firm up timing, and perhaps most important, wordlessly tell the audience in the large stadium how to feel about what they are seeing. This use of music developed in the 1970s, when Bob La Porta's understanding of the ideas and emotions he wished to express in the whale shows coincided with technical developments that made more sophisticated sound tracks possible. As he discovered what could be suggested about "relationship" by the trainers performing in the water, La Porta was also discovering how to knit animal and human movements together with layered musical tracks.

> A major breakthrough came when one of my talented people figured out a way to do the music for the ballet on eight tracks, stereo. We had to buy an eight-track recorder with a mixer, and I had the musicians create the theme for the ballet with beginning, middle, and end, yet construct it so that it could loop. On the first track was the basic theme, on the second was the same theme, measure for measure, but with driving trumpets. The third track was the theme with percussion. The fourth track was the theme played by a music box! So now the music operator could watch the whale ballet, and go from track to track, never missing a beat musically.
>
> When the trainer went up to the killer whale and hugged him, the sound operator just dissolved between track three and four. But the music kept going without a break. And it was electrifying. People were just sucked into it. Because you are not aware of the music, as you should not be, in films or anything else, but it was there. And then, as the trainer came out of the hug, and asked him to swim away and do a jump, the trumpets were right there.[112]

La Porta is describing the tape technology of the 1970s and 1980s. Today the use of computerized compact disks has replaced the spot master, making it even easier to segue, switch, and blend sound without a jolt.[113]

The extent of attention paid to music and its smooth functioning underscores that the whale show is not so much about action or story or conflict as it is about the creation of feelings and emotions. La Porta pointed to feelings: "Feelings, because that is exactly what we were doing. I mean, it wasn't just verbiage. It comes down to how people feel about the animals. That's what Sea World is all about. If Disney is fantasy, Sea World is this feeling of sharing this planet with other species and animals, and the goodness you feel about the way they are cared for, or how much that trainer loves what he's doing or appears to love what he is doing. He's doing something far more fantastical than riding over Peter Pan's village."[114]

Without "feelings" about animals, say the entertainment producers and all the park's managers, how could people learn to care about the animals and what happens to them?

In pursuit of both better visions and homogenized feelings, Sea World's entertainers rely increasingly on video. Especially since producers don't think the audience wants too much educational lecturing from the trainers, a giant-screen system has been added to the Shamu show. Like a sports arena video screen, this Jumbotron can make the live action even more visible to people in the back of the stands. But it is also used to show underwater events paralleling the terrestrial action, and it can seamlessly insert prerecorded and computer-enhanced footage into the ongoing show.

Jumbotron's uses are multiple and overlapping. It is used to divert the audience in a twenty-minute preshow quiz game.[115] It integrates canned footage of the narrator, currently actress Jane Seymour, into the live show; shots of experts talking about killer whales give the audience background information that is not easily delivered "through just talking." The big screen can also help "put the killer back in the killer whale," in Scarpuzzi's phrase, by folding in wildlife film of hunting orcas attacking a basking sea lion. The audience is taken behind the scenes and shown the care of the animals. And the new underwater cameras compensate for the distortion of the heavy glass panels, allowing the six thousand or more people in the stadium to see "what's going on underwater," including the trainers and the whales performing.[116]

Just as important, the giant screen helps make the whale performance smoother and more predictable. Video filler gives the trainers time to reinforce the animals and move them around between show segments. Scarpuzzi thought "the new show's designed so nicely for the animals because the trainers can take the time they want. When people are watching the screen, you can take the time to just rub the animal down and sit with them and get [them] ready for the next behavior that you have to send." Jumbotron also diverts the audience and fills in with prerecorded footage when the whales "shut down" or refuse a command. "We used to have to cover it all the time, y'know, you and the whale out there," he said. Now trainers can be trainers and "not have to worry about entertaining, about saying things and making sure that the lines are covered and that the people are being entertained by *you* the whole time." Indeed, by taking pressure off Scarpuzzi's trainers and whales, the big screen makes real mistakes, shut downs, and refusals less likely. "You can take some time and switch some animals around, give the animals a break and it's better."[117]

The Jumbotron has apparently eased the long-standing conflict over how educational Sea World's killer whale shows should be. Without sacrificing any of the spectacular jumps, splashes, and tail waves, the orca show has been overlaid with powerful visual messages that locate the theme park as a site of science, research, husbandry, and animal care. For example, the births of the baby killer whales are always replayed. While the trainers used to handle the oral delivery of such facts in a way that conflicted with performance, now the significance of the births can be communicated separately. And Jumbotron is television; it gives Sea World another layer of connection to the thoroughly familiar domestic medium and some of its least problematic genres, the quiz show and nature documentary.

At Sea World, much of the process of producing nature as entertainment involves figuring out what the audience already knows and likes, and shaping a kind of nature product—like any other entertainment product—that is just different enough to be received with interest and not different enough to be worrisome. Whether or not such a product is what the audience really would like is another question entirely; as in many other mass media, the theme park managers are not much interested in what the audience might find different. They have, however, developed extensive measures of what the customers will find acceptable. This is not to denigrate the talents and skills of the producers and trainers, which are sometimes impressive, but to emphasize that the demands the theme park's structure places on entertainment result in a version of nature that is a predictable novelty.

Sea World's producers are technicians of a very well defined kind of performance. Because entertainment unfolds inside the time constraints of the theme park, performances must be simple, light, safe, and familiar in their references. These are the ingredients of the acceptable, reproducible entertainment for families that is consonant with the corporate identity. And because shows are so closely connected to spending in the theme park landscape, entertainment must strike no dissonant or troubling notes. Sea World is no place to experiment with new, potentially confusing ways of displaying the killer whale. Rather, all the spectacular animals are standardized core product, and their performances must be based on familiar cultural notions about their species. Performance must make these animals visible, understandable, and content—even while it makes them amazing.

Ironically, of course, the whales stand for Sea World's metaproduct, wild nature, the value that in Western culture is supposed to epitomize the unstandardized and authentic. This definition of nature as transcendent value speaks to the theme park's audience, and it answers corporate demands for profitability as long as it can be produced in reliable and untroubling ways. Nature holds out the promise of unalienated value, and yet, through a contradictory process and with great care, the theme park can reduce the variable, mixed, and unexpected to a precise standard.

The core of predictable novelty is the living, performing animal which embodies the uneven qualities missing from the sets, scripts, and sound tracks that frame it. Despite the theme park's best efforts at turning mystery into an attraction, the performing animal remains a mystery. The formulaic novelty that has been produced all around them is the basic context for the whales, and they are manipulated, both physically and conceptually. At the same time, the killer whale's astonishing body is an irreducibly physical reality. It is what it is, but it is also what its trainers, writers, and audience make it. Perhaps it is this paradox that constitutes the real attraction at Sea World. I will explore in more detail in the next chapter how the most famous performers, the killer whales, are shown and spectacularized.

CHAPTER SIX

Dreaming of Whales

The Shamu Show

The Shamu show is the piece that pulls the entire park together for Anheuser-Busch. This powerful, if sometimes confusing, performance is seen by nearly all Sea World's customers.[1] The Shamu that audiences come to see has multiple parts to play in the theme park and is known in diverse ways. Shamu is a living animal, or rather, a part played by interchangeable trained animals that are the focus of script writing, fabulously expensive care, and detailed monitoring; it is also the park's logo and the registered trademark applied to Sea World's licensed merchandise.[2] And since Shamu is the symbol at the center of Sea World's marketing and advertising and the focus of the park's most sensitive public relations efforts, most customers arrive already knowing the killer whale. A careful look at the Shamu show reveals the peculiar processes by which the living, breathing animal is converted into spectacle and commodity, and it discloses how Shamu—not the killer whale, but the being and mass image created in performance—delivers more than one service to its corporate parent. This whale image not only efficiently communicates Sea World's central messages, it helps transmit Anheuser-Busch's view of nature.

The Shamu show carries an enormous weight. It is also confusing, because on first approach it can seem at once superficial, silly, self-serving, and profound. Indeed, in any given performance, an audience member might react with amazement and delight one moment and embarrassment the next. When I look past its superficiality, the Shamu show becomes devilishly complex to analyze. Of course, all performances are complex, and the Shamu show especially so in both ideological and structural ways. The show is a stream of words, music, actions, and video images that focus on the interactions between whales and trainers, and audiences and performers. Its spoken text is multilayered and indispensable, calling up and working with such deeply resonant and shifting cultural ideas as wildness, family, and freedom. The kinetic work of the trainers and whales both supports and runs parallel to the script; arguably, bodies in motion are here just as powerful and important as words. Another piece of complexity comes from the twenty-minute time frame: in this rapid performance compressed ideas emerge, begin to unfold, and are illustrated, only to be truncated by other, overlapping or contradictory notions. In fleeting words and gestures, the Shamu show rapidly and carefully alludes to the mixed and varied environmental predispositions of its audience; it addresses the crowd and names the particular pleasures and satisfactions it experiences.[3]

To help unpack the Shamu show's structural and ideological complexity, my analysis triangulates between performance, institutional context, and a larger cultural context. Like the performance itself, my descriptions and arguments make reference to what is said and enacted in the stadium, as well as to things done and ideas argued in the wider park and the larger world, including the world of the mass media. The Shamu shows not only take place in the institutional context of the theme park, of course, they are part of broader social and cultural discourses about many things, including animals, nature, and science.

I have tried to give my reading of the Shamu show as much historical depth as possible. For about eight years, I intermittently joined the audience in the bleachers where I watched while making detailed recordings and observations of the shows.[4] Since the Shamu show is revised about once every two years, my field notes and recordings let me trace significant continuities and changes in the ideas the show tries to represent, as well as its structure, style, and texts. (In chapter 5 I have discussed at length some of the reasons for major revisions in the Shamu show.)[5] Any version of the Shamu show is both fixed and changeable: it can be altered slightly on a performance-by-performance basis, according to the needs of the trainers and the pliability of the animals. But despite this potential for revision and flexibility, for the most part the large changes in the show have been gradual. Babies have been born and grown bigger; accidents have disrupted routines and forced script and policy changes; animal and human performers come, learn the routines, and move on. As producers have relied more on prerecorded footage and the video screen, the Shamu shows have become markedly less spontaneous and more predictable. But all these changes are attached to a fairly constant core of ideas about animals and to consistent institutional self-representations. These fundamental ideas and approaches underlie the shifting, varying surface.

The Shamu show is a kind of routinized magic. A first-time audience member is likely to experience it as a seamless whole, a package of music and pictures enveloping a series of impressive jumps by the killer whales. Such seamlessness results from a great deal of thought and work, as I have been at some pains to show in previous chapters. On leaving, the customer may notice an employee filling out an evaluation sheet that deals with all aspects of the performance, from water quality to resolution on the big screen. The customer may also see the trainers making entries in their backstage behavior log. As this continuous monitoring effort reveals, the makers of the Shamu show try to produce a consistent and homogeneous product. But almost in spite of this level of control and attention, the Shamu show is always exciting. Much of the excitement, of course, comes from the physical presence of the whales themselves. But the whales are impossible to separate from the play of contradictory ideas about whales that is the show, and perhaps these contradictions, too, add to the magic. The Shamu show makes available a range of meanings about nature and culture, humans and animals, and just as anything can happen in performance—it is possible that audience members could interpret Shamu in widely differing ways. But as I've argued in chapter 5, a great deal of care goes into creating harmony between the stories the whale can tell and the audience's perceptions, within the framework of Sea World's goals.

The following discussion is based on "Shamu New Visions," the show that opened in early 1992, with some references to "Shamu World Focus," which succeeded it in early 1995, as well as glances back to earlier versions. "New Visions" was a long-playing version of the Shamu performances; "World Focus" is a freshening up of "New Visions." Both shows were intended to be more overtly educative than earlier Shamu shows, and each focuses heavily on science, research, and reproduction. And each deals with race and gender in ways the larger park does not. Sea World's treatments of race and gender are usually only oblique or covert; in the Shamu show, these central cultural facts surface more explicitly than elsewhere, which suggests that they are staple but covert ingredients of commercially produced nature. Finally, "New Visions" and "World Focus" bracket the period of the full incorporation of Sea World into Anheuser-Busch, and they reveal the full effects of the company's infusion of millions of dollars into the park and its performances. Taken together, the two shows fill out the dimensions of Anheuser-Busch's corporate outlook, the usefulness of theme parks for its marketing, and its ideology of nature.

The killer whales perform from two to five times daily (depending on the season) in the Shamu stadium.[6] About twenty minutes before each performance, people begin to gather at the two main entrance ramps to the stadium, held back by a chain barrier and uniformed operations staff. They park their plastic-dolphin strollers along a cement curb and clump between the popcorn- and beer-vending stands and informational exhibit panels. Some people snack, some reload their cameras or reapply sunscreen, some scout for a nearby bathroom as the loud speaker system announces that the show is starting in just a few minutes. For most of these spectators the wait to get in is full of anticipation and is somewhat uncomfortable, since they have left their wanderings through shady knolls and air-conditioned exhibits to gather on the concrete, unprotected from the harsh sky. The waiting-in-line experience Sea World is so anxious to prevent is here unavoidable, but wide-brimmed hats, cold drinks, and the courteous operations staff make it tolerable.

The stadium itself is a wonder and worth a customer's attention. It consists of four deep-blue pools, filled with 5 million gallons of specially treated and filtered reconstituted seawater. The stadium is also the orcas' living space, or more accurately, they live in the "backstage" and perform in front. By craning your neck—or, if you're short, standing on tiptoe,—you can look over the beer concession, shrubs, and a concrete barrier and see dark movement in the water; drawing closer, you can hear the noisy puffs of the whales spouting vapor. For a better view, customers can walk up stairs to glassed-in skywalk galleries and look down on the four pools where three adult orcas and the new baby bask and swim. Their home is a big rectangle—two long, fifteen-foot-deep tanks meet a third, thirty-six-foot-deep tank, placed at a right angle to their western end. This deep third pool is curved and gated—the whales can't enter it at will—and it is bordered by a concrete "beach." At the intersection of the half moon and two rectangles is another, larger concrete stage. At the opposite end of the complex is a fourth, smaller tank, used for medicating, examining, and preparing animals for transport. But this work never takes place before the audience, and any closer access to the idling whales is blocked by architecture and guards. In 1992, a waiting spectator who wished to have his or her picture taken with an orca could find a fiberglass sculpture thoughtfully provided nearby. In 1995, this was replaced by a "Have Your Photo Taken with Shamu" concession. Customers pose next to the glass wall of Shamu's tank.[7]

Abruptly the barrier chain is unsnapped and the crowd can begin to move. It's time to decide, and quickly, where would be best to sit. Seats up close to the clear, raised wall of the curved tank are at a premium; those who've been here before know to sit next to the concrete beach where Shamu will later slide out to pose for snapshots. As the audience fills the stadium, they load and focus video and still cameras; huge numbers of still photographs are taken in the theme park, and the Shamu show is this park's most important photo opportunity.[8] With luck, an orca will be allowed to cruise through the tank before the performance and customers can get a candid. Indeed, sometimes, the orcas are signaled to slide out and bask on the concrete beach before the show starts, and this creates a great bustle of photographic activity. So seats around the slide-out fill up fast. The blue-painted metal benches close to the clear wall are the "soak zone," and it's risky to sit here if you want to stay dry. Teenagers and children old enough to sit alone run up and down the aisles. They are excited about the prospect of getting wet—their parents try to dissuade them. Often, a group splits up, the adults sitting higher up in the bleachers to keep themselves, their toddlers, and expensive cameras dry, the kids down below on the edge of their seats, anticipating being picked to do a trick with Shamu. Vendors race skillfully up and down the steep stairs, hawking iced drinks and bottled water, popcorn and ice cream, captain's hats, Shamu hats, and stuffed Shamu puppets. The thirsty and harassed shell out. Meanwhile, the operations staff keep latecomers moving, spread the crowd out to avoid congestion, and find seats for people at the last minute. They answer questions and give directions, clear the way for the handicapped and find places for video fanatics to unfold their tripods. The stadium permits the audience to aim their cameras down at the performance space or, at eye level, through reinforced Plexiglass windows into the tank. Children and parents walk up to and peer through the glass, into the seamless blue of the tank—hoping for a glimpse.

Sea World is worried that the audience won't have enough to see before the show begins, so the Jumbotron screen dissolves its corporate test pattern, the white, blue, and black Sea World logo, and cranks up the preshow. The preshow is mixed together by the invisible video operator, who cruises the audience *Saturday Night Live*–style, homing in on people who are looking for seats or waving to reunite befuddled family members. The faces of cute babies are frozen, snapshot style. If you look funny (but not handicapped or vulnerable), you may glance up to see your own ridiculous image on the forty-foot-square screen. (This happened to a friend of mine who made the mistake of sporting a beard and a broad-brimmed Tilley hat.) Family photography mixes with whale family photography, courtesy of an underwater camera. Fixed just below the slide-out, it allows the operator to toss up live shots of the whales cruising.

Candid photos are interspersed with quick quiz show segments about killer whales: the participants are displayed on the Jumbotron, with cheers for the winners and rude buzzers for the losers. "How many pounds of fish does a killer whale eat in a day?" Anyone who attends the show more than once realizes that the preshow texts and music are highly standardized and repetitive. Like much of the rest of the park's entertainment, they are closely modeled on television shows and the use of video and sound at mass sporting events. No-smoking messages and cautions about getting wet are folded in with ads for the Summer Nights program, annual membership passes, and the Hubbs–Sea World Marine Research Institute. And the prerecorded montage is a commercial for Sea World and Anheuser-Busch, too, including questions like, "How many Sea World parks are there?" and "Is there more to a Sea World marine family park than just fun?" The preshow uses of the camera are an odd mix: they help create a sense of informality and intimacy, blending the family video album together with mimicked mass entertainment and even familiar modes of video surveillance.[9]

Being in the stadium is an experience of distracted, multidirectional looking. We are looking: at the pool to see a killer whale; around to see what is happening; for a vendor because we're hot and thirsty; at the video to see ourselves caught looking; at the game show unfolding; and through our own camera lenses for potential snapshots or home movies. This multiple, distracted mode of seeing is central to the experience of the upcoming show.[10] On one hand, ever-multiplying vision is of a piece with Sea World's claim to continually show new and unseen things. On the other hand, the use of video is designed to fill in uncertain and undirected moments. Whereas in previous years the audience's attention had time to wander while the stadium filled, Jumbotron and the preshow help make sure that at every moment their hearing and vision have a focus—any focus—from beginning to end.[11] Simultaneously, and in contrast to the feel of movement through the rest of the park, the video camera helps create an odd sense of collectivity. The crowd sees itself on the screen, massed in the bleachers of the stadium. This is one time the crowd of customers is invited to experience itself as an audience, perhaps even a community.

"Shamu New Visions": A Dream of Swimming with Whales[12]

The introduction of momentously stringed and surging music lets us know that the show is about to begin. A male announcer delivers a public service message about the commitment of Sea World and Anheuser-Busch to the environment and how these companies are *"working for a brighter tomorrow."* The goal of all the endeavors we experience today, and especially the Shamu show, is *"to preserve that which has been given to us in trust. . . . At Anheuser-Busch, we realize that if we're to make way for the generations to come, we must preserve what we have."* A gentle female voice tells us that *"Shamu New Visions will begin in approximately three minutes,"* and bids us *"Enjoy the show!"*

For three minutes, the audience continues to settle and scout for vendors, while the music of strings, reeds, chords, and harp arpeggios sparkles and cycles with no discernible beginning or end. Now a vaguely orchestral but definite Shamu theme of several bars is repeated in different octaves and combinations of instruments, from firm horns and cymbals to soaring strings. The audience breaks into applause as four trainers in red-and-black wet suits jog onto the shallow stage. They wave. The stage is decorated with painted wooden totem poles on each side and a set of wooden waves to conceal buckets of fish. The Jumbotron screen flashes "Shamu New Visions."

Behind the stage, on the screen, killer whales are cruising and jumping, making swirls of watery bubbles. Now the bubbles dissolve into a view of frozen land and water, the aerial camera eye zooming in from high above, coming closer and closer to a glacier and, finally, focusing on the silhouetted back of a big man. He turns—it is an enormously parka-clad James Earl Jones, a hulk of red poised against the ice field.

The live trainers stand at attention, while the richly authoritative voice of the electronic Jones booms:

Ah! Alaska! [pause] *Hello, I'm glad you could join me. My name is James Earl Jones and I'm standing here in what's been referred to as God's country—the Great Northwest. Land of simple traditions and ancient legends. For centuries here in this harsh cold world, the Tlingit and Haida tribes have told stories in music and dance of a kindred spirit in the sea.* [Voice-over of soft, faded ritual chanting; the screen cuts from a shot of totem poles to Native American dancers.]

Jones: *Their mightiest totem, greater than the grizzly, greater than the myth of thunder, is* [pause] *the killer whale.*

Enter: an orca, swimming fast around the tank, forcing waves over the sides, to pulsing, rhythmic music.

Jones: *In this awesome giant, the tribesmen beheld the perfect hunter, fast and powerful and fearless.*

Combining incredible strength and agility, these mighty leviathans were not bound to the water.

It seemed almost as if they could fly.

Two whales make enormous leaps at either end of the pool—the audience gasps and cheers. The jumps are also seen on the video screen.

During an interval of rhythmic, Native American–sounding music, the whales return to stage to be stroked and fed. Now, one cruises the pool with its mouth open, displaying its conical teeth.

Jones: *These were relentless predators, with great interlocking teeth designed for ripping and tearing and a tremendous tenacity for killing and eating anything that swims in the sea.* [The screen shows footage of killer whales feeding in the wild, including a famous shot of one grabbing a sea lion in surf. Cutaway before the jaws quite close.]

Jones: *Even today we are awestruck as we witness the fearsome appetite of these majestic animals.* [Feeding footage dissolves to the Shamu logo, rendered in Northwest native style.] *In legend and reality he has earned the name killer whale.*

The whale, mouth open, tail flexed, slides up on the concrete slide-out. The audience cheers and jumps up to take photos. The whale holds the pose for several long seconds, then relaxes its spine and slides back into the water. Applause.

Now James Earl Jones appears on the screen again. He is wearing a suit and tie, and standing in a book-filled museum or library, near antique-looking Native American carvings.

Jones: *A pretty frightening sight for a simple tribesman of a thousand years ago.* [The camera focuses in on the carvings.]

While Jones speaks, the whale is being fed.

Jones: *To conquer their fears they created legends and stories about a killer whale as a friend and brother.*

> *One of the oldest legends is that of a young boy, Natsalane, who was cast out to sea and left to die by his jealous brothers. The story says that the boy carved the first killer whale of yellow cedar and brought him to life. The creature took revenge on the evil brothers and then, with Natsalane riding on his back, he returned the young boy to his village.*

Jones's narration is accompanied by still shots of illustrations of the story, which customers can later find framed in the gift shops.

> Jones: *Just a story?* [close-up of his face twisted into a wry grin] *Perhaps. But from the earliest legends of the past, to the realities of today, each of us shares deep thoughts of a relationship with these wonderful animals. A dream of swimming with the whales.*

Gentle music plays as a male trainer pats a whale and dives in to swim with it. Controlling the animal with a high-pitched whistle and other signals the trainer sits, then stands on its back and waves to the audience. Several times he makes a "How about that!" gesture: one arm on his chest, another extended, palm out, toward the orca. Standing up, he dives off the whale, and gets back on again, making a circuit around the pool. Jumping off again, he is pushed through the water on his back by the whale's snout. The video camera follows these movements, magnifying them on the jumbo screen. Now the music operator segues to a fast, modern version of the theme, a tropical iteration, keying playfulness with the plucked syncopation of synthesized marimbas.

In the middle of the pool now, the trainer inverts himself in the water, and so does the whale. With heads down they simultaneously wave feet and tail flukes at the audience.

Then the trainer positions himself on the orca's snout. He is pushed, as if by the prow of a ship, through the water. James Earl Jones makes a grand introduction, naming the whale for the first time:

> *Ladies and Gentlemen! Shamu, the Killer Whale!*

The trainer is snapped off the whale's snout and pitched back onto the concrete stage. He lands on his feet. Applause. He rewards the whale.

A second, wet-suited trainer with a remote-control microphone attached to his collar has jogged to the center of the large stage. Arms akimbo, and in a voice unfortunately much less impressive than Jones's, he cries: "Well, thank you very much ladies and gentlemen! My name is Jeff, and for twenty-five years now, we've had the privilege of knowing these unique animals, here at the world's foremost facility for killer whale research, study, and play. We're always trying to find new ways of bringing you closer to the Shamu experience. And with this special large-screen video system, we can all get closer to you!"

Shamu is being rewarded with fish. There is a zapping noise: *zzzzttt!* as the camera zooms in, and we see the trainer in extreme close-up.

Jeff [on the screen and live]: Hello out there! And what's more important, we can all get closer to Shamu, not only above the surface of the water but below it as well. These pictures are being taken by special underwater cameras, operated by remote control.

Shamu is directed to swim to the slide-out. The screen shows Shamu approaching and nuzzling the underwater lens.

Jeff: Pretty amazing? You bet! *[pause]* But that's only the beginning. Through the use of the "Shamu New Visions" screen, we can demonstrate the killer whales' excellent eyesight. Right now, Eric and a special guest from our audience will show you how!

Eric, another wet-suited trainer, gestures from the edge of the tank, stage right: "That's right, Jeff! We have Stephanie here from Phoenix, Arizona."

Cheers from the Arizonans in the audience, as the screen shows Stephanie, her name printed below her huge image.

Eric: What we're gonna do is have Stephanie help train the killer whale by giving a signal to the camera, and then see if Shamu can recognize the signal from the screen. *[pause]* So, we're gonna wait till Shamu is paying attention.

The trainer rounds Shamu up and shows Stephanie what to do. She waves to the camera. Shamu appears to regard the Jumbotron screen, rises up out of the water and "waves" back with pectoral fins. We see both Stephanie's wave and Shamu's response on the jumbo screen.

Eric: Fantastic! Okay, let's do one more.

Eric reinforces Shamu with several fish. Eric gets Stephanie to march in place; Shamu watches the Jumbotron and splashes with his flukes.

Eric: He's doing the same thing killer whale–style ! Now, let's see how you do "up close and personal."

Stephanie is asked to kneel down and gesture as if she is splashing water over her head.

Jeff: Audience, count with us! One! Two! Three!

As Stephanie gestures, Shamu spits water in Stephanie's face.

Jeff: Oh boy! How's that water feel? Cold? Yeah, that's why we're wearing wet suits, Stephanie! *[The audience laughs.]*

Stephanie is asked to give Shamu a "rubdown" as a reinforcer. We see this entire process on the big screen.

Eric: Right now you are rewarding Shamu for getting you soaking wet! We'd like to thank you for helping everybody get closer to Shamu, and we'd like to have you be part of our Shamu family album. Look up at that camera that's on top of that building and give everybody a great big wave!

Stephanie looks up, waves, Shamu "waves" pectoral fins, and the trainers wave. The audience laughs.

Eric [gesturing]: Ladies and Gentlemen, Stephanie, our honorary trainer!

As the trainers reinforce the whale and regroup, and Stephanie returns to her seat, the video screen interjects: a screen family tells a warning story about how they got splashed. The Jumbotron shows scenes of Shamu forcing huge waves of water over the Plexiglass sides of the pool. Cascading, rushing music accompanies each shot of a giant wave and close-ups of soaked, screaming children. The announcer says: "Go ahead folks, laugh it up! 'Cause if you're sitting in the lower sections, we've got news for you. You're next!"

Now the camera follows Shamu, and the screen flashes "LIVE! LIVE!"

Shamu circles the stadium pool, jumping, cruising, fluking to push water around, over, and out, onto the cheering, screaming audience. The "splashing" theme is orchestral, crashing, clashing, and spilling. The camera follows the tidal waves, and holds up the splash victims to the larger audience. After a few minutes of this, a trainer returns live to the stage and the screen.

Jeff: Well, we definitely have a whole lot of fun around here, but there's a whole lot more to it than meets the eye. Let's go behind the scenes now and show you what it takes to make a Shamu show possible.

As the trainers move to the side of the pools to reward and stroke the whales, the prerecorded Jones returns to the Jumbotron screen, this time in a hard hat and a lab coat. While he speaks, the Jumbotron cuts away to "backstage" shots of technicians working on blood samples and at computers. The scenes of technicians working are displayed in a mosaic of twelve or sixteen little divisions of the larger screen, suggesting the diversity and complexity of Sea World's operations.

Jones: *When we visit Sea World, we tend to take for granted that Shamu has been provided with a safe and comfortable habitat. Maintaining this environment creates enormous challenges for the marine specialists here at Sea World.* [upbeat music] *Over thirty professionals work behind the scenes everyday to help ensure the well-being of our animals. A full veterinary staff, using the latest in technology, constantly monitors the vital statistics of each individual animal. Animal care experts administer daily nutritional supplements with the two hundred pounds of fish that make up the killer whales' diets. And an experienced staff of animal trainers observe their social interactions as well as stimulate their mental and physical capabilities.*

Fig. 13. Shamu Does a Back Flip, 1987. The Shamu show contains a series of impressive jumps explicitly commanded by the trainer. Courtesy *San Diego Union-Tribune,* photo by Jim Baird.

Technicians are stuffing vitamins into fish, taking notes, filling out forms, patting the orcas.

Now the trainers are back onstage, and a young woman trainer takes over. She is also shown in extreme close-up on the screen.

Female trainer *[unnamed]*: Working with the killer whales is very exciting and challenging, but the most rewarding part of our day doesn't come from what we teach the whales but from what they can teach us. Each day is different, and the best part of each day is play time.

She runs to the east side of the stadium and trots along the edge of the tank. A whale follows her and they play "hide and seek." The camera traces their game, and the musical theme is picked up in gentle music box–style, with reeds, arpeggios of strings, and soft horns.

Then the music shifts to a light jazz-rock version of the Shamu theme, which gets louder as the show operator picks up the pace. The camera follows the trainer in the water as she slips into the tank to take a ride on the whale's pectoral fins. Upright in the water, the whale spins slowly. She demonstrates how the whale makes noises with its blowhole. Hopping up on the slide-out, she offers the orca a fish. Like a spoiled child, it refuses first one, then two fish, with a head shake "no." A bucket of fish gets a head shake "yes" and a laugh from the crowd. Finally she dives back in and is thrust along through the water by the whale's rostrum, her back arched and shoulders back. She lands on the stage, gives a fish to the whale, and remounts to ride back across the water to the slide-out.

The music cycles for several minutes, until the operator segues to a trumpet version of the Shamu theme we heard at the beginning of the show. The female trainer now brings a small girl out of the audience, and as Shamu glides onto the concrete beach, hoists her onto the orca's back. Triumphantly, the trainer announces, "Ladies and gentlemen, this is Christina! Our littlest trainer!" Christina's snapshot is flashed up on the Jumbotron.

The screen cuts back to James Earl Jones, who says, over suspenseful music:

> *On September 26, 1985, Sea World experienced an historic first. The birth of a killer whale. We invite you now to share in that special moment.*

The date flashes in the corner of the screen. The birth canal of a killer whale is shown in close-up, straining. Finally, the whale gives birth, swimming and spinning. Blood stains the water, and a small whale slides out and swims quickly free of its mother's body, up to the surface to breathe. We hear the taped audience cheering and screaming "Yes! Yes! Yeee-hah! Whoopee!"

Jones: *Thus began a successful killer whale–breeding program. To date we have had six new additions to the Sea World family, the latest was right here in San Diego on July 9th, 1991.*

The screen shows another birth, before a screaming, excited audience. The screen flashes "Nursing," and shows the baby orca nursing.

Jones: *Ladies and gentlemen, our own small wonder, Baby Shamu!*

We see underwater footage of baby and mother, who have entered together and swim, circling the tank. People cry, "Take a picture! Take a picture!" and jump up to do just that.

Jones is now wearing a white uniform and standing before a door with a label that reads "Curatorial."

You know, it's one thing to play with a baby, but how do you prepare yourself for an encounter with an eight-thousand-pound Orcinus orca? *The trainers are themselves trained to meet exacting physical and mental requirements. Before they enter the water with Shamu, they must be certain of every move they make.*

Trainers are shown taking tests, marking papers. Then there's a swishing zipping noise, as footage is played in fast-forward. Trainers are performing at high speed, making lots of mistakes, getting bounced off whale noses, dumped on their behinds. Like cartoon characters, they are falling, flipping, log-rolling, slipping, and somersaulting across stage, messing up spectacularly. The music is double time.

Jones [chuckling]: *Well, no one said they were perfect.* [pause] *But when trainer and killer whale are truly in synch, the results can be exhilarating.*

The male trainer enters the water, "log-rolling" on the whale's body as, swimming, it spins. The music turns jazzy and challenging. It is dominated by saxophones and modeled on the *Miami Vice* crime-drama theme music.

Trainer and killer whale perform the show's "payoff" stunts, including nose tosses and rocket rides. The trainer clings to, sits, or stands on the whale's nose, as the whale gathers speed underwater and launches them both far up and into the air, like a rocket. Sometimes the trainer is thrown or dives off, on other rides, man and whale stay close together from launch until reentry. The whale throws its whole body out of the water with enormous force. It is riveting, what most of the audience has been waiting to see, an interspecies aquatic ballet in which the enormous animal's power is highlighted by its precise coordination with the small, frail man in the water. After each "ride," the video reprises the stunt in slow motion. Then the trainer "surfs" on Shamu, waving his arms to achieve balance. Finally, he is tossed back on stage, so hard he slides belly down all the way across its wet, concrete surface. The belly slide is reprised in slow motion, too.

Trainer Eric, with extended arm: "Ladies and gentlemen: Jeff! and Nikina!" Jeff waves, acknowledging the applause, and pats Nikina.

Eric: Well, if you like that, folks, we're gonna go ahead and bring Shamu back out. So focus your cameras right on the center pool, 'cause you're gonna love this!

The Shamu theme is reprised to drums and trumpets as trainer Mike and Shamu perform big jumps, splashing the audience. The video screen alternates between shots of Shamu and trainer, the audience, and underwater views of the rocket ride.

As the trainers reward the whales, the swishing noise signals a cut to prerecorded kids' reactions to Shamu, in close-ups of faces.

Anglo boy actor: *I like the part where Shamu goes "SSSChhhooo."*
Anglo girl: *I love you, Shampoo!*
African-American boy: *I wanna be a trainer someday!*
Anglo boy: *I wanna see Shamu go "Zooom!"*
Group of kids all together as a chorus: *I want to see Shamu jump!*

For the last time, Shamu circles the pool, jumping and landing "Smack!" on its huge side, splashing the kids in the front rows who scream "EEEEEEEE!" when they're hit by the frigid water. All four whales are in the pool now, jumping and splashing in pairs. The Shamu theme is rendered in stirring horns, trumpets, and timpani.

We cut back to Jones, once again in Alaska.

Jones: *From the legendary boy Natsalane* [still shot of the carving], *to the young child of today* [snapshot of Christina on Shamu], *the same dream is shared. Here at Sea World, this dream is guiding us into the future, a future of learning and conservation. This experience has opened*

a whole world of visions for everyone at Sea World, and we hope some of them have touched you in a lasting way. And that you'll join Shamu and all of us again soon for more new visions.
Good-bye!

Jones waves. The trainers wave and exit the stage, carrying their buckets. The screen dissolves into black, white, blue, and pink computer graphics of whales; the sound track returns to circular New Age music. The audience slowly lumbers out, hauling babies and gear. Some linger to look through the thick glass plate at the whales. Screen and sound track reprise the Anheuser-Busch spot about protecting the environment, and the operations staff begins to secure and clean the stadium area.

"Shamu World Focus"

In 1995, I return to watch "Shamu World Focus," a new show that had been installed that year. Some visual changes give the stadium a new feel. The totem poles are gone from the stage, replaced by austere concrete columns framing the Jumbotron screen, and an unprecedented new color scheme has been applied to the show. After becoming so familiar with Sea World's modernist cold blue, sharp black, and clear white, I am startled to see the video screen and the huge speaker bank above it decorated in red, orange, gold, purple, and turquoise. The new colors are warm but dampened by an undertone of gray. They render an abstract, petroglyph design reminiscent of Keith Haring's subway paintings. A man with opened arms and flexed legs, a jumping whale, and a globe repeat in horizontal ranks around the dull black speaker bank and float electronically across the Jumbotron screen. "World Focus" features new theme music, too: a Los Angeles knockoff of world beat, with a hint of polyrhythms, drums, and some indecipherable chants. The new sound track contrasts with the producer's older choices of Vollenweider-esque cycling harps, although at times New Age music segments are still worked into the show. The entire effect of the retheming is to reference a vaguely pan-ethnic and postmodern vision of "one world."

But the structure of the Shamu show remains the same: the large screen video is used for the "preshow quiz," which alternates between prerecorded footage, live and underwater footage, and instant replays of bits of the ongoing action. As in "New Visions," prerecorded messages and educational facts alternate with spectacular jumps live and on-screen, participation by volunteers, and clowning around. The audio and visual styling of "World Focus" gives the show some superficial references to the idea of ethnicity (rather than any specific ethnicity), while the video screen's use to impart information about whales, Sea World, and Anheuser-Busch has been increased. An attractive wet-suited woman, "animal behaviorist" Julie Scardina-Ludwig, narrates detailed taped segments relating facts about killer whales and their training and care at Sea World.[13] Also on tape, the actress Jane Seymour, best known to Americans as the title character in *Dr. Quinn, Medicine Woman,* has bumped James Earl Jones from the celebrity spokesperson slot. Wearing a dull rose-pink sweater with a Sea World logo, Seymour takes the audience on a video tour of the straits of San Juan off the coast of Washington and British Columbia to watch Sea World staff studying and rescuing killer whales in a wild environment, and to Puerto Valdés, on the coast of Argentina, to witness the orcas catching sea lion pups. The killer is definitely back in the killer whale, now ranging the world's oceans.

In the live portions of the show, too, some things have changed. Instead of one trainer exploding out of the water on the snout of a whale, there are usually two: two whales and two trainers—male and female—erupting in unison. This gender symmetry is then broken to invert the usual order of competence. As the woman trainer elegantly completes every challenging toss, dive, and ride, the man messes up over and over again. The audience laughs at trainer Ron as he struggles to complete the tasks his colleague Cindy has mastered completely. He slips, he falls, he trips, he rolls off his whale. Shamu disobeys him, splashes him—and several times—charges him threateningly with open jaws. Lest we miss the contrast between male bumbling and victorious female competence, the trainers choose two volunteers from the audience, a man and a woman. While the woman and the orca Namu complete all the traditional training tasks with ease, the man is teased, disobeyed, spat on, and thoroughly soaked by the whale playing Shamu. When the woman trainer suggests he will have better luck with Namu, this whale humiliates him, too. At the end, he gets the consolation prize of "a big hug" from the uncooperative whale.

These are the important but slim differences between "New Visions," and its "World Focus" revision. The show's superficial connections to "authentic culture" have been redone, shifted from vaguely Northwest-coast Native American to global ethnicity. A famous African-American man, a star of stage, screen, and television, has been exchanged for a less prestigious but also celebrated white and female star of "family" television and film. Women have been given a heightened presence in all parts of the show, and some traditional notions of gender difference—that women are less competent and authoritative than men—have been ostentatiously overthrown. But underneath these changes, the structure of the performance remains fairly constant, as do its sometimes contradictory and enigmatic ideas.

In a short twenty minutes, the Shamu show shifts back and forth between several seemingly opposed ideas about the whale and its relationship to humans. Within this brief frame, the orca is transformed from a piece of elemental nature, a wild and fearsome giant, into a tame and gentle being in coordination with humankind. One moment the killer is gnashing its terrible teeth or shattering the water with a huge breach, the next moment it lies side by side in the water with its tiny trainer and accepts a caress. One moment it is docilely accepting a rub on the nose, the next it is charging its trainer with a wide-open mouth. It is on this ground of contradictory images that the show engages the audience, and the construction of contradictory feelings, their naming and resolution, is one of the principal pleasures in the performance. In the end, not only is the killer whale at times placid and apparently sensitive, it actually seems to give human beings access to their own gentle and tender feelings. The Shamu show aims to call up a spectrum of feelings in the audience, and these emotions are, of course, twisted together with concepts made explicit in performance. The delivery of emotion in the same package with information, and the fusion of sentiment with corporate image, are major effects of the Shamu show.

Fear

Early on, and again and again throughout the performance, the Shamu show aims to create a kind of fear. Indeed, in the first introduction to the live killer whale, Shamu is described as "the perfect hunter, fast, powerful, and fearless" as it speeds along to rhythmic music and forces huge waves over the tank's edge. We are told that the ancient Native Americans respected these "relentless predators."[14] As Shamu does the mouth-open swim and James Earl Jones describes the "great interlocking teeth," the big screen shows the whale attacking a sea lion. The whale's appetite, and the name "killer" are stressed: it is,

Jones says, a "pretty frightening sight." In the "World Focus" show, the producers have tried to make the killer whale even more fearsome by including video footage that shows a whale shaking sea lion pups to death. Shamu's new behavior for 1995 is to charge its trainer and threaten to bite him. If the whale could "roll its terrible eyes," like a Maurice Sendak "wild thing," it would.[15]

Is the audience really afraid, and if so, what is the quality of this fear? It seems that the fear called up in the show's opening segment is half playful and half real, and it goes at least partly unrecognized. On one hand, Shamu is always publicly referred to as a killer whale and rarely as an orca by Sea World; this widely popular name christens it as deadly. Just as relevant, members of the audience bring with them the memories of accidents and deaths that Sea World would just as soon they forgot. In the weeks and months after John Sillick was crushed between two whales colliding in performance, I frequently overheard people in the stands asking each other, "Did he die?" "Isn't this where someone got killed?" or "I wonder if someone will get hurt?" Similarly, after the death of Kandu, audience members queried, "Didn't one of these kill the other one?" or "What was it that happened?" There is no measuring the audience's expectations or background understanding on the basis of overheard comments, but they do suggest that for some customers the Shamu stadium has an aura, a half-recognized shadow hanging over it. On the other hand, much of the explicit information the park offers about the whales—in advertising, billboards, panels, and cartoon-style drawings and product promotions—emphasizes the cuddly version of the killer whale. Perhaps people's reaction to the Shamu show is much the same as Ethel Merman's: they don't know whether they want to hug the whale or cower. The presence of the human trainers in the water gives the show the same ambivalent quality as the trained lion act at the circus or a daredevil stunt: the audience is more than half-aware, perhaps even half-hoping, that something could go violently wrong. It probably won't go wrong, but it has in the past and it *could*. The show's construction of the killer whale as a fearsome and powerful giant is calculated, but the audience's perception has sources outside the show.

But having called up a half-playful fear, the show quickly pushes it into the background by introducing the idea of friendly animal-human relationships, closeness and understanding, perhaps even kinship. In the "New Visions" show, the Native American myth (only a vague provenance is offered) helps mediate this transition and draw the audience closer.[16] On one hand, the powerful whale gives the Native American boy revenge on his kin; on the other, he becomes "a friend and brother." While Jones offers that "each of us shares deep thoughts of a relationship with these wonderful animals," the trainer dives into the water, embodying the dream of swimming with the whales, of entering their own environment and perhaps becoming one of them. Sometimes you can hear a collective intake of breath as the trainer dives to the whale the first time, but that breath is let out with pleasure. As the musical theme shifts to the tropical marimbas, fear recedes and the animal has been transformed into the "wonderful animal" of dreams. The audience is asked to feel dreamy now, to use its awe to find the path to new visions.[17] Then, the trainer gets the whale to seem to imitate his actions, waving feet and flukes, arms and flippers, and nothing scary happens. It is a triumphant moment when the whale throws the trainer forcefully but precisely back onto the stage and he raises his arms, showing us he is unhurt.

This mix of subsiding fear and tender approach undergirds the rest of the emotional propositions that follow in the Shamu show.[18] Closeness to the whale is increased incrementally as the show progresses. One of the ways closeness is created is through vicarious participation, for example, through identification with the trainers who manage the animals.[19] In the show script, the trainers complete the identification and include the audience, so to speak, by using "we" to talk about "how we work" and "how we all feel" about the whales. Indeed, I frequently overheard remarks in the bleachers that reveal this identification: "He's in incredible shape!" or "I'd love to have her job!" or "He's *really* cool." Sea World also creates participation and identification through the use of representatives from the audience, as when the trainer-performers invite members of the audience to become performers themselves, to "help train a killer whale" or "have your picture taken with Shamu." And this feeling of identification can be extended: Not only does acting like a trainer help the audience to identify with the skilled employees, it invites audience members into the privileged circle of the theme park's expertise. By watching one of their own act out training (rather than just feeding or saying "hello"), the audience briefly participates in the expert killer whale care that the video and all the theme park's publicity emphasizes.[20]

On these well worn techniques of engagement and involvement, feelings of connectedness are built. Instead of watching from a distance, we are now tied in, as when we identify with Stephanie, for example, and count "one, two, three" along with her. She's been picked from the audience because she falls more or less in line with the marketing department's imagined average customer: blond, young, female, and like a lot of other customers during the summer, here from out of town.[21] And, in addition to identifying with Stephanie, we're complicit, held in when we laugh at her as she unwittingly commands the whale to spit at her. This same idea is repeated in the show's later version as men, trainer and volunteer, are tricked, disobeyed, and humiliated. Although the producers insist that the whale must never be an object of ridicule, it is positively important that humans be the butts of jokes—and not just so that animals retain dignity while humans lose theirs. Asking the audience to collude by laughing at an unwilling victim helps create commitment to the performance and the ideas it presents.[22]

Participation assimilates the audience into the caring, caretaking relationship that Sea World models between human beings and nature. There is an alternative mode of participation in the show, and interestingly, it appeals to the preteens and teenagers. Getting soaked in the screamy splash zone is one of the few child-directed experiences at Sea World. Significantly, it has no improving, educating value. Being splashed is a form of contact with the whales, but it is cold, slippery, slightly disapproved, and just a little dangerous. Like all carnivalesque activities, getting wet here is marginal: at Sea World, marginality is planned and contained, acknowledged in the video outtakes while at the same time it gives rebellious satisfaction to the young. Festive splashing, focused vision, collaborative laughter: all these modes of engagement at the Shamu show temporarily create for the crowd the sensation of belonging.

The old circus trick of humanizing the animal is one of the main techniques used to relieve half-felt fear, close the distance, and draw the audience in. Humanization is a paradox: it involves using shaped animal behaviors to get animals to act like humans, and so it simultaneously enhances similarities between the human and animals species and emphasizes their differences.[23] The symbolic reduction of the creature's essential foreignness is, of course, the ultimate exercise of domination over the animal, and since it clearly happens at the command of the trainers, it happens with the complicity of other humans, the audience, as well. Although the whales no longer wear hats and sunglasses, and Sea World managers insist that they are doing everything they can to resist "anthropomorphizing" the animals, it is impossible to interpret the orca's waving, marching, copying, or spitting as anything other than part of the long tradition of the playful delineation of species boundaries. While the audience may not understand the basics of operant conditioning or catch all the signals, it is impossible not to be aware that these humanized behaviors are commanded, and that command itself is part of what we are enjoying.[24] Put better, pleasure comes from a multilayered kind of awareness—we laugh as we see the whale douse unsuspecting Stephanie; we chuckle at the whale's impish behavior, even while we are probably aware that the behavior is not impish. Impishness, after all, is spontaneous, improvisatory, and willful. This particular impish spitting, however, is "sent," as the trainers say.[25] Laughter may come partly from awareness of the illusion—or not. But in any case, the orca is now gathered within the image of the human—it is now participating with us, acting like us, copying us, tricking us. As Bob La Porta put it, "[T]he animal is us without worry."[26]

The Shamu show raises the paradox of humanization again when it speaks about communication between whales and humans. Sea World prominently and publicly presents itself as engaged with the issue of how whales communicate, and whether or not humans can communicate with whales. In previous years, trainers showed the audience how they could "speak with baby Shamu," mainly by giving simple hand signals. In other shows, the whales' whines, clicks, and blowhole noises were amplified by a hydrophone, and accordingly, the audience could listen in on "how killer whales communicate." The notion of a potentially shared language (vague as the shows are about this) suggests that the species can move closer together and share a great deal.[27]

The most visible kind of communication displayed in the whale entertainments are the commands from the trainers to the whales and the conditioned responses from the whales. In one sense, the entire show is about the whales' ability and willingness to obey commands. Trainers command or "send" behaviors; whales usually respond, although the audience can see that at times they refuse.[28] We also see the trainers reinforce the killer whales between behaviors, although the video screen tries to distract the audience's vision from this repetitive and time-consuming task. Although the show text talks about "communication" in terms of relationships and feelings, the communicative actions performed are instrumental: a signal leads to the performance of a task or behavior, which leads to a reward from the trainer. Training results in familiar routines, although the behaviors may be startling to the audience. Communication is the flow of command given and received, movements carefully coordinated, and actions directed.

But the spoken text that raises the idea of language conflates command with communication's ability to create connection and community; the mentions of language and communication overlay commanded action with the appearance of sharing and volition. That the whales seem to wish to coordinate and communicate with the humans and take pleasure from doing so is emphasized by two techniques. First, when the whale seems to refuse an inadequate fish ration, for example, we're led to think that it is exercising some choice. Second, when the whale "plays" with the female trainer we are seeing a pantomime of spontaneity and reaching out.[29] The mention of communication in performance tries to create a willing closeness: it seems that whales want to be with us and be like their trainers, to follow the human agenda. The whales, it appears, even understand mediation—one obeys a command given by a human but delivered via TV screen. Does this mean that like us, it understands the translation into a signal of something that happens at a remove?[30] Communication and the ability to communicate are figured as an unalloyed good in American society: the more we have of it, the better off we are. Because we can now communicate with whales, the show implies, because we can create feelings of connection with them, things will only get better. Because we all want to use communication to understand more, there will be progress. Things will get better for whales.

The Shamu show switches back and forth, alternating between creating an incomplete, laughing fear of the terrible beast and a sense of reassurance. Through humanization and communication, oddly, we are reassured that the killer whale is controlled but wild, tamed but not totally dominated. Affectively and literally, we in the audience are looking down on a huge, beautiful animal that can't hurt us. We will be satisfied by this tamed bit of wild nature, and our need to see it "do something" will be met. The mini-tsunamis that crash over the Plexiglas barriers help keep open the door to the uncontrolled, even while training and communication narrow the opening to wildness.

If fear and the relief of fear are the dominant emotional axes of the Shamu show, on this structure other feelings can be built and examined. Indeed, in a way the show is a careful model of benign relationships and benign feelings. The trainers present caring, communicative, tender, and playful relationships between themselves and the orcas, the whales are shown caring for their offspring, and the audience is invited to help care for the orcas, whether by watching them with sympathy, dreaming of swimming with them, participating in their training, or just becoming more environmentally knowledgeable by visiting the nature theme park. Indeed, the audience is congratulated for being so concerned, as in the salutation "Just by being here you're showing that you care!"[31]

One particular kind of relationship is presented for inspection. Family is one of the metathemes of the Shamu show, and in it the feelings of parental, nurturant caring are called up again and again. In fact, like Sea World as a whole, the Shamu show creates a set of overlapping parallels between human families, whale families, and corporate "families." The emphasis on family is more than a pragmatic marketer's reflection of who's out there; it is a way to construct an appeal to the audience. "Family" is referenced in exhibits and programs, such as each spring's "Small Wonders" walking tour of the park's new baby animals (described in chapter 4). Brochures refer to the Anheuser-Busch "family" of parks, and the Sea World "family of corporate sponsors." The uses of candid photography in the preshow, the videos of the births of the whales, and even the title of a previous Shamu show ("Like a Family") overiterate Sea World's definition as a family place. In its advertising, Sea World usually depicts children or parent-child units making contact with marine life, implying that Sea World is a place where families learn together. Sea World identifies itself with the interests of customer families, especially their desires for education and enlightenment and clean and nonconflictual entertainment in a controlled environment. As one producer put it, families go to Sea World out of "a little bit of guilt," out of a sense that they need to provide their children with a rational recreation, and have them end up "a little enlightened."[32] Since the Shamu show is the central performance at the park, it sums up this process of enlightenment, connecting families and children with the theme park version of the important values of education, science, and rationality. The argument repeated in all these channels is that by being at Sea World, we are doing family and being family in a valuable and responsible way.

The repeated references to family and parenthood also help build parallels between the theme park's corporate parent and its audience. For example, most of the images of family are built around mothers, babies, and reproduction. In fact, reproduction is the main meaning of family at Sea World, and not least in the Shamu show. Indeed since the live births in 1988 and 1991, the most important family units on display have been the killer whale mothers and babies. In turn, the arrival of the baby prompted the revision of shows to stress maternity and reproduction, as narrators made much of the "newest addition," announcing that "the waiting is over" after twenty-five years and saluting "a time of new beginnings."[33] In the earliest of these shows, the whale mother was asked by trainers to introduce her baby to the audience: this she seemed to agree to do, like proud mothers everywhere, nodding her head and circling the stadium pool with the baby. In short, the whale baby provided a variety of ways to make parallels between the whale dyad and parents and children in the audience. By extension, the theme park itself was personalized and likened to a family that had anxiously awaited a baby.[34] Now, with the addition of video, this overlapping identification of audience families with the whale family and theme park family has become continuous and permanent, as each audience can be vicariously present at the birth. The argument that Sea World is a family that makes families whole through captive reproduction combines effortlessly with the construction of the audience as families, and Sea World as a place to be family, until Sea World's families and our families are together in this caring, family place. Whether or not the Shamu show can actually deliver all this unity and identity, the repeated references to family pull the interests and desires of the audience into congruence with the theme park's. Put another way, referring to family and the vulnerable feelings of parenthood are important ways of constructing the unified "we" that Sea World builds between its audience and itself.

The Shamu show's stories about the birth of the baby orca connect family powerfully to the whole park's motif of research and science. The appearance of Baby Shamu as a performer not only opens up the theme of family, it underscores the importance of research. Sea World has placed great public emphasis on its captive-breeding program. As is the case with the California condors (located in San Diego at the Zoological Society's Wild Animal Park) and the giant pandas (at the San Diego Zoo), efforts at species preservation through captive breeding have been portrayed as science's most important environmental effort and intervention.[35] In the case of the orcas (which, the "World Focus" show reminds us, are not listed as endangered) and the pandas and condors (both of which are), the efforts of the scientists to assist or affect the reproductive process has become a routinized or conventional story in the mass media, a story that can be written as either tragic or heroic. In such stories, the valiant efforts of dedicated scientists to help (or induce) rare and vulnerable animals to reproduce are spun out over days and weeks. The story results in the tragic loss of a precious baby and the resolve to keep trying, or, alternatively, in a miraculous victory. Perhaps not incidentally, this formulaic news story parallels similar recurrent news stories about human couples struggling with fertility problems. The Shamu babies provide the heroic variant, and fortuitously for Sea World of California, two have been born with the video cameras rolling. In either version, one important pole of the story is the selfless passion of the questing scientists, battling against the odds, as the newscasters like to say. At Sea World, the other pole is the cheering, ecstatic audience screaming its approval of the achievement. The baby orca's life and presence are a celebration of the victory of captivity in the name of progress, of research and benevolent science battling for the family.[36]

The narrative of science, technology, and research in the theme park is one of the main contexts for the Shamu show. In the show itself, human knowledge of the whales evolves from the terrain from the primitive, whether origin myth or pounding drums, and moves toward the ultramodern world of Julie Scardina-Ludwig, the professional animal behaviorist and her white-coated technician colleagues. Even if the Jumbotron screen were not there to efficiently represent the behind-the-scenes work, research as the context for the whale performance is inescapable, a backgrounded but ever present story in the larger park.[37] The display boards near the Shamu stadium, and the stadium's carefully visible "backstage," where trainers may be seen handling, feeding, and making notations about the orcas after the show; the observation deck and the uniform-like wet suits of the trainers; the guided tours and the prerecorded sound track narrations of exhibits: all these foreground the realms of science and research.[38] This determining background is drawn on and underscored in the stadium.

But very careful limits are placed on science. The screen asks such questions as "How many teeth do you think Shamu has?" "How much do you think a fully grown killer whale weighs?" "What can eat a healthy adult killer whale?" "In which oceans are killer whales found?" and "Is a killer whale a mammal or a fish?" These brief natural history facts take the form of allusions to science, rather than explore any ecological or scientific issue.[39] Some slight mentions of evolutionary history could be found in past scripts. For instance, one show mentioned the fact that whales developed from an archaic land mammal and so retain the nub of a digit in the pectoral fin. By the time of "Shamu New Visions," these vestigial mentions had been selected out, since Sea World now scrupulously avoids any mention of evolutionary theory in its education or entertainment programs. Where some kind of evolutionary process must be noted (for example, in explanation of why a whale's breathing hole is at the top of the head, rather than the front), the term "adapted" is always substituted for "evolved."[40] Brief and shallow but extraordinarily full of resonance, Sea World's images of science are myths in the sense of images to which we feel a habitual allegiance. Their effect comes in part through their omnipresence rather than any specific informational content that they convey.[41] The message is: science is powerful and good; with it, we will breed and care for these animals, and that in itself is a good thing to do.

The reproducing whale, as well as the whale as an object of research, is at the center of this mythology, and the theme park is figured as an embodiment of scientific progress, "the world's foremost killer whale research facility." As a phrase repeated in Shamu shows over the years has it: "Here at Sea World we are learning more and more about killer whales everyday."

The Shamu show focuses and intensifies the image of the park as a place of science, and mentioning science is a direct address to the audience. It helps draw them to the theme park from among the crowds at the beaches, state parks, zoos, and museums. This audience is at least partly, if ambivalently, satisfied to know that it has consumed an improving entertainment and taken part as spectator in the progress toward knowledge. There is pleasure in closeness to this kind of progress, this growing understanding—and pleasure in the congruence of one's own learning family to the world of science. The whale is one medium through which this pleasure is found. In effect, the image of science helps create and recreate the audience for the show and customers for the theme park, helping them understand themselves as, in one producer's words, "a little knowledgeable," as having done something positive and progressive for their children and for nature.[42] The marriage of science and the whale does this especially effectively: by connecting feelings of caring for the whale to research, science is converted from an intimidating and authoritative force into a kind of feeling work; and again, Shamu is the medium for this transformation.

What Is Shamu?

The emotions and ideas the Shamu show invokes are contradictory, overlapping, and circular, and I have argued that the show asks the audience to identify with the killer whale in more than one way. But what, specifically, is this multifaceted creature at the show's center?

Shamu the image is a very odd thing. In Shamu, imaginings of the freedom and power of wildness merge with the recognition that the whale is not only captive but a commodity. The celebrity–licensed-image killer whale is inextricable from the context that presents it, an environment dense with commercial imagery. At the same time that the audience focuses on the amazing animal, they are well aware that as a registered trademark, the orca is circulating everywhere: outside the park on billboards, blimps, brochures, tourist promotional magazines, and in the merchandising cross-promotions of park sponsors; inside the park on souvenirs from stuffed whales to beer steins, postcards, hats, T-shirts, posters, bumper stickers, and key chains.[43] All these mediations simultaneously sacralize and trivialize Shamu: the whale is simultaneously a transcendent being and a souvenir. Indeed, it is a question of whether the living animal or the mass image has a greater reality. In the performance there are living, spouting killer whales, whales of myth, whales of video and animation, whales as objects of various kinds of human attention, and whales for our emotions. These multiple whales create the contradictory dimensions of Shamu. Even while the show's script tells us that we are having an authentic, direct "up close and personal" experience, the performance relies heavily on all these other whales to make our experience more real. Which whale is it we are watching? What is it we are having feelings about?

Shamu certainly has a cultural provenance, if only a vague one. Its origins are based, in part, on a connection between killer whales and primitive, pre-European native peoples. Neither clearly male nor definitively female, the name Shamu itself speaks of the realm of the primitive, seemingly part of some unspecified non-European culture, although a name itself is, of course, evidence of culture.[44] The "New Visions" video specifically inserts Shamu into the Native American culture of the Pacific Northwest, with which orcas are linked touristically, geographically, and, as the video emphasizes, mythically. (Although "World Focus" drops the specificity of the origin myth and shows the killer whales at large in the world's oceans, it keeps the whales firmly in the realm of the generic primitive.) Here the Shamu show follows a long tradition of identifying captive wild animals with native peoples, in these cases either Native Americans or the more general third world.[45] Appearing in different ways in each of the shows is the same idea, rethemed as needed: the killer whale is both cultural and outside civilization, it is wild but domestically savage.

If Shamu has a vague cultural connection, what of gender? Perhaps the question is less whether Shamu has a gender than how the performance works with gender. In performance, Shamu seems to have if not an ambiguous, then a very flexible gender identity. On one hand the gender of any individual Shamu in performance is vague: trainers in performance don't emphasize the lead whale's sex, and it is not easy for the uninitiated in the audience to figure this out at a glance.[46] The first "Shamu" brought to Sea World was female, but Bob La Porta, the producer who helped create the character, thought of the whale as "him," and in the past the trademark character was distinctly male.[47] But since the late 1980s and early 1990s, with the development of shows emphasizing the whales as family groups, Shamu's gender has become less clear-cut. The strong implication remains that the fierce and mighty Shamu is male, but this alternates with the possibility that the tender and delicate Shamu is perhaps female. Certainly the video footage of births and the emphasis on captive reproduction and care tend to focus the show on maternity and what are supposedly female instincts. And as feminist critics would point out, this focus on fertility and reproduction fits tidily with the identification of the killer whale with primitive peoples. Since women have been traditionally and repetitively associated with either wild nature or tamed nature's fecund possibilities, culture, the primitive, and reproduction are here all of a piece.[48]

But while the Shamu show's emphasis on stereotypically female human traits fits with and extends the logic of familiar cultural narratives, it is also an attempt to address the women in the audience. Indeed, looked at from the perspective of marketing, "New Visions" and "World Focus" suggest that the park's managers imagine their audience as predominantly female and the average Sea World customer as a female parent with children. As the Shamu show invokes the supposedly feminine qualities of feeling, as it takes up the stereotypically female concerns with family, care, and nurturance, so the show has gradually over the years made more room for the female trainers. In the past men were almost always the central narrators and they performed the most spectacular parts of the act. In "World Focus" women have a nearly dominant role. For example, in 1995 shows the first trainer rocketed out of the water was often female (her wide-eyed face repeated on the big screen), and as we have seen, the script has her perform with superior competence while her male counterpart makes a complete fool of himself.[49] And Julie Scardina-Ludwig takes the role of the narrator who relates facts, figures, and Sea World's research and science activities. If we consider Jane Seymour's narration along with the prominence of the female trainers-performers-scientists, it is clear that the show has been progressively fem-

Fig. 14. Animal Behaviorist Julie Scardina-Ludwig Works with a Newly Arrived Orca, 1994. Women trainers play an increasingly important role in the Shamu show, as the show's scripts seem to speak to women in the audience. Courtesy *San Diego Union-Tribune,* photo by Nelvin Cepeda.

inized, with women inserted as fictional doctors and actual narrators, knowledgeable behaviorists and powerful athletes. This gender shift has been incremental over a long time, but now that it is accomplished, it is solid.

It seems especially telling that James Earl Jones, the African-American narrator of "New Visions," has been replaced in "World Focus" by the actress and model Jane Seymour.[50] Best known to American audiences from a Sunday night prime-time television show, Jane Seymour is a white, family entertainment icon. She plays a vigorous, intelligent, and chaste frontier doctor in a show that stresses community, healing, and caring and has little overt violence. In short, she is a positive female role model from what's seen as safe television for children. The shifting "primitive" theme, the interchangeability of the black celebrity and the white female authority show that although race and gender find little explicit place in the rest of the theme park, in fact can barely be detected there, they are central to the meanings Sea World constructs around the whale. Perhaps race and gender in any particular killer whale show matter less than the fact that Shamu must, somehow, be connected to femininity and racial difference. When Jones is replaced by Seymour and the totem poles vanish, Shamu doesn't lose ethnicity and connection to the primitive and nonwhite world. Rather, these fleeting references to women and nonwhites help construct a stance for the theme park and its audience. Like world beat music and the animated petroglyphs, references to race and a new construction of the female are there to speak to the largely white audience of difference, of change, of multiculturalism and progress, within the carefully controlled theme park definition and frame. Difference is carefully arranged—against a field of white, so to speak—so that, unthreatening, it can be incorporated.

Against a background of alternating associations, the meanings of Shamu are built up. Throughout the show, the audience is subtly asked to confront the question of the whale's essential nature. What is it? It is animal and humanlike, wild and tame, threatening and gentle, primitive and tied in with progressive science, obedient and rebellious, female and male. The image of the killer whale slides back and forth across these contradictory grounds to make meanings for Shamu.

Finally, the way Bob La Porta saw his work seems true today, too. The central story of the Shamu show is the story of relationships: between whales and humans, between humans and nature. One of the uses of references to culture and racial difference is to place Shamu in a universal cultural tradition. In "New Visions," the Native American connections, signaled at once by the mock totem pole set and underscored in the video by the dances, carvings, and discussions of myth, argue that orcas and humans go way back. In fact, the Tlingit and Haida claimed their ancestors carved the whales into existence. A continuity is thus established for the interaction between humans and orcas, a long continuous tradition of dreaming about and wishing for interspecies contact and communication. In the Shamu show, this ongoing wish for a relationship follows two paths, the spiritual and the scientific. In each case, the end point of the journey through tradition is Sea World and Anheuser-Busch.

On the spiritual path, "New Visions" suggests that the audience is like the Tlingit or Haida, in search of communion with animals. By making connections to Native American culture, Sea World inserts itself into a stream of spiritual communication between animals and humans.[51] This longing of the civilized for the primitive is commonplace in American culture, and this mystical version of it has surfaced in earlier Sea World shows. For example, in the 1989 Shamu show a trainer's speech compared Sea World's research with space exploration, and the killer whales to extraterrestrial beings: "It's been said that space is the final frontier. If this is true, then the current frontier must certainly be the oceans of our own planet. Now with the birth of Baby Shamu and her cousins in Florida and Texas, we have been given an incredible opportunity at interspecies communication. Some people feel that before we ever speak to animals and creatures from outer space, we might be able to speak or communicate with animals of the sea. Dolphins, whales, maybe even Baby Shamu!"

As in much other American entertainment, this version of the Shamu show asked the audience to imagine themselves as explorers, and it called up the familiar idea that American society continually progresses outward in search of new spaces to occupy. This is a reference to a broader cultural science fantasy: since the continent is used up and so, increasingly, is the environment, inventive Americans could start new high-tech colonies—somewhere out there. At the same time, the fantasy of interspecies communication and exploration hooks back into another idea familiar to the affluent middle class: that the process of movement is now inward rather than outward, a therapeutic (rather than chemical) process of expanding consciousness. One door to the new frontier inside is the animal world, real or imagined. In the variants of so-called New Age philosophy, the oceans and cetaceans figure not only as material resources, but as channels of what New Age practitioners call "energy" and "awareness." Dolphins and whales are literally the mind in the waters, as John Lilly and Joan McIntyre speculated in the 1960s—conduits to and embodiments of higher consciousness.[52] Cetaceans connect humans to a "more aware" way of being. This mention of the search for contact fits with the popular enthusiasms for dolphins and whales as spiritual healers and sources of energy, as many popular therapies, fads, and Sea World's own "touch the dolphins" attractions attest. It helps obliquely link the Shamu show to ideas found in the widely diffused and varied philosophies called "New Age."[53]

Sea World thus offers "an incredible opportunity" not only for contact with marine mammals, but perhaps for transcendence. In the Shamu show this is a brief reference, and the sort of transcendence is unclear, but the trainers' mentions of outward movement, nationhood, and hopes bordering on the religious make this fleeting moment a central point in the construction of meanings around the whale. In this emphasis, if orcas are "a kindred spirit in the sea," it is also possible that they are not just a parallel consciousness, but greater than humans. Perhaps they are animal gods or beings with access to a less visible reality. Perhaps whales and dolphins are more human than we, but, finally, Sea World doesn't say. Like the themes of family and science, the theme of spiritual exploration is clipped and beckoning, universalized but covert.

A second, more dominant meaning of the interspecies contact called up by the Shamu show is science. In the 1992 show, James Earl Jones speaks of "the dream of a kindred spirit in the water," "a dream guiding us into the future," of a "whole world of visions" opening up. Contact and communion with the whales will bring us whole new perceptions, "a future of learning and conservation" based on scientific knowledge. Throughout the show, the big screen and voice-overs have presented the audience with multiple images of Sea World's scientific expertise, its research on and high-tech care for the whales. The connection between science, expertise, and caring for animals is repeated in all the park's materials: the park map features a blurb asserting that "your visit today makes possible our . . . programs," and an earlier version of the Shamu show advised, "Just by being here, you're showing that you care."[54] Whether the interspecies connection is made by paying admissions, making a donation to the Hubbs–Sea World Research Institute, or by watching the show, Sea World offers a participatory spectatorship in science, a way the audience can "make contact." Science and research are part of the "shared dream," the door opening to the future.

Finally the Shamu show is inseparable from the context that produces it, the corporate theme park. What is the relationship between the killer whale and its parent? Since Sea World is a public relations venue for Anheuser-Busch, one that stresses the company's social responsibility, conservation-mindedness, and environment-friendliness, there is a tight connection between the killer whale and the giant brewer that literally makes the whale's life in captivity possible. But Shamu creates feelings and dispenses an image for something larger than Anheuser-Busch. The

Fig. 15. Close Contact, 1987. Warm feelings, intimacy, and communication between killer whales and people are central themes of the Shamu show, suggesting that the corporate owner makes transcendent understanding possible. The Sea World logo is in the background. Courtesy *San Diego Union-Tribune,* photo by Tammy Ljungblad.

whale stands for something so central that it cannot be turned too obviously into a trademark the way the Clydesdale horses, for example, can stand for Budweiser and breweries. The celebrity whale helps convey a set of ideas more expansive than the particular interests of the theme park and its owners. The killer whale represents a general view of the natural world, one written from the perspective of corporate interests generally, and presented in such a value-free and universal way that the audience can engage and identify with it.[55]

This nature is built up out of wildness, but wildness is tamed and locked firmly inside the benevolent paddock of science and research. And the farm is being run by private business explicitly in the interest of preserving natural resources. For example, as billboards around the old dolphin pool told visitors, research on how to harvest fish without killing dolphins is being conducted by Sea World in conjunction with the tuna industry. At Sea World scientific research as an activity is located socially nowhere; it takes place for the purpose of developing techniques of rational exploitation in the service of private enterprise. Rational exploitation is supported by conservation. The park saves beached animals to see what they can tell us about blood diseases; studies of diving seals will help us help submarine crews; the resources of the ocean and Antarctica are charted so that they may be harvested in a more orderly fashion to feed a generalized population called "mankind."[56] This kind of universalized rhetoric is very familiar—from the industry pavilions of Walt Disney World to television specials on science and industry. There is no discussion of who will be exploiting resources, in whose interests, or toward what goal. This same myth of benign research floats through the Shamu show as well—in the construction of the whale trainers as scientists, in the attention to captive reproduction as a mode of knowledge, in the assertion that Sea World is unlocking the secrets of cetacean communication. Research seems to proceed mutually and voluntarily, as in the repeated statements about what we are teaching Shamu and what Shamu is teaching us.

At Sea World, nature and the human world are finally, firmly separate. "Nature" is "out there"—distant, deep, far away, and frozen until research steps in. Research puts a gentle face on the human penetration and control of nature, and conversely, human penetration of the natural world and environment can be seen only as rational investigation. Gone is the older Western notion of nature as howling wilderness, as threat to humankind, as potent force to be vanquished. Gone too are the intimate but brutal old relationships of agriculture, where animals were both sources of power and protein.[57] Gone, but not forgotten. Now that fear has been conquered, animals and the marine environment are figured as "our resources," as holding benevolent secrets which will eventually yield to patient efforts at decryption.

Behind the notion of "our resources" is the argument that nature should now be managed by experts, and this view is now global, not local or national. Some of the old sting of racism, ethnocentrism, and North American superiority has disappeared, to be replaced by a hazy vision of a new world order guided by experts and technicians. Research is a benign tool of this managing project, the theme park is its working model, and the beneficiaries are a loosely defined "us": Anheuser-Busch, Sea World, and the audience, acting together. This concerted, coordinated harmonious action is one of the basic structures of the Shamu show, and one of its explicit themes. But at Sea World, research is never a tool of unrestrained extraction, a producer of polluting technologies, a means of developing more efficient exploitation and expanded consumption. Science never goes off the tracks to build dams or nuclear power plants or develop eugenics projects. At Sea World pollution and extinction and endangerment are only obliquely mentioned; when they are, they come up as problems that more research will solve. They have no discernible social locations or causes. Nature itself is remote and decontextualized. It is simply an object for pity and consumption.

Here Shamu has a very important and complex part to play. The orca is a humanizable, huggable, consumable part of the great power we call nature, a bit of the nonhuman world we can both love and compare ourselves to. We can participate as an audience in its management. As a member of the highly celebrated order of whales, Shamu also draws sentiment and emotion. As a spectacular animal, Shamu's protection through careful, corporate husbandry, elaborate technology, and thoughtful research can come to model the protection of all nature. But first Shamu must be made into something very close to human, and then into something much less than human, in order that we might feel both powerful and benevolent. As Yi-Fu Tuan has written, dominance and affection go hand in hand.[58]

Finally, the work of creating feelings and relationships interlocks with the task of helping the audience understand their own relationship to Sea World and its corporate parent. In the process of loving and taming, investigating and breeding, Shamu becomes a mediator between the audience, Anheuser-Busch, and the larger corporate world. These multinational economic actors must indeed have our best interests at heart if they care so much about the killer whale. And here at Sea World, in their own domain, we the audience learn to love them, as we learn to see the mighty beast as the tame prankster who will kiss a little girl. Through Shamu's apparent free will, playful rebellions, and final cooperation we learn that the real nature of being in the world is to cooperate and conform. Nature is separate from our world but it exists in harmony with private enterprise. Wildness itself is really obedient. It is obedient to human beings, and it is cheerful in the face of research, and it is, after all, not as vulnerable as we feared, for it presents itself as willing to be managed.

Perhaps, though, the Shamu show draws some of it strength and popularity from an opposite set of understandings. Seeing the body of the orca, seeing its size, physical power, and undeniable beauty—the audience may also thrill in the possibility that this time, maybe, Shamu won't or can't be managed. The possibility that the whale will prove unmanageable is very real, because accidents and injuries are fresh in the minds of many in the audience, and because new reports of accidents, mishaps, and catastrophes cluster around the killer whale by virtue of its celebrity. It may be that at some level the audience watches in hopes that just this one time . . .

Yet most of the time, in most shows, there are no accidents and few real disruptions of order. Disasters are rare, and controllable violations of conformity are written into the performance. In other words, what hopes there may be for rebellion are satisfied by small mistakes and resistances, and the show moves toward its conclusion. As a spectacular animal, Shamu is fearsome and gentle, it rebels and conforms. Similarly, through the Shamu show, Sea World and Anheuser-Busch propose the corporate view of nature in the specific context of contemporary public awareness of ecological threat and disaster. At least for the duration of the show, conflicted understandings are resolved.[59] The actors from whom the audience might have feared the most for the future of their world—oil companies, agribusiness, chemical manufacturers, banks, even scientists themselves—have lined up to tell us that their immeasurable riches and skills are at the disposal of the killer whale and all who love it. All we have to do is accept their definition of our world and their work.

Conclusion

I returned to Sea World for follow-up fieldwork several times during fall 1995. By this time, I had spent so much time there and thought so long about its landscapes, performances, and educational products that each visit seemed harder than the last. This was, in part, the normal exhaustion that comes with winding up a long project. But as I thought about it, I realized I felt not just weary but overwhelmed by the very aspects of Sea World I had been trying to describe and explain. On one hand, following the logic of the attraction, the theme park kept revising itself. Something was always under construction, and Anheuser-Busch's enormous financial resources meant that each new variation on Sea World's core ideas was expensive and elaborate. The old Cap'n Kid's World activity area has been replaced by Shamu's Happy Harbor—a multistory, wet and dry, postmodern, tropical-colored playland that is wildly popular with children. Similarly, the Shamu Stadium is being expanded into an even more complex site for whale viewing. A Shamu Backstage habitat gives customers close-up, underwater views of the orcas in a seventy-foot-long viewing gallery. Shamu Backstage promises customers a chance to "interact" by playing hide-and-seek with the whales or taking part in "feeding, play, husbandry and training sessions. . . ." And almost unbelievably, the backstage also features a beachlike controlled-contact area where customers can wade into the water and touch a killer whale.[1]

While Sea World generates grand new exhibits based on its traditional patterns, it improvises ways to make the old landscape richer and denser. Interactive programs, inexpensive, flexible ways to generate revenue are

Fig. 16. Dolphin Encounter. In 1995, Sea World extended its emphasis on selling interspecies communication when it opened its own wade-with-the-dolphins program at Rocky Point Preserve. Customers pay extra to don a wet suit and make contact. Courtesy *San Diego Union-Tribune,* photo by Don Kohlbauer.

being nestled around the existing animal shows and petting pools. In November 1995, Sea World inaugurated a "wade with the dolphins" experience in which, for an extra $120, customers receive ninety minutes of instruction and then slip into a wet suit for twenty minutes of communion. "It borders on a religious experience," said one dolphin-hugger.[2] Similarly, the pleasures of contact can be overlaid with instruction for families who order a catered, poolside "Dinner with Shamu" and the trainers at Shamu Stadium.[3] And the living landscape is yet again being replanted to make the flatter, eastern area of the park more inviting. Raised beds filled with palms, pines, shrubs, and fashionable perennials give this part of Sea World the up-to-date and privileged feel of an Orange County mall.[4] And speaking of malls, souvenir novelties have been multiplied. There is a photo service for people who want their portraits taken with Shamu, and the gift shops display expensive Northwest Native American–styled crafts, infusing the corporate setting with authenticity. Sea World and Anheuser-Busch pack formulaic diversity into the theme park frame with such intensity that I was forced to realize that no one person could keep up with its institutional creativity, at least not for long.

The scale of the changes in the park reminded me of my initial impressions of Sea World. Eight years earlier when I had begun exploring it closely, the park sometimes seemed incoherent to me. I found it fun to work there because while I could see the physical and rhetorical ways its landscape and shows succeeded, I could also see the ways they failed. For every lounge chair artfully placed to help the harried feel at home, there was a bed of red, white, and blue petunias that clashed absurdly with the underwater environment theme. Landscape architect Anne Spirn had commented on this incoherence, suggesting that "perhaps Sea World is just a collection of things people said they like, identified through market research."[5] True enough, and up until recently, the park's landscape showed its uneven, collated history. Different owners had each given it their stamp.

But now I thought that some of that earlier clumsiness was probably only a stumble on the path to success, missteps made worse when beleaguered Harcourt Brace Jovanovich milked the park of cash. Since 1989, Anheuser-Busch has poured tens of millions of dollars back into Sea World of California alone—and it shows. In its command of the details of landscape, the theme park has become more overbearingly persuasive, more beautiful and likable. Its efforts to shape perceptions and feelings work, at least a lot of the time. If the park juxtaposes animals, artifacts, and performances in sometimes clashing ways, still, overall, Sea World is a manicured and convincing institution. In fact, as it moves toward the year 2000, what Sea World has is authority. Once inside the park, I found it harder than before to imagine an alternative to it. It was hard to imagine a different San Diego landscape, the rest of Mission Bay, another kind of park—another way of looking at animals and thinking about environments. I came home from one of these visits and scribbled in my field journal, "They won!"

What did it mean to say "They won"? That the theme park is an authoritative institution, performs a public role, and offers credible shapes of nature and glimpses of the future—these premises Sea World is anxious to have its customers share. But have theme parks really succeeded in displacing older public spaces, in making everything outside themselves irrelevant? If Disneyland and shopping malls provide literal models for cities and communities, if they are the simulacra America aspires to become, is it possible that theme parks provide models for the future of nature? This suggestion is usually made in jest. Could places like Sea World come to typify our contact with nature better than walks on the beach, hikes in the hills, or struggles with the garden? And if theme parks do become our commonsense models for nature, should we care?

In a recent op-ed piece in the *New York Times,* Jennifer Whitaker, an environmental policy analyst, makes a satirical case for theme park nature. She writes that with free market ideologues threatening to erode environmental regulations and protections, the commodification of everything is at hand, including the commodification of the seemingly absolute values of wilderness and nature. "Even though the Contract with America establishes the primacy of property values of nature," she writes, environmentalists should cheer up. "If we trash the real world, there will be big bucks in environmental theme parks." Since "the biosphere doesn't stand a chance against the market . . . [a]s habitats and species disappear, we can reinvent them as entertainment." If nature was once boring or incomprehensible, repackaging will make it compelling. Themes will be varied and diverse, interactive technologies will allow customers to touch and participate, and virtual reality will collapse great distances. "Moreover," Whitaker claims, "most people will get a lot more education out of the bio-world experience than they ever did out of nature in the raw. The very fact that they are paying for it will make them pay attention to what they are getting."[6]

As we have seen, Whitaker's modest proposal already exists fully formed at places like Sea World. Without irony, this theme park seriously offers nature in the very promotional terms Whitaker borrows to mock the anti-environmentalists and deregulators. Sea World's managers talk explicitly about their whale shows, for example, as a close-to-home, affordably priced nature tourism opportunity; they speak of their entertainments as not only informative but a useful form of conservation action. If their exhibits have to navigate the Scylla and Charybdis of customer prejudice and corporate ideology, managers say that they are still reasonably good representations of the real.

In fact, theme parks may be called on to substitute for national and state parks as these terrains are closed or sold off, their public support and very existence undermined by federal spending cuts and the dismantling of regulations and government bureaucracies. As the touristic appeal of wilderness lands loses out to logging, mining, and grazing, as national and state parks are ill-maintained, theme parks and their corporate owners might compensate the public by taking up the slack. Entertainment companies might be—and have been—invited in to run super-popular sites like Yosemite, which, as Dean McCannell argues, has already been extensively theme-parked by the agencies charged with interpreting it to and protecting it from its public. In McCannell's view, the commodification of nature and the urbanization of wilderness in the national parks happens because nature sights must be delivered to tourists. Nature theme parks are the logical next step in a long historical process of integrating the Anglo-American valuation of wilderness with the world of commerce.[7]

The commercial production and circulation of nature experiences and commodities are so far advanced that it seems entirely possible that theme parks could become a dominant way of experiencing nature. Nature's value as transcendence and compensation inflates simultaneously with popular understanding that the biosphere is threatened and vulnerable. And if nature compensates for the urban world, offers cultural capital, provides a path to self-improvement, and proposes to help people transcend everyday life, the nature entertainments of the theme park may at once become the real thing and its system of distribution.

But spectacular nature is more than a simulacrum or substitute. In fact, it is corporate culture's philanthropic answer to a world of environmental emergencies. Here the theme park is an advanced experiment in wildlife preservation, modeled to the needs, worries, and expectations of the affluent. In fact this is how the Disney company, in consultation with the Wildlife Conservation Society, frames its plan for a five hundred–acre theme park called Wild Animal Kingdom, to open near Orlando in 1998. According to the *New York Times,* Disney plans to spend between $600 million and $800 million to make a "habitat for more than 1,000 animals, some of them endangered."[8] "[A]n advisory panel of wildlife experts" sees the park as a way to "excite" the public about wildlife issues. Sea World's familiar arguments reappear here: according to William Conway of the Wildlife Conservation Society, Wild Animal Kingdom will promote environmental protection by creating feelings and awareness; rather than extend support for environmental legislation or regulation, its goal is to expand preservationist sentiment by "broadening the audience and the level of caring." Conway points to attempts to weaken the Endangered Species Act as evidence not of a concerted political campaign to allow business to expand its profits, but of a lack of the appropriate feelings in the public at large. "[W]e're at a time" Conway says, "when population is growing so rapidly that the only wildlife we'll be able to save is the one we care about [*sic*]." If Disney can replicate and sell community in "Celebration," its updating of the company town tradition, there's no reason it can't produce something that looks like both social action and an ecosystem, wrapped up in appropriate, institutionally created emotions. Here the possibility of alternatives collapses into the consumption of images.[9]

There are, of course, real limits to this fantastic process, as the vicissitudes of the Biosphere II project, a blend of tourism and science, have shown. It seems very unlikely that any scientific project can quickly build a working ecosystem, although tourists will pay to see science try. The question is not whether fake nature is preferable to real nature, or whether entertainment companies might find it profitable to hire scientists to try to save endangered species or habitats. Nature simulations made of paint, concrete, and living plants and animals have been part of Western culture for centuries; virtual ecosystems on the computer screen extend that tradition. The questions that we should raise about theme park nature are political and cultural ones: it is the uses to which nature simulations are put that we should worry about, the stories about environmental crisis that are left untold and the limits on our ability to imagine solutions. What is invisible at Sea World, and places like it, are the selective ways nature is shaped into something that can be looked at.

Like all cultural displays, theme parks are definitional projects: that is, they work to model reality by defining what issues are open for consideration, what problems can be solved, and what concepts can be used in thinking issues through. The marine theme park, with its powerful references to the idea of nature, is selective in the sense described by Raymond Williams, that is, it revises a long cultural history of thought about and representation of the natural world.[10] At Sea World, marine nature in particular and the biosphere in general are separated from their human uses past and present and abstracted from a history of exploitation and conflicts over resources. Most important, in Sea World's stories about itself and the marine world, the oceans and the oceans' vast resources are infinitely "manageable" by corporate capital and, at the same time, protected from abuse and pollution. Narrow interest comes to stand for general interest, and private businesses have nature and the public's best interests at heart. In these stories, extraction and pollution can never be connected to exploitation in the human world, to inequalities between classes, peoples, and nations. At the same time that Sea World and its proliferating cousins erase a human history, they claim to be, in and of themselves, a path to preservation, conservation, and environmental action. That these private, entertainment spaces claim the status of collective social action is an extraordinary commonplace of the 1990s, a feature of the cultural landscape that urgently needs to be addressed.

The corporate emphasis of Sea World's definitional project can be seen in the company's assertions that it is a research institution. As noted in chapter 2, Anheuser-Busch and the park sponsor research, conferences, and publications through their nonprofit adjunct, the Hubbs–Sea World Research Institute.[11] Though fiscally and administratively separate from the theme park, for public relations purposes the research institute and Sea World are one. As one of Sea World's brochures argues, the park itself offers a "world of research" as part of an attraction explicitly focused on "a continuing effort to discover better ways to evaluate and manage the resources of the sea for the benefit of both the environment and mankind."[12] The argument continues: "We must learn not only how to conserve and manage the populations occupying the oceans, but to properly conserve and manage their environment as well. . . . We believe a deepening knowledge and understanding of the oceans, based on extensive scientific study, represents the only real hope of preserving the living resources of the sea . . . and the future of mankind may well depend on our success. . . ."[13] Here, as in the rest of the park, the statement is a response to popular concern. The oceans, and indeed all of the living parts of the material world, are threatened and in need of preservation. But in the Sea World version, the oceans are manageable and their species ultimately replaceable; that is, the future is possible as long as the experts are in charge. The theme park thus models the research agenda of multinational business, in which change and progress are directed from above in the absence of redistribution of resources and power.[14]

Despite the details offered by the brochure, the general, public image of "research at Sea World" is little more than a sketchy idea that research is done there.[15] The park itself helps keep this picture vague. For example, a twenty-minute videotape at the Penguin Encounter details the daunting voyage of Sea World biologists to the tip of South America to collect eggs for the penguin hatchery. In the same building, texts emphasize the commitment of ARCO, an exhibit sponsor, to understanding the Antarctic ecosystems and resources. The Antarctic, it is argued, is an incompletely explored area—full of resources that could be used for the benefit of humankind. We might suspect that the Antarctic has resources of specific interest to ARCO, but this is never stated nor is the question of energy or mineral exploration raised. Rather, the narrative of exploration, research, and resources is loosely juxtaposed around the recreated penguin colony. This exhibit could be read as an assertion that petroleum companies deserve to play some role in deciding what happens to this unpeopled and seemingly unexploited continent—but nothing is quite so definite. Indeed, much like the underwater views in the aquariums, Antarctica at Sea World appears culture-free and outside of events, and this enhances the neutrality of the story it tells. The Penguin Encounter leaves the impression that Antarctica, perhaps the wildest of the wild, is being rationally, benevolently explored—with no company or country's particular interest in mind—just as the penguins are being so lovingly hatched for their own sake. To ride the moving walkway into the cold, through the dark, and past Antarctica's frozen and vibrant world of life, is to enjoy the wonders of exploration and identify with the researchers and their benevolent sponsors: Sea World, ARCO, and the National Science Foundation.

Research here is two things: it is something that takes place, an activity that really goes on, and it is a piece of Sea World's public image.[16] Like environmental management, research always appears as a neutral and positive activity; it is never presented as controversial or problematic. As in so much of the advertising and public relations–driven world of commercial culture, separating the image of research from its actuality is tricky. Recently, over the protests of neighbors and environmentalists, the Hubbs–Sea World Research Institute has constructed a fish hatchery on the Agua Hedionda Lagoon in Carlsbad, about twenty miles north of Mission Bay. The hatchery is an environmental mitigation project: by helping fund the propagation and release of millions of fingerling white bass, Southern California Edison is compensating the State of California for the effects of its San Onofre nuclear generating plant, some of which are the loss of a huge kelp bed, habitat of a now-depleted fish population.[17] The image of the hatchery and its experiment in fish replacement circulate through the local media, publicizing Hubbs–SWRI while giving the theme park ancillary publicity. And although not on display at Sea World, the hatchery project is a perfect example of the environmental management philosophy the theme park embodies. If a mode of extraction ruins the living resources of the ocean, wise managers will add back another resource to compensate and balance the books. Stories like this appear in the press and other media dozens of times in any given year, helping to construct environmental research as instrumental: it is melioration and management, it is what can be practically accomplished as things now stand.

Taking a different view of research, nature, and science, however, it would be extremely interesting for a wide public—not just a small group of experts—to know, for example, the extent of habitat loss near San Onofre, what caused it, what its long-term effects might be, and whether a well-informed regional citizenry approved that loss as a reasonable cost of the production of electricity.[18] It would be fascinating to have some idea whether scientists think that habitat loss is measurable and replaceable, and by what criteria breeding white bass for fisherman is environmental rehabilitation. But to raise these questions would be to let the powerful public awareness of the North American exploitation of the natural world leak into the theme park, and it would call up the general feeling that limits to exploitation will shortly be met. Certainly the crisis of nuclear power is evidence of those limits, and whether or not Sea World's customers worry about the safety and necessity of nuclear power plants in general or nearby San Onofre in particular, environmental concern is part of what draws customers to Sea World. But questions of the real extent of destruction and loss cannot be opened within the framework of corporately produced entertainment, and so the Carlsbad hatchery, the park's rehabilitated oil-spill otters, and its rescued baby sea lions are simply items displayed to confirm "corporate responsibility."

Whatever research is, it is not a contested social process. As we have seen, the Hubbs–Sea World Research Institute is a kind of backstage for the theme park, and the park's displays and performances gain authority and authenticity when the curtain slips back and Hubbs–SWRI can be glimpsed. The mention of research is a part of the pleasure of the theme park, since it gives the customer contact with the power of science and tells him or her that Sea World is working to make everything turn out all right. Not the least bit accidentally, Sea World's publicity brochures also help customers to feel that they contribute to this process of enlightened progress with their admissions fees. One neighbor of mine told me that she didn't really mind paying the high entrance fees for her family because she felt they did "such good things for the ocean there." "It's really worth it," she emphasized. But research, the good things for the ocean, does not articulate problems, nor is it open to question: it simply solves problems, or appears to. Its worth is to be judged, if at all, only by other experts.[19]

The definition of the biosphere as a general economic resource is utilitarian and, in this case, shaped by corporate standards of utility. Dolphins, krill, fingerling bass, the oceans' ecosystems are not allowed to be useless or to just exist beyond human fathoming: the whole natural world is there *for something*. While this stance acknowledges that all human material life comes from interaction with and work on nature, it doesn't confront or even raise issues such as who would benefit from the management of the biosphere, which kinds of claims on resources can be fairly made, and which kinds must be limited.[20] In the Sea World view, the major threat to the environment is from careless individuals who litter, or just don't care. And although Anheuser-Busch presents itself as a solidly proconservation corporation, what forms even conservation—a very limited, protective strategy—takes are unclear. Does the biosphere need to be protected from human exploitation for the short or long term? Who is conservation for, and what is it for? Are the world's natural resources fairly distributed? All these matters trouble American public opinion, but Sea World is quiet about them. At the same time, however, displays that stress the research activities of sponsors imply that particular companies and business in general are prudent stewards who have a legitimate say and a leading role in making decisions about the allocation of the rights to extraction and use. This say or title is earned, in part, through the investment in expertise and research, but also, perhaps, through the construction of exquisite displays and exhibits for education. Here the work of Sea World becomes almost circular: the theme park is a way for corporate America to make public its own free market environmental views; its research, conservationist, and educational surfaces serve as testimony to the supposedly public and disinterested origins of these views.

Sea World is not so much a substitute for nature as an opinion about it, an attempt to convince a broad public that nature is going to be all right. Even when its exhibits say nothing about benevolent corporations, they are literal models of stewardship proposing a version of nature that is at once a reassurance and promise. The dioramas, aquariums, and whole environments provide a model of what nature should be: remote, pure, balanced, and teeming with life. In these formats, as on television, nature is an up-close far-away. We know, even though we would like not to know, that our industrial system of extraction, production, and consumption has thrown the biological world into a tailspin. But insofar as we think about that, our awareness of it is suppressed by the beauty and seeming wholeness of the theme park version we're watching. It is on display for our consumption and connection, through the dolphin and whale performances. Sometimes it is even available for close connection through physical touch, available for our feelings when the lovingly managed animal docilely loves us back.

All this relationship feels good, it may even feel like social action, but it bears no connection to lives in the city or suburbs. Just as Sea World bears no legible relation to the environmental history of Mission Bay, so its nature vision is abstracted from Southern California life in general. Indeed, using images of an unaltered natural order, Sea World takes part in a rationalized process of extraction: it extracts profits from the labor of its workers and its animals, from the manipulation of its landscape, and from the desires of its customers. But, as Raymond Williams pointed out in *The Country and the City,* the idea of unaltered nature helps hide that fact of extraction. In just the same way, the theme park usually hides its own hard work. As Disneyland serves as an improved version of American history—the way its privileged producers wish it was, rather than the way it is or has been—so Sea World's relationship to the rest of everyday life is one of reassurance and compensation for everything. Compensation for the chaparral, the open space, the air quality, the water quality that the Southern California growth machine consumes so rapidly and cannot put back. At other times, Sea World's nature is simply an enjoyable way for the affluent to forget, for a while, that destruction.[21]

Indeed, despite all the arguments Sea World's public relations department makes about how the company "gives back" to San Diego through taxes, charities, recycling projects, beach cleanups, animal rescue, and education, none of these activities answer the very pressing environmental needs of San Diego's (or any city's) population. There is need for open space, for free time, and recreational space and activities, for some respite from the pressures of both commercial culture and routinized work. There is need too for the cleanup of toxics, and for clean air and water, real public transportation, affordable housing, and good jobs. In other words, San Diego and other American communities have vast, unmet needs. Not least among the things missing is a broad understanding that environmental problems are problems of whole economies and ways of life, and that solutions must go far beyond "don't litter" lectures and beach cleanups.

But why should a theme park be berated for failing to provide these things? In this case, because Sea World makes claims to environmental and educational expertise and responsibility. As an institution crossing the public-private boundary, it embodies now-common claims for the influence of private enterprise on public issues. As we have seen, Sea World has acquired an increasingly museum-like face, and its role in public education is expanding. The authority of the museum and the school give weight and an important feeling of objectivity to the theme park's oblique and self-serving definitions of environmental problems and solutions. By taking the right to have an authoritative opinion, by extending itself into the schools, and by calling itself a research institution, Sea World has made itself into a private-public actor.

Given these claims to responsibility, it's fair to ask what public needs the theme park does fill. On the level of customer as individual, Sea World urges us to think about our relationship to the world by having feelings that it helps design; it puts seeing and touching, contact and emotion on center stage for the customer, while it argues that the experts will take care of the complicated scientific and technical parts. More generally, Sea World is a material argument for private business solutions to environmental problems that, though unequal in their origins and effects, are of course not private but collective and social in the most profound sense. And perhaps most important, like all major theme parks Sea World is an advertisement for and a triumphal, material celebration of the wonders that the private corporation and multinational capital can produce. A public service needs to be assessed in terms of how broadly positive, effective, and equally accessible its benefits are. Unless we think that public service means creating audience emotions that in turn validate and promote private solutions, it is hard to see what progress is made here. Of course, Sea World does serve its corporate parent admirably, providing both a good return on investment and excellent public image benefits. But this is a completely private service despite the fact that the imagery of public effort has been channeled to produce it.

To return to the outburst I scribbled in my notebook, what did it mean to say, "They won"? What has been won, and by whom, in this battle for markets, dollars, length of stay, and feelings? Increasingly sophisticated in its vision and persuasive in its messages, Sea World is clearly getting more elaborate and beautiful all the time. That it is so popular, that it takes up ever more psychic and social space, that it is ever more skillful at packaging consumption as a form of public action—this could all be interpreted as victory.

However, there is a sense in which the theme park world can never really "win." Sea World is a machine that profits by selling people's dreams back to them—dreams of a happy family, congenial public spaces free of fear, a peaceful community, meaningful social action, unalienated labor and true leisure, a just and clean and provident physical world. And this is a process so contradictory that it can never completely work. Although in the future these dreams might result in inclusive and democratic outcomes, in their theme park versions they are based on exclusion, on the control and order of a closed world. Although American culture is astoundingly good at creating commodities that promise these dreams, none of these desires can be reached through the process of consumption, not least because the culture of high consumption depends on the exploitation of people, on awesome human and material waste. And although criticism of consumption unfolds mainly on the margins of American discourse, it is unlikely that, except for a brief suspension of disbelief, most of the theme park's customers think it can deliver on its promises. The problem is to find another place and way to dream.

Notes

Introduction

1. Annual reports and Securities and Exchange Commission filings list Anheuser-Busch's extensive holdings and operations. Anheuser-Busch Corporation, *1992 Annual Report* (St. Louis: Anheuser-Busch Corporation, 1992); Securities and Exchange Commission, "Form 10-K: Anheuser-Busch Companies, Inc." (Washington, D. C: Securities and Exchange Commission, 1992). Busch's annual reports also contain details of the company's environmental and conservation programs.

2. Susan G. Davis, *Parades and Power: Street Theatre in Nineteenth-Century Philadelphia* (Philadelphia: Temple University Press, 1986); On the history and transformations of public space, see Roy Rosenzweig and Elizabeth Blackmar, *The Park and the People: A History of Central Park* (Ithaca and London: Cornell University Press, 1992); David Harvey, *The Condition of Postmodernity: An Inquiry into the Conditions of Cultural Change* (Oxford: Basil Blackwell, 1989); Herbert I. Schiller, *Culture Inc.* (New York: Oxford University Press, 1991).

3. A detailed analysis of Disneyland as a total, ideological universe is developed in Michael Real, *Mass Mediated Culture* (Englewood Cliffs, N.J.: Prentice-Hall, 1977). Herbert I. Schiller, in *The Mind Managers* (Boston: Beacon Press, 1973), was arguably the first to dissect the politics of innocence and neutrality in Disney entertainment products in general (pp. 79–103). Armand Mattelart and Ariel Dorfman anatomized Disney products in the Chilean context, in *How to Read Donald Duck: Imperialist Ideology in the Disney Comic,* trans. David Kunzle (New York: International General, 1975). The work of Schiller, Real, Mattelart, and Dorfman was profoundly influenced by, and part of, the popular radicalism of the 1960s. For a contemporary approach to the same issues, see Henry Giroux, "Beyond the Politics of Innocence: Memory and Pedagogy in the 'Wonderful World of Disney,'" *Socialist Review* 23, no. 2 (1993): 79–107; and Giroux, "Animating Youth: The Disneyfication of Children's Culture," *Socialist Review* 24, no. 3 (1994): 23–55.

4. One exception is Michael Wallace, "Mickey Mouse History: Portraying the Past at Disney World," in *Radical History Review* 32 (1985):33–57.

5. Much work on theme parks, especially Disneyland and Disney World, has emphasized the form's consensual meanings and culturally normative uses. See, for example, Margaret J. King, "The New American Muse: Notes on the Amusement/Theme Park," and "Disneyland and Walt Disney World: Traditional Values in Futuristic Form," in *Journal of Popular Culture* 15 (Summer 1981): 56–62; 116–40; Alexander Moore, "Walt Disney World: Bounded Ritual Space and the Playful Pilgrimage Center," *Anthropological Quarterly* 53, no. 4 (October 1980).

6. Roy Rosenzweig, *Eight Hours for What We Will: Workers and Leisure in an Industrial City, 1870–1920* (Cambridge and New York: Cambridge University Press, 1983); Kathy Peiss, *Cheap Amusements: Working Women and Leisure in New York City, 1880 to 1920* (Philadelphia: Temple University Press, 1985); David Nasaw, *Going Out: The Rise and Fall of Public Amusements* (New York: Basic Books, 1993); John F. Kasson, *Amusing the Million: Coney Island at the Turn of the Century* (New York: Hill and Wang, 1978); Robert W. Rydell, *All the World's a Fair: Visions of Empire at America's International Expositions, 1876–1916* (Chicago: University of Chicago Press, 1984); Robert W. Rydell, *World of Fairs: The Century of Progress Expositions* (Chicago: University of Chicago Press, 1993); Paul Greenhalgh, *Ephemeral Vistas: The Expositions Universelles, Great Exhibitions and World's Fairs, 1851–1939* (Manchester: Manchester University Press, 1988); the history of American theme and amusement parks is traced by Judith Adams, *The American Amusement Park Industry: A History of Technology and Thrills* (Boston: Twayne Publishers, G. K. Hall and Co., 1991).

7. Michael Sorkin, ed., *Variations on a Theme Park: The New American City and the End of Public Space* (New York: Hill and Wang, 1992); Mike Davis, *City of Quartz* (New York and London: Verso Books, 1990); Edward Soja, *Postmodern Geographies: The Reassertion of Space in Critical Social Theory* (New York and London: Verso Books, 1989).

8. Carol Lawson, "Disney's Newest Show Is a Town," *New York Times,* November 16, 1995, p. B-1.

9. For a look at recent theme park history, see Susan G. Davis, "Theme Park: Global Industry and Cultural Form," in *Media, Culture and Society* 18, no. 3 (July 1996): 399–422.

10. This newer literature covers historical and ethnographic accounts of the parks, the economic workings of the Disney empire, new biographical treatments of Disney himself, and of course, cultural critique of Disney media products; see Mike Wallace, "Mickey Mouse History;" Ruth E. Knack, "The Mouse That Ate Orlando," *Planning* 45, no. 2 (February 1979): 17–21; Diana Mara Henry, "Future Food?" *Southern Exposure* (November–December 1983): 22–26; John M. Findlay, *Magic Lands: Western Cityscapes and American Culture after 1940* (Berkeley and Los Angeles: University of California Press, 1992), pp. 52–116; Susan Willis, "Disney World: Public Use/Private State," *South Atlantic Quarterly* 92, no. 1 (winter 1993): 119–137; The Project on Disney, *Inside the Mouse: Work and Play at Disney World* (Durham, N.C.: Duke University Press, 1995); and Stephen M. Fjellman, *Vinyl Leaves: Walt Disney World and America* (Boulder, Colo.: Westview Press, 1992); Alexander Wilson, *The Culture of Nature* (Oxford and New

York: Basil Blackwell, 1992); Disney hagiography has been undermined by Mark Eliot, *Walt Disney: Hollywood's Dark Prince* (New York: Harper Paperbacks, 1993).

11. In this view, nature is located in the furthest reaches of the physical world—away from urban settlement, human density, and daily lives. It is found in remote wildernesses and national parks, rather than at tourist attractions surrounded by asphalt parking lots.

12. Lynn Smith, "For Some, Dolphins Bring Spiritual Inspiration," *Los Angeles Times,* August 16, 1989, sec. V, p. E-8. Smith reports that in 1989, more than three thousand "people and organizations [were] involved in dolphin projects. At least 300 of them involve[d] attempts at interspecies communication, despite the lack of scientific evidence that it is possible." Smith quotes Beth Gawaine of Maui, Hawaii, describing dolphins as "very good Buddhists." To my knowledge, the connections between dolphins, whales, and popular spiritual movements remains unstudied.

13. On landscape painting, for example, see Anne Bermingham, *Landscape and Ideology: The English Rustic Tradition, 1740–1860* (Berkeley and Los Angeles: University of California Press, 1986); on photography, see Peter B. Hales, *William Henry Jackson and the Transformation of the American Landscape* (Philadelphia: Temple University Press, 1988); on advertising, see T. J. Jackson Lears, *Fables of Abundance: A Cultural History of Advertising in America* (New York: Basic Books, 1994); and Roland Marchand, *Advertising the American Dream: Making Way for Modernity, 1920–1940* (Berkeley and Los Angeles: University of California Press, 1985). The beginnings of a history of nature and landscape film are found in Derek Bouse, "The Wilderness Documentary: Film, Video and the Visual Rhetoric of American Environmentalism" (Ph.D. diss., University of Pennsylvania, 1991).

14. On television, nature programming makes up a significant proportion of network and cable broadcast hours, yet nature TV has received no sustained attention from media scholars. We have no accurate picture of how much nature TV is broadcast, who produces it, when it is broadcast and whom it reaches. But, see William Hoynes, *Public Television for Sale: Media, the Market and the Public Sphere* (Boulder, Colo.: Westview Press, 1994), particularly pp. 89–114. Hoynes stresses the public relations uses of nature programming for multinational corporations. Cf. Charles Seibert, "The Artifice of the Natural: How TV's Nature Shows Make All the Earth a Stage," *Harper's,* February 1993, 43–51; Louise McElvogue, "Running Wild: Executives Find Value in Natural History Programs," *Los Angeles Times,* February 13, 1996, pp. D-1, D-6; Mindy Sink, "The Call of the Wildlife Show," *New York Times,* April 15, 1996. McElvogue writes that "[m]any companies, particularly those with international interests, have jumped into the field of natural history programming [because it can easily cross cultural and language barriers]. Well-done programming has a long shelf-life and can be reused in different markets," (p. D-1). Five of the top producers of nature shows on television are Discover Communications (with sixty-five hours of programming produced in 1995), National Geographic (eighty-five hours in 1995), Turner Productions, BBC Natural History Unit, and Survival Anglia.

15. Nature is, however, deeply implied in these concepts. Judith Williamson's *Decoding Advertisements: Ideology and Meaning in Advertising* (New York: Mar-

ion Boyars, 1984) is an exception to the lack of contemporary critical attention; there is an excellent discussion of "nature's" connection to contemporary food marketing in Warren J. Belasco, *Appetite for Change: How the Counterculture Took On the Food Industry, 1966–1988* (New York: Pantheon Books, 1989); on race, gender, and nature, see Marianna Torgovnic, *Gone Primitive: Savage Intellects, Modern Lives* (Chicago: University of Chicago Press, 1990), especially pp. 3–72.

16. Raymond Williams, "Ideas of Nature," in *Problems in Materialism and Culture* (London: Verso Editions, 1980), pp. 67–85; and Williams, *The Country and the City* (New York: Oxford University Press, 1980).

17. Carolyn Merchant, *The Death of Nature: Women, Ecology, and the Scientific Revolution,* 1st ed. (San Francisco: Harper and Row, 1980); Donna Haraway, *Primate Visions: Gender, Race, and Nature in the World of Modern Science* (New York: Routledge, 1989). Angus Gillespie and Jay Mechling explore how Americans use wild animals "to think" about society and social group in the volume they edited, *American Wildlife in Symbol and Story* (Knoxville: University of Tennessee Press, 1987).

18. There are exceptions, most of which deal with news reporting conventions; see Anders Hansen, ed., *Mass Media and Environmental Issues* (Leicester and New York: Leicester University Press, 1993); Craig L. LaMay and E. Everette Dennis, eds. *Media and the Environment* (Washington, D.C.: Island Press, 1991); "Covering the Environment," special issue, John Corner and Philip Schlesinger, eds., *Media, Culture and Society* 13, no. 4 (October 1991), especially Jacqueline Burgess, Carolyn Harrison, and Paul Maitney, "Contested Meanings: The Consumption of News about Nature Conservation" (459–519); on documentary, see Roger Silverstone, "The Agonistic Narratives of Television Science," in *Documentary and the Mass Media,* ed. John Corner (London: Edward Arnold, 1986), pp. 81–106; on entertainment culture, see Stephen Papson, "Cross the Fin Line of Terror: Shark Week on the Discovery Channel," *Journal of American Culture* 15, no. 4 (winter 1992): 67–81. In general, there is a missing connection between environmental activism, media activism, and media scholarship. See the criticism of the DuPont corporation's "Ode to Joy" television ad in "Hold the Applause" (Friends of the Earth, Washington, D.C., 1992, photocopy).

19. Cf. Alice M. Geffen and Carol Berglie, *Eco-Tours and Nature Getaways: A Guide to Environmental Vacations around the World* (New York: Clarkson Potter, 1993).

20. Cultural tourism is better studied than nature tourism as an economic complex that reproduces imperial relationships. Jamaica Kincaid offers a biting meditation in *A Small Place* (New York: Penguin Books, 1981).

21. See, for example, Jennifer Price, "Looking for Nature at the Mall: A Field Guide to the Nature Company," in *Uncommon Ground: Toward Reinventing Nature,* ed. William Cronon (New York: W. W. Norton, 1995), pp. 186–202.

22. Cf. Wilson, *The Culture of Nature.*

23. The illustrations in this book reflect this struggle for control: Sea World will not permit its own publicity materials to be used in an environment they do not control. At the same time, like Disney World, Sea World claims to "strictly prohibit" the publication of photographs taken on its premises. Since I would not allow prepublication review of the manuscript, I am unable to include

examples of the flood of images that make up Sea World's institutional self-representation. Instead, I have made use of the more independent sources of news photographers who, of course, also work only with Sea World's permission and under its sponsorship.

As I researched the illustrations at the San Diego Historical Society and the *San Diego Union-Tribune,* it became clearer how closely Sea World controls visual images of the park and, especially, of its animals. In its earliest years and the pre-Anheuser-Busch period (before 1989), Sea World's public relations department regularly invited newspaper photographers to the park for photo opportunities. As Sea World expanded, it developed its own, in-house photographic operations to illustrate its brochures, maps, and books and provide news reporters with excellent images, which accompanied Sea World's press releases, to illustrate articles. By the late 1980s, these very high quality photos began to replace the staff news photographers' own work, and thus gave Sea World more effective control of how its animals and landscapes would be represented visually. Images of whales and dolphins especially are limited to Sea World's proprietary images, which are carefully thought out and composed. Today, an onsite photographic workshop turns out these standardized, proprietary images by the thousands, but none of them could be used to illustrate this book. In choosing photographs to give readers a sense of the physical park and its animals, I had to work around these limits, looking for published photos credited to more independent sources.

24. The closest I have come to animal rights activism is making occasional donations to Greenpeace. While I am sympathetic to the animal rights critique of the irrationality of "rational" capitalist research, science, and food production, especially the critiques of animal testing and experimentation and factory farming, I am at the same time put off by the animal rights movement's apparent disinterest in an already well-developed tradition of criticism of the exploitation of human beings. Animal rights critics of Sea World tend to focus on the issues of captivity and performance; as will become plain, I am developing a broader approach in this study.

25. Given my goal of researching the institution, I had little choice but to conduct officially sponsored interviews. Other alternatives would have been to contact Sea World officials and employees outside their workplace, or to conduct clandestine research, perhaps by using a fictitious resume and taking a job at the theme park. The first strategy seemed to likely to go nowhere; had it been successful it might have jeopardized peoples' jobs. The clandestine alternative is for spies. I conducted no interviews with employees at Sea World without the knowledge and sponsorship of management. Most formal interviews were tape recorded.

26. One curator flatly refused to meet with me, saying he hated doing interviews.

27. Each of these longtime former employees had been fired by Sea World during one corporate crisis or another, yet each seemed to identify with Sea World's enterprise. These were not grudge-airing or dirt-dishing sessions, and the interviewees were engaged, I think, because they were pleased that someone was interested in the work that had occupied them for so many years.

28. Except for the most informal and fleeting contacts, all interviews were conducted with informed consent, recorded on audiotape, with the approval of and following the guidelines set out by the University of California at San Diego Committee on Research on Human Subjects. Interviewees were informed of the nature and scope of the project, and they knew that my research results, including parts of interviews, would be published. When I interviewed children, I followed the committee's protocol for gaining both the child's and the parent's permission and informed consent.

29. A long tradition of critical research in communication makes this case—most early and eloquently, Schiller, *The Mind Managers;* and Erik Barnouw, *The Sponsor: Notes on a Modern Potentate* (New York: Oxford University Press, 1978).

30. For a cogent examination of the politics of privatization in education, see Michael W. Apple, "Whittling Away at Democracy: The Social Context of Channel One," in *Watching Channel One: The Convergence of Students, Technology and Private Business,* ed. Anne De Vaney (Albany: State University of New York Press, 1994), pp. 167–188. The delivery of courses, on-site and off-site, is well under way in other theme park companies, notably Disney, which offers American studies and science course credits for teachers and high school students at the EPCOT Center. The Carter Company of Boston, Inc., collaborates with Walt Disney World, Sea World, and the Kennedy Space Center to offer "Earth Shuttle: The Ultimate Field Trip," a social science and sciences tour program, to teachers and students in grades three through twelve. See the promotional brochure *Earth Shuttle* (Boston, Mass.: Carter Company, 1989). Thanks to JoEllen Fisherkeller for this reference. Disney also has plans for a "Disney University" of continuing education at its Orlando sites. See, for example, Tim O'Brien, "Industry Getting Involved in Educating America's Youth," *Amusement Business,* February 25, 1991, 5.

31. Apple, "Whittling Away at Democracy."

1. Another World

1. John Berger, "Why Look at Animals?" *About Looking* (New York: Pantheon Books, 1980), pp. 1–26.

2. Michael Sorkin, "See You in Disneyland," in *Variations on a Theme Park: The New American City and the End of Public Space,* ed. Michael Sorkin (New York: Hill and Wang, 1992), pp. 205–232; William F. Mangels, *The Outdoor Amusement Industry from Earliest Times to the Present* (New York: Vantage, 1952).

3. On the history of Coney Island, see John F. Kasson, *Amusing the Million: Coney Island at the Turn of the Century* (New York: Hill and Wang, 1978).

4. By 1919 the United States had between fifteen hundred and two thousand amusement parks. Every major city boasted a "trolley park" developed by street railway companies to promote and subsidize transportation. Judith Adams, *The American Amusement Park Industry: A History of Technology and Thrills* (Boston: Twayne Publishers, G. K. Hall and Co., 1991), p. 57.

5. Roy Rosenzweig, *Eight Hours for What We Will: Workers and Leisure in an Industrial City, 1870–1920* (Cambridge and New York: Cambridge University

Press, 1983); Kathy Peiss, *Cheap Amusements: Working Women and Leisure in New York City, 1880 to 1920* (Philadelphia: Temple University Press, 1985); David Nasaw, *Going Out: The Rise and Fall of Public Amusements* (New York: Basic Books, 1993); Robert W. Rydell, *All the World's a Fair: Visions of Empire at America's International Expositions, 1876–1916* (Chicago: University of Chicago Press, 1984); Rydell, *World of Fairs: The Century of Progress Expositions* (Chicago: University of Chicago Press, 1993); Paul Greenhalgh, *Ephemeral Vistas: The Expositions Universelles, Great Exhibitions and World's Fairs, 1851–1939* (Manchester: Manchester University Press, 1988).

6. Adams, *American Amusement Park Industry,* p. 67.

7. Margaret D. Pacey, "For Fun and Profit: Amusement Parks Are a Hit at the Box Office and in the Boardroom," *Barron's,* July 12, 1971, 11, 20–21.

8. Bro Uttal, "The Ride Is Getting Scarier," *Fortune,* December, 1977, 167–84. The business was not without uncertainty. Bally (with interests in gaming and casinos), Taft (broadcasting), and Marriott (hotels and resorts) disengaged by the early 1980s largely because "the parks, acquired as a sideline to other, more dominant interests demanded expanding resources in the areas of capital expenditures, operating procedures, and managerial attention." Adams, *American Amusement Park Industry,* p. 122. The parks were sold and recombined into still larger leisure businesses.

9. Tim O'Brien, "North American Parks Have Banner Season," *Amusement Business,* January 2, 1994, 65, 68, 69.

10. O'Brien, "Banner Season," 68–69; in 1995, the ten largest North American theme parks accounted for more than 49 percent of attendance (or 76.4 million visitors) at the top fifty amusement and theme parks (out of a total 155,127,000 visitors). Tim O'Brien, "Attendance Climbs 7% at Top North American Parks," *Amusement Business,* December 18–31, 1995, 1, 76–78, 104.

11. Richard Schickel, *The Disney Version: The Life, Times, Art, and Commerce of Walt Disney* (New York: Avon Books, 1968), pp. 295–337. Schickel's is still the definitive account of how this was done, but see also George Lipsitz, "Discursive Space and Social Space: Television, Highways, and Cognitive Mapping in the 1950s City" (paper presented at the annual meeting of the American Studies Association, Toronto, Canada, November 4, 1989); and Sorkin, "See You in Disneyland."

12. Patricia Bates, "Disney Parks Write the Book on Corporate Sponsorship," *Amusement Business,* March 28, 1987, 4; Douglas Gomery, "Disney's Business History: A Reinterpretation," in *Disney Discourse: Producing the Magic Kingdom,* ed. Eric Smoodin (New York and London: Routledge, 1994), pp. 81–82.

13. For example, on Kraft's worldview as expressed at Disney World, see Diana Mara Henry, "Future Food?" *Southern Exposure* (November–December 1983): 22–26; Stephen M. Fjellman, *Vinyl Leaves: Walt Disney World and America* (Boulder, Colo.: Westview Press, 1992), pp. 319–347.

14. Product association and coordinated point-of-sale advertising—for example, on Carnation milk packages sold to families with children—also help theme parks deliver the correct image to the right audience segment.

15. For a planner's assessment of the possibilities, see David L. Brown, "Thinking of a Theme Park?" *Urban Land* (February 1980): 5–11. John M. Find-

lay, *Magic Lands: Western Cityscapes and American Culture after 1940* (Berkeley and Los Angeles: University of California Press, 1992), pp. 52–116.

16. Orlando is thought to be the most visited destination in the world. On Orlando, see Fjellman, *Vinyl Leaves,* pp. 127–149.

17. Sea World's former president Jan Schultz, interview by author, La Jolla, Calif., March 19, 1992.

18. Adams, *American Amusement Park Industry,* pp. 107–108.

19. This rhetoric of parental control over recreation was paralleled in discussions of television; see Lynn Spigel, *Make Room for TV: Television and the Family Ideal in Postwar America* (Chicago: University of Chicago Press, 1992), pp. 36–72.

20. Travel to theme parks and destination resorts is increasingly organized by corporate employers, either in the form of conventions or "incentive travel," that is, rewards or bonuses to middle management. It may be that the theme park's corporate outlook is being strengthened, or underlined, by the corporate recruitment of its clientele.

21. Amy Wallace, "Like, It's So L.A.!: Not Really," *Los Angeles Times,* February 29, 1992, San Diego County edition, pp. 1, 22–23.

22. Susan G. Davis, "Theme Park: Global Industry and Cultural Form," *Media Culture and Society* 18, no. 3 (July 1996): 399–422.

23. O'Brien, "Attendance Climbs," 76–78.

24. Ibid., and O'Brien, "Banner Season."

25. O'Brien, "Attendance Climbs"; and O'Brien, "Banner Season."

26. Michael Bristol, "Acting Out Utopia: The Politics of Carnival," *Performance* 1 (May–June 1973): 13–28.

27. Derek Walker, *Animated Architecture* (London: Architectural Design, 1982), p. 20. As Walker puts it, "[D]etail is the language that makes the land of believable dreams possible."

28. Theme parks do subcontract some performances and services, but on a limited basis. Shows using outside "talent" are usually written and produced in-house.

29. Adams, *American Amusement Park Industry,* pp. 106–107.

30. Historically, Disney specialized in film and animation: so did MGM (now in a park partnership with Disney), Universal, the Rank Organization (now in a partnership with MCA), Paramount, and Time-Warner. But MCA is also involved with music recording and media technologies, as is Disney; Viacom owns MTV, VH-1, and Nickelodeon; products from these channels and many others are promoted in the Paramount parks. The theme park provides a context for the renarration and enhancement of filmed commodities, because it creates a material space and place for them.

31. To take a recent example, 1994 sales of merchandise themed to the animated film *The Lion King* were projected at as much as $1 billion, while the film's box office was estimated at about $267 million for its initial run. Claudia Eller, "A Peek at *Pocahontas* When *Lion King* Returns," *Los Angeles Times,* October 20, 1994, pp. F-1, F-10; Kate Fitzgerald, "'Lion' Is New King of Licensing Jungle," *Advertising Age* 65, no. 28 (July 4, 1994).

32. In 1993 Busch contracted the William Morris Agency to represent and coordinate its Hollywood interests.

33. Thomas C. Hayes "Harcourt Near Sale of Sea World," *New York Times,* August 14, 1989, pp. D-1, D-6; Thomas C. Hayes, "Anheuser Is Buying Parks from Harcourt," *New York Times,* September 29, 1989, pp. D-1, D-16. The parks were sold for $1.1 billion.

34. Recently the name was changed to Busch Gardens, Tampa Bay.

35. The *Sesame Street* theme of Sesame Place is rented, with limitations, from the Children's Television Workshop, rather than owned outright.

36. Total attendance at the Disney parks far outranks that of any other major contender.

37. In addition to the four Sea Worlds, the two Busch Gardens and Sesame Place, Busch operates two water-ride parks, also in Tampa and Williamsburg. Busch Entertainment Corporation brought $55 million in profits to the larger corporation in 1992, up 22 percent from the previous year (but still less than in 1990). Richard Melcher, "Anheuser-Busch Says *Skoal, Salud, Prosit,*" *Business Week,* September 20, 1993, 76.

38. Julia Flynn Siler, "Even August Busch Can Only Handle So Much Beer," *Business Week,* September 25, 1989, 182–187.

39. Melcher "*Skoal, Salud, Prosit,*" 76–77; on Asia, see Evelyn Iritani, "Beer Battle Brewing in China," *Los Angeles Times,* July 25, 1995, pp. A-1, A-9.

40. Growth in the beer market in the United States has been flat for more than a decade, with numbers of young drinkers falling since the 1970s; Sea World's family image certainly extends to Busch's beers, and it may help market "light" beer to women, one of the few segments of the market that is seen to have room for expansion. Seth Lubove, "Get 'Em before They Get You," *Forbes,* July 31, 1995, 88–93. Thanks to Dan Schiller for this point. The August Busch family of St. Louis is a proponent of wildlife management efforts, such as the Ducks Unlimited organization, which urges rational management of wildfowl populations for recreational hunters.

41. Cf. Iritani, "Beer Battle Brewing." Anheuser-Busch calls attention to its recycling approach to solid waste production in its annual reports, and in its brochure, "A Pledge and a Promise" (St. Louis: Anheuser-Busch Companies, 1993).

42. A Shamu-based television show remains a possibility. In spring 1996 Busch announced a new nature- and animal-rescue-themed television show, *Second Noah,* filmed at Busch Gardens, Tampa Bay. *Second Noah* aired on the ABC network.

43. Due to a series of bad licensing and media decisions, Shamu's uses have been limited to small ventures, such as audiotapes, toys, and children's pajamas. Unknown to Busch when it purchased the Sea Worlds, all the rights to the image were held by Watson General Pictures, and Busch had to purchase them separately. Kim Kowsky, "Busch to Buy Rights to Films about Shamu," *Los Angeles Times* January 5, 1990, pp. D-1, D-2. In 1995, an animated Shamu character could be seen in "Don't Trash Where You Splash" television public service announcements. Sea World's public relations department claims Shamu has a "Q score" (the score is a measure of the warm feelings the character evokes) equal to that of Mickey Mouse. Dan LeBlanc, interview by author, San Diego, Calif., March 3, 1992.

44. Free Willy Foundation, *Free Willy: Keiko Adoption Kit* (San Francisco:

Free Willy Foundation, 1995). On Keiko, see Jane Galbraith, " A Whale of an Actor in a Killer Part," *Los Angeles Times,* May 16, 1993, Sunday Calendar, pp. 23–24; on increased interest: Sea World's director for public relations, Diane Oaks, interview by author, San Diego, Calif., September 13, 1994.

45. Stuart Elliot, "Whale of a Promotion, by Southwest Airlines Is a Killer," *USA Today,* May 25, 1988, 1-B. Sponsorship partners' names were much more visible when I began fieldwork than they would be in the middle 1990s. For example, the penguin exhibit was prominently labeled the "ARCO Penguin Encounter" when it opened; by 1995 it was designated the "Penguin Encounter," although ARCO continues to be listed as part of Sea World's "family of sponsors" on maps and brochures. Sea World may be subtly trying to make its environment seem less commercial, in pursuit of an impossible contradiction. Another explanation may be that direct sponsorships were more important when the Sea Worlds were owned by Harcourt Brace Jovanovich. Anheuser-Busch's pockets are much deeper.

46. This may be especially important in an era of public concern over advertising alcoholic beverages to youth, and over commercial connections between beer, rock music, and sports. Beer companies' extensive sponsorship of rock concerts and band tours has been criticized by health professionals and advocates of drunk driving prevention. Paul Grein, "Suds 'n' Bucks 'n' Rock 'n' Roll: Beer Companies' Rock Sponsorships Stir Controversy," *Los Angeles Times,* July 30, 1989, Sunday Calendar, pp. 8, 85, 86. Budweiser has been the major sponsor for U.S. concerts by Mick Jagger and the Rolling Stones, most recently providing millions of dollars for the 1994 "Voodoo Lounge" tour. Anheuser-Busch has come under criticism in San Diego for the promotional uses of the park; see "What's Brewing at Sea World? Baby Shamu or Shamu Light?" *Prevention File* (San Diego County Edition, summer 1992) (published by UCSD Extension, University of California at San Diego, La Jolla, Calif.), inset, pp. S.D. 4–S.D 5. A protest flier circulated in August 1993 urged raised public awareness of "the mixed messages that are sent to our communities, particularly our youth, through beer company sponsorship" of sports events. San Diego Advocates for Responsible Alcohol Advertising, "Bud Light Triathlon? Athletes Become Human Billboards for Beer Company" (San Diego Advocates for Responsible Alcohol Advertising, Solana Beach, Calif., n.d., photocopied). See also, Jennifer Loven, "Spirited Group of Nuns Takes on Big Business," *San Diego Union-Tribune,* August 27, 1995, pp. I-1, I-6, for the Adrian Dominican Sisters' criticism of Anheuser-Busch's advertising to youth.

47. Joel Bleifuss discusses the limits of recycling as environmental action in "The First Stone: Pavlov's Pack Rats," *In These Times,* November 13–26, 1995, 12–13; see also Jim Schwab, "California: Fighting for Life and Breath," in *Deeper Shades of Green: The Rise of Blue Collar and Minority Environmentalism in America* (San Francisco: Sierra Club Books, 1994), pp. 44–76 for a discussion of solid waste and toxic waste in California.

48. Raymond Williams, "Ideas of Nature," in *Problems in Materialism and Culture* (London: Verso Editions, 1980) p. 67–85.

49. Raymond Williams, *The Country and the City* (New York: Oxford University Press, 1980).

50. Williams, "Ideas of Nature."

51. Ibid.; and Williams, *The Country and the City,* pp. 87–107.

52. Jonas Frykman and Orvar Lofgren, *Culture Builders: A Historical Anthropology of Middle-Class Life,* trans. Alan Crozier (New Brunswick: Rutgers University Press, 1987), pp. 42–87.

53. Frykman and Lofgren are arguing that late nineteenth-century Sweden was both particular and typical of the rest of Europe in the general development of its bourgeois culture. They view the recasting of nature in Sweden as rather abrupt and harsh, due to the rapid pace of industrialization there. However, the intellectual and ideological developments they cite were widespread. Their study is useful for thinking about theme parks in its ethnographic emphasis on practices and customs of everyday life, as opposed to the critical study of fine arts and literature. They are able to tell a great deal about how nature was "lived" by its appreciators, and to contrast this with the experience of the peasantry and farm laborers.

54. Peter J. Schmitt, *Back to Nature: The Arcadian Myth in Urban America* (Baltimore: Johns Hopkins University Press, 1990). Mid- and late-nineteenth-century English nature appreciators invented the small aquarium to preserve and make visible the small animals and plants they gathered at the seaside. Lynn Barber, *The Heyday of Natural History, 1820–1870* (Garden City, N.Y.: Doubleday, 1980).

55. Schmitt, *Back to Nature,* pp. 77–95. It is notable that indigenous working-class traditions of outdoor recreation have been little studied (and little appreciated by historians of environmental movements) except where they have clashed with the recreations of the propertied. See, for example, Edward D. Ives, *George Magoon and the Down East Game War: History, Folklore, and the Law* (Urbana: University of Illinois Press, 1988). See also Schwab, *Deeper Shades of Green;* and Robert Gottlieb, *Forcing the Spring: The Transformation of the American Environmental Movement* (Washington, D.C.: Island Press, 1993), pp. 15–46.

56. Harriet Ritvo, *The Animal Estate: The English and Other Creatures in the Victorian Age* (Cambridge: Harvard University Press, 1987), pp. 205–242. The literal nature of this emblematic function is underlined when we note that humans—for example, pygmies—were displayed along with animals in menageries, parks, and zoos. See, for example, Carl Hagenbeck, *Beasts and Men* (London: Longmans and Green, 1910) and Bob Mullan and Gary Marvin, *Zoo Culture* (London: George Weidenfeld and Nicholson, 1987), pp. 85–88. Imperialist representation through animals could also leak out of the zoo. From early on, London's animal dealers supplied wealthy scientists as well as the purveyors of popular city amusements. Exotic animals became part of an urban world of cheap recreation, joining older diversions such as cockfighting and bearbaiting.

57. Mary Louise Pratt, *Imperial Eyes: Travel Writing and Transculturation* (New York and London: Routledge, 1992), pp. 15–37; John Michael Kennedy, "Philanthropy and Science in New York City: The American Museum of Natural History, 1868–1968" (Ph.D. diss., Yale University, 1968); Donna J. Haraway, *Primate Visions: Gender, Race and Nature in the World of Modern Science* (New York: Routledge, 1989), pp. 1–58.

58. Ritvo, *Animal Estate*, pp. 205–242. The social history of the popular uses of the American zoo is much less developed. See also Mullan and Marvin, *Zoo*

Culture, pp. 89–137. The San Diego Zoo features more modest, more directly didactic trained animal performances than does Sea World. Although it is a nonprofit, the zoo's revenues are also heavily dependent on concession sales.

59. The term *selective tradition* is Raymond Williams's, from *Marxism and Literature* (Oxford: Oxford University Press, 1977), pp. 115–120.

60. For example, Paul Bouissac, *Circus and Culture* (Bloomington: Indiana University Press, 1976); John Culhane, *The American Circus: An Illustrated History* (New York: Henry Holt and Company, 1990). For descriptions of nineteenth-century menageries, Ritvo, *Animal Estate,* pp. 206–213; on traveling menageries, see E. H. Bostock, *Menageries, Circuses and Theatres* (London, 1927; reprint, New York: Benjamin Blom, 1972); on twentieth-century American menageries, see George W. "Slim" Lewis, *The Ape I Knew* (Caldwell, Idaho: Caxton Printers, 1961). At Sea World, the techniques of animal training derive indirectly from the circus tradition, as I show in chapter 5.

61. Dean McCannell formulates the tourist as a pilgrim to sacred ideas in *The Tourist: A New Theory of the Leisure Class* (New York: Schocken Books, 1976). For a discussion of tourist pilgrimages to nature, see John F. Sears, *Sacred Places: American Tourist Attractions in the Nineteenth Century* (New York: Oxford University Press, 1989).

62. For an examination of the theme of touch and contact in Sea World ads, see Susan G. Davis, "Touch the Magic," in *Uncommon Ground: Toward Reinventing Nature,* ed. William Cronon (New York: W. W. Norton, 1995), p. 204–217.

63. Much to Sea World management's dismay, many of its activist critics view the theme park and the contemporary circus as identical, and call for limits not only on the park's ability to obtain dolphins and whales for performances, but on the animal performance and display across the board. For example, in 1995 animal rights activists and marine mammal protectionists put forward the California Marine Mammal Protection Act (California Assembly Bill 1737), which would have banned the display of whales, dolphins, and other sea mammals that had begun their lives in the wild. On the rationality of the park's displays, representatives of Sea World debated representatives from the Humane Society of the United States and People for the Ethical Treatment of Animals on "These Days," a local radio call-in show on station KPBS, on June 12, 1995. See also "Protest Held on Mission Bay Drive," *San Diego Union-Tribune,* May 29, 1995, p. B-2.

64. "Sea World Attendance," *Amusement Business,* April 4, 1987, p. 20.

65. Each of the Sea Worlds commissions extensive market and "psychographic" (lifestyle) research on its customers. Sea World of California's market research consultants interview as many as five hundred customers per month in person and the department distributes numerous take-home questionnaires to others. Sea World's senior vice president for marketing, Bill Thomas, interview by author, San Diego, Calif., March 11, 1992.

66. It is unclear whether this identification is based on observation or self-description, and whether it refers to color, historical identity, or mother tongue. Leo J. Schapiro and Associates, "Sea World of California Market Research Summary," January–May 1992, Chicago, Illinois, table 203–1. The figure for the me-

dian income for San Diego County comes from the United States Department of Commerce, Bureau of the Census, summarized in an untitled flier circulated in 1992 by the San Diego Association of Governments (SanDAG) and the Economic Research Bureau of the Greater San Diego Chamber of Commerce. (A revealing contrast may be made between the $35,000 average annual income, which would include rents and investment income, and average annual pay, which was $22,956 in San Diego County in 1992.)

67. The 1990 federal census shows that San Diego County's approximately 2.5 million population is 74.9 percent white, 6.4 percent black, 0.8 percent American Indian, 7.9 percent Asian, and 9.9 percent other. In federal statistics, the category "Hispanic origin" overlaps all others; about 20.5% of San Diego county claims Hispanic origin.

68. Schapiro and Associates, "Market Research Summary," table 203–1. The average age in San Diego County in 1992 was 31.9 years.

69. In California, "gang members" can serve as a code word for minority youth generally. See, for example, Linda Deckard, "Great America's Gang Profiles Targeted by ACLU," *Amusement Business,* July 15, 1991, 1. Deckard reports that while Great America (in Santa Clara, California) rescinded its "gang profile" screening in 1991, metal detector wands are used on "every adult and child entering the park."

70. Frykman and Lofgren, *Culture Builders,* pp. 42–87; Yi-Fu Tuan, *Dominance and Affection: The Making of Pets* (New Haven: Yale University Press, 1984), especially pp. 115–131; Schmitt, *Back to Nature,* pp. 77–124.

71. See, for example, Richard Louv, *Childhood's Future* (Boston: Houghton Mifflin, 1990).

72. Frykman and Lofgren, *Culture Builders,* pp. 42–87. When thinking about what children "need," it is useful to distinguish contact with nature from unstructured play or autonomous activities. In the case of Sea World, there is little that is unstructured or autonomous about the "nature" children encounter there.

73. Schmitt, *Back to Nature,* pp. 77– 124.

74. While Sea World managers claim that their park has a broad audience and "universal appeal," they acknowledge, at the same time, that the price of admission places it out of reach of many. The managers all said in effect, "We know there's price resistance out there, but there's only so much we can do about it."

75. Frank Clifford, "Opening Parks to All of America," *Los Angeles Times,* November 24, 1994, pp. A-1, A-34, A-35.

76. Mike Davis, "Behind the Orange Curtain: Legal Lynching in San Clemente" *Nation,* October 31, 1994, 485. Sea World's picnic areas are limited, with small tables, and perhaps discouraging to extended-family outings. On the other hand, Sea World is unusual among theme parks in that it does not prohibit people from bringing in their own food.

77. Of course, none of the cultural categories referred to by Sea World and offered to its audience are stable. For example, although defined as a family-oriented park, in 1995 Sea World inaugurated "gay night," risking, perhaps, the disapproval of customers with a very conservative definition of family but gaining some attendance and good will from affluent gays.

78. See for example, Schwab, *Deeper Shades of Green;* see also Everett C. Ladd,

"What Do Americans Really Think about the Environment?" *The Public Perspective* 1, no. 4 (May–June 1990): 11–13; on business reaction to wide popular concern over pollution, toxics, and environmental degradation, see David Helvarg, "The Big Green Spin Machine: Corporations and Environmental PR," *The Amicus Journal* 18, no. 2 (summer 1996): 13–21. Helvarg's examples show that Sea World is part of a much larger and very well developed corporate environmental public relations strategy.

2. The Park and the City

1. Histories of the development of tourism economies remain few. Fewer still are histories that link the rise of tourism to structures of space, power, and politics in a city or, more appropriate when describing San Diego, a sprawling exurban region. Essays in Michael Sorkin, ed., *Variations on a Theme Park: The New American City and the End of Public Space* (New York: Hill and Wang, 1992) are suggestive; see also Mike Davis, *City of Quartz* (New York and London: Verso Books, 1990) and Kevin Starr, *Inventing the Dream: California through the Progressive Era* (New York: Oxford University Press, 1985) on Southern California's history of settlement promotion. Earl Pomeroy's *In Search of the Golden West* (New York: Alfred A. Knopf, 1957) remains important on California's general tourist development. San Diego's social history remains incomplete; the standard narrative source is Richard Pourade's multivolume *The History of San Diego* (La Jolla, Calif.: Copley Books, 1960–1977).

2. A tourism economy devotes a considerable part of its resources and infrastructure to creating the attractions that bring spending visitors to a region; a proportion of both human and fiscal resources are employed to produce services for those visitors. By contrast, a manufacturing economy devotes infrastructure to heavy or light industrial production, supporting the manufacture and distribution of goods. Its workforce is largely involved in the production and movement of goods, its services in supporting this production. Tourism tends to draw its labor force into the low-waged, seasonal, and often part-time production of experiences—such as those produced by entertainment, tours, restaurants, and attractive concessions—and services such as waiting tables, cleaning hotels, and performing other janitorial tasks. State and city governments and regional governmental coalitions collaborate to promote tourism growth by subsidizing investment in hotels, convention centers, and historical and themed shopping districts, which directly benefits the real estate, construction, and hotel industries. See John Urry, *The Tourist Gaze: Leisure and Travel in Contemporary Societies* (London: Sage, 1990); on the semiotic structure and integration of attractions, see Dean McCannell, *The Tourist: A New Theory of the Leisure Class* (New York: Schocken Books, 1976).

3. During the time I conducted interviews for this book, Sea World of California was moving its in-house design and engineering department to St. Louis and retiring its senior architect. Up until 1992, Sea World of California designed its own buildings and landscape, occasionally contracting with Southern California firms. Now, design decisions for all the chain are centrally made.

4. The figure in 1989 was $3.5 billion. Union-Tribune, *Union-Tribune Annual Review of Business* (San Diego: Union-Tribune, 1990), p. 45.

5. San Diego has proven more or less immune to the military base closings that have hit the rest of California so hard. Nonetheless, as in the rest of the country, most job growth has been in the low-wage, service sector or in exports, that is, industries exporting materials for assembly in foreign processing centers. The local picture has been one of little manufacturing job growth and income stagnation. Cf. Uri Berliner, "Inflation Outpacing Incomes Here," *San Diego Union-Tribune,* October 26, 1995, p. C-1. A report by Bank of America in mid-1995 noted that while exports of equipment to Mexico were up, and bankruptcies and unemployment were dropping in the county, the city continued to lose high-paying jobs, "with little prospect of regaining them." "[I]ncreasing demands for services placed on counties and municipalities are pushing some of them to the breaking point." Uri Berliner, "San Diego Economy Charts a Healthy Course," *San Diego Union-Tribune,* August 4, 1995, pp. C-1, C-2.

6. Bill Brotherton, executive director of the San Diego Convention and Visitors' Bureau, quoted in the *San Diego Union,* December 27, 1970, B-1 (cited in Joy E. Hayes, "Tourism in San Diego," unpublished paper in the author's possession, 1990, p. 1).

7. Pomeroy, *In Search of the Golden West,* pp. 26–27; further information on early tourism promotion in San Diego is from Hayes, "Tourism in San Diego"; *San Diego Union,* September 2, 1882; and *San Diego Union,* July 10, 1884.

8. Cf. Mark Sauer, "The Changing Tide," *San Diego Union-Tribune,* August 13, 1995, pp. D-1–2,

9. The first exposition drew over 3.5 million visitors to the San Diego area. Hayes, "Tourism in San Diego," p. 5.

10. On the expansion of auto tourism generally, see Pomeroy, *In Search of the Golden West;* Warren J. Belasco, *Americans on the Road : From Autocamp to Motel, 1910–1945* (Cambridge, Mass.: MIT Press, 1979). According to Hayes, "In the days of rail travel, San Diego's tourism was limited by that fact that it was situated on a branch line from Los Angeles. But with the opening of the transcontinental Lee Highway between Washington, D.C., and San Diego in 1923 and Highway 80 between Savannah, Georgia, and San Diego in 1927, the city hoped to draw tourists directly from the East and bypass Los Angeles." Hayes, "Tourism in San Diego," p. 6, n. 3.

11. The first renovations of the exposition buildings took place in the early 1920s. The Presidio Park and museum were dedicated in 1929. Partial restoration of the San Diego Mission was first attempted in 1931. On the expansion of tourism infrastructure, see Richard F. Pourade, *The Rising Tide: The History of San Diego,* vol. 6 (La Jolla, Calif.: Copley Books, 1967) pp. 31, 37, 87, 127, 138–9, 159; and Pourade, *City of the Dream: The History of San Diego,* vol. 7 (La Jolla: Copley Books, 1977), p. 245; Hayes, "Tourism in San Diego," pp. 5–7.

12. Matthew Morbello, "Zoo-Veneers: Animals and Ethnic Crafts at the San Diego Zoo," *Communication Review* 1, no. 4 (1996) in press. Cf. Harry M. Wegeforth and Neil Morgan, *It Began with a Roar! The Beginnings of the World Famous San Diego Zoo* (San Diego: Zoological Society of San Diego, 1953).

13. Pourade, *City of the Dream,* pp. 127–163; 167–182.

14. Pourade, *The Rising Tide,* p. 139; and *City of the Dream,* p. 40.

15. Roberta Ridgely, "How Others See Us," *San Diego Magazine,* April 1954, 23–24, quoted in Hayes, "Tourism in San Diego."

16. Pourade, *City of the Dream,* pp. 102, 145, 148. Actually these lands had long had recreational as well as significant ecological importance. As wetlands they were sites of hunting and fishing, in addition to waste dumping, and were very important for the reproduction of birds and fish. See Sauer, "Changing Tide."

17. San Diego City Planning Department, *Report on Mission Bay–San Diego* (San Diego, August 20, 1954), ii, quoted in Hayes, "Tourism in San Diego," p. 14.

18. Commercial development remains set at that level in the master plan. Pourade, *City of the Dream* , pp. 58–59, 67, 102; on the 1958 Mission Bay Master Plan, ibid., p. 134; San Diego City Planning Department, *History and Development of Mission Bay* (San Diego, January 1957), maps 5, 7. Bay dredging and channel restructuring were performed by the Army Corps of Engineers and paid for largely with federal grant money, an example of federal offices and monies subsidizing local touristic development. As dredging proceeded and nearby landowners began to understand that bay development would provide an important boost to local speculative land values, the vision of the way the bay might be used began to change. A theoretical discussion of the role of private interest in the development of tourist economies, with much relevance to the history of San Diego, is found in Harvey Molotch and John Logan, "The City as Growth Machine," in *Urban Fortunes: The Political Economy of Place,* ed. Molotch and Logan (Berkeley and Los Angeles: University of California Press, 1987), pp. 50–98.

19. Roger M. Showley, "Aquatic Park Mirrors the San Diego Lifestyle," *San Diego Union-Tribune,* July 31, 1994, pp. H-1, H-5. The process of converting Mission Bay from marsh into playground was not uncontested: see Roger M. Showley, "It All Began as a Retreat for Hunters," and sidebar: "A Mission Bay History Lesson," *San Diego Union-Tribune,* July 31, 1994, p. H-5. Similarly, from the beginning, San Diegans had divergent views of the plans for Mission Valley: see Roger M. Showley, "Tracking the Valley," *San Diego Union-Tribune,* December 10, 1995, pp. H-1, H-7. One 1950s plan for the valley envisioned it as an open space greenbelt in the heart of a growing city, with trails connecting to Old San Diego and Mission Bay Park. Development would be kept atop nearby mesas, and retail retained and preserved in the downtown. The clamor of real estate speculation was stronger than the planners' voices. Through the years, however, radical revisions of open space have not gone unchallenged. San Diego owes much of its open space and fragile ecosystem preservation schemes to the work of many small but determined groups of activists who continue to resist the forces of growth. For example, one such group helped protect the Tijuana River Estuary from the fate of Mission Bay in the mid-1970s. Frank Klimko, "He's Why the Marsh Wasn't Swamped," *San Diego Union-Tribune,* August 5, 1995, pp. B-8, B-9.

20. Showley, "Aquatic Park Mirrors the San Diego Lifestyle," pp. H-1, H-5. See also, Julie Tamaki, "Struggle Shapes for Use of Mission Bay Land," *Los Angeles Times,* March 3, 1992, San Diego County edition, pp. B-1, B-3. Wetlands in California generally are gravely endangered: approximately 96 percent have been

destroyed during this century. Cf. *Life on the Edge: A Guide to California's Endangered Natural Resources: Wildlife,* vol. 1 (Santa Cruz, Calif.: BioSystems Books, 1994), pp. 121–22; 156–157; 289–290.

21. "For a short time after the war, improved irrigation and world market demand combined to push agriculture ahead of tourism." Hayes, "Tourism in San Diego," p. 2.

22. Spending rose from approximately $60 million to over $150 million. "100,000 Visit Daily," *San Diego Union,* January 9, 1973, p. X-42 (supplement).

23. *San Diego Union,* January 8, 1964, p. C-5.

24. The averaged daily visitor count was 68,493 in 1960 and 78,082 in 1965. San Diego Convention and Visitor's Bureau, *Visitor Industry Report for San Diego County* (San Diego, 1965).

25. By 1965, the aggregate daily spending averaged $675,879, an increase of nearly a third over 1960's figure of $533,000. San Diego Convention and Visitor's Bureau, *Visitor Industry Report* (San Diego, 1965).

26. *San Diego Union,* January 9, 1973, p. X-42. The late 1960s saw the expansion of elegant golf resorts and health spas in the San Diego area, including the La Costa Country Club.

27. *San Diego Union,* October 8, 1968, p. B-1. "In 1946 the San Diego-California Club changed its name to the San Diego Tourists' Bureau. In 1954 it merged with the San Diego Convention Bureau, which had started in 1928, to become the San Diego Convention and Tourist Bureau. In 1965 this organization changed its name to the San Diego Convention and Visitors Bureau." Hayes, "Tourism in San Diego," n. 2. ConVis serves to coordinate promotions and fund travel research. This research deals with demographic categories of visitors, arrival and departure statistics, hotel occupancy rates, and the relative effectiveness of the city's attractions in drawing visitors. ConVis's main goal is to help determine where and how to advertise San Diego as a destination, keeping in mind the interests of the hotel and motel industry as well as some of the convention service industries. In 1966, a survey of hotel consultants ranked the city third among the leading American destination cities. San Diego Convention and Visitor's Bureau, *Visitor Industry Report, 1966.*

28. For a mid-1970s assessment of the direction and possibilities of these changes, see Kevin Lynch and Donald Appleyard, *Temporary Paradise? A Look at the Special Landscape of the San Diego Region* (Cambridge: Department of Urban Studies and Planning, MIT, 1974).

29. Union-Tribune, *The Union-Tribune Annual Review of Business,* p. 45; Hayes, "Tourism in San Diego."

30. In *The Tourist* Dean McCannell argues that modern tourism is a cultural form based on the production and consumption of differentiations, as against everyday life. Tourist attractions are structured around stories about differences from everyday life in the modern world, stories about "authentic" nature, culture, work, the primitive, the past, the future. Any attraction or cluster of attractions, McCannell argues, is a symbolic form which offers tourists the opportunity to pay homage to these central cultural myths. McCannell, *The Tourist.* Cf. John D. Dorst, *The Written Suburb: An American Site, an Ethnographic Dilemma* (Philadelphia: University of Pennsylvania Press, 1988).

31. Cf. Pomeroy, *In Search of the Golden West;* and Starr, *Inventing the Dream.*

32. Although San Diego has a number of authentic architectural remnants of the Spanish settlement and numerous, more fragile relics of its deep Native American history, the Panama-California Exposition set the baroque "Spanish Renaissance" style that would, for most of the rest of the century, decorate fashionable hotels and public spaces. Acts of recovery of local memory have focused on neighborhood histories—for example, in the "Searching for San Diego" programs of the California Council for the Humanities.

33. Martha K. Norkunas, *The Politics of Public Memory: Tourism, History, and Ethnicity in Monterey, California* (Albany: State University of New York Press, 1993).

34. In this, as Earl Pomeroy has shown, they followed the lead of numerous California real estate developers. Pomeroy contends it was not the West itself that the first gentlemen tourists sought, but imitations and recreations of Italy and the romantic areas of the Old World. *In Search of the Golden West,* pp. 32–38.

35. *San Diego "Our Italy"* (San Diego: San Diego Chamber of Commerce, 1895). In 1925, "John D. Spreckles, developer, civic leader, and owner of the Hotel del Coronado, hoped that his new Mission Beach amusement development would become the 'Venice of America.'" Pourade, *City of the Dream,* p. 57.

36. CIC Research, Inc., *Economic Impact of Sea World on San Diego* (San Diego: CIC Research, 1992). The CIC Report (which was commissioned by Sea World) argues that about 35 percent of Sea World's 2.92 million out-of-town visitors say that the theme park is their main reason for coming to San Diego (p. 5). A tourism promotion video, "Spirit of the City" (San Diego Convention Center, 1992), produced for the convention market, stresses "cultural diversity," "arts," and "heritage" as important attractions of the city; nevertheless, Sea World's performing whales are the first and most prominent images of San Diego offered to the viewer, a kind of key to or summary of the city.

37. The development of a complex tourist attraction depends on, Dean McCannell has pointed out, an interpenetrating infrastructure of institutions and media which continually recreate the region as an attraction or set of attractions. Put another way, city governments, councils, and planning bodies, along with chambers of commerce and the media of news, entertainment, and public relations, all have an important part to play in the construction of a region as an attraction, in the translation of a place and its lived experience into a set of images of a place. Dean McCannell, *The Tourist.*

38. San Diego City Planning Department, *Report on Mission Bay—San Diego,* pp. ii, 101–102; Sea World Lease File 1, City of San Diego, City Clerk's Office.

39. There are no documents recording any public discussion of the granting of the original Sea World lease. By contrast, in the 1990s, with open space at a premium in the city, proposed revisions of Mission Bay's master plan come under close public scrutiny.

40. Sea World seems unique in the theme park industry in that it does not occupy its own real estate but holds a long-term lease with the city; the park must negotiate major landscape changes with the city planning commission and city manager's office. In return the park pays a percentage of profits in rent, prop-

erty taxes, and state sales taxes, some of which end up in city coffers. According to an economic impact report commissioned by Sea World, the park collected $3.3 million in state sales taxes in 1990 on revenues of $102 million. It added $500,000 to San Diego's general fund and $500,000 to city transport funds; it paid $3.9 million in rent to the city and $1.5 million in property taxes. Thus, out of $102 million in revenues, $6.4 million stayed in San Diego. Sea World's consultants estimate that about double this figure is actually pumped into the city, due to the "multiplier" effect. That is, since some people come to San Diego mainly to see the theme park, taxes collected on their spending outside the park can also be credited to Sea World's "account." CIC Research, Inc., *Economic Impact,* p. 2.

41. "Visitor Industry: Sights and Sublime Climate Lure Tourists" *San Diego Union,* April 12, 1964, p. 18 (supplement).

42. As of May 1995, Long Beach has revived its plans for an aquarium at the harbor. J. Michael Kennedy, "It's Sink or Swim for Aquariums," *Los Angeles Times,* May 26, 1995, pp. A-1, A-36–37.

43. Denise Carabet, "Sea World after 15 Years," *San Diego Union* March 27, 1979 (from the San Diego Historical Society, Vertical File 562).

44. On homegrown exoticism, see for example, Kasson, *Amusing the Million: Coney Island at the Turn of the Century* (New York: Hill and Wang, 1978); on imagery at San Diego's expositions, see Robert W. Rydell, *All the World's a Fair: Visions of Empire at America's International Expositions, 1976–1916* (Chicago: University of Chicago Press, 1984), p. 222–223, 230–231. According to Rydell, the overall cultural impact of the expositions' exhibits and attractions was to demonstrate that the white man's technological advance and presumed racial supremacy were simply two sides of the same wave of progress. The progress of white civilization was celebrated within the stately walls of a Spanish city that seemed to promise a way for the civilized to consume foreign cultures without being lowered or tainted by them. The legacy of this fair was all the more enduring, Rydell states, "for the simple reason that it never ended" (p. 231–232).

45. "Sea World Park 80% Complete," *San Diego Union*, December 20, 1963, p. A-21.

46. On Hawaii, see Noel J. Kent, *Hawaii: Islands under the Influence* (New York and London: Monthly Review Press, 1983). This transition is traced in the film *Blue Hawaii,* directed by Norman Taurog and starring Elvis Presley (1962).

47. Among the televised images of Hawaii was the popular program, *Adventures in Paradise,* which aired from October 1959 to April 1962.

48. "Visitor Industry: Sights and Sublime Climate Lure Tourists," *San Diego Union,* April 12, 1964, p. 18 (supplement); "Oceanarium New Magnet for Visitors," *San Diego Union,* January 8, 1964, p. C-5; "April Travel . . . in and beyond Southern California," *Sunset,* April 1964, p. 3.

49. "The Indispensable Visitors," *Journal of Business* [San Diego State College] (spring 1965): 14–15; Pourade, *City of the Dream,* p. 167–185; "San Diego's Mission Bay Park: Sea World Oceanarium," *Architectural Record* 138 (July 1965): 164–165.

50. "April Travel," 3; "Sea World's Motif Carved By Artist, 27," *San Diego Evening Tribune,* March 20, 1964, p. 22.

51. From an undated brochure, *Sea World: World's Greatest Show* (San Diego: Sea World), San Diego Public Library, California Room, Sea World Clip File; Carl Plain, "Sea World Park Promises to Become Tourist Magnet," *San Diego Union,* September 22, 1963, from San Diego Public Library, California Room, Sea World Clip File; "San Diego's New Oceanarium Living Pageant of the Pacific," *San Diego Evening Tribune*, March 20, 1964, p. A-14.

52. In its first year, seven of Sea World's eight shows and exhibits were performed underwater. "April Travel," 3.

53. Richard Schickel, *The Disney Version: The Life, Times, Art, and Commerce Of Walt Disney* (New York: Avon Books, 1968), p. 300.

54. Cliff Smith, "Six Girls Splash into Spotlight," *San Diego Union,* April 18, 1964, p. 10; "Sea World Needs Dolphin Kissers," *San Diego Union,* January 17, 1965, p. A-18.

55. On development patterns in San Diego, see Lynch and Appleyard, *Temporary Paradise?*

56. These descriptions of Sea World's original landscape are based on contemporary newspaper descriptions, photographs, blueprints (from the City of San Diego, City Clerk's Office, Sea World Lease Files 1–13); and Sea World's publicity materials.

57. Sea World Lease File 4, City of San Diego, City Clerk's Office. For the representation of research, technology, and even nuclear technology as benign in the entertainment media, see for example, the contemporaneous Disney film, *The Absent-Minded Professor* (1962).

58. Of the downtown, Lynch and Appleyard wrote in 1974: "[T]he streets of San Diego, except for a few locations such as Horton Plaza, La Jolla, or Mission Beach, are remarkable for their emptiness at almost any hour, and all the more remarkable when we consider the mild climate." At the same time, they noted, "downtown is the principal shopping and entertainment center for the low income neighborhoods around it. Their residents are more dependent on the facilities that downtown affords and use its public space more intensively. Yet they have the least to say about its transformation." *Temporary Paradise?* pp. 21–22. The building of the Bay Bridge to Coronado, which placed huge pilings and an overpass in the center of the largely Chicano neighborhood of Logan Heights, revealed the general relationship of the city's poor and minority neighborhoods to the tourism economy. A dispute broke out over the bridge's construction, and the neighbors demanded a public park. The Chicano Park murals, which later decorated the concrete pylons of the bridge, have slowly (and with no sense of irony) been worked into the city's official roster of tourist sights.

59. "'Sea World' Filmed Here: Channel 10 Offers New Series," *San Diego Union,* April 24, 1964, p. A-10. Within months of opening, Sea World achieved the ultimate theme park seal of approval, a visit from Walt Disney. Carl Plain, "Sea World Even Pleases Disney," *San Diego Union,* October 4, 1964, p. I-10.

60. Carl Plain, "Danny Thomas: Network TV Show Set at Sea World," *San Diego Union,* August 1, 1967, p. B-1; Donald Freeman, "As Hugh Downs Sees *Today* Role," *San Diego Union,* April 25, 1967, p. D-3; Donald Freeman, "Getting a Shark for TV 'Kingdom,'" *San Diego Union,* July 11, 1968, p. C-7. Richard Schickel examines the importance of TV to Disneyland in *The Disney Version:*

The Life, Times, Commerce and Art of Walt Disney, rev. ed. (New York: Touchstone Books, 1985), p. 295–338. *Flipper* ran from September 19, 1964 to May 14, 1967. On the history of the Miami Seaquarium and its relation to television, see Craig Phillips, *The Captive Sea: Life behind the Scenes at the Great Modern Oceanariums* (Philadelphia: Chilton Books, 1964). Miami's Marine Studios, the first Seaquarium, or large oceanarium, in the United States was actually built as an underwater film studio; such campy classics as *The Creature from the Black Lagoon* were filmed there.

61. George Lipsitz describes Disney's use of television and televisual space in "Discursive Space and Social Space: Television, Highways, and Cognitive Mapping in the 1950s City" (paper presented at the annual meeting of the American Studies Association, Toronto, Canada, November 4, 1989); see also Lynn Spigel, *Make Room for TV: Television and the Family Ideal in Postwar America* (Chicago: University of Chicago Press, 1992).

62. One of the most important managers directing the Hollywood connection was Bob La Porta, who arranged celebrity visits to Sea World and sometimes had the celebrities sign their names in concrete near the Shamu Stadium.

63. The public relations department's television productions frequently cross the boundaries between news, entertainment, and advertisement. To accommodate its expanding televisual promotion, Sea World maintains sophisticated direct broadcast satellite uplinks and is developing its own video production capabilities. On broadcasting from the park, see chapter 4.

64. "It's a Whale of a Day," *San Diego Union*, December 20, 1965, p. B-5. On the subsequent importance of Shamu and Shamu's financial valuation, see Peter Waldman and Richard Turner, "Park Wars: Shamu Is the Big Prize Buyer of Sea World Will Get for Its Money," *Wall Street Journal,* August 28, 1989, pp. A-1, A-2.

65. Marineland remained competitive and added its own killer whale shows. But its location on the tip of the Palos Verdes Peninsula, with little highway access, denied it room for physical expansion. Finally, in 1987, Marineland was bought by Harcourt Brace Jovanovich; after a bitter public struggle over its future, the park was closed and its whales transferred to Sea World. Especially desirable for breeding purposes was the acquisition of Orky, an adult male. Nina Easton, "The Death of Marineland," *Los Angeles Times Magazine* , August 9, 1987, 6–10, 23–26.

66. Comparing Sea World's rapid growth from a small start, to the stasis of Disneyland during the 1960s and 1970s (but a major competitor then and now), an executive recalled, "We used to laugh at what a sleepy little company Disney was. We used to wonder what would happen if they ever woke up." Sea World's former president Jan Schultz, interview by author, La Jolla, Calif., March 19, 1992.

67. (The economic and spatial logic of the attraction will be discussed in more detail in chapter 3.) Space is a central, peculiar resource in the amusement park industry: as real estate, it appreciates over the very long term for most parks. In the short term it is something which must be used intensively. Space must be used to extend length of stay and expand concession sales; therefore, there must be many attractions, as close together as possible, and there must be as many

concessions as practicable. But space must be used carefully: people must not feel crowded, or they will stop spending money. Space must be pleasant to stand in and move through, but visitors must keep moving. Harold Vogel, *Entertainment Industry Economics: A Guide for Financial Analysis,* 2nd ed. (New York: Cambridge University Press, 1986), p. 277.

68. One marketing department survey breaks Sea World's present-day clientele into four regions: San Diego County, Southern California minus San Diego County, Arizona, and the rest of the world. The second category is considered critical for advertising purchases. For most of Sea World's history a significant proportion of its customers, as many as 50 percent, have come from within a day's drive of San Diego, which can, of course, include Phoenix, Tucson, Yuma, Las Vegas, and San Francisco. Of these travelers, a significant but smaller number (roughly 17–20 percent) come from San Diego itself. CIC Research, Inc., *Economic Impact,* p. 35; Leo J. Schapiro and Associates, Sea World of California Market Research Summary, January–May 1992, Chicago, Illinois, table 203–1.

69. Longtime San Diego residents recall using Sea World as a public park or garden, as a place to stroll with small children. My study of school children and other fieldwork suggests that today many well-off North County families own annual passes to Sea World and the zoo, and that they use the park much as other people use a free, public, or tax supported space. For the affluent, the park is a place for a casual picnic or a few hours spent outdoors. The parks' controlled spaces—that is, its very lack of social openness—appeal to the parents of small children. On the privatization of public play spaces, compare Leah Brumer, "Up the Sandbox: Safe Fun in 'America's Playground,'" *East Bay Express,* August 26, 1994, p. 6, 8.

70. "It's a Whale of a Day," *San Diego Union,* December 20, 1965, p. B-5; society events included the Scripps Memorial Hospital charity benefit, the Brandeis National Women's Committee benefit, and the annual dinner of the Chamber of Commerce. On Scripps Hospital, see Judith Blakeley, "Hospital Auxiliary Slates Gala Event at Sea World," *San Diego Union,* February 19, 1964, p. 27; on Brandeis, see Judith Blakeley, "Fathoms of Fun Fete Set by Brandeis U. Unit," *San Diego Union,* March 1, 1964, p. D-6; on the Chamber of Commerce, see *San Diego Union,* June 28, 1968, p. B-4; on the Japanese festival, see Kay Jarvis, "'Natsu Matsuri' Designed to Entice Japanese Gods," *San Diego Union,* August 7, 1966, p. D-1. Other early community events held at the park included North Island Naval Air Station employees' day barbecue: *San Diego Union,* October 9, 1966, p. H-8; and a benefit for Southeast San Diego's Theater Workshop: *San Diego Union,* August 25, 1967, p. B-4; on date night, see "Date Night Schedule Listed by Sea World," *San Diego Union,* June 7, 1964, p. A-10.

71. Carl Plain, "Sea World Sets Course on Water," San Diego *Union,* March 16, 1972 (from the San Diego Historical Society, Vertical File 562).

72. "Upscale Amusement Parks," *New York Times*, April 27, 1984, p. D-3; Bro Uttal, "The Ride is Getting Scarier for Theme Park Owners," *Fortune,* December 1977, 67–84; Margaret Thoren, "Fun and Profit: Amusement Parks Shrug Off First Bad Season in Years," *Barron's,* November 3, 1980, 11.

73. Cf. Sally Fitz, "Exploit the Fun of Theme Parks for Meetings," *Success-*

ful Meetings, July 1980, 29. Fitz lists the specially "themed" meals available for conventions at Sea World: Oktoberfest, Mexican Fiesta, Western Barbecue, Old San Diego, and of course, Luau. As San Diego's convention business has grown, Sea World's marketers have found that corporate meetings and conventioneers "help fill in the relatively slow periods in the tourist season" and offer "a cost effective way for parks to better utilize their animals, trainers and facilities." Greg Johnson, "Zoo and Sea World Seek to Lure Corporate Groups," *Los Angeles Times,* October 6, 1992, San Diego County edition, p. D-2.

74. "San Diego Symphony at Sea World," *Evening Tribune,* April 8, 1977, p. A-5.

75. The new Horton Plaza, designed by John Jerde and built by shopping center developer Ernest Hahn, was completed in 1985. Roger M. Showley, "Still the One: 10 Years Later, Horton Plaza Is 'Universal Success' Story," *San Diego Union-Tribune,* August 13, 1995, p. H-2.

76. Plain, "Sea World Sets Course." (One early environmental goal was to help avert the destruction of area tide pools by overzealous nature classes by channeling students into the park.) Ken Hudson, "New Schooling Plan Mapped by Sea World," *San Diego Union,* December 26, 1970, pp. B-1, B-7. See also "School's Open Monday for Sea World's Kids," *San Diego Union,* January 29, 1970, p. B-2. Sea World proclaimed itself "a gigantic free classroom" for the children of San Diego, as it introduced a program of free access for school groups, as well as programs to train teachers in how to use the park. Ken Hudson, "50 Acre Classroom Planned at Sea World," *San Diego Union,* June 12, 1972 (from the San Diego Historical Society, Vertical File 562).

77. "Sea World Acquires Quarterly Magazine," *San Diego Union* August 28, 1977.

78. Cecil Scaglione, "Sea World Has Much More Than Entertainment; Research, Too," *San Diego Union,* September 2, 1977, p. C-8; "Film Series Plunges into Sea Mysteries," *San Diego Evening Tribune,* December 28, 1977, p. B-1; "If You Can't Come to Us, We'll Come to You," Sea World flier stamped "October 1985," San Diego Public Library, California Room, Sea World Clip File; Vicki Torres, "Sea World Aids Library Program," *San Diego Evening Tribune,* June 9, 1983, p. B-20.

79. Ken Hudson, "50 Acre Classroom Planned"; Plain, "Sea World Sets Course on Water"; "Shamu and Seamore's Classroom," *Image,* supplement to *San Diego Sentinel,* June 29, 1977, p. 33 (from the San Diego Historical Society, Vertical File 562).

80. Homer Clance, "Sea World Will Expand by 32 Acres," *San Diego Union,* September 25, 1968; "Sea World Outlines Plan for Oceanographic Exhibit" (from an unmarked clipping from the San Diego City Clerk's Office, Sea World Lease File 7).

81. To the playground space Anheuser-Busch later added a games arcade and a pond for remote-controlled boats, both designed to expand the spending of families with children. In 1994, Cap'n Kid's World was rethemed "Shamu's Happy Harbor," an elaborate, multistory, wet-dry tropical playground, garden, arcade, and performance space.

There was some controversy over the children's play area and its relationship to education at Sea World. Soon after their establishment in 1972, the educational programs were no longer free. Disputes erupted in 1975 about how much, if anything, they should cost, who would provide and plan curricular materials, and who would teach students. San Diego City Clerk's Office, Sea World Lease Files, 6th Lease amendment.

82. On corporate sponsorship in science museums, cf. Howard Learner, "White Paper on Science Museums," (Washington, D.C.: Center for Science in the Public Interest, 1979).

83. Which is exactly what happened. By 1992, the San Diego Natural History Museum was opening "blockbuster"-style exhibits (including "Giants of the Deep," featuring robotic whales) in an attempt to revitalize flagging attendance and membership. Priscilla Lister, "Natural History Museum Gains in Due Recognition," *San Diego Daily Transcript,* March 26, 1992, pp. 1-A, 6-A. In 1994, the Natural History Museum's attendance was flagging, due in part to a year of more "intellectual" exhibits on environments and their problems. Preston Turegano, "Museums Didn't Exhibit Robust '94 Attendance," *San Diego Union-Tribune,* March 13, 1995, p. D-5.

84. From the brochure, *Sea World* (San Diego: Sea World, 1978), pp. 43–45.

85. Cf. Joan McIntyre, *Mind in the Waters: A Book to Celebrate the Consciousness of Whales and Dolphins* (New York: Scribners, 1974). See John Lilly, "A Feeling of Weirdness," in McIntyre, *Mind in the Waters,* pp. 71–77. For a summary of the explosion of popular interest in dolphin and whale consciousness, see David Day, *The Whale War* (San Francisco: Sierra Club Books, 1987), pp. 148–158.

86. Individuals and environmental organizations such as the Sierra Club protested Sea World's practices before the city council and in environmental impact hearings. They questioned the treatment of dolphins and whales, the park's dumping of copper-sulfate treated water into the bay, the effects of water-ski shows on the bay's ecosystem, and Sea World's effect on the local environment generally. Sea World Lease Files 8 and 9, San Diego City Clerk's Office. Michael J. Bean, *The Evolution of National Wildlife Law* (New York: Praeger, 1983), pp. 281–317, describes the purview and implementation of the Marine Mammal Protection Act.

87. Indeed, the record-keeping provisions of the Act and the workings of the National Marine Fisheries Service and the Department of Agriculture help wildlife and animal rights activists to monitor the treatment of marine mammals at Sea World. Sea World's curator of mammals, Jim Antrim, interviews by author, San Diego, Calif., April 1, 1992 and April 7, 1992. See also, Lisa Petrillo, "Law Quashed Ex-King of Dolphin Trade," *San Diego Union-Tribune,* August 29, 1993, pp. B-1, B-4.

88. Sea World president David Demotte argued that the "large number of bills aimed at zoos and marine parks is overwhelming. . . . If all the proposed legislation went through, it would make it very difficult to earn any return on equity." Sea World organized a group called ZooAct and started a petition gathering drive to protect their interest in performing whales. "Help in Fighting Zoo Foes Urged," *San Diego Union*, May 9, 1975, p. C-7.

89. On the capture controversy, see Cliff Smith, "Sea World Whale Hunt Stymied," *San Diego Union,* March 11, 1976, p. 1; "Whale Ban Plan Draws Crit-

icism," *San Diego Union,* March 31, 1976, p. B-9; "Killer Whales Debated," *San Diego Union,* May 5, 1976, p. B-3; "Whale Capture Ban Ruled Out," *San Diego Union,* September 18, 1977, p. B-11; Gina Lubrano, "Sea World Plan to Catch Whales Fought," *San Diego Union,* August 17, 1983, p. B-1; Elizabeth Wong, "Killer Whale Hunt Sparks Concern," *San Diego Evening Tribune,* May 12, 1983 (from the San Diego Public Library, California Room, Sea World Clip File); Elizabeth Wong, "Killer Whale Plan Faces Opposition," *San Diego Evening Tribune,* August 15, 1983, p. A-6; Gina Lubrano, "Sea World Plan to Get Hearing," *San Diego Union,* August 15, 1983, p. 1. For the conclusion, see "US Judge Sinks Sea World Plan to Catch Whales," *San Diego Evening Tribune,* January 22, 1985, pp. B-1, B-5. Sea World and other parks have been accused of "whale laundering," that is, obtaining through foreign animal dealers orcas captured outside the purview of United States law. John Hall, a former Sea World employee, describes such an arrangement in "Whale Laundering Exposed," *Earth Island Journal,* fall, 1993, 14.

90. Carl Hubbs was a professor emeritus at the Scripps Institute of Oceanography. Cliff Smith, "$50 million Ocean Research Lab Formally Dedicated at Sea World," *San Diego Union,* May 25, 1977, p. B-1.

91. "Sea Study Backed," *San Diego Union,* June 17, 1982, p. B-14.

92. Scaglione, "Sea World Has Much More," p. C-8; Cliff Smith, "Sea World Begins Research Work Designed to Aid Public," *San Diego Union,* May 27, 1981, p. B-1. Sea World Research Institute, "Sea World Research Institute Publications," (San Diego: Sea World Research Institute, c. 1992) (unpublished, undated bibliography).

93. For a recent description, see Neil Morgan, "Tortoises on the Dance Floor at Sea World," *San Diego Union-Tribune,* July 9, 1995, p. A-2.

94. The first Baby Shamu to survive in captivity was born at Sea World of Florida in 1985; several others were born that did not survive. Sea World of California's first Baby Shamu was born September 23, 1988. John Wilkens and Dayna Lynn Fried, "Kandu Death Imperils Breeding Program," *San Diego Union,* August 24, 1989, p. B-1.

95. For a description of the Center for the Reproduction of Endangered Species (CRES), see Zoological Society of San Diego, *Annual Report, 1995,* published in *ZooNooz* 68, no. 7 (July 1995): 5–6. The CRES is an important aid to fund-raising and, very likely, also a help in defusing concerns about animal abuse and the morality of captivity. On the debate on captive reproduction generally, see Bryan G. Norton, Michael Hutchins, Elizabeth F. Stevens, and Terry L. Maple, *Ethics on the Ark: Zoos, Animal Welfare, and Wildlife Conservation* (Washington: Smithsonian Institution Press, 1995), p. 127–208.

96. R. B. Brenner, "Whale Accident Seriously Injures Trainer," *San Diego Union,* November 22, 1987, p. B-3. Following the accident, in which trainer John Sillick was nearly crushed to death, several executives were fired, and the whale shows were rewritten so that the trainers did not enter the water. John MacLaren and David Hasemeyer, "Injuries Prompt Top Level Firings at Sea World," *San Diego Tribune,* December 2, 1987, p. A-1; "Routines Revised for Whale Show," *San Diego Union,* November 25, 1987, p. B-3. "Orky," the whale that injured Sillick, had a long history of aggressive behavior; in addition, Sea World's train-

ing methods, a high turnover among trainers, and pressure to produce performers for the opening of the Texas park seem to have been contributing causes of the accident. Ed Jahn, "Sea World Official Faults Entertainment Emphasis," *San Diego Union,* December 6, 1987, p. A-1. Jim Okerblum, "Sea World Felt the Pressure?" *San Diego Union,* December 4, 1987, p. A-1.

97. Richard Core and John R. Lamb, "Killer Whale's Death Shocks Sea World," *San Diego Tribune,* August 22, 1989, p. A-1; Pat Flynn and Lisa Petrillo, "Crowd Views Sea World Tragedy," *San Diego Union,* August 22, 1989, p. A-1. For Sea World's analysis of the accident, see Dayna Lynn Fried and John Wilkens, "Kandu Bled to Death after Accident," *San Diego Union,* August 23, 1989, p. A-1. There has been an ongoing controversy over Sea World and whales and dolphins in captivity: activists have protested Sea World's collaboration with Chicago's Shedd Aquarium to capture dolphins off the Southern California coast; see Marla Cone, "Free Flipper," *Los Angeles Times ,* November 14, 1993, pp. A-3, A-32; Steve Schmidt, "Activists Eluded; Dolphins Caught," *San Diego Union-Tribune,* November 29, 1993, pp. B-1, B-4. Several animal rights and whale protection groups have urged Sea World to release one of its older orcas, Corky, arguing that since her pod (social group of origin) has been identified, she can rejoin it. For example, the "Collage" program broadcast "The Corky Debate" on radio station KPCC (Pasadena), July 29, 1992; see also Stuart Elliott, "Thanks to Hollywood, Anheuser-Busch is Working to Avoid a Whale of an Image Problem," *New York Times,* August 4, 1993, p. C-2; Michael Granberry, "Free Corky?: Calls to Release Sea World Orca Grow Louder," *Los Angeles Times,* August 11, 1993, pp. A-3, A-24.

98. San Diego added population quickly during the 1980s, housing nearly fifty thousand new residents a year for a decade, largely in the county's northern and eastern suburbs. But Sea World's local attendance fell absolutely during this period. The local customers have made up slightly less than 20 percent of the paying customers annually, but this is a reliable bedrock that buys annual passes, keeps the park active in the off-season, and makes up the audience for special events.

99. On this trend in the zoo world, see Melissa Greene, "No Rms, Jungle View," *Atlantic Monthly,* December 1987, 62, 64–68, 70–72, 74, 76–78.

100. Cliff Smith, "$50 million Ocean Research Lab Formally Dedicated at Sea World," *San Diego Union,* May 25, 1977, p. B-1; Daniel C. Carson, "Sea World Plan May Include Artificial Blizzard," *San Diego Union,* February 13, 1979, pp. B-1, B-4; "Sea World's Penguin Show Wins Award," *San Diego Union,* September 21, 1984, p. B-8.

101. They also announce, albeit vaguely, that the Hubbs–Sea World Research Institute's Antarctic research receives funding from the National Science Foundation.

102. Bat Ray Shallows opened in spring 1990, rebuilt on the site of the former Japanese Village; Rocky Point Preserve is copied from an exhibit at the Point Defiance Aquarium in Tacoma, Washington.

103. On this history, see Anthony Corso, "San Diego: The Anti-City" in *Sun Belt Cities: Growth and Politics Since World War II,* ed. Richard M. Bernard and Bradley R. Rice (Austin: University of Texas Press, 1983), pp. 328–344.

104. Mike Wallace makes a similar argument about the difference between Disneyland's and Walt Disney World's versions of American history in "Mickey Mouse History: Portraying the Past at Disney World," *Radical History Review* 32 (1985): 33–57.

105. Senior vice president for marketing, Bill Thomas, interview by author, San Diego, Calif., March 11, 1992; "Theme Parks Pull for the Home Team," *Los Angeles Times,* November 27, 1990, San Diego County edition, p. D-2.

106. Sea World employs over fifteen hundred people; CIC Research, Inc., *Economic Impact,* p. 2. Sea World's management asserts that the park is the largest single employer of high school students in the county.

107. It was hoped Horton Plaza would coax developer money back into the downtown. Mayor Pete Wilson and Hahn's goal was to bring department stores downtown, "something no major city has been able to do in the era of suburban shopping malls," to "revitalize downtown retailing, spur redevelopment of housing, offices and mass transit, and most important to generate new taxes in an area that had been a net loss to the city treasury." Despite the plaza's "49 color palette," the takeoff of downtown has not happened. Showley, "Still the One."

108. Annual passes cost about $59.00 per person in 1995; Sea World reported having about 80,000 annual pass holders in 1992, roughly equivalent to 3.3 percent of the countywide population of about 2.4 million.

109. Many state beaches and parks in San Diego County now charge the public fees for parking and entrance. City lifeguard services and trash collection have been sharply reduced. See also Sauer, "The Changing Tide."

110. It is doubtful that this commodified space can accommodate the spontaneous, mixed, and flexible uses possible in older public spaces such as Balboa Park. Demonstrations, protests, gatherings of the politically unpopular or socially undesirable seem unlikely in the theme park. Since the park expanded and gated its parking lots in 1993–94 and began charging five dollars to park, it is even harder for animal rights demonstrators to occupy the park's perimeter. Unlike the old amusement park or the beach areas, the park cannot be entered freely from other nearby activities. Although a system of bike trails through Mission Bay skirts Sea World, the park is connected mainly to its own maze of parking lots.

3. Producing the Sea World Experience

1. As a friend pointed out to me, the smell of the ocean is missing. Sea World's dominant odors are the scent of popcorn, fish, and chlorinated salt water.

2. A vast literature is devoted to commentary on the design of theme parks. See, for example, Derek Walker, *Animated Architecture* (London: Architectural Design, 1982); "Entertainment Landscapes," special issue of *Landscape Architecture* 80, no. 6 (June 1990).

3. Former vice president for communications, Jackie Hill, interview by author, San Diego, Calif., March 13, 1992. "Somewhere along the line, someone somewhere made the connection that [per capita spending] is up when in-park stay is up. So you give people more things to do to stay longer."

4. Sea World's senior vice president for marketing, Bill Thomas, interview by author, San Diego, Calif., March 11, 1992.

5. Hill, interview, March 13, 1992.

6. Ibid.

7. Bill Thomas, interview by author, San Diego, Calif., April 1, 1992.

8. Hill, interview, March 13, 1992.

9. "Good merchandise per caps is critically important in this day and age, and becoming more important since you cannot raise your gate high enough to support the operations and the profit. There's a limit on how far we can go, but we don't know what that is. You have to make up your operating costs and your profit out of something else. You do it out of food and merchandise." Hill, interview, March 13, 1992.

10. Bad weather in January and February is predictable, but 1992's disastrous March rains were unexpected and hit Sea World's attendance hard. However, no one foresaw that the riots in 1992 and fires in 1993 might scare tourists away from Los Angeles and toward San Diego and Sea World. And there are other factors the planners can't control: the moveable character of the Easter holiday week, for example, always creates problems because it does not articulate in predictable ways with public school calendars. Similarly, the movement to year-round schooling with holiday breaks scheduled around the year instead of in summer, plays havoc with attendance projections, especially since some districts in the San Diego area have year-round schedules, and some do not. Although it is open all year, Sea World gets more than 50 percent of its attendance in the summer months. But what if summer vacations become a thing of the past?

11. Hill, interview, March 13, 1992.

12. Ibid.

13. Sea World's vice president for operations, Steve Geiss, interview by author, San Diego, Calif., April 28, 1992; also Hill, interview, March 13, 1992.

14. Sea World discounts very heavily against a high admission price, using a range of cross-promotional arrangements with many different kinds of business. Thomas, interview, March 11, 1992.

15. In 1992, Sea World had between 80,000 and 90,000 annual pass members, each of whom was thought to visit the park four to five times yearly (that is, 320,000–450,000 visits). The lower estimate is probably closer. Thomas, interview, March 11, 1992.

16. Sea World's vice president for design and engineering, Ferris Wankier, interview by author, San Diego, Calif., April 1, 1992.

17. As part of this same effort to communicate "class," all the park's buildings are freshly painted every year. Upgrading may often require more intensive efforts. During spring 1992, construction workers replaced Sea World's complicated network of asphalt walkways with light-colored, patterned concrete. Asphalt is dark, does not show dirt, and presumably needs less cleaning, but I was told that this decision was made largely for stylistic reasons. Concrete, according to Steve Geiss, the director of operations, looks "high-class," whereas asphalt looks urban and presumably "low-class." Sea World's vice president for operations, Steve Geiss, interview by author, San Diego, Calif., March 11, 1992.

18. Wankier, interview, April 1, 1992.

19. Ibid.
20. Ibid.
21. Geiss, interview, April 28, 1992.
22. Hill, interview, March 13, 1992.
23. Ibid.
24. Running the park, as we will see below, involves not only creating physical structures and temporal patterns; it involves getting animals to perform and efficiently deploying the park's hundreds of service employees. Marine mammals and birds, food servers, janitors, parking lot attendants, ticket-takers, ride operators, and maintenance people are all part of this human and architectural machine.
25. Geiss, interview, March 11, 1992.
26. Ibid.
27. Ibid.
28. Ibid.
29. Arlie R. Hochschild, *The Managed Heart: Commercialization of Human Feeling* (Berkeley and Los Angeles: University of California Press, 1983). See also "Working at the Rat," in The Project on Disney, *Inside the Mouse: Work and Play at Disney World* (Durham: Duke University Press, 1995), pp. 110–162.
30. Operations is one of the largest park departments. The number of Sea World employees nearly doubles during the summer.
31. "We do a lot of part-time hiring. So we can make up for the fact that we don't have an actual forty-hour, full-time person there with a couple of twenty-hours people." Geiss interview, March 11, 1992. Sea World tends to hire people with other commitments or part-time jobs around which they can fit some Sea World hours. Management claims to prefer local college student employees as more mature and trainable, and as more likely to keep commitments to return to work full-time during holiday breaks. According to Sea World management, they place a premium on the employment of students from the several local colleges and universities, and it is true that San Diego's public university students increasingly need to work at least part-time, and more often full-time, to support their studies. Sea World even offers educational assistance plans for employees of several years' tenure, paying for books and fees in return for a commitment to continual part-time work. As beneficent and flexible as this sounds, it also reflects the weakness of the San Diego economy and the low wages generally available in an economy heavily reliant on tourism. Although Sea World also hires high school graduates, the fact that college-age men and women are willing to start at a very low wage means that other, less educated workers are even more hard-pressed. Geiss, interview, March 11, 1992. Various kinds of part-time permanent and temporary work are common in the theme park industry. For a comparison to work at Walt Disney World, see "Working at the Rat," pp. 110–162.
32. Seen from the point of view of Sea World management, the younger, less educated part of the workforce does not take easily to the basic principles of work discipline. This may be another reason college students are preferred. Geiss, interview, March 11, 1992.
33. Hochschild, *The Managed Heart,* p. 89–136.
34. Geiss, interviews, March 11, 1992 and April 28, 1992.
35. Hochschild points out that airline flight attendants face a similar demand

to use emotional labor to reduce customers' alienation. *The Managed Heart,* pp. 89–136.

36. Geiss, interview, March 11, 1992.

37. Sea World management would not share details of this training process. Geiss, interview, March 11, 1992.

38. Ibid.

39. David White, interview by author, San Diego, Calif., April 7, 1992. This also asks service employees to identify with the high status, well-paid trainers.

40. "If you see them dealing with a guest in an appropriate manner or going out of their way to satisfy a guest or just do a better job, we give them a Showtime! card. Once a month there is a drawing and you can win nice prizes." White, interview, April 7, 1992.

41. Ibid.

42. Geiss, interview, March 11, 1992.

43. However, if employees are underscheduled, they will lose interest in a job that doesn't provide enough hours and quit or become unreliable. "So there's always all those seemingly conflicting interests going on in the show schedules." Geiss, interview, April 28, 1992. Accurate counts of attendance can make a big difference to the food service department. "It usually happens that if we've overhired, a lot of kids will leave and find another job so they can get some kind of income. They expect forty hours when they are hired, but if our attendance goes off 5 percent, then our man-hours are going to go down at least 5 percent." White, interview, April 7, 1992.

44. White, interview, April 7, 1992.

45. Theme park industry analysts assume that in any party, a food purchase will be made every two hours, so the longer people stay, the more they eat and drink.

46. On labor relations and work patterns in the fast-food industry in general, see Ester Reiter, *Making Fast Food: From the Frying Pan into the Fryer* (Montreal: McGill-Queen's University Press, 1991).

By means of a "line schedule," managers divide up food service workers' hours into twenty-minute blocks. Tasks are blocked out for the worker at each station so that no paid time will be wasted. According to White, to make up the line schedules, "we collect data in the facilities, sales data, and data on tasks, and we sit down and write schedules based on the task and how much time it takes. And, it's all based on attendance. The data we collect tell us, for example, we need two cashiers for three thousand people and three cashiers for five thousand people." Each "facility," whether restaurant or food stand, has work stations, and each worker is assigned a schedule of instructions about which stations to staff and which tasks to perform. These tasks are determined by time-motion studies of the same sort in use in American factories since the early twentieth century. The definitions of stations (or locations) and tasks show how finely work processes are broken down. For example, "a location might be a cash register, it might be putting hamburgers on the hamburger machine, it might be catching them when they come off, or having a certain quadrant of the patio to keep clean." White, interview, April 7, 1992.

47. White, interview, April 7, 1992.

48. Ibid.

49. Ibid.; Hill, interview, March 13, 1992.

50. Judith Adler, "The Origins of Sightseeing," *Annals of Tourism Research*, vol. 16 (1989): 7–29. Adler also argues that seeing and viewing are inseparable from processes of physical movement of the viewer. John F. Sears, *Sacred Places: American Tourist Attractions in the Nineteenth Century* (New York: Oxford University Press, 1989).

51. This looking-across-the-landscape technique was developed in German zoos at the turn of the century and frequently was used to create the impression that different species shared the same terrain. At Sea World it is used on a smaller scale to give the viewer the impression that he or she has been inserted into nature and has come upon birds and turtles unexpectedly. Bob Mullen and Gary Marvin, *Zoo Culture* (London: George Weidenfeld and Nicholson, 1987), pp. 46–89.

52. It is an interesting question whether and how much the park materializes what has already been televised. In the last forty years, largely through the leadership of Disney films but also through the television works of Marlin Perkins and Jacques Cousteau, previously remote and unseeable animal sights have been brought to television audiences. So, while today many species that were previously little known have had their fifteen minutes of fame, in the larger picture they are still new, still animal curiosities.

53. On the history and ideological structure of travel literature, see Mary Louise Pratt, *Imperial Eyes: Travel Writing and Transculturation* (London: Routledge, 1992); on nature, knowledge, and empire, see Harriet Ritvo, *The Animal Estate: The English and Other Creatures in the Victorian Age* (Cambridge: Harvard University Press, 1987), pp. 1–44; on *National Geographic*, see Herbert I. Schiller, *The Mind Managers* (New York, Beacon Books, 1974) pp. 79–103, and Catherine A. Lutz and Jane L. Collins, *Reading National Geographic* (Chicago: University of Chicago Press, 1993).

54. There are, for example, no displays dealing with or referring to European, Mediterranean, Eurasian, or Atlantic nature or marine life.

55. Sears, *Sacred Places*, pp. 12–30.

56. To appeal to the mix of ages in the audience, the Shark Encounter is constructed as simultaneously a frightening adventure and nothing to be afraid of. Tunnels are frequently used in aquariums around the world to create the powerful illusion of entering the other environment.

57. Bob Mullan and Gary Marvin, *Zoo Culture*, pp. 46–89. See also Kenneth J. Polakowski, *Zoo Design: The Reality of Wild Illusions* (Ann Arbor: University of Michigan, School of Natural Resources, 1987).

58. Quoted is marketing director John Racanelli, *Amusement Business*, April 29–May 5, 1991, p. 26.

59. Wankier, interview, April 1, 1992.

60. Ibid.

61. Ibid.

62. Ibid. The same kind of moving walkway is installed in the Shark Encounter's acrylic tube.

63. Ibid.

64. Sears, *Sacred Places*, pp. 12–30; 182–216.

65. Sea World's vice president for entertainment, Don Ludwig, interview by author, San Diego, Calif., March 11, 1992.

66. Geiss, interview, March 11, 1992.

67. As one visitor put it jocularly, "*You* pay to feed *their* animals!"

68. Beyond these feeding-touching modes of engagement, the people who really get "up close and personal" with the animals (to use a Sea World-ism) are the trainers, and it is by proxy, as a crowd watching trainers perform, that the audience goes beyond superficial contact with the captive animals. (In chapter 5, I take up the issue of what the audience participates in through watching the trainers.)

69. Wankier, interview, April 1, 1992.

70. Sea World's curator of mammals, Jim Antrim, interview by author, San Diego, Calif., April 1, 1992.

71. Wankier, interview, April 1, 1992.

72. The Point Defiance exhibit is called Rocky Shores; it "replicates an area near Cape Flattery, Washington, and offers close up and above water and below water viewing of Pacific walrus, white whales, dolphins, sea otters, seals, sea lions, puffins and auklets." Anthony L. Pacheco and Susan E. Smith, *Marine Parks and Aquaria of the United States: A Reference Guide* (New York: Lyons and Burford, 1989), p. 102. Dean McCannell has traced the process of pile-up and overlay of mass media images in tourism in his *The Tourist: A Theory of the New Leisure Class* (New York: Schocken Books, 1976), pp. 123–131.

73. Many Sea World offices are decorated with official Sea World images—posters and photographs. But sometimes they are also decked with what might be thought of as touristic "originals"—a postcard featuring a view of Telegraph Cove, for example, a famous place to spot wild killer whales. Janet Gotch pointed to such a postcard during our interview and said, "I've been there to see the killer whales, but most of our guests will never be able to go. You can't go up to the Puget Sound and, [even if you do] you may see killer whales but you will see them from the surface only. You'll see their dorsal fin, or see them taking a breath or breaching. And that's if you can afford to go up there and see them. So, Sea World gives you a chance to see these animals in a way that you never would in real life." Sea World entertainment department producer and director, Janet Gotch, interview by author, San Diego, Calif., April 14, 1992.

Of course, this process of creating better versions of recognizably foreign places is commonplace in theme parks, but it is more recognizable when the parks deal in culture-scapes. "City Streets" at Sea World was closely modeled on a blend of the Lower East Side of Manhattan and Newburgh, New York. Sea World of Florida is currently producing an improved model Key West, so that its customers will feel they've really seen Florida. "Theme Park to Replicate a Nearby Exotic Locale," *New York Times*, November 19, 1995, p. 20.

74. Antrim, interview, April 1, 1992.

75. Wankier, interview, April 1, 1992. According Ferris Wankier, the perceptions of the employees who care for and present the animals are also important, and they too favor the realistic look.

76. Ben Deeble, Greenpeace spokesperson, quoted in Nancy Cleeland, "Captive or Coddled: Debate Lingers on Whale Habitat," *San Diego Union*, October 18, 1987, p. A-13.

77. Cleeland, "Captive or Coddled," pp. A-1, A-2, A-13.

78. Wankier, interview, April 1, 1992.

79. Ibid. By contrast, the San Diego Zoo sometimes uses "nature" sound tracks or recordings of ambient sound to enhance its "bioclimatic zone" exhibits.

80. It is well known that Muzak can enhance spending in gift shops. Background music also masks other people's conversations: a sound envelope helps maintain the illusion that the small group is sequestered from strangers and crowds. It is impossible to get away from prerecorded music at Sea World. I found the seamless sound track an obstacle to my fieldwork: I was always looking for excuses to get away from the music in order to be alone with my thoughts, and the only way to do that was to leave the park. But this apparently is not a widely shared reaction. Sea World, along with its audience, finds the electronic aural theming of every bit of space completely unremarkable, perhaps because both television and inexpensive sound technologies for the home and automobile have proliferated, and the penetration of workplaces and public spaces by "mood music" is so advanced. Its managers seem to think that if they did not add music to its landscapes, visitors might feel something was missing and experience the park as incomplete. On the dominance of prerecorded and specifically themed and customized music in commercial spaces, see Simon C. Jones and Thomas G. Schumacher, "Muzak: On Functional Music and Power," *Critical Studies in Mass Communication* 9 (1992): 156–169.

81. Park officials say that "When I Take the Time" is very popular. The entertainment department gets requests for copies of that CD and other areal sound tracks. "It's a pretty message and the music is emotional—people request it all the time," says the vice president for entertainment. "It goes, 'When I take the time to look around . . . ,' and so on." Don Ludwig, interview by author, San Diego, Calif., April 7, 1992.

82. Thomas, interview, March 11, 1992.

83. Ibid.

84. Ibid.

85. Ibid.

86. Hill, interview, March 13, 1992.

87. Ibid.

4. Enlightenment Lite

1. The specifically educational uses of entertainment media have been very little studied, as Elizabeth Ellsworth points out in "Educational Media, Ideology, and the Presentation of Knowledge through Popular Cultural Forms," in *Popular Culture, Schooling and Everyday Life,* ed. Henry A. Giroux, Roger Simon, and Contributors (Granby, Mass.: Bergin and Garvey, 1989), pp. 47–66.

2. The most sustained period of my research took place during the academic year 1991–92. During this time I interviewed Sea World education department personnel and San Diego city and county school teachers and program coordinators, observed Sea World's education programs for different age groups in the theme park and in several schools and day care centers, and spent time observing

students and staff at one of Sea World's sponsored "magnet schools," Emerson-Bandini in Logan Heights in south San Diego. I also interviewed a small sample of eight- to eleven-year-old school children about their relationship to theme parks generally and Sea World in particular. From 1992 to 1995, I conducted follow-up fieldwork in the park and with teachers and tracked the development of Sea World's forays into new communication media.

3. As every museum and zoo curator knows well, visitors often treat the information offered by museum and zoo exhibits as distractions from the real attractions.

4. In 1995, this photographic aspect of the tide pool was more pronounced: Sea World had added a huge, bright orange plastic sculpture of a sea star, with touchable suction cups on the underside of its legs. It was clearly added as a picture-taking opportunity, but was thronged by children fascinated with its textures. The sculpture offered a powerfully magnified, visible whole starfish—a better, more explorable version of the living stars in the pool.

5. In these selections from my field notes, I have given pseudonyms to teachers, students, and Sea World staff (with the exception of vice president for education Joy Wolf) who spoke with me during field trips to Sea World; I have given pseudonyms to schools as well.

6. They hadn't. The next day I crossed paths with Joy Wolf, the vice president for education, who said, a little anxiously, "I hear you ran into a teacher with a complaint yesterday. They just went to the CD [compact disc]," she explained, and the sound track couldn't be interrupted. "I talked to Entertainment about it. . . . I'd wanted them to put a longer break in between repetitions of the song. But they just custom-pressed the CD, and that's expensive to change." The frustrating problem of fitting themselves into an entertainment landscape they did not control was familiar to the education staff.

7. Karen Pryor recalls that "training" each other to do odd things was both a popular parlor trick and a way of teaching animal trainers operant conditioning theory at Sea Life Park in the 1960s. *Lads before the Wind: Diary of a Dolphin Trainer,* 2nd ed. (North Bend, Wash.: Sunshine Books, 1991), pp. 119–123.

8. Deborah Ely-Lawrence, "Writing Classroom Materials That Make the Grade," *Public Relations Journal* 50, no. 4 (April 1994): 26. Ely-Lawrence describes the ways companies can use educational resources to get their points of view and products into the classroom, and she outlines the requirements for successful classroom materials. Materials should be short with clear goals, easily fitted into already extant units, grade appropriate, and multidisciplinary; they should also have a socially "hot" topic and yet be carefully written to avoid controversy in districts prone to censorship. She suggests that teachers have input into the development of curricular materials, and that materials be field-tested on students to see how they work. Ely-Lawrence might also have mentioned that it helps a great deal if the materials are free—and very colorful. For a critical perspective on corporate public relations materials in the classroom, see Consumers Union, *Captive Kids: Commercial Pressures on Kids at School* (Yonkers, N.Y.: Consumers Union Educational Services, 1995); Michael F. Jacobson and Laurie Ann Mazur, *Marketing Madness: A Survival Guide for a Consumer Society* (Boulder: Westview Press, 1995), pp. 21–38.

9. "My biggest fear," public relations director Dan LeBlanc told me, "isn't with animal rights [activists] themselves, it's with the public at large and what they are listening to. Are we doing a good enough job communicating what it is that we do? That goes back to talking more about education. It involves publicizing beached animal [rehabilitation] or getting involved in beach cleanups. It's part of the reason we do those things. Some of them are programs we just started, some of them we've had forever. We're finding out we'd better start letting people know we do these things, because these guys, as crazy as some of the things are that they're saying, people believe in it. And also, [we need to] undo the damage of the accidents in 1987, 1989." He went on to say, "We really rely on the San Diego community to allow us to do a lot of things." Dan LeBlanc, interviews by author, San Diego, Calif., March 11, 1992 and April 14, 1992.

10. From the promotional brochure *Earth Shuttle* (Boston, Mass.: Carter Company, 1989).

11. Disney Educational Productions produces classroom videotapes, interactive videodiscs, and laser discs for all grade levels in the sciences and social sciences, as well as educational commercial television programming. Completely separate from its educational products division but related conceptually are Disney's book, magazine publishing, and music divisions, as well as its consumer products division. Suffice it to say here that the educational reach of the Disney empire is extensive and largely unstudied. For some sense of the potential scope, see *The Walt Disney Company 1995 Annual Report* (Burbank: Walt Disney Company, 1996), pp. 16–43.

12. Nor do I mean to say that Sea World is the only park chain that uses education or conservation as a public relations and marketing tool. Six Flags parks have long had a reading promotion program, well suited to help the image of the parks, which themselves serve as advertising for television programs. See Tim O'Brien, "Six Flags-IAAPA Programs Encourage Youth to Read for Fun," *Amusement Business,* February 4, 1991, 5. For details on a range of theme park industry programs, see O'Brien, "Industry Getting Involved in Educating America's Youth," *Amusement Business,* February 25, 1991, 5.

13. Sea World's former vice president for communications, Jackie Hill, interview by author, San Diego, Calif., March 26, 1992. The movement for privatizing public schools aims, in its overall thrust, at more control over the content and direction of education and training so that corporate manpower and skills needs can be met in the next century. But this movement also intersects with a principled right-wing effort to de-liberalize and de-secularize public education. See Michael W. Apple, "Whittling Away at Democracy: The Social Context of Channel One," in *Watching Channel One: The Convergence of Students, Technology, and Private Business,* ed. Anne De Vaney (Albany: State University of New York Press, 1994), pp. 167–188. Sea World probably has no intention of taking over or running a public school. It does sponsor four "magnet schools," three in San Diego and one in Arizona. But the fact that Sea World donates minimal resources to each of these schools seems to indicate that what is hoped for is a public relations gain, the image of being a solid citizen, rather than a close and directing relationship.

14. Busch's introduction of *Second Noah,* a network television series with an

animal-saving theme, in 1996, and Sea World's increased offerings of "educational" park-based sound tracks and videos seem to indicate that the company is experimenting with nature education as a new profit center.

15. These examples are based on my interviews with teachers at the elementary and preschool level in neighborhoods ranging from very poor to extraordinarily wealthy, and on discussions with Sea World's education staff. I also draw on discussions with a small sample of school-age children, parents, and documentary sources.

16. Sea World of California, *Sea World of California Education Department Year-End Report, 1993* (San Diego: Sea World Education Department, 1993), p. 17. Ocean Discovery's 1993 attendance rose by more than 500 students from the previous year. Ibid., p. 10.

17. The parent-child participation fee is relatively high, about $30, but not as much as a whole day at Sea World would cost. Children and parents are therefore escorted out—a bit unceremoniously—at 11 a.m. Figures for the preschool-parent participation classes are not disaggregated in *Year-End Report, 1993,* but are listed in the category "grades pre[school]–5" for the Camp Sea World summer programs (see below). However, the preschool–5 category is Camp Sea World's largest, with 1,446 of an attendance total 2,116 that year. Sea World of California, *Year-End Report, 1993,* p. 13.

18. This work was conducted at two San Dieguito Boys and Girls Club after-school programs for three months in fall 1991. I observed roughly one hundred elementary school children and interviewed seventeen. This was an ethnically diverse but largely middle-class group of children by virtue of its location in coastal North County; however, several children from working-class and poor families were included in my interview group.

19. Sea World of California, *Year-End Report, 1993,* p. 5.

20. Ibid., p. 4. Field trip attendance, while steadily growing, fluctuates throughout the year. In 1993, the biggest months for instructional field trip attendance were, in order, May, March, April, and June. To give a sense of the rising and falling tides of visiting students, May, with attendance of nearly thirty-three thousand children and teachers, contrasted with a more average month, February, with about forty-eight hundred student visitors. School groups want to avoid San Diego's sometimes rainy late fall and early spring weather.

21. Total outreach participation in 1993 was 146,766, up from 123,702 in 1992. Sea World of California, *Year-End Report, 1993,* p. 4.

22. College students are not disaggregated from the other students in the *Year-End Report,* but they make up a small proportion of the in-park field trip visitors. The Office of Education counted about 504, 800 students enrolled in 1993. This figure includes special education programs and some adult vocational classes run by the districts. Information from San Diego County Office of Education, fall 1994.

23. Most class visits to the zoo, for example, are free. The zoo's education department probably sees several hundred thousand school children annually. From an undated report on the zoo's financial contribution to San Diego: *A Hidden Value* (San Diego: San Diego Zoo and Wild Animal Park, n.d.).

24. Joy Wolf, interview by author, San Diego, Calif., April 7, 1992.

25. Jonathan Kozol explains the property tax–based funding patterns which

have perpetuated the stark division of impoverished from affluent public school districts in *Savage Inequalities: Children in America's Schools* (New York: Crown Publishers, 1991).

26. The results of my interviews with children tend to confirm this, although the sample is very small. Children from professional families in wealthy neighborhoods tended to talk about Sea World as another park to play in, a place to go on weekends for a few hours. Children who lived in the poor neighborhoods and trailer parks bordering and supporting the wealthy suburbs spoke of Sea World as a place to "study," "look things up," and "learn."

27. Camps following a "science" theme are offered at the Natural History Museum, the zoo, the UCSD campus, and through many other educational, service, and private for-profit institutions. The market is growing as more school districts move to year-round schooling, and working parents face more complex scheduling tasks.

28. Sea World of California, *Year-End Report, 1993,* p. 12

29. It is probably not the poorest of families that are making sacrifices to let their kids "dive into learning." Most of the more than two thousand children who attended Camp Sea World during 1993 were there for less than three hours per day—which implies other arrangements were available: an at-home or vacationing parent, baby-sitter, or another camp. Further, more than half of the Camp Sea World members in 1993 were 12-Month Pass members, meaning their parents had bought an expensive year's admission pass to the park.

Other ways the park encourages families to use Sea World as a private public space include the park's program of customized birthday parties and educational sleep-over parties in the Shark Encounter aquarium.

30. Sea World education department's year-end report does not break down attendance for the instructional field trips by grades; however, the first four days a week are devoted to the elementary grades; junior high school, high school, and college classes are fitted in on Fridays. Thus preschool and elementary school students make up most of the field trip clientele.

31. Similarly, Gifted and Talented Education (GATE) programs are customized. Although many schools have GATE classes, in some wealthy districts where test scores are high, entire schools are classified as Gifted and Talented.

32. Sea World of California, *Year-End Report, 1993,* p. 15.

33. In the past, the University of California at San Diego and San Diego State University Extension both delivered Sea World courses; in 1993–94, only San Diego State did.

34. These courses have been hard hit by fee increases at the state university level, and these increases have apparently been responsible for reducing attendance.

35. Joy Wolf, interview, April 7, 1992.

36. California State Department of Education, *Science Framework for California Public Schools, Kindergarten through Grade Twelve* (Sacramento, 1989), pp. 1–9; California State Department of Education, *Science Model Curriculum Guide: Kindergarten through Grade Eight* (Sacramento, 1987). Some of Sea World's education staff sat on the Science Framework Advisory Committees.

37. A hundred special courses were held in 1993, for about twenty-two hundred students.

38. This degree of positive regard, I suspect, also involves feelings of de-

pendence and indebtedness. Such feelings have surfaced when teachers listen to my presentations on Sea World. On one occasion, a teacher became stridently angry at me for raising criticisms of the theme park, in effect arguing that I had no right at all to question the work of such a generous corporate donor.

39. For years the park's marketing department has produced, and Sea World of California has contributed to, annual "Shamu specials" carried on network television. The marketing director saw this blend of entertainment and advertising as essential work. Vice president for marketing, Bill Thomas, interview by author, San Diego, Calif., March 11, 1992.

40. Sea World of California, *Year-End Report, 1993,* pp. 18–19.

41. The success of the 1–800–23-SHAMU connection led Sea World to keep it open forty hours a week.

42. Sea World does advise teachers that its tapes have a kind of shelf life—their information may become dated in a few years.

43. The free rebroadcast strategy is likely a way to capture a central place in the instructional TV market, and it is possible that charges will be introduced later, once the product has gained acceptance.

44. Joy Wolf, interviews by author, San Diego, Calif., March 17, 1992 and October 3, 1994.

45. Wolf, interview, March 17, 1992.

46. Anheuser-Busch has been accused of doing just this at the theme park by local health and antialcohol activists, and it has had to respond publicly (see chapter 2).

47. Joy Wolf, interview by author, San Diego, Calif., October 3, 1994. The education department's year-end reports contain lists of goals accomplished and goals set for the upcoming year. They include statements like: "Achieved: To continue support for Marketing, Group Sales, and Public Relations. . . . To alter public presentations to be proactive representing controversial Sea World issues." Sea World of California, *Sea World of California Education Department Year-End Report, 1991* (San Diego: Sea World Education Department, 1991), p. 1.

48. Sea World is not alone in creating promotional curricular materials for the classroom, as reported in the recent study by Consumers Union. Consumers Union, *Captive Kids.* These materials have been the subject of pointed criticism from several positions on the political spectrum. Frank Clifford, "Battle over the Environment Moves into the Classroom," *Los Angeles Times*, November 13, 1995, pp. A-1, A-20.

49. During fieldwork, my associate Nic Sammond observed Sea World staff discussing phoning in their own questions to the experts. There are "ringers" in the audience.

50. For certain specialized broadcast editing skills, staff from the local cable company can be contracted for a day or two.

51. Even outside the classroom context, *Shamu TV* as educational programming is multiply useful by virtue of the flexibility of videotape and the availability of cable. The taped programming can be repositioned, suited, perhaps, to a different use or fitted into a slightly different market niche. Or it can be reedited, with new pieces of footage added to change it slightly. For example, the education and marketing departments have also experimented with creating

"family learning" events, rebroadcasts of *Shamu TV* programs in the evenings (that is, family viewing time) in several cities. The transition from classroom material to family learning event is a question of marketing rather than major reworking. Sea World of California, *Year-End Report, 1993,* pp. 19–20.

52. Media and technology specialist for the San Diego Unified School District, Carol Kearney, interview by author, San Diego, Calif., October 31, 1995; cf. Apple, "Whittling Away at Democracy."

53. Cf. Consumers Union, *Captive Kids;* Apple, "Whittling Away at Democracy."

54. This is a paraphrase of responses I've met in conversations with public school teachers, for example, at the summer California Social Science History Institute at the University of California at San Diego.

55. Anheuser-Busch brochure, *A Pledge and a Promise* (St. Louis: Anheuser-Busch Companies, 1993).

56. The student reporters were recruited from a local performing arts high school; the minority classroom scenes were likely shot at one of the Sea World magnet schools. The magnet coordinator at one school, when asked what the school gave Sea World in return for its magnet sponsorship, told me, "We let them use our kids for photo shoots."

57. *A Pledge and a Promise.* Baba Dioum is described in this material as a "[n]oted African environmentalist." No more direct citation for Dioum's maxim is given and I have been unable to turn up its original context. The quote is also used at the San Diego Zoo and Wild Animal Park.

58. Wolf, interview, March 17, 1992. Wolf said that her department's environmental educational philosophy is culled from similar programs and the publications of wildlife conservation organizations, such as American Wildlife Federation's *Ranger Rick* magazine. I asked her if her department were ever criticized as being not environmentalist enough, as not going far enough to present environmental information to the park's customers and education audience. She said no, although this criticism was made sometimes by park staff. She commented that the marketing department was very nervous about hitting customers "over the head" with a heavy environmental message. "We just hope that later, when they're out there making a decision later on, it will come through: the positive feeling about the environment, the positive feeling about animals, and the importance of preserving and protecting it. But we're trying not to come out and say, 'Don't do this and don't do that. [Do follow this program or] don't follow that one.' Because each [of us] have our own individual choices in here, awareness levels."

59. Cf. Consumers Union, *Captive Kids.* Interestingly, even this "morality play" environmental education is offensive to some industry groups: they would like it banished from the schools altogether, not because it is feeble and ineffectual, but because they see it as biased political advocacy. Clifford, "Battle over the Environment Moves to the Classroom," p. A-20.

60. Wolf, interview, April 7, 1992.

61. Ibid.

62. The answer does, however, fit with the education department's goal to "be proactive representing controversial Sea World issues." Sea World of Cali-

fornia, *Year-End Report, 1991,* p. 1. Sea World's life span estimates are disputed by Humane Society activists and their researchers, who claim that Sea World lowballs the life span estimates to make captivity look as if it is good for whales, or at least neutral; some scholars claim that the life span of wild killer whales may be nearly twice that of those at Sea World. So, it is a question of whether they die in captivity "just like" they die in the wild. On life span controversies, see Bruce Obee, "The Great Killer Whale Debate," *Ocean Realm,* July 1993, 40–55. Mortality statistics are closely guarded, but figures up to 1987 are reported in Nancy Cleeland, "Captive or Coddled: Debate Lingers on Whale Habitat," *San Diego Union,* October 18, 1987, pp. A-1, A-12, A-13. By 1987, twelve of the twenty-four whales acquired by Sea World since it opened had died in captivity.

63. For example, Kenneth S. Norris, *Dolphin Days: The Life and Times of the Spinner Dolphin* (New York: Avon Books, 1991); or Stephen Leatherwood and Randall R. Reeves, *The Sierra Club Handbook of Whales and Dolphins* (San Francisco: Sierra Club Books, 1983).

64. Cf. Catherine Dold, "Toxic Agents Found to Be Killing Off Whales," *New York Times,* June 16, 1992, p. B-10; and Rae Corelli, "A River of History," *Maclean's,* January 15, 1990, 38–39.

65. Cf. Frank Clifford, "Battle over the Environment Moves to the Classroom," pp. A-1, A-20; Joel Bleifuss, "The First Stone: Pavlov's Pack Rats," *In These Times,* November 13–26, 1995, 12–13.

5. Routine Surprises

1. The history of dolphin shows remains unwritten, but see Karen Pryor, *Lads before the Wind: Diary of a Dolphin Trainer,* 2nd ed. (North Bend, Wash.: Sunshine Books, 1991); and Ralph Nading Hill, *Window in the Sea* (New York: Rinehart and Company, 1956). According to Hill, in 1949 a porpoise named "Flippy" (probably a bottle-nosed dolphin) was trained at Marineland Oceanarium in Marineland, Florida, and became the first known performing dolphin, pp. 177–182. Hill says that "Flippy" was trained by Adolph Frohn, a circus trainer specializing in lions and tigers. See also, Craig Phillips, *The Captive Sea: Life behind the Scenes of the Great Modern Oceanariums* (Philadelphia: Chilton Company, 1964), pp. 60–98; and Don C. Reed, *Notes from an Underwater Zoo* (New York: Dial Press, 1981).

2. This was spring 1992. There is currently no "all animal" show without visible trainers, although this has been attempted in the past, according to Sea World's former vice president for entertainment, Bob La Porta, interview by author, La Jolla, Calif., April 3, 1992.

3. Another job of the entertainment department's producers is to make sure the contracted performers fit into Sea World's entertainment style and "vision."

4. Sea World's producer and director, Janet Gotch, interview by author, San Diego, Calif., April 14, 1992.

5. The entertainment department fields managers and coordinators for all shows; their job is to keep the acts up to company standards, anticipate problems, and suggest changes, revisions, or shifts of emphasis in performance. Since shows may be repeated six, seven, or more times a day, maintenance is a formi-

dable task involving attention to scheduling, technique, script, equipment, animal-human interactions, and morale. The department is also responsible, with the operations department, for writing show schedules, the complicated process of manipulating time described in chapter 3. Other aspects of what the management calls "ambience," or ways the audience experiences the park, fall under the aegis of entertainment: the entertainment department sends out mimes, seemingly spontaneous skits and concerts, and "occasional," or walk-around, costumed characters (whales, penguins, pirates) who hug and greet children.

6. For the history of killer whales in captivity, see Eric Hoyt, *Orca: The Whale Called Killer* (Camden East, Ontario: Camden House, 1981), pp. 250–259; K. Burgess, "The Behavior and Training of a Killer Whale, *Orcinus Orca,* at San Diego Sea World," *International Zoo Yearbook* 6 (1968): 202–205. On Namu, the first killer whale successfully kept in captivity, see Erik Sletholt, *Wild and Tame: A View of Animals,* trans. Oliver Stallybrass (New York: Charles Scribner's Sons, 1975), pp. 16–24.

7. On the connections between Hollywood film and Marine Studios, see Gregg Mitman, "Hollywood Technology, Popular Culture, and the American Museum of Natural History," *Isis* 84, no. 4 (December 1993): 637–661. *Flipper,* the film by Ivan Tors, was shot at Marineland. Tors also made *Namu* (1965), the first theatrical release film starring an orca. Ivan Tors, *My Life in the Wild* (Boston: Houghton Mifflin, 1979), pp. 134–149.

8. Cf. Hill, *Window in the Sea,* pp. 177–182. Marineland of the Pacific was the first oceanarium on the West Coast (ibid., p. 198). Marineland of the Pacific was eventually purchased by Harcourt Brace Jovanovich in order to transfer its valuable orcas to Sea World.

9. It is clear that circus skills and circus tricks were translated directly into work with marine mammals. Sea World of California's head trainer, Mike Scarpuzzi, says early dolphin trainers borrowed their techniques from people who worked with sea lions. When Sea World brought its first "Shamu" from Washington State for display and training, the park drew on the knowledge developed from working with dolphins. Mike Scarpuzzi, interview by author, San Diego, Calif., June 2, 1992. When Karen Pryor began her famous dolphin training at Sea Life Park in Hawaii, she felt she was a novice. She drew on two sources: her own practical experience working with ponies and dogs, and a detailed operant conditioning manual that translated Skinnerian theory into an outline for practical work with animals. Pryor, *Lads before the Wind,* pp. 1–42.

Pryor also gives details about the connections between dolphin training and naval research in the 1960s. The navy was interested in the kinds of military and salvage tasks dolphins could be trained to do, as well as more basic research subjects such as bioacoustics and biomechanics. Ibid., pp. 147–205, and passim.

10. Mike Scarpuzzi, interview by author, San Diego, Calif., April 14, 1992.

11. Ibid., and Scarpuzzi, interview, June 2, 1992.

12. Keeping the whales alive was a trial and error process. Cf. Sletholt, *Wild and Tame,* pp. 16–24; Scarpuzzi, interview, April 14, 1992. See also Dennie Eskow, "Killers' High-Tech Haven," *Popular Mechanics,* March 1985, 108.

13. Scarpuzzi, interview, June 2, 1992.

14. Sea World of California's own entertainment department comprises a staff of several hundred, and it works with a production budget of about $5 million

annually. There have been ups and downs: the "reduction in force" during the period of HBJ ownership meant that entertainment lost staff and for a long time had to produce a lot of entertainment with very little money and few personnel.

15. "Reality Revisited," in The Project on Disney, *Inside the Mouse: Work and Play at Disney World* (Durham, N.C.: Duke University Press, 1995), pp. 12–33; Michael Bristol, "Acting Out Utopia: The Politics of Carnival," *Performance* 1 (May–June 1973): 13–28.

16. "If there is a good show down in Florida, why not bring it here, or take the best of it and embellish it, make it even better when it comes here?" Sea World's vice president for entertainment, Don Ludwig, interview by author, San Diego, Calif., March 11, 1992. There are many examples of this standardization and portability: a water-ski show first tried out in Ohio was successfully moved to the other parks, and Sea World of California housed "Beach Blanket Ski Party," a water-ski show written for Florida and translated for the California park's layout and water conditions. But there are, producers commented, "creative" and personnel problems with this strategy: why keep producers on staff to dream up new shows only to import productions from another park?

17. Mike Scarpuzzi, interview, June 2, 1992.

18. Ibid.; and Scarpuzzi, interview, April 14, 1992. He also noted that treatment of the valuable trainers must be uniform: "[We need to be sure] that we're treating the trainers the same way, the pay scale, the benefits."

19. Of course, the marketers presume a very specific and concrete audience located in space and time, and as pointed out in chapters 1 and 2, Sea World's bedrock customers are Southern Californians. But local time, history, and concrete space conflict with the rationalized time and fluid space of tourism. In any year, special marketing programs that take account of local life and culture are designed to bring more of the San Diego audience into the park: "Snow World" features pseudosnow for local children who rarely see a snowflake, much less a drift to sled on. "Yellow Ribbon Summer" in 1991 played to the military connections of a large number of San Diego families, offering special "salute" programs and discounts for active personnel. But localness is always a marketing decision, always an intensification of the appeal to the local base within an understanding of the tourist market. It is telling that while this tourist attraction has a severely limited sense of local embeddedness, Sea World's shows and exhibits are about intense connections between people and animals.

20. Gotch, interview, April 14, 1992.

21. On the struggle over culture for children, see Henry Giroux, "Beyond the Politics of Innocence: Memory and Pedagogy in the "'Wonderful World of Disney,'" *Socialist Review* 23, no. 2 (1993): 79–107; and Giroux, *Disturbing Pleasures: Learning Popular Culture* (New York and London: Routledge, 1994).

22. Sea World's marketers are quite specific about which shows they will buy advertising time on. The very popular *Roseanne,* with its view of a stressed-out, underemployed, and cantankerous family in which the teenage children are sexually active, was one they anathemized in the early 1990s. Sea World's senior vice president for marketing, Bill Thomas, interview by author, San Diego, Calif., March 11, 1992.

23. "Reality Revisited" and "The Family Vacation," *Inside the Mouse,* pp. 12–33 and 34–53. For a historical view of Disney's ability to connect merchandising to

definitions of childhood, see Richard DeCordova, "The Mickey Mouse in Macy's Window," in *Disney Discourse: Producing the Magic Kingdom,* ed., Eric Smoodin (New York: Routledge, 1994), pp. 203–213.

24. Cf. "The Family Vacation," pp. 34–53.

25. Sea World managers often claimed that market research told them their customers were "families" and "families with young kids," rather than "children." Thomas, interview, March 11, 1992. Cf. John M. Findlay, *Magic Lands: Western Cityscapes and American Culture after 1940* (Berkeley and Los Angeles: University of California Press, 1992), pp. 52–116.

26. When guessing what parents want kids to do and see, entertainment producers tend to use themselves as models or informants. One told me, "I think the audience is pretty much like me." Ludwig, interview, March 11, 1992; and Don Ludwig, interview by author, San Diego, Calif., April 7, 1992.

27. No countercultural forms of dress or personal ornamentation are permissible among the staff. Death is an off-limits subject: education workers have not been able to mount a display using a dolphin skeleton, lest visitors realize that dolphins die at Sea World.

28. Bob La Porta, interview by author, La Jolla, Calif., May 21, 1992. La Porta noted, "When I first came to Sea World, the sea maids could not wear two-piece bathing suits!"

29. La Porta, interview, May 21, 1992.

30. Gotch, interview, April 14, 1992.

31. Ibid.

32. Ibid.

33. In 1992, one killer whale trainer was on the U.S. Olympic kayaking team. Sea World has regularly hosted the Miss California beauty pageant, another performance holding up physical and moral role models connected to advertising culture. The theme park offers the pageant organizers the special advantage of respite from feminist antipageant protesters, since the park is a controlled private space.

34. Of course, as I have been at pains to show in chapter 3, Sea World's landscape is designed to do the thinking for its customers. Cf. "Reality Revisited."

35. Thomas, interview, March 11, 1992; and Bill Thomas, interview by author, San Diego, Calif., April 1, 1992.

36. Ludwig, interview, March 11, 1992. Apparently the show ratings and pressure from marketing do convince entertainment producers that de-theatricalizing and scientizing the presentation of animals "is deadly," and pragmatically Ludwig fears his show ratings will fall if he "preaches" to the audience. His statement, along with phrases like "Joe and Betty Six-Pack," seems to suggest that producers flexibly and strategically construe the audience as socially and intellectually like or different from themselves when making arguments about what entertainment should contain, and that the final point of reference is the ratings.

37. Ludwig, interview, March 11, 1992.

38. The Vancouver Aquarium has experimented with a killer whale performance that attempts to discuss the relationship between behavior in the wild and behavior in captivity. See Elin Kelsey, "Conceptual Change and Killer Whales: Constructing Ecological Values for Animals at the Vancouver Aquarium," *International Journal of Science Education* 13, no. 5 (1991): 551–559.

39. This pressure has intensified since 1995, when animal rights activism

forced the closing and dispersal of collections of the Vancouver Zoo. Craig Turner, "In Canada, Animal Rights Activists Bag Their First Zoo," *Los Angeles Times,* October 16, 1995, p. A-1. Sea World's circus relatives are under intense public attack from groups like People for the Ethical Treatment of Animals and the Humane Society of the United States.

40. Gotch, interview, April 14, 1992.

41. Ludwig, interview, March 11, 1992.

42. Sea World's former vice president for corporate communication, Jackie Hill, interviews by author, San Diego, Calif., March 13, 1992 and March 26, 1992. Cf. "Chickens of the Sea," *Harper's,* May 1992, 35; this excerpt from a Sea World of Florida training manual appeared in the November 24, 1991, issue of *Florida,* the Sunday magazine of the *Orlando Sentinel.*

43. Ludwig, interview, March 11, 1992.

44. Ibid.

45. Gotch, interview, April 14, 1992.

46. Hill, interview, March 26, 1992.

47. Ludwig, interview, April 7, 1992.

48. The original "City Streets" show was an upbeat retelling of the gang fight scenes in *West Side Story,* with a conflict-resolution ending that made sure the audience left feeling cheery about city life.

49. La Porta, interview, April 3, 1992.

50. Ibid.

51. Ibid.

52. A well-known Shakespearean and Broadway actor, Jones has also been featured in a prime-time television series and as a popular voice in advertisements. He is perhaps best known to the mass audience as the voice of Darth Vader in *Star Wars.* His is also the voice of CNN. It would be hard to find a more prestigious and well-known male actor.

53. In 1995, *Baywatch* had approximately 1 billion viewers worldwide. Its star, David Hasselhoff, is also a pop music idol in Europe and Great Britain. Certainly, Sea World had its international tourist customers in mind when it struck a licensing deal with *Baywatch.*

54. And certainly, the market research that the entertainment department relies on does not emphasize creating new understandings for the audience, nor discovering the audience's reactions in any depth. The audience is already well known to producers as a collection of demographic characteristics, so their goal is to produce an acceptably good, somewhat refreshed version of an already well-understood product.

55. Another important function of the trainers is behavioral maintenance: training must be kept alive, kept accurate, and up to par in the animals.

56. Newspaper polling following the death of Kandu in 1989 appeared to bear out this desire to see contact and connection. Barry M. Horstman, "San Diegans Favor Keeping Whale Shows," *Los Angeles Times,* August 30, 1989, San Diego County edition, pp. A-1, A-17. Fully 65 percent of those polled thought the whale shows should be continued, while 23 percent thought they should be discontinued and 12 percent said they didn't know.

57. In *Lads before the Wind,* Pryor stresses Skinnerian theory in her work with dolphins. At Sea World, the "bridge" is usually a high-pitched whistle. Said Mike

Scarpuzzi, "There are two different reinforcers: there are primary reinforcers and there are secondary reinforcers. Primary reinforcement is what they need to live: they need food, they need water, they need air, they need sex; those are primary—they have to do that to continue to thrive. Secondary reinforcers are other things that are in their environment that take on reinforcing properties. Like rubbing on each other, rubbing on rocks, things like that are out in the wild. We add ice cubes, back rubs, belly rubs, tongue wiggles, eye massages, spraying them with water, giving them different massages or giving them a toy, smiling at them, getting excited, running over here and diving in, . . . all those things are secondary reinforcers that we have to teach them [to find] reinforcing, that's the key. When you start to go out there and just start giving them a back rub, it doesn't mean anything, so we have to teach them [to associate it with primary reinforcement]. And the way you do that is by pairing it." Scarpuzzi, interview, April 14, 1992.

58. "We are not consistent in reinforcement: that's something that takes a while for people to understand. That's the key, that's what Sea World taught me. My uncle was consistent in what he taught me in reinforcement: The animals do it right, they get their reinforcement; the animals do it wrong, they don't get their reinforcement. Sea World taught me that is not the best way to motivate animals, and indeed they are correct. What I found out coming here to Sea World was, that when an animal performs a behavior correctly, if he indeed finds out that he's going to get a variety of reinforcers, he'll be more motivated to go out and perform the behavior to find out what you're going to give him. If he knows you're only going to give him food, as soon as he is satiated with food, there is no motivation to go out and do the behavior; so once he's full, why go perform, see?" Scarpuzzi, interview, April 14, 1992.

59. Ibid.

60. "At the bottom, you write comments: 'She started to understand the mouth-open, however, her speed on the fast swim is very slow. Need to work on speed, along with the mouth-open.' So the next trainer that walks in there picks up the record which is right there. Before he goes out and works with Kasatka that day, he looks at Kasatka's records and says, 'Oh, . . . I see where they are on the mouth-open fast swim. I'd better go talk to Mike and get some more details about what's going on.'" Scarpuzzi, interview, June 2, 1992.

61. Ibid.

62. Ibid. This level of control is desirable because of the reporting requirements of the National Marine Fisheries Service, but also to prevent unpredictable behavior that can lead to accidents.

63. For whales or dolphins imported from other countries, the baseline is nonexistent and must be constructed. But for whales born at Sea World, "We've got everything." Scarpuzzi, interview, June 2, 1992.

64. Karen Pryor's shows at Sea Life Park, divided between "Whaler's Cove" and "Ocean Science Theater," similarly embodied such a fiction-fact distinction. *Lads before the Wind,* pp. 1–20.

65. For example, see Emmanuel Dvinsky, *Durov and His Performing Animals,* trans. Phyl Griffith (Moscow: Foreign Languages Publishing House, n.d.).

66. La Porta, interview, April 3, 1992.

67. Ibid.

68. This emphasis on feelings has been present in the Shamu show since the

middle 1980s. See Bob Mullan and Gary Marvin, *Zoo Culture* (London: Weidenfeld and Nicholson, 1987), pp. 19–23.

69. As I will detail in chapter 6, other means of humanization or anthropomorphizing are possible without the use of costumes.

70. Is it humorless to add that humans rank low on the political sensitivity scale? They belong to the only species employed to wear the hot, heavy, fuzzy, and ridiculous walk-around suits.

71. Sea World's director of public relations, Dan LeBlanc, interview by author, San Diego, Calif., March 11, 1992.

72. La Porta, interview, April 3, 1992.

73. Ibid.

74. La Porta, interview, May 21, 1992.

75. Ibid.

76. Ibid.

77. Ibid.

78. On neoteny, see Elizabeth A. Lawrence, "Neoteny in American Perceptions of Animals," *Journal of Psychoanalytic Anthropology* 9, no. 1 (winter 1986): 41–54; Stephen Jay Gould, "A Biological Homage to Mickey Mouse," in *The Panda's Thumb* (New York: W. W. Norton, 1980), pp. 95–107.

79. La Porta, interview, April 3, 1992.

80. Ibid.

81. Ibid.

82. La Porta, interview, May 21, 1992.

83. La Porta, interview, April 3, 1992.

84. Cf. Scarpuzzi, interviews, April 14, 1992 and June 2, 1992.

85. La Porta, interview, April 3, 1992.

86. It's an interesting question where "new" behaviors in animal shows come from. Novelty often comes out of experiments in the training process, as trainers get ideas and see if they can be carried out. But animals, with their own need for stimulation, seem also to invent new things to do. Sea World trainers and producers make much of the notion that everything they train is an extension of something the animal does in the wild—that the animals are not asked to do anything "unnatural." For example, the audience is told that small leaps out of the water are extensions of sighting behaviors and that larger jumps are extensions of "spy hops" (another orienting behavior). But Karen Pryor's account of dolphin training suggests that dolphins in captivity have invented things to do in their tanks that no ethologist has ever observed in the wild. Pryor, *Lads before the Wind,* pp. 234–254. Educators at the Vancouver Aquarium have experimented with interpreting whale behaviors as responses to and compensations for captivity. See Kelsey, "Conceptual Change and Killer Whales," 551–559. But it would be unacceptable at Sea World to claim that the conditions of captivity itself generate something new; this would undermine the "naturalness" of Sea World.

87. La Porta, interview, April 3, 1992. La Porta uses the term "lads" to refer to dolphins, borrowing this from Karen Pryor, who borrowed it from Herman Melville's *Moby Dick.* Pryor, *Lads before the Wind,* p. vi.

88. La Porta, interview, April 3, 1992.

89. Ibid.

90. Ibid.
91. Ibid.; cf. Ludwig, interview, March 11, 1992.
92. La Porta, interview, April 3, 1992.
93. Ibid.
94. According to La Porta, "Now trainers have more control. . . . It's going back to the way it was. Because it's the only retaliation to the objections, to the people who don't believe animals should be doing this. We were considered the enemy. The bad guy. We're *entertainment.* 'You make these animals jump, for applause!' [he phrases the angry accusation]. 'You make them go through rings!'" La Porta, interview, April 3, 1992.

But the trainers' intimate relationship with the animals is, finally, limited. In old-fashioned circuses or carnivals, trainer-owners organized animals into acts and contracted with a larger show. In the theme park, performing animals are corporate property and part of a large-scale entertainment design.

95. Ibid.
96. Ludwig, interview, March 11, 1992.
97. La Porta, interview, April 3, 1992.
98. Ludwig, interview, April 7, 1992.
99. Ibid.
100. Ludwig, interview, March 11, 1992.
101. Ludwig, interview, April 7, 1992.
102. Janet Gotch described the uncertainty and unpredictability of the trained bird show that she produced. Narration, human characters, and quizzing the audience were used as filler when birds became uncooperative, as they often did. Gotch directed birds of prey performing in the same area with parrots and other potential victims. The prospects for disruption led her to fold into the script what couldn't be hidden: "We're starting to work on the uncertainty now. The more we know about the birds and what they don't do, we write lines for the mistakes we know are going to happen. Not mistakes, but just the times when they decide to bail!" Gotch, interview, April 14, 1992.
103. Cf. Paul Williams, "Mistakes Are Made" (student paper, UCSD Department of Communication, 1989), on built-in mistakes in the Commerson's dolphin performance at Sea World; Paul Bouissac, *Circus and Culture: A Semiotic Approach* (Bloomington: Indiana University Press, 1976), pp. 108–150.
104. La Porta, interview, May 21, 1992.
105. Ibid.
106. Ludwig, interview, April 7, 1992.
107. La Porta, interview, May 21, 1992.
108. Ibid. I will have more to say about humanization, a complicated form of mastery through dominative play that underlines the animal qualities of the animal, while seeming to distort or obscure them, in chapter 6.
109. La Porta, interview, May 21, 1992. Interestingly, the "Shamu Backstage" exhibit added in 1996 replicates some of La Porta's ideas for "Triad."
110. Scarpuzzi, interview, June 2, 1992. Dolphin shows have been produced that were based entirely on remote commands and underwater tones; see Pryor, *Lads before the Wind,* pp. 43–72.
111. Ludwig, interview, April 7, 1992.

112. La Porta, interview, April 3, 1992.

113. Music is handled by a "show operator" located in a booth at the very top of the stadium. It is this person's job to watch the performance carefully, know the script, and anticipate variations from it. The show operator also provides special sound effects: for example, wet smacking noises when animals "throw kisses" or whimsical audio doodles that let the audience know something silly has happened. The show operator's job is an extremely complex one of manipulating various electronic sources of sound in ways that create a perception of unity for the audience.

114. La Porta, interview, April 3, 1992.

115. Not surprisingly, the head trainer speaks about the preshow's educational function in straight behaviorist terms: "The cameras go right on you in the audience; it's a question asked: How many teeth does a killer whale have? And you have choice of, you know, twelve, twenty-four, forty-four, and the camera comes right on you, and you're up on the screen and you have to put up a finger, one, two, or three—you answer one, two, or three and you get either a fun sound to say, 'Yea, you got it right!' or 'Boo, you got it wrong.' *And you don't know if you're going to get picked or not, and so everybody is alert and so they're learning.*" Scarpuzzi, interview, April 14, 1992 (my emphasis).

116. Ibid.

117. Ibid.

6. Dreaming of Whales

1. Sea World's marketers report that about 90 percent of its customers see the Shamu show.

2. Several adult whales take turns performing as Shamu, and the baby or juvenile plays Baby Shamu. In 1992, the whales were: Kasatka, Nikina, Corky, and Orkid, the baby; in 1995, there were five: Corky, Kasatka, Splash (imported from Canada), Ulises (a breeding male imported from a theme park in Spain), and Orkid, still called Baby Shamu though growing fast.

3. On the complex and emergent qualities of live performance, see Dell H. Hymes, "Breakthrough into Performance," in *Folklore: Performance and Communication,* eds. Dan Ben-Amos and Kenneth S. Goldstein (The Hague: Mouton, 1975), pp. 11–74.

4. I watched the Shamu show many times between 1987 and 1992 and returned to check up on new shows between 1993 and 1995. My method of recording usually included a taped audio track keyed to handwritten notes; on many occasions, I used still photography as well. My reading is informed more extensively than another audience member's would be by this documentation, by my background reading about orcas generally, and by my understanding of the institutional context defining the performance. I am not claiming that I have lately had the same sensations or reactions as someone who has seen the show once or twice.

5. I've also found it useful to compare my descriptions of the Shamu show with those of other observers and analysts, including Bob Marvin and Gary Mullen, *Zoo Culture* (London: George Weidenfeld and Nicholson, 1987), pp. 19–

23; and Jane C. Desmond, "Performing 'Nature': Shamu at Sea World," in *Cruising the Performative: Interventions into the Representation of Ethnicity, Nationality, and Sexuality,* ed. Sue-Ellen Case, Phil Brett, and Susan Foster (Bloomington: Indiana University Press, 1995), pp. 217–236. Desmond's analysis is the most recent, and though produced entirely separately from mine, it comes to many similar conclusions about the structure and meanings of the Shamu show. She is, however, less concerned than I am about locating the Shamu show in the context of corporately produced entertainment.

6. These do not include the educational Shamu shows that are given to school groups about nine months out of the year, night performances during the height of the summer season, and special performances scheduled for guests, dignitaries, or group events in the park.

7. By 1995, several changes had been made in access to the killer whales. Sea World had set up a small dining area near the examination bay, where customers could, for a special fee, eat "Dinner with Shamu." In fall 1995, a massive new killer whale exhibit, Shamu Backstage, was under construction. It is designed as an underwater viewing area, an adjunct to what can be seen from above the whale pools. Visitors can walk alongside the expanded tanks, down to see the orcas at eye level, much as they do in the Shark Encounter.

8. Cf. "Kodak and Disney: Corporate Utopia?" *AfterImage,* April 1980, 21. Careful consideration has also been given to what the audience should not take pictures of. Somewhere nearby is an enormous tarp that can be unrolled to protect the whale pool from aerial photography in the event of a whale disaster.

9. The most important invisible participant in the show is the show operator, seated in a booth above the stadium, who coordinates music tapes, CDs, and prerecorded videos with the movements of whales and humans and a spoken, partly prerecorded text. His tasks interlock with those of a video operator working a camera with a zoom lens.

10. On distracted seeing, see Margaret Crawford, "The World in a Shopping Mall," in *Variations on a Theme Park: The New American City and the End of Public Space,* ed. Michael Sorkin (New York: Hill and Wang, 1992), pp. 3–30. The multisource quality of the performance also means that, as with television, different levels of attention are possible among the audience. While a trip to Sea World is a more marked and heightened ritual than watching television, the distracting structure of the Shamu show means that it is possible to be distracted, even bored. It is almost as if all the distractions—the big screen, the quiz show, the vendors, the music—are there to keep the imagination from wandering off on its own. And indeed, this is part of what the trainers and producers mean when they say the Jumbotron "supports" the Shamu show: it relieves the performing humans of the task of keeping the audience focused on facts and commentary.

11. This parallels the inescapability of recorded sound at the park.

12. A note on conventions for rendering this performance as a text: utterances and actions by live performers are rendered in plain text. Prerecorded oral statements are presented in italics.

13. Julie Scardina-Ludwig is a Sea World trainer and performer with long experience, not a hired spokesperson.

14. This is something new, although there have been hints, in earlier shows, of killer whale attacks on humans. For example, at one point in the 1988 show, the audience was asked to imagine itself a sea lion basking on an iceberg, a potential mouthful for Shamu.

15. Although earlier versions of the show emphasized that the orca is a "predator," "the ocean's top predator," and "a giant," this is a stronger emphasis than in the past. Members of the audience sometimes respond negatively to the sea lion pup footage with comments like, "I *really* don't need to see this," and covered eyes. And the audience gasps when Shamu charges Ron, so overwhelming are the size and physical power of the whale.

16. Killer whales do figure in Tlingit and Haida myths, but Sea World's public relations office was unable to tell me from which myth or which cultural tradition the story of Natsalane was drawn.

17. The narrative gesture to the Native Americans, although brief, is supposed to remind us of our earlier childlike and primitive selves, full of wonder. As the Sea World commercial theme goes, "Do you remember the feeling of wonder . . . reach back and touch the child inside of you. . . ."

18. There are of course in the audience the bored, the appalled, the suffering, the condescending, as well as the pleased and delighted. I am not homogenizing the audience experience, but I am pointing out that Sea World aims to create a predominant experience beneath the surface unevenness and variety it presents.

19. Polling has shown that the park's audiences find the trainers indispensable to the Shamu show, even while many of Sea World's customers harbor doubts about keeping whales captive. Barry M. Horstman, "San Diegans Favor Keeping Whale Shows," *Los Angeles Times,* August 30, 1989, San Diego County edition, pp. A-1, A-17.

20. That the trainers are the special representatives of the audience is underscored by their whiteness. For the most part the trainers, male and female, are blonde and seemingly Anglo. Their accents are white Southern Californian.

21. Stephanie has been selected from the audience by operations staff, who follow carefully defined demographic and personal criteria in choosing audience representatives. Entertainment staff say they often try to choose "a young mom," because that brings "the best 'Awww . . .'" from the audience. Sea World's vice president for entertainment, Don Ludwig, interview by author, San Diego, Calif., April 7, 1992. Cf. director of operations, Steve Geiss, interview by author, San Diego, Calif., March 11, 1992.

22. Over the years, the Shamu show has almost always had a human serve as the butt of an animal joke. And audience complicity is an old trick at Sea World. The "Dolphinesia" show in 1984, for example, had the audience urge an apparently shy and reluctant young woman to pet the dolphins. She resisted, was coerced, and finally lost her footing and fell in the lagoon—to reemerge soaking, but riding on the backs of two dolphins.

23. Cf. Paul Bouissac, *Circus and Culture: A Semiotic Approach* (Bloomington: Indiana University Press, 1976), pp. 108–150; and Elizabeth A. Lawrence, *Rodeo: An Anthropologist Looks at the Wild and the Tame* (Knoxville: University of Tennessee Press, 1982).

24. Those who object to trained animal acts make this point with great poignancy, and they claim that the enjoyment of domination is what causes them distress.

25. This is not to say that whales and dolphins and many other animals cannot be spontaneous and invent tricks for their trainers—by most accounts they can. But this is not what we are watching when we watch the trained animal show. By Pryor's account, dolphins can be trained through operant conditioning to creatively generate new behaviors.

26. Bob La Porta, interview by author, San Diego, Calif., May 21, 1992.

27. Trainers told me that they are at work on whale language, or tonal systems, with the goal of developing an automatic human-whale "communication" system of command that can be carried out through broadcast tones rather than hand or whistle signals. Head of Sea World's animal training department, Mike Scarpuzzi, interview by author, San Diego, Calif., June 2, 1992. Killer whales echolocate like dolphins; some researchers think that pods (groups) of killer whales have their own recognizable "dialects." But the "what" of what is being communicated by the killer whales' clicks and vocalizations remains unclear. John K. B. Ford, "Family Fugues," *Natural History,* March 1991, 68–76. What is clear is that some humans profoundly wish to believe that animals have something like human language and are trying to reach out to them. Compare the critique of animal language experiments in Thomas A. Sebeok and Robert Rosenthal, eds., *The Clever Hans Phenomenon: Communication with Horses, Whales, Apes, and People* (New York: New York Academy of Sciences, 1981). By 1992, earlier references to language seemed to have been displaced to the education shows produced for school children (discussed in chapter 4).

28. However, as argued above, the big screen TV is used to dampen this awareness of refusal. And the audience does not see the use of the "least reinforcing stimulus" to let the whales know they've made an incorrect move.

29. The "play" segment in the show is modeled on an "enrichment" session, a training and maintenance technique practiced behind the scenes. Enrichment is an attempt to keep whales healthy and alert by compensating for the lack of challenge in the captive environment.

30. Animal trainer Vicki Hearne thinks that the fact of trainability and the process of training itself indicate ability in domestic animals to act at a remove, to enter with humans a common frame of comment on their own acts. Vicki Hearne, *Adam's Task: Calling Animals by Name* (New York: Vintage Books, 1987), especially pp. 1–116.

31. This phrase was used in the 1989 Shamu show.

32. Vice president for entertainment, Don Ludwig, interview by author, San Diego, Calif., March 11, 1992.

33. "The Waiting Is Over" and "Like a Family" are also Shamu show theme songs used after 1988.

34. This was how trainers and animal care staff, who care deeply about the whales, experienced the event.

35. It is not clear that captive reproduction *is* a solution to the problem of extinction, which is, after all, a problem of habitat destruction. Recently, critics of zoos in British Columbia successfully argued for the closing of the Van-

couver Zoo, in part on the grounds that money spent on captive reproduction would be better used in habitat conservation efforts. Craig Turner, "In Canada, Animal Rights Activists Bag Their First Zoo," *Los Angeles Times,* October 16, 1995, p. A-1.

36. Science and research received increasing emphasis and foregrounding over the years I observed the Shamu show, from very little in the late 1980s to a large proportion of the twenty minutes in 1992. If the adults in the core audience come from the professional and technical classes, they may strongly identify with the image of scientists struggling for species preservation and, by extension, environmental salvation.

37. While in earlier years "educational" and "scientific" facts had been worked into the interstices of whale performance, by 1992 the video quiz show had broken up the didactic monologue. With the addition of the Jumbotron screen, we no longer depend on the trainers to talk to us about blood-sampling techniques or to mime "research" on killer whale "language" (the tonal systems). The huge video images of scientists at work at computers make all this more concise and more detailed. Where entertainment producers worried about scripts seeming to "talk at" the audience, now the video screen does the lecturing with pictures, and the audience presumably feels less lectured at.

38. Sea World is repetitively constructed as a site of research in its mass media image: Local news broadcasts in the San Diego area routinely report on research or animal saving at the park. Sea World's directors of research, mammalogists, and veterinarians (and not just public relations flacks) are frequently quoted in the press and television. National news broadcasts have covered the birth of baby orcas, and prime-time magazine shows feature the parks and invariably discuss Sea World's research identity.

39. Of course, a close look at the verbal and performed text of the Shamu show reveals very little actual scientific or natural historical information, and discussions of research goals and discoveries are hazy. True, not much can be packed into a twenty-minute performance, but a look at what is included is revealing. The audience is asked whether Shamu is a fish or a mammal and is told that it is a mammal—but the definition of mammals, or the significance of mammalian status, or the importance of the differences between marine mammals and fish is never discussed. There are brief mentions of adaptation and evolution—but these, as I've argued above, serve mainly to locate the orca parallel to humans in a natural hierarchy. Some versions of the show have briefly discussed the evolution of the terrestrial precursor's articulated foot into a flipper, noting the cetaceans' retention of a finger- or toelike nub of bone. But this mention, and a brief mention it is, serves only to help construct the whale as "like" human beings, rather than to discuss the remotely related and long-gone quadruped. We are presented with a fact to remember, but no reason to remember it.

40. "Chickens of the Sea," *Harper's,* May 1992, 35; this excerpt from a Sea World of Florida training manual appeared in the November 24, 1991, issue of *Florida,* the Sunday magazine of the *Orlando Sentinel.* The manual states: "Evolve: because evolution is a controversial theory, use the word 'adapt.'" This is one measure of how serious Sea World's science education is, so exquisitely sensitive is it to market pressures. Sea World may be sensitive not only to antievo-

lutionists among its commercial audience, but to the growing number of private Christian schools in its education market.

41. Cf. Roland Barthes, *Mythologies,* trans. Annette Lavers (New York: Hill and Wang, 1970).

42. Ludwig, interview, March 11, 1992.

43. For example, the image of the jumping killer whale is so closely associated with the city of San Diego itself as a tourist destination that, despite the licensing limitations placed on the image, "generic" jumping killer whales sneak into local tourist items and are found on postcards and memorabilia (such as coffee cups, maps, postcards, and refrigerator magnets). This association grows out of tourism marketing, since there is no close ecological association between the *Orcinus orca* and San Diego's waters. In Dean McCannell's terms, all these modes of circulation help create Shamu as an attraction. McCannell, *The Tourist: A New Theory of the Leisure Class* (New York: Schocken Books, 1976), pp. 109–134.

44. Animal performers have frequently been given "primitive" names that help distinguish them from conquering, civilized humans (while enculturating them) and let them stand in for foreign peoples and exotic places. See Harriet Ritvo, *The Animal Estate: The English and Other Creatures in the Victorian Age* (Cambridge: Harvard University Press, 1987), pp. 205–242.

45. Ritvo, *The Animal Estate,* pp. 205–242.

46. Orcas of both sexes have slits that contain their reproductive organs; males have one slit, the females, three: one for the birth canal and one for each nipple. When they're flipped over, it's easy enough to tell male from female, but the killer whales only turn belly up briefly and quickly in performance. In any case, no narrator points out genitalia during the performance. During the 1992 research for this chapter, all the whales at Sea World in San Diego were female; in 1994, a new male was acquired. This haziness regarding the sex of the whales has also to do with struggles over the content of shows between trainers and entertainment writers. Trainers who work with whales daily know their real names and sex. (The shortage of male orcas in captivity makes it likely that during any given performance a female orca will play Shamu.)

47. Bob La Porta, interview by author, San Diego, Calif., April 3, 1992; and interview, May 21, 1992; cf. Ivan Tors, *My Life in the Wild* (Boston: Houghton Mifflin, 1979), pp. 182–192. In early cartoon ads, Shamu had a gravelly voice and wore a sailor's hat. "Willy" in the Time-Warner film *Free Willy* is male.

48. Marianna Torgovnic, *Gone Primitive: Savage Intellects, Modern Lives* (Chicago: University of Chicago Press, 1990), pp. 3–41; Donna J. Haraway, *Simians, Cyborgs and Women: The Reinvention of Nature* (New York: Routledge, 1991).

49. The head trainer, discussing the gender balance of his staff, asserted that women offered the show more avenues to work with and displayed "feelings and emotions." Scarpuzzi, interview, June 2, 1992.

50. Jones is familiar to a wide audience through television, advertising, and film, and his Broadway and Shakespearean credentials give him the heft of prestige. His powerfully cultured and resonant baritone is literally one of the most widely heard and recognizable in the world today, but unlike voices of many other black men, his has high cultural associations: he is a safe, serious, and responsible representative of color.

51. This communication is explicitly cited in the Haida or Tlingit myth and more vaguely hinted at in other Shamu shows.

52. Joan McIntyre, *Mind in the Waters: A Book to Celebrate the Consciousness of Whales and Dolphins* (New York: Scribners, 1974).

53. Swim-with-the-dolphins programs are widely known in Southern California and are popular with tourists in Southern California, Florida, and Hawaii. Outside the world of commercial culture, dolphins are part of a thus far unstudied popular mysticism and are integrated into Southern California alternative therapies. In one such, word of mouth has it, women give birth in tanks with dolphins in order to access "dolphin energy." Sea World inaugurated its own dolphin-contact attraction in fall 1995. Karen Kucher, "Entering Another World: The Dolphin's," *San Diego Union-Tribune,* December 5, 1995, pp. B-1, B-2.

54. This line appeared in the Shamu show of 1990. Despite the fact that admission and concession spending go directly to the theme park's bottom line and return only indirectly to research programs, such a statement construes a visit to Sea World as a kind of science philanthropy. At some exhibits (for example, the Shark Encounter) visitors can pick up brochures soliciting donations to the Hubbs–Sea World Research Institute.

55. Interestingly, Shamu is free of the other, overlapping sponsorship arrangements that mark the rest of Sea World's landscape and animal shows, although its trademark image does appear outside the park on tied-in products and in cross-promotions. In the versions of the show that I tracked since 1987, unlike every other animal performance at the park the Shamu show seemed to have little to do with corporate sponsorship. There was no advertising imagery except the blue, black, and white leaping killer whale logo on the video screen, and no outside brand-names were repeated. Two small exceptions proved this rule—there was a brief mention at the end of the performance that the wet suits had been provided by Bodyglove (a brand popular with surfers) and a small Kodak logo at the bottom of billboards presenting information about killer whales. Since 1991, these have vanished. If the physical environment of the Sea World park is constructed as an advertising and public relations venue, why does the sponsor's advertising let up so noticeably just as one approaches the park's most celebrated attraction? One obvious explanation is that the association with Shamu itself is an attractive benefit of sponsorship for corporations affiliated with Sea World. By not associating any particular sponsor with Shamu, all sponsors are able to claim a sort of general association with the idea, the character, and the image. However, this consideration may be less important in recent years, since Anheuser-Busch may have less need for sponsorship than HBJ had, and since the brewer is developing its own, extensive promotional uses for the parks.

56. This rhetoric is familiar from corporate image advertising on television and in print and, to a great extent, from nature and wildlife television. The connections between corporate image advertising and nature television are very close, especially in public broadcasting. William Hoynes, *Public Television for Sale: Media, the Market and the Public Sphere* (Boulder, Colo.: Westview Press, 1994), pp. 89–114. See also Susan G. Davis, "Touch the Magic," in *Uncommon Ground: Toward the Reinvention of Nature,* ed. William Cronon (New York: W. W. Norton, 1995), pp. 204–217.

57. John Berger, "Why Look at Animals?" *About Looking* (New York: Pantheon Books, 1980), pp. 1–26.

58. Yi-Fu Tuan, *Dominance and Affection: The Making of Pets* (New Haven: Yale University Press, 1984).

59. Although personal reactions to the Shamu show are variable, some in the audience have powerfully negative responses to the show. I was struck by one acquaintance's reaction to a talk I gave on my research. I touched a nerve when I discussed the ways Sea World's exhibits create illusions of endlessness and boundlessness, and connected this illusion to the problematic discourse of captivity, free will, and corporate responsibility that is so prominent in the killer whale show. After a discussion of how Sea World tries to help its audience feel about killer whales, a woman about my age (I will call her Helen) came up to me, nearly in tears, and said, "I can't tell you how much I hate that place." When I asked her to explain what she meant, she responded with a long letter that I excerpt here, with her permission.

> Dear Susan,
>
> I had an "incorrect" response to Sea World when I went there a couple of years ago. I started sobbing right after I got to the whale tank and didn't settle down for hours after I left the place. It didn't surprise me that I started crying, but I couldn't console myself at all, and of course I was trapped out there with a group of friends. . . .
>
> What hit me hardest were the obvious attempts to create illusions of "endless space" within the tanks where huge animals are trapped. Orcas are so big, and in the wild they do whatever they want. They are the most efficient predator in the sea. They would eat other whales' babies if there wasn't anything else around. Those tanks never seem like a good substitute for the oceans of the world.
>
> I confess that orcas have been my "favorite animal" for a long, long time—maybe 20 or 30 years, and I often dream about them. Rather, they enter my dreams, always swimming around in oceans, and always showing up as a favor to me, usually as a reward for my goodness of heart. (God knows what these symbols "mean" but, whatever, orcas make really interesting vehicles for dream symbols, and conveniently, they can also just represent themselves if I want them to.) [February 23, 1995]

In her letter, Helen went on to relate examples of Northwest Coast folklore; some of it she said derived from Native Americans and white fisherfolk, some of it apparently from floating popular wisdom about orcas. For three single-spaced pages, she offered thoughts on the popularity of orcas, the idea of communication with wild animals, analyses of the style of killer whale display at the Vancouver Aquarium, thoughts about the place of dolphins in science fiction writing, and more discussion of how Sea World presents killer whales. Although Helen's reaction was intensely negative, most of Sea World's audience approves the whales in performance and their presence in the theme park. But her thoughts about killer whales show how the mix of ideas and arguments at Sea World's shows intersect with and draw on those presented in the mass media, other popular recreations, and in folklore.

Helen's letter is fascinating because it sheds light on a tiny part of the rich world of ideas about, and individuals' personal experiences with, animals and nature that people bring with them to Sea World. When Helen writes, "They are the most efficient predators in the sea," this is straight out of Sea World's scripts; when she relates stories about orcas rescuing women and children (but not men) from shipwrecks, this is popular whale lore from the Northwest Coast, where she has lived for a long time. When she says that in order to see orcas in the wild one has to be either "very lucky, or very, very deserving," we are perhaps at a crossroads where old folklore and new mysticism intersect.

Conclusion

1. Text from a Sea World's "Pass Times" advertising flier. Sea World, "Pass Times" (Sea World, San Diego, Calif., winter 1995). The play area is modeled on other schemes, such as the Discovery Zone chain playgrounds, that reproduce public playgrounds inside private pay-to-enter spaces.

2. Farrell Timlake, quoted in Karen Kucher, "Entering Another World: The Dolphin's," *San Diego Union-Tribune,* December 5, 1995, pp. B-1, B-2.

3. Sea World charges extra fees for the dolphin experience and dinner with Shamu. These programs not only enhance the theme park experience, but enhance the revenue stream.

4. Not all Sea World's visitors can recognize the plants or know their names, but many can, and they visit the park in part to enjoy its gardens. For the horticulturally informed, Sea World's replacement of annuals by perennials and its replacement of some of its common Southern California landscaping plants of the 1970s (such as lantana, bottlebrush, and ceanothus) with more novel and fashionable plants (such as sages and New Zealand flax) communicates up-to-dateness. Karen C. Wilson, "Sea World's Quiet Splash," *San Diego Union-Tribune,* December 3, 1995, pp. H-1, H-7.

5. Anne Whiston Spirn, field notes, and letter to the author, February 7, 1994. Thanks to Anne Spirn for sharing her observations with me.

6. Jennifer S. Whitaker, "Virtual Ecosystems," *New York Times* v144 (May 5, 1995): A15.

7. The National Park Service contemplates selling off architectural as well as natural assets. Patricia Leigh Brown, "National Parks at Crossroads over What to Save," *San Diego Union-Tribune,* August 27, 1995, pp. H-7, H-11; Dean MacCannell, "Nature, Incorporated," in *Empty Meeting Grounds: The Tourist Papers* (New York and London: Routledge, 1992), pp. 114–127.

8. Mireya Navarro, "Disney Announces Plans for a Wildlife Theme Park," *New York Times,* June 21, 1995, p. A-14.

9. Carol Lawson, "Disney's Newest Show Is a Town," *New York Times,* November 16, 1995, p. B-1. Indeed, the Disney Company's duchy in South Florida spans two county boundaries and is governed by its own company-designed environmental regulations, which in some cases sidestep state and federal standards. For a look at Disney's ideas on environmental governance as expressed in its Florida Reedy Creek Improvement District, see Ruth Knack, "The Mouse That Ate Orlando," *Planning,* 45, no. 2 (February 1979): 17–21; and Stephen Fjellman, *Vinyl Leaves: Walt Disney World and America* (Boulder: Westview Press, 1992), pp. 109–150, and notes. On institutionally created emotions, "Working at the Rat," in The Project on Disney, *Inside the Mouse: Work and Play at Disney World* (Durham: Duke University Press, 1995), pp. 110–162.

10. Raymond Williams, "Ideas of Nature," in *Problems in Materialism and Culture* (Oxford and New York, Oxford University Press, 1980), pp. 67–85; see also Williams, "Socialism and Ecology, 1982," in *Resources of Hope: Culture, Democracy, Socialism,* ed. Robin Gable (London and New York: Verso Books, 1989), pp. 210–227.

11. Hubbs receives money mainly from Anheuser-Busch, although it has other contributors.

12. The nonprofit institution conducts research in the following areas: "bioacoustic and behavioral studies of marine mammals, sharks and birds; various types of environmental monitoring; and mariculture. . . . Numerous Institute programs are carried out in conjunction with academic establishments, government agencies, other private institutions, and with Sea World." Sea World, *Sea World* (San Diego, Calif.: Sea World, 1978), p. 1. This brochure is nearly twenty years old, but Sea World's contemporary publicity materials endlessly rehearse the same theme, while inviting "audience participation" in the activity of earth saving through entertainment. For example, Sea World–Busch Gardens offers an "Animal Information Database" on the Internet, with educational animal facts, conservation career information, and publicity for Busch Gardens and Sea World, all of which repeat the argument that research at places like Sea World represents hope for the oceans and wildlife.

13. Sea World, *Sea World,* pp. 43–45.

14. By late 1995, Sea World could suggest that its customers might act politically to affect the environment. A modest display at Rocky Point Preserve suggested the customers write letters and vote on undefined conservation issues.

15. Undergraduate students often report that they think Sea World is a nonprofit institution. The park certainly would like to effect this impression, at least some of the time.

I think it is significant that descriptions of research and research agendas are more likely to be textual, conveyed by printed materials like labels, signs, guidebooks, and brochures than by the performances. It is well known in the museum field that it is extraordinarily difficult to get people to read such materials on-site or later. Claims about research may be kept out of oral or performed media for fear that they will be "boring." However, texts in print or on laminated museum-style "labels" may be more authoritative and give strength to claims for the theme park's research identity.

16. I don't mean to say that research is not done at Sea World. Sea World's scientists are serious scholars, publishing their findings in reviewed journals. They receive federal and corporate funding for their projects, and experience the same pressures as academic researchers. What is interesting about the theme park as research site is that there does not seem to be a close relationship between research as conducted and its representation at Sea World. For example, a bibliography of publications of the Hubbs–SWRI staff seems to show very little connection to the research that is talked about in Sea World performances.

17. Alan Abrahamson, "Edison Sued over Harm to Fish near San Onofre," *Los Angeles Times,* November 9, 1990, p. A-36; Amy Wallace, "San Onofre Mitigation Plan Wins Approval," *Los Angeles Times,* July 17, 1991, pp. A-3, A-15; Tony Perry, "Edison Settles Damage Suit for $15 Million," *Los Angeles Times,* January

27, 1993, pp. A-3, A-12. The cooling systems at the twin-towered nuclear power plant near San Clemente draw in seawater at a rate of 1.6 million gallons an hour. One effect of the seawater cooling has been the decimation of the three hundred–acre San Onofre kelp bed, a reduction of light to the ocean floor, and the loss of about twenty tons of fish and billions of fish eggs annually. In 1995, citing soaring costs of environmental rehabilitation, Southern California Edison proposed "a significant weakening of the mitigation package." Deborah Schoch, "Nuclear Plant Asks to Cut Back Marine Life Projects," *Los Angeles Times,* November 2, 1995, p. A-3.

18. In fact, the construction of the San Onofre plant was bitterly contested; there have been continual questions and doubts about the safety of the reactors' location and the adequacy of its construction. Leslie Wolf details the controversy in "N-Plant Is Neither Ogre nor Angel to Ocean, Study Finds," *Los Angeles Times,* September 7, 1989, pp. B-1, B-9. Does a "mitigation project" help fog public awareness of such long-running controversy?

19. This conflict-free construction of entertainment is parallel to the general conception of "entertainment" in American culture, discussed by Herbert I. Schiller, in *The Mind Managers* (Boston: Beacon Press, 1973). Sea World's presentation of itself as an educational institution has relied on this same construction of neutrality.

20. Cf. Williams, "Socialism and Ecology, 1982," pp. 210–227, on the central importance of discussions of production "for what" in political arguments for environmental action.

21. As Raymond Williams put it, "Out of the ways in which we have interacted with the physical world, we have made not only human nature and an altered natural order; we have also made societies." Williams, "Ideas of Nature," p. 84; see also Williams, *The Country and the City* (New York: Oxford University Press, 1973).

INDEX

Page numbers appearing in italics refer to pages containing maps or illustrations.

Indexer: Jill Bergman
Designer: Nola Burger
Compositor: Integrated Composition Systems
Text: 10/13 Galliard
Display: Galliard
Printer: Haddon Craftsmen, Inc.
Binder: Haddon Craftsmen, Inc.